# Management Accounting
## for Non-Specialists

THIRD EDITION

# Management Accounting
## for Non-Specialists

**Peter Atrill**

and

**Eddie McLaney**

**FT** Prentice Hall
FINANCIAL TIMES

*An imprint of* **Pearson Education**

Harlow, England • London • New York • Boston • San Francisco • Toronto • Sydney • Singapore • Hong Kong
Tokyo • Seoul • Taipei • New Delhi • Cape Town • Madrid • Mexico City • Amsterdam • Munich • Paris • Milan

**Pearson Education Limited**
Edinburgh Gate
Harlow
Essex CM20 2JE
England
and Associated Companies throughout the world

*Visit us on the World Wide Web at:*
www.pearsoneduc.com

---

Second edition published 1999 by Prentice Hall Europe
**Third edition published 2002 by Pearson Education Limited**

© Prentice Hall Europe 1999
© Pearson Education Limited 2002

ISBN 0273 65591 4

**British Library Cataloguing-in-Publication Data**
A catalogue record for this book is available from the British Library

**Library of Congress Cataloging-in-Publication Data**
Atrill, Peter.
    Management accounting for non-specialists / Peter Atrill and Eddie McLaney.—3rd ed.
        p. cm.
    Includes bibliographical references and index.
    ISBN 0-273-65591-4
    1. Managerial accounting.   I. McLaney, E. J.   II. Title.
    HF5657.4 .A873 2002
    658.15′11—dc21                                    2001050184

10  9  8  7  6  5  4
07  06  05  04  03

Typeset in 9.5/12pt Stone serif by 35
Printed by Ashford Colour Press Ltd., Gosport

# Contents

## 5 Managing in a competitive environment                               96

## 6 Budgeting                                                          124

## 7 Accounting for control

## 10 Measuring and controlling divisional performance

# Acknowledgements

We are grateful to the following for permission to reproduce copyright material:

Exhibit 6.4 from *Financial Management and Working Capital Practices in UK SMEs*, by Chittenden, F., Poutziouris, P. and Michaelis, N., 1998, reprinted by permission of Manchester Business School; Exhibit 6.6 from 'Beyond budgeting' by J. Hope and R. Fraser, published in *Management Accounting*, January 1999, reprinted by permission of Chartered Institute of Management Accountants; Figure 11.9 and Exhibit 11.4 from 'Using the balanced scorecard as a strategic management system' by Robert Kaplan & David Norton, Vol. 76, January–February 1996, Harvard Business Review, © 1996 by the President and Fellows of Harvard College, all rights reserved.

In some instances we have been unable to trace the owners of copyright material, and we would appreciate any information that would enable us to do so.

# Preface

Management accounting is concerned with the provision and use of information which should help managers to make better decisions and try to ensure that what has been decided actually occurs. This book seeks to introduce management accounting, particularly to those people who wish or need to have an understanding of the subject, without going into a lot of unnecessary technical detail.

The book is directed primarily at non-accounting students who are following a short course in management accounting, perhaps as part of a university or college course majoring in some other area, such as business studies, tourism or engineering. It is also directed at readers who are studying independently, perhaps with no qualification in mind.

Specialist accounting students should also find the book useful as an introduction to the principles of management accounting, which can be used as a foundation for deeper study.

In writing the book, we have been mindful of the fact that most of the book's readers will not have studied management accounting before. We have therefore tried to write in an accessible style, avoiding technical jargon. Where technical terminology is unavoidable, we have tried to give clear explanations. At the end of the book there is a glossary of technical terms, which can be used to refresh the minds of readers if they come across a term whose meaning is in doubt.

The book is written in an 'open learning' style. That is to say, it tries to involve the reader in a way not traditionally found in textbooks. The book tries to approach its contents much as a good lecturer would do. We have tried to introduce topics gradually, explaining everything as we go. We have also included a number of questions and tasks of various types to try to help readers to understand the subject fully, in much the same way as a good lecturer would do in lectures and tutorials. More detail of the nature and use of these questions and tasks is given in the 'How to use this book' section immediately following this preface.

The open learning style has been adopted because we believe it to be more 'user friendly' to readers. Whether they are using the book as part of a taught course or for personal study, we feel that the open learning approach makes it easier for readers to learn.

Chapter 1 provides a broad introduction to the nature and purpose of management accounting. Chapters 2, 3, 4 and 5 are concerned with identifying cost information and using it to make short-term and medium-term decisions. Chapters 6 and 7 deal with the use of management accounting in the process of planning and trying to ensure that plans are actually achieved. Chapter 8 considers the use of management accounting information in making investment decisions, typically long-term ones. Chapter 9 looks at the way in which management accounting can help in the control of short-term assets, like stock and cash. Chapter 10 deals with the role of management accounting in trying to deal with the problems which arise from managing businesses which operate, as most businesses do, through a divisional structure. Finally, Chapter 11, a completely new chapter in this edition, deals with 'strategic management accounting'. This is an increasingly important area of management accounting that focuses on factors outside the organisation, that have a significant effect on the success of the organisation.

In this third edition, we have taken the opportunity to make improvements to the book. We have included more material which relates to management accounting in practice. We should like to thank our colleague at the University of Plymouth Business School, John Boston, for supplying two of the cases included.

We should also like to thank the Chartered Association of Certified Accountants for permission to include questions from the Certified Diploma in the book.

Finally, we should like to thank everybody at Pearson Education for their support and encouragement in writing this book. Without their help the book would not have materialised.

We hope that readers will find this book readable and helpful.

*Peter Atrill*
*Eddie McLaney*

# How to use this book

Whether you are using the book as part of a lecture/tutorial-based course or as the basis for a more independent mode of study, the same approach should be broadly followed.

## Order of dealing with the material

The contents of the book have been ordered in what is meant to be a logical sequence. For this reason, it is suggested that you work through the book in the order in which it is presented. Every effort has been made to ensure that earlier chapters do not refer to concepts or terms which are not explained until a later chapter. If you work through the chapters in the 'wrong' order, you may encounter points which have been explained in an earlier chapter which you have not read.

## Working through the chapters

You are advised to work through the chapters, from start to finish, but not necessarily in one sitting. Activities are interspersed with the text. These are meant to be like the sort of questions which a good lecturer will throw at students during a lecture or tutorial. Activities seek to serve two purposes:

1. To give you the opportunity to check that you understand what has been covered so far.
2. To try to encourage you to think beyond the topic which you have just covered, sometimes so that you can see a link between that topic and others with which you are already familiar. Sometimes, activities are used as a means of linking the topic just covered to the next one.

You are strongly advised to do all the activities. The answers are provided immediately after the activity. These answers should be covered up until a solution has been deduced, when the solution deduced by you should be compared with the suggested answer provided.

Towards the end of Chapters 2–11, there is a 'self-assessment question'. This is rather more demanding and comprehensive than any of the activities. It is intended to give you an opportunity to see whether you understand the main body of material covered in the chapter. The solutions to the self-assessment questions are provided at the end of the book. As with the activities, it is very important that you have a thorough attempt at the question before referring to the solution. If you have real difficulty with a self-assessment question you should go back over the chapter again, since it should be the case that complete study of the chapter would enable completion of the self-assessment question.

## End-of-chapter questions

At the end of each chapter, there are four 'review' questions. These are short questions requiring a narrative answer, and intended to enable you to assess how well you can recall main points covered in the chapter. Suggested answers to these questions are included on the student Web site. Again, a real attempt should be made to answer these questions before referring to the solutions.

At the end of each chapter, there are normally eight exercises. These are more demanding and extensive questions, mostly computational, and should further reinforce your knowledge and understanding. We have attempted to provide questions of varying complexity.

Answers to five out of the eight exercises in each chapter are provided at the end of the book. Those marked with a coloured number are provided with an answer. Solutions to the three exercises that are not marked with a coloured box are given in a separate teacher's manual. Yet again, a thorough attempt should be made to answer these questions before referring to the answers.

### A Companion Web Site accompanies *Management Accounting for Non-Specialists* 3rd edition by Peter Atrill and Eddie McLaney

Visit the *Management Accounting for Non-Specialists* Companion Web Site at www.booksites.net/atrillmclaney to find valuable teaching and learning material including:

**For Students:**
- Study material designed to help you improve your results
- Multiple Choice Questions to help test your learning
- Case study
- Links to relevant sites on the World Wide Web

**For Lecturers:**
- A secure, password protected site with teaching material
- Complete, downloadable Instructor's Manual
- Extra questions with solutions for use with your students
- PowerPoint slides for use with the book

**Also:** This regularly maintained and updated site has a syllabus manager, search function, and email results function.

## CHAPTER 1

# Introduction to management accounting

## Introduction

Welcome to the world of management accounting! In this first chapter, we shall begin by considering the role and nature of accounting in general. We shall identify the main users of accounting information and discuss the ways in which accounting can improve the quality of the decisions that they make. We shall then go on to consider the needs of managers and the role of management accounting information in meeting those needs. As this book is concerned with management accounting for private sector businesses, we shall also consider what the key financial objective of a business is likely to be. The particular objective chosen will exert an important influence on what is reported and how it is reported.

### OBJECTIVES

**When you have completed this chapter, you should be able to:**

- Explain the role and nature of accounting.
- Explain the distinction between management and financial accounting.
- Identify the main users of accounting information and discuss their needs.
- Explain how management accounting can fulfil the needs of managers.
- Discuss the possible financial objectives of a business.

## What is accounting?

➡ When studying a new subject it is often helpful to begin with a definition. The literature contains various definitions of **accounting**, but the one we find most appealing is that provided by the American Accounting Association which defines accounting as:

> the process of identifying, measuring and communicating information to permit informed judgements and decisions by users of the information.

This rather broad definition is appealing because it highlights the fact that accounting exists for a particular purpose. That purpose is to help users of accounting information to make more informed decisions. If accounting information is not capable of helping to make better decisions then it is a waste of time and money to produce. Sometimes, the impression is given that the purpose of accounting is simply to prepare financial reports on a regular basis. Whilst it is true that accountants undertake this kind of work, it does not represent an end in itself. The ultimate purpose of the accountant's work is to influence the decisions of users of the information produced. This decision-making perspective of accounting is a major theme of the book and will shape the way in which we deal with each topic.

## Who are the users?

For accounting information to be useful, the accountant must be clear about *for whom* the information is being prepared and *for what purpose* the information will be used. There are likely to be various user groups with an interest in a particular organisation, in the sense of needing to make decisions about that organisation. The most important groups which use accounting information about private sector businesses are shown in Figure 1.1.

| Figure 1.1 | **Main users of financial information relating to a business** |
| --- | --- |

The figure shows that there are several user groups with an interest in the accounting information relating to a business. The majority of these are outside the business but nevertheless, they have a stake in the business. This is not meant to be an exhaustive list of potential users; however, the user groups identified are normally the most important.

| Activity 1.1 | Why do each of the user groups identified above need accounting information relating to a business? |

Your answer may be as follows:

| User group | Use |
| --- | --- |
| Customers | To assess the ability of the business to continue in business and to supply the needs of the customers. |
| Competitors | To act as a benchmark when evaluating their own performance. To assess the competitive strength of the business and to identify significant changes which may signal future actions (e.g. stockbuilding as a prelude to market expansion). |
| Employees (non-management) | To assess the ability of the business to continue to provide employment and to reward employees for their labour. |
| Government | To assess how much tax the business should pay, whether it complies with agreed pricing policies, whether financial support is needed, etc. |
| Community representatives | To assess the ability of the business to continue to provide employment for the community, to use community resources, to help fund environmental improvements, etc. |
| Investment analysts | To assess the likely risks and returns associated with the business in order to determine its investment potential and to advise clients accordingly. |
| Suppliers | To assess the ability of the business to pay for the goods and services supplied. |
| Lenders | To assess the ability of the business to meet its obligations and to pay interest and to repay the principal. |
| Managers | To help them to make decisions and plans for the business and to help them to exercise control to try to ensure that plans come to fruition. |
| Owners | To assess how effectively the managers are running the business and to make judgements about likely levels of risk and return in the future. |

You may have thought of other reasons why each group would find accounting information useful.

This book is concerned with providing accounting information for the penultimate group mentioned above, that is, managers. This is a particularly important group. Managers have day-to-day responsibility for running the business and so their decisions and actions will influence its financial health. We shall see how planning for the future and exercising day-to-day control over a business involves various tasks and requires a great variety and quantity of accounting information.

## Not-for-profit organisations

Though the focus of this book is accounting as it relates to private sector businesses, there are many organisations which do not exist mainly for the pursuit of profit yet produce accounting information for decision-making purposes. Examples of such organisations include charities, clubs and associations, universities, local government authorities, churches and trades unions. Accounting information about these types of organisation is needed by user groups. These groups are often the same as, or similar to, those identified for private sector businesses. They may have a stake in the future viability of the organisation and may use accounting information to check that the wealth of the organisation is being properly controlled and used in a way that is consistent with the objectives of the organisation.

## How useful is accounting information?

No one would seriously claim that accounting information fully meets the needs of the various user groups identified. Accounting is still a developing subject and we still have much to learn about user needs and the ways in which these needs should be met. Nevertheless, the information contained within accounting reports should reduce uncertainty over the financial position and performance of the business. It should help to answer questions concerning the availability of cash to pay owners a return for their investment or to repay loans, etc. Often there are no close substitutes for the information contained within accounting reports (for example, reports which measure profit generated during a period) and so they are usually regarded as more useful than other sources of information which are available regarding the financial health of the business.

There are arguments and convincing evidence that accounting information is at least *perceived* as being useful to users. There have been numerous studies that asked users to rank the importance of accounting information, in relation to other sources of information, for decision-making purposes. Generally speaking, these studies have found that users rank accounting information more highly than other sources of information. There is also considerable evidence that businesses choose to produce accounting information for users which exceeds the minimum requirements imposed by accounting regulations. (For example, businesses often produce a considerable amount of management accounting information, which is not required by any regulations.) Presumably, the cost of producing this additional accounting information is justified on the grounds that users believe it to be useful to them. Such arguments and evidence, however, leave unanswered the question as to whether the information produced is actually being used for decision-making purposes, that is, does it affect people's behaviour?

It is normally very difficult to assess the impact of accounting on decision-making; however, one situation arises where the impact of accounting information can be observed and measured. This is where the shares (portions of ownership of a business) are traded on a stock exchange. The evidence reveals that, when a business makes an announcement concerning its accounting profits, the prices of shares traded and the volume of shares traded often change significantly following the announcement. This suggests that investors are changing their views about the future prospects of the business as a result of this new information available to them and that this, in turn, leads them to either buy or sell shares in the business.

Thus, we can see there is evidence that accounting reports are perceived as being useful and are used for decision-making purposes. However, it is impossible to measure just how useful accounting reports are to users and whether the cost of producing those reports represents value for money. Accounting information will usually represent only one input to a particular decision and the precise weight attached to the accounting information by the decision maker and the benefits which flow as a result cannot be accurately assessed. We shall see below, however, that it is at least possible to identify the kinds of qualities which accounting information must possess in order to be useful. Where these qualities are lacking, the usefulness of the information will be diminished.

# Accounting as a service function

One way of viewing accounting is as a form of service. Accountants provide economic information to their 'clients', who are the various users identified in Figure 1.1. The quality of the service provided will be determined by the extent to which the information needs of the various user groups have been met. It can be argued that, to be useful, accounting information should possess certain key 'qualitative' characteristics. These are:

➡ ■ **Relevance**. Accounting information must have the ability to influence decisions. Unless this characteristic is present, there is really no point in producing the information. The information may be relevant to the prediction of future events (for example, in predicting how much profit is likely to be earned next year) or relevant in helping confirm past events (for example, in establishing how much profit was earned last year). The role of accounting in confirming past events is important because users often wish to check on the accuracy of earlier predictions that they have made.

➡ ■ **Reliability**. Accounting should be free from significant errors or bias. It should be capable of being relied upon by users to represent what it is supposed to represent. Although both relevance and reliability are very important, the problem that we often face in accounting is that information that is highly relevant may not be very reliable, and that which is reliable may not be very relevant.

| Activity 1.2 | To illustrate this last point, let us assume that a manager is charged with selling a custom-built machine owned by the business and has recently received a bid for it. What information would be relevant to the manager when deciding whether to accept the bid? How reliable would that information be? |
| --- | --- |

The manager would probably like to know the current market value of the machine in order to decide whether or not to accept the bid. The current market value would be highly relevant to the final decision, but it might not be very reliable because the machine is unique and there is likely to be little information concerning market values.

Where a choice has to be made between providing information that has either more relevance *or* more reliability, the maximisation of relevance should be the guiding rule.

➡ ■ **Comparabilty**. This quality will enable users to identify changes in the business over time (for example, the trend in sales over the past five years), also to evaluate the performance of the business in relation to other similar businesses. Comparability is achieved by treating items that are basically the same in the same manner for measurement and presentation purposes and by making clear the policies that have been adopted in measuring and presenting the information.

➡ ■ **Understandability**. Accounting reports should be expressed as clearly as possible and should be understood by those at whom the information is aimed.

| Activity 1.3 | Do you think that accounting reports should be understandable to those who have not studied accounting? |
|---|---|

This may prove to be an impossible challenge for those preparing accounting reports. The complexity of financial events and transactions cannot normally be so easily reported. It is probably best that we regard accounting reports in the same way as we regard a piece of modern art (an interesting thought!). To understand both, we really have to do a bit of homework. Generally speaking, accounting reports assume that the user not only has a reasonable knowledge of business and accounting but is also prepared to invest some time in studying the reports.

➡ ■ **Materiality**. When preparing accounting reports, we should make sure that all material information is provided. Information will be regarded as material if it is likely to have an influence on the decisions made by users. If information is not regarded as material, it is best to exclude it from the reports as it will merely clutter up the reports and, perhaps, interfere with the users' ability to interpret the financial results.

## Costs and benefits of accounting information

In the previous section, the five key characteristics of relevance, reliability, comparability, understandability and materiality were identified. In fact, there is also a sixth key characteristic which is very important.

| Activity 1.4 | Suppose an item of information is capable of being provided. It is relevant to a particular decision, it is also reliable, comparable and can be understood by the decision maker concerned and is material.<br>    Can you think of a reason why, in practice, you might choose not to produce the information? |
|---|---|

The reason that you may decide not to produce, or discover, the information is that you judge the cost of doing so to be greater than the potential benefit of having the information. This cost–benefit issue, like comparability, understandability and timeliness, will place limits on the usefulness of accounting information.

In theory, financial information should only be produced if the costs of providing that piece of information are less than the benefits, or value, to be derived from its use. Figure 1.2 shows the relationship between the costs and value of providing additional financial information. The figure shows how the value of information received by the decision maker eventually begins to decline, perhaps because additional information becomes less relevant, or because of the problems which a decision maker may have in processing the sheer quantity of information provided. The costs of providing the information, however, will increase with each additional piece of information. The point at which the gap between the value of information and the cost of providing that information is at its greatest is indicated by a broken line. This represents the optimal amount of information that can be provided. This theoretical model, however, poses a number of problems in practice, as discussed below.

| Figure 1.2 | **Relationship between costs and the value of providing additional financial information** |

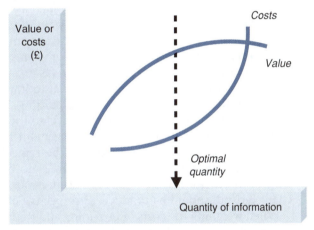

The figure shows how the benefits of financial information will eventually decline. The cost of providing information, however, will rise with each additional piece of information. The optimal level of information provision is where the gap between the value of the information and the costs of providing it is at its greatest.

To illustrate the practical problems of establishing the value of information, suppose that you wish to buy a particular portable radio which you have seen in a local shop for sale at £25. You believe that other local shops may have the same model of radio on offer for a lower price. The only ways that you can find out the prices at other shops are either to telephone them or to visit them. Telephone calls cost money and involve some of your time. Visiting the shops may not involve the outlay of money, but more of your time will be involved. Is it worth the cost of finding out the price of the radio at various shops? The answer, as we have seen, is that if the cost of discovering the price is less than the potential benefit, it is worth having that information.

To identify the various selling prices of portable radios there are various points to be considered including:

- How many shops will you telephone or visit?
- What is the cost of each telephone call?
- How long will it take to make all the telephone calls or visits?
- How much do you value your time?

The economic benefit of having the information on the price of radios is probably even harder to assess and the following points need to be considered:

- What is the cheapest price that you might be quoted for the radio?
- How likely is it that you will be quoted prices cheaper than £25?

As you can imagine, the answers to these questions may be far from clear. When assessing the value of accounting information we are confronted with similar problems.

The provision of accounting information can be very costly; however, the costs are often difficult to quantify. The direct, out-of-pocket costs such as salaries of accounting staff are not really a problem, but these are only part of the total costs involved. There are also less direct costs such as the costs of the manager's time spent on analysing and interpreting the information contained in reports. In addition, costs will also be incurred if the accounting information is used to the disadvantage of the business by users. For example, if suppliers discovered from the accounting reports that the business was in a poor financial state, they might decide to refuse to supply further goods or to impose strict conditions.

The economic benefit of having accounting information is even harder to assess. It is possible to apply some 'science' to the problem of weighing the costs and benefits, but a lot of subjective judgement is likely to be involved. Whilst no one would seriously advocate that the typical business should produce no accounting information, at the same time, no one would advocate that every item of information which could be seen as possessing one or more of the key characteristics should be produced, irrespective of the cost of producing it.

When weighing the costs of providing additional financial information against the benefits, there is also the problem that those who bear the burden of the costs may not be the ones who benefit from the additional information. The costs of providing accounting information are usually borne by the owners, but other user groups may be the beneficiaries.

The characteristics which influence the relevance and reliability of accounting information and which have been discussed in this section and the preceding section are set out in Figure 1.3.

## Accounting as an information system

Another way of viewing accounting is as a part of the total information system within a business. Users, both inside and outside the business, have to make decisions concerning the allocation of scarce economic resources. To try to ensure that these resources are allocated in an efficient manner, users require economic information on which to base decisions. It is the role of the accounting system

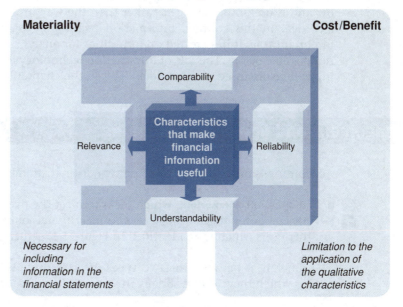

**Figure 1.3**

### The characteristics that influence the usefulness of accounting information

**Materiality**  **Cost/Benefit**

Comparability

Characteristics that make financial information useful

Relevance   Reliability

Understandability

*Necessary for including information in the financial statements*

*Limitation to the application of the qualitative characteristics*

The figure shows that there are four main qualitative characteristics that influence the usefulness of accounting information. In addition, however, accounting information should be material and the benefits of providing the information should outweigh the costs.

to provide that information and this will involve information gathering and communication.

The **accounting information system** has certain features that are common to all information systems within a business. These are:

- Identifying and capturing relevant information (in this case economic information)
- Recording the information collected in a systematic manner
- Analysing and interpreting the information collected
- Reporting the information in a manner that suits the needs of users.

The relationship between these features is set out in Figure 1.4.

**Figure 1.4**

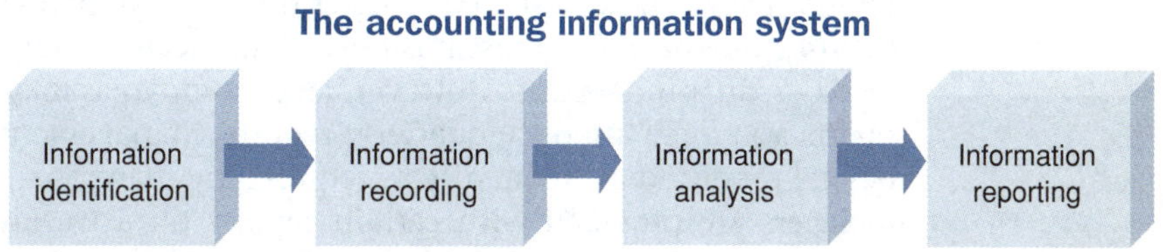

### The accounting information system

Information identification → Information recording → Information analysis → Information reporting

The figure shows the four sequential stages of an accounting information system. The first two stages are concerned with preparation, whereas the last two stages are concerned with using the information collected.

Given the decision-making emphasis of this book, we shall be concerned primarily with the final two elements of the process – the analysis and reporting of financial information. We shall consider the way in which information is used by, and is useful to, managers rather than the way in which it is identified and recorded. In this context, information technology is playing an increasingly important role. It has created opportunities for analysis and reporting that were not possible before. The role of information technology in management accounting will be discussed in more detail later in the chapter.

## Management and financial accounting

Accounting is usually seen as having two distinct strands. These are:

 ■ **Management accounting**, which seeks to meet the needs of managers; and
■ **Financial accounting**, which seeks to meet the accounting needs of all of the other users which were identified in Figure 1.1, earlier in the chapter.

The differences between the two types of accounting reflect the different user groups which they address. Briefly, the major differences are as follows:

■ *Nature of the reports produced.* Financial accounting reports tend to be general-purpose reports. That is, they contain financial information which will be useful for a broad range of users and decisions rather than being specifically designed for the needs of a particular group or set of decisions. Management accounting reports, on the other hand, are often specific-purpose reports. They are designed either with a particular decision in mind or for a particular manager.

■ *Level of detail.* Financial accounting reports provide users with a broad overview of the performance and position of the business for a period. As a result, information is aggregated and detail is often lost. Management accounting reports, however, often provide managers with considerable detail to help them with a particular operational decision.

■ *Regulations.* Financial reports, for many businesses, are subject to accounting regulations which try to ensure they are produced according to a standardised format. These regulations are imposed by law and the accounting profession. Because management accounting reports are for internal use only, there are no regulations from external sources concerning the form and content of the reports. They can be designed to meet the needs of particular managers.

■ *Reporting interval.* For most businesses, financial accounting reports are produced on an annual basis. However, large companies may produce half-yearly reports and a few produce quarterly reports. Management accounting reports may be produced as frequently as required by managers. In many businesses, managers are provided with certain reports on a weekly or monthly basis, which allows them to check progress frequently. In addition, special-purpose reports will be prepared when required (for example, to evaluate a proposal to purchase a piece of machinery).

■ *Time horizon.* Financial accounting reports reflect the performance and position of the business for the past period. In essence, they are backward looking. Management accounting reports, on the other hand, often provide information concerning future performance as well as past performance. It is an oversimplification, however, to suggest that financial accounting reports never incorporate expectations concerning the future. Occasionally, businesses will release forecast information to other users in order to raise capital or to fight off unwanted take-over bids.

■ *Range and quality of information.* Financial accounting reports concentrate on information that can be quantified in monetary terms. Management accounting also produces such reports, but is also more likely to produce reports which contain information of a non-financial nature such as measures of physical quantities of stocks and output. Financial accounting places greater emphasis on the use of objective, verifiable evidence when preparing reports. Management accounting reports may use information that is less objective and verifiable, but provides managers with the information they need.

We can see from the above that management accounting is less constrained than financial accounting. It may draw from a variety of sources and use information which has varying degrees of reliability. The only real test to be applied when assessing the value of the information produced for managers is whether or not it improves the quality of the decisions made.

| Activity 1.5 | Do you think this distinction between management accounting and financial accounting may be misleading? |
|---|---|

Is there any overlap between the information needs of managers and the needs of other users?

The distinction between management and financial accounting suggests that there are differences between the information needs of managers and those of other users. Whilst differences undoubtedly exist, there is also a good deal of overlap between these needs. For example, managers will, at times, be interested in receiving an historic overview of business operations of the sort provided to other users. Equally, the other users would be interested in receiving information relating to the future, such as the forecast level of profits and non-financial information such as the state of the order book and product innovations.

The distinction between the two areas reflects, to some extent, the differences in access to financial information. Managers have much more control over the form and content of information they receive. Other users have to rely on what managers are prepared to provide or what the financial reporting regulations state must be provided. Though the scope of financial accounting reports has increased over time, fears concerning loss of competitive advantage and user ignorance concerning the reliability of forecast data have led businesses to resist providing other users with the detailed and wide-ranging information that is available to managers.

# Management accounting information and management decisions

We saw earlier that management accounting information is designed to help managers to manage. If we view accounting as a form of service, then managers can be viewed as the 'clients' of management accounting information. You may wonder what kind of information these 'clients' require. Management accounting information is usually required to help managers make decisions which fall within the following broad areas:

■ *Developing long-term plans and strategies.* Managers are responsible for establishing the objectives of the business and then developing long-term plans and strategies to achieve these objectives. Management accounting information can play a valuable role in providing forecast reports which set out the likely financial outcomes from the proposed courses of action. These reports can be used by managers to evaluate each course of action and then to select the appropriate course(s) of action for inclusion in the long-term plan.

■ *Performance evaluation and control.* Having set a particular course for the business, or segments of the business, managers need to know whether things are going according to plan. By providing information relating to the actual outcomes of the business, the relative performance of the business can be determined. Thus, the actual outcomes will be compared with the planned outcomes to see whether the performance is better or worse than expected. Where there is a significant difference between the planned level of performance and the actual level, some investigation should be carried out and corrective action taken where necessary. In this way, performance may be controlled by the managers more effectively.

**Figure 1.5**

**Management decisions requiring management accounting information**

Developing long-term plans and strategies

Performance evaluation and control

Management accounting information

Determining costs and benefits

Allocating resources

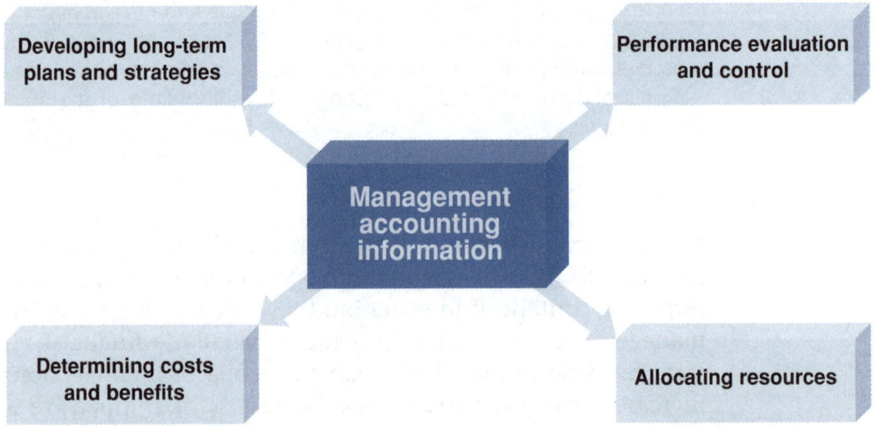

The figure shows that management accounting information is required to help managers to make decisions in four broad areas: developing long-term plans and strategies, performance evaluation and control, allocating resources and determining costs and benefits.

■ *Allocating resources.* Rescources available to a business are limited and it is the responsibility of managers to try to ensure that the scarce resources available are used in an efficient and effective manner. Decisions concerning such matters as the optimum level of output, the optimum mix of products and the appropriate type of investment in new equipment will all require management accounting information.

■ *Determining costs and benefits.* Many management decisions require a knowledge of the costs and benefits of pursuing a particular course of action such as providing a service, or producing a new product or closing down a department. The decision will involve weighing the costs against the benefits. The management accountant can help managers by providing details of particular costs and benefits. In some cases, costs and benefits may be extremely difficult to quantify; however, some approximation is usually better than nothing at all.

These areas of management decision making are set out in Figure 1.5.

## Management accounting and human behaviour

It is important to appreciate that the process of measuring and evaluating performance is intended to have an effect on behaviour within the business. Unfortunately, the behaviour change caused by management accounting is not always beneficial. One possible effect is that managers and employees will concentrate their attention and efforts on the aspects of the business that are being measured and will give much less attention to the items that are not. It is said that 'The things that count are the things that get counted.' This rather narrow view, however, can have undesirable consequences for the business.

| Activity 1.6 | Can you think of an example where concentrating efforts on 'the things that get counted' can have undesirable consequences? |
| --- | --- |

Undesirable consequences can often arise where a particular measure is being used, or is perceived as being used, as a basis for evaluating performance. For example, a manager of a department may be given a particular expenditure limit to keep within. To demonstrate cost consciousness, the manager may underspend during the period by cutting back on staff training and development. Though the effect on expenditure incurred may be favourable, the effect on staff morale and longer-term profitability may be extremely unfavourable for the business. These unfavourable effects may go unrecognised, at least in the short term, where the expenditure limit is the focus of attention.

Attempts may be made to manipulate a particular measure where it is seen as important. For example, a manager may continue to use old, fully depreciated, pieces of equipment to keep depreciation charges low and, therefore, boost profits. This may be done despite knowledge that the purchase of new equipment would produce higher-quality products and help to increase sales over the longer term. Attempts at manipulation are often related to improving rewards. For example, profit-related bonuses may provide the incentive to manipulate reported profits in the way described.

In some cases, the particular targets against which performance is measured are the object of manipulation. For example, a sales manager may provide a deliberately low forecast of the size of the potential market for the next period if he or she believes that the forecast will form the basis of future sales targets. This may be done either to increase rewards (for example, where bonuses are awarded for exceeding sales targets) or to ensure that future sales targets can be achieved with relatively little effort.

The management accountant must be aware of the impact of accounting measures of performance on human behaviour. When designing accounting measures, it is important to try to ensure that all key aspects of performance are taken into account, even though certain aspects may be difficult to measure. When operating an accounting measurement system, it is important to be alert to behaviour aimed at manipulating particular measures rather than achieving the goals to which they relate.

## The changing nature of management accounting

Over the past two decades, the environment in which businesses operate has become increasingly turbulent and competitive. Various reasons have been identified to explain these changes. These include:

- The increasing sophistication of customers
- The development of a global economy where national frontiers become less important
- Rapid changes in technology
- The deregulation of domestic markets (for example, electricity, water and gas)
- Increasing pressure from owners (shareholders) for good returns
- The increasing volatility of financial markets.

The effect of these environmental changes has been to make the role of managers more complex and demanding. It has meant that managers have had to find new ways to manage their business. Changes in management practice inevitably lead to changes in management accounting. It must respond to the changing needs of managers.

Increasingly, successful businesses are those which are able to secure and maintain competitive advantage over their rivals. To obtain such advantage, businesses have become more 'customer driven' (that is, concerned with satisfying customer needs). This has led to a need for management accounting information which provides details of customers and the market such as customer evaluation of services provided and market share. Customer focus has also led to greater concern for quality and for developing new, innovative products.

Many types of management accounting information are not expressed in financial terms.

To compete successfully, businesses must also find ways of reducing costs. The cost base of modern businesses is under continual review and this, in turn, has created a need to develop more sophisticated methods of measuring and controlling costs. It has also created a need for information about the costs incurred by rival businesses. These can be used as 'benchmarks' by which to gauge competitiveness.

**Activity 1.7**

Imagine that you are the manager of a manufacturing business. What kinds of information may be relevant to help you evaluate:

- **The quality of the products manufactured?**
- **The level of innovation in developing new products?**

Quality of products may be evaluated using the following information:

- Customer perception surveys
- Defects produced as a percentage of total production
- Percentage of sales returned by customers
- Percentage of products requiring re-working.

Level of innovation may be evaluated using the following information:

- New products launched over the past two years compared with competitors
- Percentage of total revenue generated by new products
- Time taken to develop new products
- New products launched as a percentage of new product proposals.

You may have thought of other information which may be relevant.

The changes described above have meant that management accounting has become more outward looking in its focus. In the past, information provided to managers has been largely restricted to that collected within the business. However, the attitude and behaviour of customers and rival businesses have now become the object of much information gathering. The changes have also meant that management accounting has become increasingly concerned with non-financial reporting such as quality, product innovation, product cycle times, delivery times, etc.

**Activity 1.8**

It can be argued that non-financial measures, such as those mentioned above, do not, strictly speaking, fall within the scope of accounting information and, therefore, could (or should) be provided by others. What do you think?

It is true that this kind of information need not be collected by the management accounting system. The reason for it to be regarded as management accounting is, perhaps, that the accounting system is often regarded as the most important element of the management information system and it can be readily adapted so as to provide a broad range of information necessary for economic decisions. The boundaries of accounting are not fixed and so it is possible to argue that this kind of information should be collected by the management information system, as it is often linked inextricably to financial outcomes.

## Management accounting and information technology

The impact of information technology on the development of management accounting is difficult to overstate. The ability of information technology to process large amounts of information means that routine reports can be produced quickly and accurately. This is vital to the businesses operating in the kind of environment described above as they can no longer risk the damage to competitive advantage which can occur where decisions are based on inaccurate and misleading information.

Information technology has allowed management reports to be produced in greater detail and in greater variety than could be contemplated under a manual system. In addition, it has allowed sophisticated measurement systems to be provided at relatively low cost. Managers can use information technology to help assess proposals by allowing variables (such as product price, output, product cost and so on) to be changed easily. By pressing a few keys on a computer keyboard, managers can increase or decrease the size of key variables to create a range of possible scenarios.

The information revolution is gathering pace and so information technology is likely to play an increasingly important role in management accounting in the future. Particularly interesting developments are occurring in the area of financial information evaluation. Computers are becoming more capable of making sophisticated judgements which, in the past, only humans were considered capable of doing. Increasingly, information technology in management accounting is viewed not only as a means of improving the timeliness and accuracy of management reports but as an important source of competitive advantage.

## The changing role of the management accountant

Given the changes described above, it is not surprising that the traditional role of the management accountant within a business has changed. Information technology has released the management accountant from much of the routine work associated with preparation of financial reports. In the past, the management accountant's role has been confined to assisting managers by providing information in the areas discussed earlier. Whilst this role is still vitally important, management accountants are increasingly seen as part of the management team. As a team member, the management accountant is expected to be directly involved in the planning and decision-making process. Thus, management accountants are now working more closely with other managers to improve profit performance.

This expanded role for the management accountant has benefits for the development of management accounting as a discipline. It provides the management accountant with a greater awareness of operational matters and the information needs of managers which can, in turn, improve the quality of information provided by the management accounting system. As a consequence, we can see increasing evidence that management accounting systems are being designed to fit the particular structure and processes of the business rather than the other way round.

The changes identified are largely in response to changes in the external environment in which management accounting exists. Given the increasing rate of change in the external environment, we can expect management accounting to change at an even faster pace in the future.

# Business objectives

Throughout this book we shall assume that *increasing the wealth of the owners* is the principal financial objective of a business. To justify this assumption, we shall briefly consider other financial objectives that have been identified, by various commentators, as likely practical targets for businesses. We shall then expand on the wealth enhancement objective a little more.

Popular suggested objectives include:

1. *Maximisation of sales revenue.* Most businesses seek to sell as much of their goods or services as possible. As a business objective, however, it is far from adequate. Almost any business could sell enormous quantities of goods and/or services if it were to lower its prices to gain market share. This may well, however, lead to the business collapsing as a result of the sales revenues being insufficient to cover the costs of running the business.
2. *Maximisation of profit.* This is probably an improvement on sales maximisation as it takes account both of sales revenues and of expenses. It is probably also too limited as a business goal.

| Activity 1.9 | Can you think of any reasons why making the maximum profit possible this year may not be in the best interests of the business and those who are involved with it? We could think of several reasons. |

The reasons which we thought of are:

- *Risk.* It may be achieved by taking large risks, like not having expensive quality-control mechanisms. This may make the business profitable, but it could lead to disaster sooner or later.
- *Short-termism.* Concentrating on the short term and ignoring the long term may lead to immediate profits. For example, cutting out spending on things which are likely to pay off in the longer term, such as research and development, and training, can have short-term benefits at the expense of longer-term ones.
- *Size of the investment.* Expanding the business, through increased investment, could lead to higher profit, but the benefits of the investment may diminish with each additional amount invested.

3. *Maximisation of return on capital employed.* This suggestion overcomes the last of the three objections to the profit maximisation suggestion, since it takes account both of the level of profit and of the investment made to achieve it. It still suffers, however, from the risk and short-termist weaknesses of profit maximisation.
4. *Survival.* Businesses obviously aim to survive; however, this is unlikely to be enough, except in exceptional short-term circumstances. Businesses must normally have a more challenging reason for their existence.
5. *Long-term stability.* Though businesses may pursue this goal to some extent, it is not a primary objective for most businesses in that, like survival, it is insufficiently challenging.

6. *Growth.* This is probably fairly close to what most businesses aim for. It seeks to strike a balance between long-term and short-term benefits. It also encompasses survival and, probably, long-term stability. Growth is probably not specific enough to act as a suitable target. Is any level of growth acceptable or is a specific level of growth aimed for? Is it growth of profits, of assets or, perhaps, of something else?

7. *Satisficing.* It has been argued that all of the other suggested objectives are much too concerned with profits and the welfare of the owners of the business. The business can be seen as an alliance of various 'stakeholders' which includes owners, but it also includes the employees, suppliers, customers and the community in which the business operates. Thus, it is suggested, the objective should not be to maximise the returns of any one of these stakeholders, but to try to give them all a satisfactory return. It is difficult to argue with this general principle, but it is not clear how this can be stated as a practical touchstone for making business decisions.

8. *Enhancement/maximisation of the wealth of the owners.* This means that the business would take decisions such that the owners would be worth more as a result of the decision. When valuing businesses, people logically tend to take account of future profitability, both long-term and short-term, and of the risk attaching to future profits. Thus, all of the valuable features of suggestions 1 to 6 (above) are taken into account by this wealth enhancement objective.

   This objective probably has the maximum potential to satisfy all the stakeholders (suggestion 7) as it can be argued that any decision that failed to consider the position of the various stakeholders could be a bad one from a wealth enhancement point of view. For example, a decision that led to customers being exploited, and not getting a satisfactory deal, would pretty certainly not be one which would have a wealth-enhancing effect for the owners. This is because disenchanted customers would avoid dealing with the business in the future and would, possibly, influence others to do the same.

   Though wealth enhancement of owners may not be a perfect description of what businesses seek to achieve, it is certainly something that they cannot ignore. Unless the owners feel their wealth is being enhanced there would be little reason for them to continue the business.

For the remainder of this book we shall treat enhancement/maximisation of owners' wealth as the key objective against which decisions will be assessed. There will usually be other non-financial/non-economic factors that will also tend to bear on decisions. The final decision may well involve some compromise.

## Summary

In this chapter, we identified the main users of accounting and examined their information needs. We saw that accounting exists in order to improve the quality of economic decisions made by users. Unless accounting information fulfils this purpose, it has no real value. We considered two views of accounting that help us to understand its essential features. The first view is that accounting is a form of service and that the information provided should contain certain key characteristics or qualities to ensure its usefulness. The second view is that accounting is a part of the total information system of a business which is concerned with identifying, recording, analysing and reporting economic information. These two views are not competing views of the subject. By embracing both views we can achieve a better understanding of the nature and role of accounting.

We went on to consider the particular purpose of management accounting, which is to help managers to manage their business. We saw that management accounting differs from financial accounting in a number of important respects and that these differences reflect, to some extent, difference in access to financial information. Managers have greater control over the form and content of information provided than other user groups. We also saw that management accounting was changing as a result of changes in the business environment and changes in technology. These changes will continue and so management accounting must continue to adapt and develop in order to provide relevant information for decision-making purposes in the future.

Finally, we discussed the kind of financial objectives which have been suggested for businesses. We argued that enhancement/maximisation of owner wealth is the key objective against which the managers' actions and decisions will be assessed.

 **Key terms**

| | |
|---|---|
| Accounting   p. 1 | Understandability   p. 6 |
| Relevance   p. 5 | Accounting information system   p. 9 |
| Reliability   p. 5 | Management accounting   p. 10 |
| Comparability   p. 6 | Financial accounting   p. 10 |

## Further reading

If you would like to explore the topics covered in this chapter in more depth, we recommend the following books:

**Management Accounting**, *Atkinson, A., Banker, R., Kaplan, R.* and *Young, S.,* 3rd edn, Prentice Hall, 2001, chapter 1.

**Management and Cost Accounting**, *Drury, C.,* 5th edn, Thomson Learning, 2000, chapter 1.

**Cost Accounting: A managerial emphasis**, *Horngren, C., Foster, G.* and *Datar, S.,* 10th edn, Prentice Hall, 2000, chapter 1.

**Management Accounting: A review of recent developments**, *Scapens, R.,* 2nd edn, Macmillan, 1991, chapters 1 and 2.

## ❓ REVIEW QUESTIONS

**1.1** Identify the main users of accounting information for a university. Do these users, or the way in which they use accounting information, differ very much from the users of accounting information for private-sector businesses?

**1.2** Management accounting has been described as 'the eyes and ears of management'. What do you think this expression means?

**1.3** Management accounting information is often provided for groups of managers rather than individual managers. These groups of managers may make decisions which may not always be in the best interests of the business as a whole. Why is this?

**1.4** 'Accounting information should be understandable. As some managers have a poor knowledge of accounting we should produce simplified financial reports to help them.'

To what extent do you agree with this view?

## CHAPTER 2

# Relevant costs

## Introduction

In this chapter we shall consider the identification and use of costs in making management decisions. We shall see that not all costs surrounding an area are relevant to a particular decision. It is important to distinguish carefully between costs (and revenues) that are relevant and those that are not, since failure to do so could well lead to bad decisions being made.

**OBJECTIVES**    When you have completed this chapter, you should be able to:

- Define and distinguish between relevant costs, outlay costs and opportunity costs.
- Identify and quantify the costs that are relevant to a particular decision.
- Use the relevant costs to make decisions.
- Set out the analysis in a logical form so that the conclusion may be communicated to managers.

## What is meant by 'cost'?

The answer to this question is, at first sight, very obvious. Most people would say that **cost** is how much was paid for an item of goods being supplied or a service being provided.

**Activity 2.1**    You own a motor car, for which you paid a purchase price of £5,000 – much below list price – at a recent car auction. You have just been offered £6,000 for this car. What is the cost to you of keeping the car for your own use? *Note*: ignore running costs and so on; just consider the 'capital' cost of the car.

The real economic cost of retaining the car is £6,000, since this is what you are being deprived of to retain the car. Any decision that you make with respect to the car's future should logically take account of this figure. This cost is known as the 'opportunity cost' since it is the value of the opportunity forgone in order to pursue the other course of action. In this case, the other course of action is to retain the car.

In one sense, the cost of the car in Activity 2.1 is £5,000 because that is how much you paid for it. However, this cost, which for obvious reasons is known as the **historic cost**, is only of academic interest. It cannot logically ever be used to make a decision on the car's future. If you disagree with this point, ask yourself how you would assess an offer of £5,500, from another person, for the car. You would obviously compare the offer price of £5,500 with the **opportunity cost** of £6,000. You would not accept the £5,500 on the basis that it was bigger than the £5,000 you paid in the first place; you would reject it on the basis that it was less than the £6,000 offered. The only other figure that should concern you is the value to you, in terms of pleasure, usefulness and so on, that retaining the car would provide. If you valued this more highly than the £6,000 opportunity cost, you would reject both offers.

It may occur to you that the £5,000 is to some degree relevant here because, if you sold the car, either you would make a profit of £500 (£5,500–£5,000) or £1,000 (£6,000–£5,000). Since you would choose to make the higher profit, you would sell the car for £6,000 and make the right decision as a result. But ask yourself what decision you would make if the car cost you £4,000 to buy? Clearly you would still sell the car for £6,000 rather than for £5,500. What is more, you would reach the same conclusion whatever the historic cost was. Thus the historic cost can never be relevant to a future decision.

You should note particularly that even if the car cost, say, £10,000, the historic cost would still be irrelevant. If you have just bought a car for £10,000 and find that shortly after it is only worth £6,000, you may well be fuming at your mistake, but this does not make the £10,000 a **relevant cost**. The only relevant factors, in a decision on whether to sell the car or to keep it, are the £6,000 and the value of the benefits of keeping it.

Historic cost is normally used in accounting statements, like the balance sheet and the profit and loss account. This is logical, however, since these statements are intended to be accounts of what has actually happened and are drawn up after the event. In the context of decision making, which is always related to the future, historic cost is always irrelevant.

To say that historic cost is an **irrelevant cost** is not to say that the effects of having incurred that cost are always irrelevant. The fact that you own the car and you are thus in a position to exercise choice as to how you use it is not irrelevant.

It might be useful to formalise what we have discussed so far.

## A definition of cost

Cost may be defined as the amount of resources, usually measured in monetary terms, sacrificed to achieve a particular objective. The objective might be to retain a car, to buy a particular house, to make a particular product or to render a particular service. If we are talking about a **past cost**, we are talking about historic costs. If we are considering the future, we are interested in future opportunity costs and future **outlay costs**.

## Relevant costs: opportunity and outlay costs

An opportunity cost can be defined as the value in monetary terms of being deprived of the next-best opportunity in order to pursue the particular objective.

An outlay cost is an amount of money that will have to be spent to achieve that objective. We shall shortly meet plenty of examples of both of these types of future cost.

To be relevant to a particular decision, a cost must satisfy both of the following criteria:

■ *It must relate to the objectives of the business.* Most businesses have some wealth-enhancement objective; that is, they are seeking to become richer (see Chapter 1). Thus, to be relevant to a particular decision, a cost must have an effect on the wealth of the business, assuming a wealth-enhancement objective.
■ *It must differ from one possible decision outcome to the next.* Only items that are different between outcomes can be used to distinguish between them. Thus the reason that the historic cost of the car that we discussed earlier is irrelevant, is that it is the same whichever decision is taken about the future of the car. This means that all past costs are irrelevant because what has happened in the past must be the same for all possible future outcomes.

It is not only past costs that are the same from one decision outcome to the next; future costs may also be the same. Take, for example, a road haulage business that has decided that it will buy a new lorry and the decision lies between two different models. The load capacity, the fuel and maintenance costs are different for each lorry. The potential costs and revenues associated with these are relevant items. The lorry will require a driver, so the business will need to employ one; but a qualified driver could drive either lorry equally well, for the same wage. The cost of employing the driver is thus irrelevant to the decision as to which lorry to buy. This is despite the fact that this cost is a future one.

If, however, the decision were whether to operate an additional lorry or not, the cost of employing the driver would be relevant because here it would be a cost that would vary with the outcome.

| Activity 2.2 | A garage has an old car standing around that it bought several months ago for £3,000. The car needs a replacement engine before it can be sold. It is possible to buy a reconditioned engine for £300. This would take seven hours to fit by a mechanic who is paid £8 an hour. At present the garage is short of work, but the owners are reluctant to lay off any mechanics or even to cut down their basic working week because skilled labour is difficult to find and an upturn in repair work is expected soon. |
|---|---|

Without the engine the car could be sold for an estimated £3,500. What is the minimum price at which the garage would have to sell the car, with a reconditioned engine fitted, to justify doing the work?

The minimum price is:

|  | £ |
|---|---|
| Opportunity cost of the car | 3,500 |
| Cost of the reconditioned engine | 300 |
| Total | 3,800 |

The original cost of the car is irrelevant. It is the opportunity cost that concerns us. The cost of the new engine is relevant because, if the work is done, the garage will have to pay out the £300; if the job is not done, nothing will have to be paid. This is known as an outlay cost.

The labour cost is irrelevant because the same cost will be incurred whether the mechanic undertakes the work or not. This is because the mechanic is being paid to do nothing if this job is not undertaken; thus the additional cost arising from this job is zero.

It should be emphasised that the garage will not seek to sell the car with its reconditioned engine for £3,800; it will seek to charge as much as possible for it. On the other hand, any price above the £3,800 will make the garage better off financially than not undertaking the job.

---

**Activity 2.3**

Assume exactly the same circumstances as in Activity 2.2, except that the garage is quite busy at the moment. If a mechanic is to be put on the engine replacement job, it will mean that other work that the mechanic could have done during the seven hours, all of which could be charged to a customer, will not be undertaken. The garage's labour charge is £12 an hour.

What is the minimum price at which the garage would have to sell the car, with a reconditioned engine fitted, to justify doing the work under these altered circumstances?

The minimum price is:

|  | £ |
|---|---|
| Opportunity cost of the car | 3,500 |
| Cost of the reconditioned engine | 300 |
| Labour cost (7 × £12) | 84 |
| Total | 3,884 |

The relevant labour cost here is that which the garage will have to sacrifice in making the time available to undertake the engine replacement job. While the mechanic is working on this job, the garage is losing the opportunity to do work for which a customer would pay £84. Note that the £8/hour mechanic's wage is still not relevant. This is because the mechanic will be paid the £8 irrespective of whether it is the engine replacement work or some other job that is undertaken.

---

**Activity 2.4**

A business is considering offering a tender to undertake a contract. Fulfilment of the contract will require the use of two types of raw material, a quantity of both of which is held in stock by the business. All of the stock of these two raw materials will need to be used on the contract. Information on the stock required is as follows:

| Stock item | Quantity (units) | Historic cost (£/unit) | Sales value (£/unit) | Replacement cost (£/unit) |
|---|---|---|---|---|
| A1 | 500 | 5 | 3 | 6 |
| B2 | 800 | 7 | 8 | 10 |

Stock item A1 is in frequent use in the business on a variety of work. The stock of item B2 was bought a year ago for a contract that was abandoned. It has recently become obvious that there is no likelihood of ever using this stock if the contract currently being considered does not proceed.

Management wishes to deduce the minimum price at which it could undertake the contract without reducing its wealth as a result. This can be used as the baseline in deducing the tender price.

How much should be included in the minimum price in respect of the two stock items detailed above?

Stock item:  A1  £6 × 500 = £3,000
B2  £8 × 800 = £6,400

Since A1 is frequently used, if the stock is used on the contract it will need to be replaced. Sooner or later, if this stock is used on the contract, the business will have to buy 500 units (currently costed at £6 per unit) of it additional to that which would have been required had the contract not been undertaken.

Under the circumstances, the only reasonable behaviour of the business, if the contract is not undertaken, is to sell the stock of B2. Thus, using this stock has an opportunity cost equal to the potential proceeds from disposal, reckoned at £8 per unit.

**Activity 2.5**

HLA Ltd is in the process of preparing a quotation for a special job for a customer. The job will have the following material requirements:

| Material | Units req'd | Units currently held in stock | | | |
| --- | --- | --- | --- | --- | --- |
| | | Quantity | Cost (£/unit) | Saleable value (£/unit) | Replacement cost (£/unit) |
| P | 400 | 0 | – | – | 40 |
| Q | 230 | 100 | 62 | 50 | 64 |
| R | 350 | 200 | 48 | 23 | 59 |
| S | 170 | 140 | 33 | 12 | 49 |
| T | 120 | 120 | 40 | 0 | 68 |

Material Q is used consistently by the company on various jobs. Materials R, S and T are in stock as the result of previous overbuying. No other use can be found for R, but the 140 units of S could be used in another job as a substitute for 225 units of material V that are about to be purchased at a price of £10 per unit. Material T has no other use and the company has been informed that it will cost £160 to dispose of the material currently in stock.

What is the relevant cost of the materials for the job specified above?

| | £ |
| --- | --- |
| Material P will have to be purchased at £40 per unit (400 × £40) | 16,000 |
| Material Q will have to be replaced; therefore the relevant price is (230 × £64) | 14,720 |
| 200 units of material R are in stock and could be sold. The relevant price of these is the sales revenue forgone (200 × £23) | 4,600 |
| The remaining 150 units of R would have to be purchased (150 × £59) | 8,850 |

| | |
|---|---:|
| Material S could be sold or used as a substitute for material V. The existing stock could be sold for £1,680 (140 × £12); however, the saving on material V is higher and therefore should be taken as the relevant amount (225 × £10) | 2,250 |
| The remaining units of material S must be purchased (30 × £49) | 1,470 |
| A saving on disposal will be made if material T is used | (160) |
| Total relevant cost | £47,730 |

## Sunk costs and committed costs

➡ **Sunk cost** is simply another way of saying past cost and the two expressions can
➡ be used interchangeably. A **committed cost** is also, in effect, a past cost to the extent that an irrevocable decision has been made to incur the cost because, for example, the business has entered into a binding contract. As a result, it is more or less a past cost despite the fact that the cash may not be paid in respect of it until some point in the future. Since the business has no choice as to whether it incurs the cost or not, a committed cost cannot be a relevant cost.

It is important to remember that, to be relevant, a cost must be capable of varying according to the decision made. If the business is already committed by a legally binding contract to a cost, that cost cannot vary with the decision.

| | |
|---|---|
| *Activity 2.6* | **Past costs are irrelevant costs. Does this mean that what happened in the past is irrelevant?** |

No, it does not mean this. The fact that the business has an asset that it can deploy in the future is highly relevant. What is not relevant is how much it cost to acquire that asset. This point was examined in the discussion which followed Activity 2.1.

Another reason why the past is not irrelevant is that it generally – though not always – provides us with our best guide to the future. Suppose that we need to estimate the cost of doing something in the future to help us to decide whether or not it is worth doing. In these circumstances our own experience, or that of others, on how much it has cost to do the thing in the past may provide us with a valuable guide to how much it is likely to cost in the future.

Figure 2.1 summarises the relationship between relevant, irrelevant, opportunity, outlay and past costs.

## Qualitative factors of decisions

Though businesses must look closely at the obvious financial effects when making decisions, they must also consider factors that are not directly economic. These are likely to be factors that have a broader but less immediate impact on the business. Ultimately, however, these factors are likely to have an economic effect – that is, to affect the wealth of the business.

**Figure 2.1**

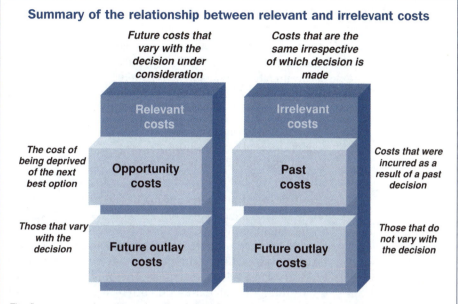

### Summary of the relationship between relevant and irrelevant costs

*Future costs that vary with the decision under consideration*

*Costs that are the same irrespective of which decision is made*

Relevant costs

Irrelevant costs

*The cost of being deprived of the next best option*

**Opportunity costs**

**Past costs**

*Costs that were incurred as a result of a past decision*

*Those that vary with the decision*

**Future outlay costs**

**Future outlay costs**

*Those that do not vary with the decision*

The figure summarises the main points relating to the identification of relevant and irrelevant costs. Note in particular that future outlay costs may be either relevant or irrelevant costs depending on whether they vary with the decision. Future opportunity costs and outlay costs, that vary with the decision, are relevant; future outlay costs, that do not vary with the decisions, and all past costs are irrelevant.

**Activity 2.7**

Activity 2.3 was concerned with the cost of putting a car into a marketable condition. Apart from whether the car could be sold for more than the relevant cost of doing this, are there any other factors that should be taken into account in making a decision as to whether or not to do the work?

We can think of three points:

- Turning away another job in order to do the engine replacement may lead to customer dissatisfaction.
- On the other hand, having the car available for sale may be useful commercially for the garage, beyond the profit that can be earned from that particular car sale. For example, having a good stock of second-hand cars may attract potential customers.
- There is also the more immediate economic point that it has been assumed that the only labour opportunity cost is the charge-out rate for the seven hours concerned. In practice, most car repairs involve the use of some materials and spare parts. These are usually charged to customers at a profit to the garage. Any such profit from a job turned away would be lost to the garage, and this lost profit would be an opportunity cost of the engine replacement and should, therefore, be included in the calculation of the minimum price to be charged for the sale of the car.

You may have thought of additional points.

It is important to consider 'qualitative' factors carefully. They can seem unimportant because they are virtually impossible to assess in terms of their ultimate economic effect. This effect can nevertheless be very significant.

**Self-assessment question 2.1**

JB Limited is a small specialist manufacturer of electronic components and much of its output is used by makers of aircraft, for both civil and military purposes. One of the aircraft manufacturers has offered a contract to JB Limited for the supply, over the next 12 months, of 400 identical components. The data relating to the production of each component are as follows:

(i)  *Material requirements*:
     3 kg of material M1 (see note 1 below)
     2 kg of material P2 (see note 2 below)
     1 part no. 678 (see note 3 below)

     *Note 1*: Material M1 is in continuous use by the company; 1,000 kg are currently held in stock. Their original cost was £4.70/kg, but it is known that future purchases will cost £5.50/kg.
     *Note 2*: 1,200 kg of material P2 are held in stock. The original cost of this material was £4.30/kg. The material has not been required for the last two years. Its scrap value is £1.50/kg. The only foreseeable alternative use is as a substitute for material P4 (in current use) but this would involve further processing costs of £1.60/kg. The current cost of material P4 is £3.60/kg.
     *Note 3*: It is estimated that part no. 678 could be bought in for £50 each.

(ii)  *Labour requirements*:  Each component would require five hours of skilled labour and five hours of semi-skilled. An employee possessing the necessary skills is available and is currently paid £7/hour. A replacement would, however, have to be obtained at a rate of £6/hour for the work, which would otherwise be done by the skilled employee. The current rate for semi-skilled work is £5/hour and an additional employee could be appointed for this work.

(iii) *General manufacturing costs*:  It is JB Limited's policy to charge a share of the general costs (rent, heating and so on) to each contract undertaken at the rate of £20 for each machine hour used. If the contract is undertaken, the general costs are expected to increase over the duration of the contract by £3,200.

Spare machine capacity is available and each component would require four machine hours. A price of £150 per component has been offered by the potential customer.

**Required:**
(a) Should the contract be accepted? Support your conclusion with appropriate figures to present to management.
(b) What other factors ought management to consider that might influence the decision?

## Summary

In this chapter we have seen that 'cost' can have several meanings. Relevant costs are those that relate to the objectives of the decision-making business and they will vary with the decision. Relevant costs include not only outlay costs, but opportunity costs as well. Past costs are always irrelevant because they will be the same irrespective of the course of action taken in the future. Some future costs will also be irrelevant – where they are the same, irrespective of the decision. We saw that financial/economic decisions almost inevitably have qualitative aspects, which the financial analysis probably cannot really handle, and that these aspects are typically very important.

## Key terms

| | |
|---|---|
| **Cost**  p. 21 | **Past cost**  p. 22 |
| **Historic cost**  p. 22 | **Outlay cost**  p. 22 |
| **Opportunity cost**  p. 22 | **Sunk cost**  p. 26 |
| **Relevant cost**  p. 22 | **Committed cost**  p. 26 |
| **Irrelevant cost**  p. 22 | |

## Further reading

If you would like to explore the topics covered in this chapter in more depth, we recommend the following books:

**Accounting for Management Decisions**, *Arnold, J.* and *Turley, S.*, 3rd edn, Prentice Hall International, 1996, chapter 10.

**Management and Cost Accounting**, *Drury, C.*, 5th edn, Thomson Learning, 2000, chapter 9.

**Cost Accounting: A managerial emphasis**, *Horngren, C., Foster, G.* and *Datar, S.*, 10th edn, Prentice Hall International, 2000, chapter 11.

**Cost and Management Accounting**, *Williamson, D.*, Prentice Hall International, 1996, chapter 12.

## ? REVIEW QUESTIONS

**2.1** To be relevant to a particular decision, a cost must have two attributes. What are they?

**2.2** Distinguish between a sunk cost and an opportunity cost.

**2.3** Define the word 'cost' in the context of management accounting.

**2.4** What is meant by the expression 'committed cost'?

## ? EXERCISES

Exercises 2.7 and 2.8 are more advanced than 2.1–2.6. Those with coloured numbers have answers at the back of the book.

**2.1** Lombard Ltd has been offered a contract for which there is available production capacity. The contract is for 20,000 items, manufactured by an intricate assembly operation, to be produced and delivered in the next financial year at a price of £80 each. The specification per item is as follows:

| | |
|---|---|
| Assembly labour | 4 hours |
| Component X | 4 units |
| Component Y | 3 units |

There would also be the need to hire equipment at an outlay cost of £200,000.

The assembly is a highly skilled operation and the workforce is currently under-utilised. It is the business's policy to retain this workforce on full pay in anticipation of high demand in a few years' time, for a new product currently being developed. Skilled workers are paid £10 per hour.

Component X is used in a number of other subassemblies produced by the business; it is readily available, and a small stock is held and replenished regularly. Component Y was a special purchase in anticipation of an order that did not in the end materialise. It is, therefore, surplus to requirements and 100,000 units that are in stock may have to be sold at a loss. An estimate of alternative values for components X and Y provided by the materials planning department is as follows:

| | X £/unit | Y £/unit |
|---|---|---|
| Historic cost | 4 | 10 |
| Replacement cost | 5 | 11 |
| Net realisable value | 3 | 8 |

It is estimated that any additional costs associated with the contract will amount to £8 per item.

**Required:**
Analyse the information in order to advise Lombard on the desirability of the contract.

**2.2** The local authority of a small town maintains a theatre and arts centre for the use of a local repertory company, other visiting groups and exhibitions. Management decisions are taken by a committee that meets regularly to review the accounts and plan the use of the facilities.

The theatre employs a full-time staff and a number of artistes at costs of £4,800 and £17,600 per month, respectively. They mount a new production every month for 20 performances. Other monthly expenditure of the theatre is as follows:

|                                                      | £     |
|------------------------------------------------------|-------|
| Costumes                                             | 2,800 |
| Scenery                                              | 1,650 |
| Heat and light                                       | 5,150 |
| A share of the administration costs of local authority | 8,000 |
| Casual staff                                         | 1,760 |
| Refreshments                                         | 1,180 |

On average the theatre is half full for the performances of the repertory company. The capacity and seat prices in the theatre are:

> 200 seats at £6 each
> 500 seats at £4 each
> 300 seats at £3 each

In addition the theatre sells refreshments during the performances for £3,880 per month. Programme sales cover their costs but advertising in the programme generates £3,360.

The management committee has been approached by a popular touring group to take over the theatre for one month (25 performances). The group is prepared to pay half of its ticket income for the booking. It expects to fill the theatre for 10 nights and achieve two-thirds capacity on the remaining 15 nights. The prices charged are 50p less than normally applies in the theatre.

The local authority will pay for heat and light costs and will still honour the contracts of all artistes and pay the full-time employees who will sell refreshments, programmes and so on. The committee does not expect any change in the level of refreshments or programme sales if they agree to this booking.

*Note*: The committee includes the share of the local authority administration costs when making profit calculations. It assumes occupancy applies equally across all seat prices.

**Required:**
(a) On financial grounds should the management committee agree to the approach from the touring group? Support your answer with appropriate workings.
(b) Assume the group will fill the theatre for ten nights as predicted. What occupancy is required for the remaining 15 nights for the committee to:
  (i) exactly cover all of its costs for the month?
  (ii) be financially indifferent to the booking?
(c) What other factors may have a bearing on the decision by the committee?

**2.3** Andrews and Co. Ltd has been invited to tender for a contract. It is to produce 10,000 metres of a cable in which the business specialises. The estimating department of the business has produced the following information relating to the contract:

- *Materials.*   The cable will require a steel core, which the business buys in. The steel core is to be coated with a special plastic, also bought in, using a special process. Plastic for the covering will be required at the rate of 0.10 kg/metre of completed cable.
- *Direct labour.*  Skilled:      10 minutes/metre
  Unskilled:    5 minutes/metre

The business already has sufficient stock of each of the materials required to complete the contract. Information on the cost of the stock is as follows:

|  | Steel core £/metre | Plastic £/kg |
|---|---|---|
| Historic cost | 1.50 | 0.60 |
| Current buying-in cost | 2.10 | 0.70 |
| Scrap value | 1.40 | 0.10 |

The steel core is in constant use by the business for a variety of work that it regularly undertakes. The plastic is a surplus from a previous contract where a mistake was made and an excess quantity ordered. If the current contract does not go ahead, this plastic will be scrapped.

Unskilled labour, which is paid at the rate of £5 an hour, will need to be taken on specifically to undertake the contract. The business is fairly quiet at the moment which means that a pool of skilled labour exists that will still be employed at full pay of £7 an hour to do nothing if the contract does not proceed. The pool of skilled labour is sufficient to complete the contract.

**Required:**
Indicate the minimum price at which the contract could be undertaken, such that the business would be neither better nor worse off as a result of doing it.

**2.4** SJ Ltd has been asked to quote a price for a special contract that will take the business one week to complete. Information relating to labour for the contract is as follows:

| Grade of labour | Hours required | Basic rate/hour |
|---|---|---|
| Skilled | 27 | £9 |
| Semi-skilled | 14 | £7 |
| Unskilled | 20 | £5 |

A shortage of skilled labour means that the necessary staff to undertake the contract would have to be moved from other work that is currently yielding an excess of sales revenue over labour and material cost of £8 per hour.

Semi-skilled labour is currently being paid at semi-skilled rates to undertake unskilled work. If the relevant staff are moved to work on the contract, unskilled labour will have to be employed for the week to replace them.

The unskilled labour actually needed to work on the contract will be employed for the week.

All labour is charged to contracts at 50 per cent above the rate paid to the employees, so as to cover the contract's fair share of the various production overheads of the company. It is estimated that the cost of overheads will increase by £50 as a result of undertaking the contract.

Undertaking the contract will require the use of a specialised machine for the week. The business owns such a machine, which it depreciates at the rate of £120 per week.

This machine is currently being hired out to another business at a weekly rental of £175 on a week-by-week contract.

To derive the above estimates, the business has had to spend £300 on specialised drawings. If the contract does not proceed, the drawings can be sold for £250.

An estimate of the contract's fair share of the business rent and rates is £150 per week.

**Required:**
Deduce the minimum price at which SJ Ltd could undertake the contract such that it would be neither better nor worse off as a result of undertaking it.

**2.5** A business in the food industry is currently holding 2,000 tonnes of material in bulk storage. This material deteriorates with time, and so in the near future it needs to be repackaged for sale or sold in its present form.

The stock was acquired in two batches: 800 tonnes at a price of £40 per tonne and 1,200 tonnes at a price of £44 per tonne. The current market price of any additional purchases is £48 per tonne. If the business were to dispose of the material, it could sell any quantity but only for £36 per tonne; it does not have the contacts or reputation to command a higher price.

Repackaging of this bulk material may be undertaken to develop either product A or product X. No weight loss occurs with repackaging; that is, one tonne of material will make one tonne of A or X. For product A, there is an additional cost of £60 per tonne, after which it will sell for £105 per tonne. The marketing department estimates that 500 tonnes could be sold in this way.

In the development of product X, the business incurs additional costs of £80 per tonne for repackaging. A market price for X is not known and no minimum price has been agreed. The management is currently engaged in discussions over the minimum price that may be charged for product X in the current circumstances.

**Required:**
Identify the relevant unit cost for pricing the increments of Product X, given sales volumes of X of:

(a) up to 1,500 tonnes
(b) over 1,500 tonnes, up to 2,000 tonnes
(c) over 2,000 tonnes.

Explain your answer.

**2.6** A local education authority is faced with a predicted decline in the demand for school places in its area. It is believed that some schools will have to close in order to remove up to 800 places from current capacity levels. The schools that may face closure are referenced as A, B, C or D. Their details are as follows:

- *School A.* (capacity 200) was built 15 years ago at a cost of £1.2 million. It is situated in a 'socially disadvantaged' community area. The authority has been offered £14 million for the site by a property developer.
- *School B.* (capacity 500) was built 20 years ago and cost £1 million. It was renovated only two years ago at a cost of £3 million to improve its facilities. An offer of £8 million has been made for the site by a company planning a shopping complex in this affluent part of the town.
- *School C.* (capacity 600). The land for this school is rented from a local company for an annual cost of £30,000. The school cost £5 million to build five years ago.

■ *School D.* (800 capacity) cost £7 million to build eight years ago; last year £1.5 million was spent on an extension. It offers considerable space, which is currently used for sporting events. This factor makes it popular with developers, who have recently offered £9 million for the site.

In the accounting system, the local authority depreciates fixed assets based on 2 per cent per year on the original cost. It also differentiates between one-off, large items of capital expenditure or revenue, and annually recurring items.

The land rented for school C is based on a 100-year lease. If the school closes, the property reverts immediately to the owner. If school C is not closed, it will require a £3 million investment to improve safety at the school.

If school D is closed, it will be necessary to pay £1.8 million to adapt facilities at other schools to accommodate the change.

The local authority has a central staff, which includes an administrator for each school costing £20,000 per year each, and a chief education officer costing £40,000 per year in total.

**Required:**
(a) Prepare a summary of the relevant cash flows (costs/revenues) under the following options:
  (i)   no closures
  (ii)  closure of D only
  (iii) closure of A and B
  (iv)  closure of A and C.
  Show separately the one-off effects and annually recurring items, rank the options open to the local authority, and briefly interpret your answer. *Note*: Various approaches are acceptable providing they are logical.
(b) Identify and comment on any two different types of irrelevant cost contained in the information given.
(c) Discuss other factors that might have a bearing on the decision.

2.7 Rob Otics Ltd, a small business that specialises in building electronic control equipment, has just received an order from a customer for eight identical robotic units. These will be completed using Rob Otic's own labour force and factory capacity. The product specification prepared by the estimating department shows the following:

■ Material and labour requirements per robotic unit:
  Component X     2 per unit
  Component Y     1 per unit
  Component Z     4 per unit.
■ Other miscellaneous items:
  Assembly labour     25 hours per unit (but see below)
  Inspection labour    6 hours per unit.

As part of the costing exercise, the business has collected the following information:

■ *Component X.* This is a stock item normally held by the business as it is in constant demand. The 10 units currently in stock were invoiced to Rob Otics at £150 per unit, but the sole supplier has announced a price rise of 20 per cent effective immediately. Rob Otics has not yet paid for the items in stock.
■ *Component Y.* 25 units are in stock. This component is not normally used by Rob Otics but is in stock because of a cancelled order following the bankruptcy of a customer. The stock originally cost the company £4,000 in total, although Rob

Otics has recouped £1,500 from the liquidator. As Rob Otics can see no use for it, the finance director proposes to scrap the 25 units.

- *Component Z.* This is in regular use by Rob Otics. There is none in stock but an order is about to be sent to a supplier for 75 units, irrespective of this new proposal. The supplier charges £25 per unit on small orders but will reduce the price by 20 per cent to £20 per unit for all units on any order over 100 units.
- *Other miscellaneous items.* These are expected to cost £250 in total.

Assembly labour is currently in short supply in the area and is paid at £10 per hour. If the order is accepted, all necessary labour will have to be transferred from existing work, and other orders will be lost. It is estimated that for each hour transferred to this contract £38 will be lost (calculated as lost sales revenue £60, less materials £12 and labour £10). The production director suggests that, owing to a learning process, the time taken to make each unit will reduce, from 25 hours to make the first one, by 1 hour per unit made.

Inspection labour can be provided by paying existing personnel overtime which is at a premium of 50 per cent over the standard rate of £12 per hour.

When the company is working out its contract prices, it normally adds an amount equal to £20 per assembly hour to cover overheads. To the resulting total, 40 per cent is normally added as a profit mark up.

**Required:**
(a) Prepare an estimate of the minimum price that you would recommend Rob Otics to charge for the proposed contract, and provide explanations for any items included.
(b) Identify any other factors that you would consider before fixing the final price.

2.8 A business places substantial emphasis on customer satisfaction and to this end delivers its product in special protective containers. These containers have been developed in a separate department, which has recently been assessed to be too expensive to continue. As a result, tenders have been issued for the provision of these containers by an outside supplier. A quote of £250,000 a year has been received for a volume that compares with current internal provision.

An investigation into the internal costs of container manufacture is undertaken and the following emerges:

(a) The annual cost of material is £120,000 according to the stores records maintained at actual historic cost. Three-quarters of this represents material that is regularly stocked and replenished. The remaining 25 per cent of the material cost is a special foaming chemical that is not used for any other purpose, and there are 40 tonnes still in stock. It was bought in bulk for £750 per tonne. Today's replacement price for this material is £1,050 per tonne but it is unlikely that the business could realise more than £600 per tonne if it had to be disposed of owing to the high handling costs and special transport facilities required.
(b) The annual labour cost is £80,000 for this department, however, most are casual employees or recent starters, and so, if an outside quote were accepted, little redundancy would be payable. There are two long-serving employees who would each accept as a salary £15,000 a year until they reached retirement age in two years' time.
(c) The department manager has a salary of £30,000. The closure of this department would release him to take over another department for which a vacancy is about to be advertised. The status and prospects are similar.

(d) A rental charge of £9,750 based on floor area is allocated to the containers department. If the department were closed, the floorspace released would be used for warehousing and, as a result, the company would give up the tenancy of an existing warehouse for which it is paying £15,750 a year.

(e) The plant cost £162,000 and was expected to be exhausted in nine years. Its market value now is £28,000 and it could continue for another two years.

(f) Annual plant maintenance costs are £9,900 and allocated general administrative costs £33,750 for the coming year.

**Required:**

Calculate the annual cost of manufacturing containers for comparison with the quote using relevant figures for establishing the cost or benefit of accepting the quote. Indicate any assumptions or qualifications you wish to make.

## CHAPTER 3

# Cost-volume-profit analysis

## Introduction

This chapter is concerned with the relationship between volume of activity, costs and profit. Broadly, costs can be analysed between costs that are fixed, relative to the volume of activity, and those that vary with it. We shall consider how we can use knowledge of this relationship to make decisions and assess risk, particularly in the context of short-term decisions.

**OBJECTIVES**

When you have completed this chapter you should be able to:

■ Distinguish between fixed costs and variable costs.
■ Use knowledge of this distinction to deduce the break-even point for some activity.
■ Make decisions on the use of spare capacity using knowledge of the relationship between fixed and variable costs.
■ Make decisions about the acceptance (or continuance) or rejection of a particular contract or activity, based on knowledge of the relationship between fixed and variable costs.

## The behaviour of costs

It is an observable fact that, for many commercial/business activities, costs may be broadly classified as follows:

■ Those that stay fixed (the same) when changes occur to the volume of activity.
■ Those that vary according to the volume of activity.

➡ These are known as **fixed costs** and **variable costs** respectively.

We shall see in this chapter that knowledge of how much of each type of cost is involved with some particular activity can be of great value to a decision maker.

### Fixed costs

The way in which fixed costs behave is depicted in Figure 3.1. The distance 0F represents the amount of fixed costs in an activity, and this stays the same irrespective of the level of activity.

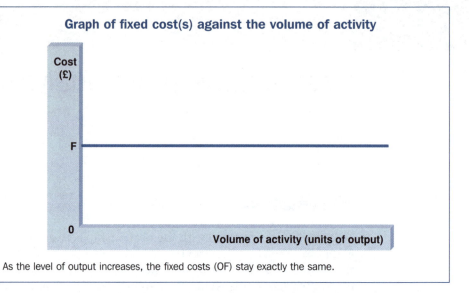

**Figure 3.1**

**Graph of fixed cost(s) against the volume of activity**

As the level of output increases, the fixed costs (OF) stay exactly the same.

**Activity 3.1**

A business operates a small chain of hairdressing salons. Can you give some examples of costs that are likely to be fixed for this business?

We came up with the following:

- Rent
- Insurance
- Cleaning costs
- Staff salaries.

These costs seem likely to be the same irrespective of alterations in the number of customers wanting their hair cut or styled.

Staff salaries and wages sometimes tend to be referred to as always being variable costs. In fact, they tend to be fixed. People are generally not paid according to the level of output and it is not normal to sack staff when there is a short-term downturn in activity. If there is a long-term downturn in activity, or at least if it looks that way to management, redundancies may occur, with fixed-cost savings. This, however, is true of all costs. If there is seen to be a likely reduction in demand, the business may decide to close some branches and make rental-cost savings. Thus 'fixed' does not mean set in stone for all time; it usually means fixed over the short to medium term.

Nevertheless, in some circumstances, labour costs are variable, but probably in a minority of cases.

It is important to be clear that 'fixed', in this context, only means that the cost is not altered by changes in the **level of activity**.

Fixed costs are likely to be affected by inflation. If rent (a typical fixed cost) goes up owing to inflation, a fixed cost will have increased, but not owing to a change in the level of activity.

More generally, the level of fixed costs does not stay the same irrespective of the time period involved. Fixed costs are almost always 'time-based'; that is, they vary with the length of time concerned. The rental charge for two months is normally twice that for one month. You should note that when we talk of fixed costs being, say £1,000, we must add the period concerned, say £1,000 a month.

**Activity 3.2**

Do fixed costs stay the same irrespective of the level of output, even where there is a massive rise in that level? Think in terms of the rent cost for the hairdressing business.

In fact, the rent is only fixed over a particular range (known as the 'relevant' range). If the number of people wanting to have their hair cut by the business increases, and the business wishes to meet this increased demand, it would have to expand its physical size eventually. This might be by opening additional branches, or perhaps by moving existing branches to larger premises in the same vicinity. It may be possible to cope with minor increases in activity by using existing space more efficiently, or having longer opening hours. If activity continued to expand, increased rental charges would seem inevitable.

**Figure 3.2**

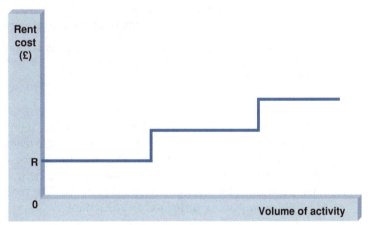

**Graph of rent cost against the volume of activity**

As the volume of activity increases from zero, the rent (a fixed cost) is unaffected. At a particular point, the volume of activity cannot increase without additional space being rented. The cost of renting the additional space will cause a 'step' in the rent cost. The higher rent cost will continue unaffected if volume were to rise further until, eventually, another step point would be reached.

Thus, in practice, the situation described in Activity 3.2 would look something like Figure 3.2. At lower levels of activity the rent cost shown in Figure 3.2 would be OR. As the level of activity expands, the accommodation becomes inadequate and further expansion requires an increase in premises and, therefore, cost. This higher level of accommodation provision will enable further expansion to take place. Eventually, further costs will need to be incurred if further expansion is to occur. Fixed costs that behave like this are often referred to as **stepped fixed** **costs**.

**Exhibit 3.1**

**Debenhams's fixed costs**

Debenhams plc, the department store chain, has a level of fixed costs that amount to less that 10 per cent of its total sales revenue for 2000, according to that year's annual report and accounts.

The fact that this information is reported indicates that businesses actually analyse their costs between fixed and variable. It is unusual, however, for a business to report its level of fixed costs as Debenhams has done.

The retail trade is relatively unusual in having such a small fixed cost element.

## Variable costs

Variable costs are costs that vary with the level of activity. In a manufacturing business, for example, these would include raw materials used.

| Activity 3.3 | **Can you think of some examples of variable costs in the hairdressing business?** |
| --- | --- |

We can think of a couple:

■ Lotions and other materials used
■ Laundry costs to wash towels used to dry the hair of customers.

As with many types of business activity, variable costs of hairdressers tend to be relatively light in comparison with fixed costs; in other words fixed costs tend to make up the bulk of total costs.

Variable costs can be represented graphically as in Figure 3.3, which shows that, at zero level of activity, the variable cost is zero. This cost increases in a straight line as activity increases. The straight line for variable cost on this graph implies that the cost of materials will normally be the same per unit of activity irrespective of the level of activity concerned. We shall consider the practicality of this assumption a little later in this chapter.

| Figure 3.3 | **Graph of the cost of a hairdresser's materials against the volume of activity** |
| --- | --- |

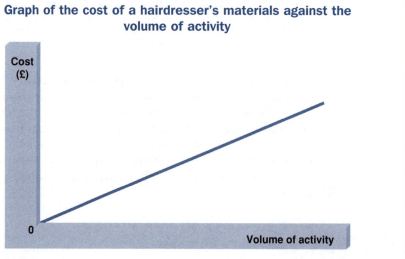

At zero activity, there are no variable costs. As the level of activity increases, so does the variable cost.

## Semi-fixed (semi-variable) costs

→ In some cases, costs have both an element of fixed and of variable cost about them. They can be described as **semi-fixed (semi-variable) costs**.

| Activity 3.4 | Can you suggest a couple of costs that are likely to be semi-fixed/semi-variable for a hairdressing business? |
|---|---|

We thought of:

- Electricity charges
- Telephone charges.

Some of the electricity charge will be for heating and lighting, and this part is probably fixed, at least until the volume of activity expands to a point where longer opening hours or larger premises are necessary. The other part of the cost will vary with the level of activity. Here we are talking about such things as power for hairdryers and so on.

Similarly with telephone charges. There would be rental, which is fixed; there are also certain calls that would be made irrespective of the volume of activity involved; yet increased business would be likely to lead to the need to make more telephone calls.

Usually it is not obvious how much of each element a particular cost contains. It is normally necessary to look at past experience. If we have data on what the electricity cost has been for various levels of activity – say the relevant data over several three-month periods (electricity is usually billed by the quarter) – we can estimate the fixed and variable portions. This may be done graphically, as shown in Figure 3.4. We tend to use past data here purely because it provides us with an estimate of future costs; past costs are not, of course, relevant for their own sake.

| Figure 3.4 | **Graph of electricity cost against the volume of activity** |
|---|---|

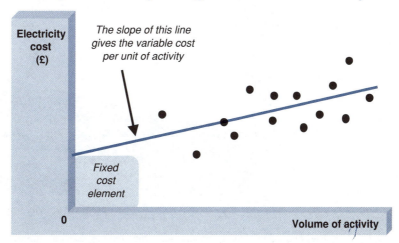

Here the electricity bill for a time period (for example, three months) is plotted against the volume of activity for that same period. This is done for a series of periods. A line is then drawn which best 'fits' the various points on the graph. From this line we can then deduce both the cost at zero activity (the fixed element) and the slope of the line (indicating the variable element).

Each dot in Figure 3.4 is a reading of the electricity charge for a particular level of activity (probably measured in terms of sales revenue). The diagonal line is the 'line of best fit'. This means that, to us, it looked like the line that best represents the data. A better estimate can usually be made using a statistical technique (least-squares regression), which does not involve drawing graphs and making estimates. In practice, though, it usually makes little difference which approach is taken.

From the graph we can say that the fixed element of the electricity cost is the amount represented by the vertical distance from the origin at zero (bottom left-hand corner) to the point where the line of best fit crosses the vertical axis. The variable cost per unit is the amount that the line of best fit rises for each unit increase in the volume of activity.

By analysing semi-fixed costs into their fixed and variable elements in this way, we are left with only two types of cost. This means that we can use the information for further analysis.

Now that we have considered the nature of fixed and variable costs, we can go on to do something useful with that knowledge – carry out a **break-even analysis**.

## Break-even analysis

If, in respect of a particular activity, we know the total fixed costs for a period and the total variable cost per unit, we can produce a graph like Figure 3.5.

The bottom part of the figure shows the fixed cost area. Added to this is the variable cost, the wedge-shaped portion at the top of the graph. The uppermost line represents the **total cost** at any particular level of activity. This total is the

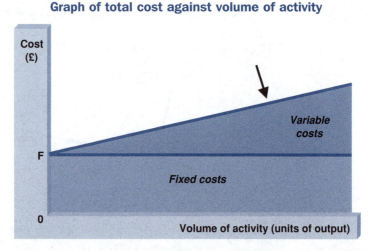

**Figure 3.5**

**Graph of total cost against volume of activity**

Cost (£)

Variable costs

F

Fixed costs

0

Volume of activity (units of output)

The bottom part of the graph represents the fixed cost element. To this is added the wedge-shaped top portion, which represents the variable costs. The two parts together represent total cost. At zero activity, the variable costs are zero, and so total cost equals fixed costs. As activity increases, so does total cost, but only because variable costs increase. We are assuming that there are no steps in the fixed costs.

| Figure 3.6 |
|---|

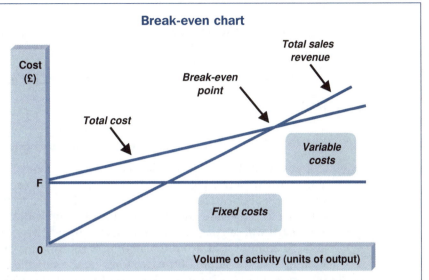

**Break-even chart**

The sloping line starting at 0 represents the sales revenue at various levels of activity. The point at which this finally catches up with the sloping total-cost line, which starts at F, is the break-even point. Below this point a loss will be made, above it a profit.

vertical distance between the horizontal axis and the uppermost line, for the particular level of activity concerned. Logically enough, the total cost at zero activity is the amount of the fixed costs. This is because, even where there is nothing going on, the business will still be paying rent, salaries and so on, at least in the short term. The fixed cost is augmented by the amount of the relevant variable costs, as the volume of activity increases.

If we superimpose onto this total-cost graph a line representing total revenue for each level of activity, we obtain the **break-even chart** shown in Figure 3.6.

Note, in Figure 3.6, that at zero level of activity (zero sales) there is zero sales revenue. The profit (total sales revenue less total cost) at various levels of activity is the vertical distance between the total sales line and the total cost line, at that particular level of activity. At **break-even point**, there is no vertical distance between these two lines and thus there is no profit or loss, and the activity breaks even. Below break-even point, a loss will be incurred; above break-even point, there will be a profit. The further below break-even point, the greater the loss; the further above, the greater the profit.

As you might imagine, deducing break-even points by graphical means is a laborious business. It may have struck you that since the relationships in the graph are all linear (the lines are all straight), it would be easy to calculate the break-even point.

We know that at break-even point (but not at any other point):

$$\text{Total revenues} = \text{Total costs}$$

That is,

$$\text{Total revenues} = \text{Fixed costs} + \text{Total variable costs}$$

If we call the number of units of output at break-even point $b$, then

$$b \times \text{Sales revenue per unit} = \text{Fixed costs} + (b \times \text{Variable costs per unit})$$

thus,

$$(b \times \text{Sales revenue per unit}) - (b \times \text{Variable costs per unit}) = \text{Fixed costs}$$

and,

$$b \times (\text{Sales revenue per unit} - \text{Variable costs per unit}) = \text{Fixed costs}$$

giving

$$b = \frac{\text{Fixed costs}}{\text{Sales revenue per unit} - \text{Variable costs per unit}}$$

If you look back at the break-even chart, this looks logical. The total-cost line starts with an 'advantage' over the sales revenue line equal to the amount of the fixed costs. Because the sales revenue per unit is greater than the variable cost per unit, the sales revenue line will gradually catch up with the total cost line. The rate at which it will catch it up is dependent on the relative steepnesses of the two lines, and the amount that it has to catch up is the amount of the fixed costs. Bearing in mind that the slopes of the two lines are the variable cost per unit and the selling price per unit, the above equation for calculating $b$ looks perfectly logical.

Though the break-even point can be calculated quickly and simply, as shown, it does not mean that the break-even chart is without value. The chart shows the relationship between cost, volume and profit in a form that can readily be understood by non-financial managers. The break-even chart can therefore be a useful device for explaining this relationship.

| Example 3.1 | Cottage Industries Ltd makes baskets. The fixed costs of operating the workshop for a month total £500. Each basket requires materials that cost £2. Each basket takes two hours to make and the business pays the basketmakers £5 an hour. The basketmakers are all on contracts such that if they do not work for any reason, they are not paid. The baskets are sold to a wholesaler for £14 each.

What is the break-even point for basketmaking for the business?

The break-even point (in number of baskets) is:

$$\frac{\text{Fixed costs}}{\text{Sales revenue per unit} - \text{Variable costs per unit}}$$

$$= \frac{£500}{£14 - (2 + 10)} = 250 \text{ baskets per month}$$

Note that the break-even point must be expressed with respect to a period of time.

| Exhibit 3.2 | **Break-even point at British Airways plc (BA)**

In its annual report and accounts for 2000, BA reported that it breaks even at a level of about 66 per cent. In general terms, if BA's planes fly at about two-thirds full, the business will break even. During the late 1990s the break-even point was, on average, a percentage point or two below the 2000 level.

The fact that BA has mentioned this implies that, in practice, businesses consider cost–volume relationships when assessing their financial performance.

**Activity 3.5**

Can you think of reasons why the managers of a business might find it useful to know the break-even point of some activity that they are planning to undertake?

The usefulness of being able to deduce a break-even point is to compare the planned or expected level of activity with the break-even point and so make a judgement about risk. Operating only just above the level of activity necessary in order to break even may indicate that it is a risky venture, since only a small fall from the planned level of activity could lead to a loss.

**Activity 3.6**

Cottage Industries Ltd (see Example 3.1) expects to sell 500 baskets a month. The business has the opportunity to rent a basket-making machine. Doing so would increase the total fixed costs of operating the workshop for a month to £3,000. Using the machine would reduce the labour time to one hour per basket. The basket makers would still be paid £5 an hour.

(a) How much profit would the business make each month from selling baskets, assuming first that the basket-making machine is not rented and then assuming that it is rented?

(b) What is the break-even point if the machine is rented?

What do you notice about the figures that you calculate?

(a) Estimated profit, per month, from basket making:

| | Without the machine | | With the machine | |
|---|---|---|---|---|
| | £ | £ | £ | £ |
| Sales (500 × £14) | | 7,000 | | 7,000 |
| Less  Materials  (500 × £2) | 1,000 | | 1,000 | |
| Labour  (500 × 2 × £5) | 5,000 | | | |
| (500 × 1 × £5) | | | 2,500 | |
| Fixed costs | 500 | | 3,000 | |
| | | 6,500 | | 6,500 |
| Profit | | 500 | | 500 |

(b) The break-even point (in number of baskets) with the machine is:

$$\frac{\text{Fixed costs}}{\text{Sales revenue per unit} - \text{Variable costs per unit}}$$

$$= \frac{£3,000}{£14 - (2 + 5)} = 429 \text{ baskets per month}$$

The break-even point without the machine is 250 baskets per month (see Example 3.1 (above)).

There seems to be nothing to choose between the two manufacturing strategies regarding profit, at the estimated sales volume. There is, however, a distinct difference between the two strategies regarding the break-even point. Without the machine, the actual level of sales could fall by a half of that which is expected (from 500 to 250) before the business would fail to make a profit. With the machine, a 14 per cent fall (from 500 to 429) would be enough to cause the business to fail to make a profit. On the other hand, for each additional basket sold, above the estimated 500, an additional profit of only £2 (£14 – (2 + 10)) would be made without the machine, whereas £7 (£14 – (2 + 5)) would be made with the machine.

(Note that knowledge of the break-even point and the planned level of activity gives some basis of assessing the riskiness of the activity.)

We shall take a closer look at the relationship between fixed costs, variable costs and breaking even, together with any advice that we might give the management of Cottage Industries Ltd, after we have briefly considered the notion of contribution.

## Contribution

→ The bottom part of the break-even formula (sales revenue per unit less variable costs per unit), is known as the **contribution** per unit. Thus, for the basket-making activity, without the machine the contribution per unit is £2 and with the machine it is £7. This can be a useful figure to know in a decision-making context. It is referred to as 'contribution' because it contributes to meeting the fixed costs and, if there is any excess, it also contributes to profit.

→ The variable cost per unit will usually be equal to the **marginal cost** – that is, the additional cost of making one more basket. Where making one more will involve a step in the fixed costs, the marginal cost is not just the variable cost but will include the increment, or step, in the fixed costs.

## Margin of safety and operating gearing

→ The **margin of safety** is the extent to which the planned level of output or sales lies above the break-even point. Going back to Activity 3.6, we saw that the following situation exists:

|  | Without the machine | With the machine |
|---|---|---|
| Expected level of sales | 500 | 500 |
| Break-even point | 250 | 429 |
| Difference (margin of safety): | | |
|     Number of baskets | 250 | 71 |
|     Percentage of estimated level of sales | 50% | 14% |

**Activity 3.7**

**What advice would you give Cottage Industries Ltd about renting the machine on the basis of the figures for margin of safety?**

It is a matter of personal judgement, which in turn is related to individual attitudes to risk, as to which strategy to adopt. Most people, however, would prefer the strategy of not renting the machine since the margin of safety between the expected level of activity and the break-even point is much greater.

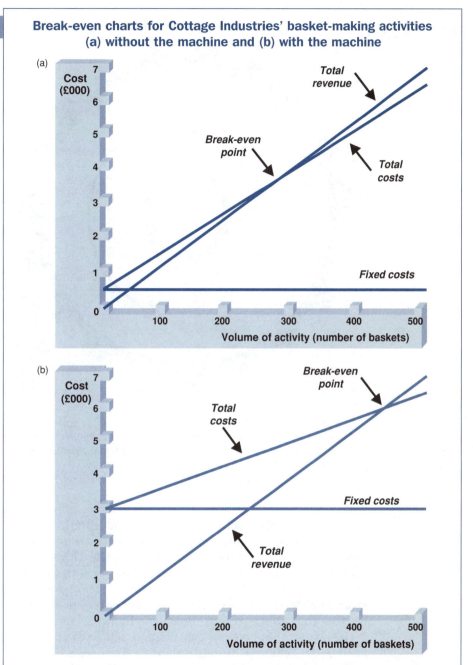

**Break-even charts for Cottage Industries' basket-making activities (a) without the machine and (b) with the machine**

Without the machine the contribution per unit is low. Thus, each additional basket sold does not make a dramatic difference to the profit or loss. With the machine, however, the opposite is true; and small increases or decreases in the sales volume will have a marked effect on the profit or loss.

The relative margins of safety are directly linked to the relationship between the selling price per basket, the variable costs per basket and the fixed costs per month. Without the machine, the contribution (selling price less variable costs) per basket is £2; with the machine, it is £7. On the other hand, without the

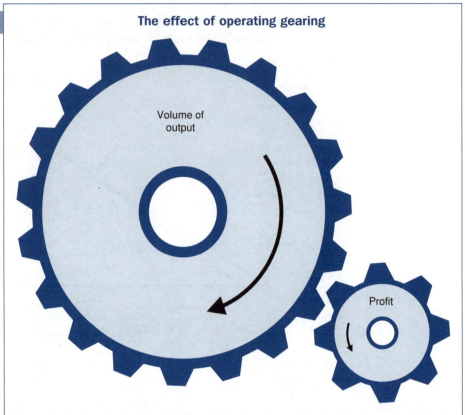

**Figure 3.8**

**The effect of operating gearing**

Volume of output

Profit

Where operating gearing is relatively high, as in the diagram, an amount of circular motion in the volume wheel causes a greater amount of circular motion in the profit wheel. An increase in volume would cause a disproportionally greater increase in profit. The equivalent would be true of a decrease in activity, however.

machine the fixed costs are £500 a month and with the machine they are £3,000. This means that, with the machine, the contributions have more fixed costs to 'overcome' before the activity becomes profitable. However, the rate at which the contributions can overcome fixed costs is higher with the machine, because variable costs are lower. This means that one more, or one less, basket sold has a greater impact on profit than it does if the machine is not rented. The contrast between the two scenarios is shown graphically in Figure 3.7.

The relationship between contribution and fixed costs is known as **operating gearing**. An activity with relatively high fixed costs compared with its variable costs is said to have high operating gearing. Thus, Cottage Industries Ltd is more highly operating geared with the machine than without it. Renting the machine quite dramatically increases the level of operating gearing because it causes an increase in fixed costs, but at the same time it leads to a reduction in variable costs per basket.

The reason why the word 'gearing' is used in this context is that, as with inter-meshing gear wheels of different circumferences, a movement in one of the factors (volume of output) causes a disproportionately greater movement in the other (profit), as illustrated by Figure 3.8.

We can demonstrate operating gearing with Cottage Industries Ltd's basket-making activities, as follows:

|  | Without the machine | | | With the machine | | |
|---|---|---|---|---|---|---|
| Volume | 500 | 1,000 | 1,500 | 500 | 1,000 | 1,500 |
|  | £ | £ | £ | £ | £ | £ |
| Contributions | 1,000 | 2,000 | 3,000 | 3,500 | 7,000 | 10,500 |
| *Less* Fixed costs | 500 | 500 | 500 | 3,000 | 3,000 | 3,000 |
| Profit | 500 | 1,500 | 2,500 | 500 | 4,000 | 7,500 |

where contributions are calculated as £2 per basket without the machine and £7 per basket with it.

Note that without the machine (low operating gearing), a doubling of the output from 500 to 1,000 brings a trebling of the profit. With the machine (high operating gearing), doubling output causes profit to rise by eight times.

**Activity 3.8**

In general terms, what types of business activity tend to be most highly operating geared? *Hint*: Cottage Industries Ltd might give you some idea.

In general, activities that are capital intensive tend to be more highly geared, since renting or owning capital equipment gives rise to fixed costs but can also give rise to lower variable costs.

## Profit–volume charts

➡ A slight variant of the break-even chart is the **profit–volume (PV) chart**. A typical PV chart is shown in Figure 3.9.

**Figure 3.9**

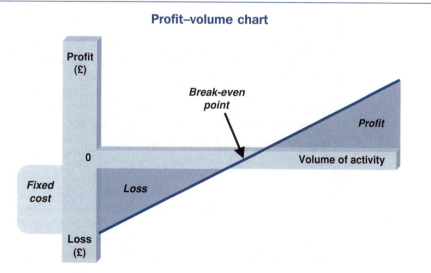

The sloping line is profit plotted against volume of activity. As activity increases, so does total contribution (sales revenue less variable costs). At zero activity there are no contributions, and so there will be a loss equal in amount to the total fixed costs.

The PV chart is obtained by plotting loss or profit against volume of activity. The slope of the graph is equal to the contribution per unit, since each additional unit sold decreases the loss, or increases the profit, by the sales revenue per unit less the variable cost per unit. At zero level of activity, there are no contributions and so there is a loss equal to the amount of the fixed costs. As the level of activity increases, the amount of the loss gradually decreases until break-even point is reached. Beyond break-even point, profits increase as activity increases.

It may have occurred to you that the PV chart does not tell us anything not shown by the break-even chart. Though this is true, information is perhaps more easily absorbed from the PV chart. This is particularly true of the profit at any level of volume. This information is provided by the break-even chart as the vertical distance between the total cost and total sales revenue lines. The PV chart, in effect, combines the total sales revenue and total variable cost lines, which means that profit (or loss) is plotted directly.

## The economist's view of the break-even chart

So far in this chapter we have treated all the relationships as linear – that is, all of the lines in the graphs have been straight. This is typically the approach taken in accounting, though it may not be strictly valid.

Consider, for example, the variable cost line in the break-even chart; accountants would normally treat this as being a straight line. Strictly, however, the line perhaps should not be straight because at high levels of output **economies of scale** may be available to an extent not available at lower levels. For example, a raw material (a typical variable cost) may be able to be used more efficiently with higher volumes of activity. Similarly, the relatively large quantities of material and services bought may enable the business to benefit from bulk discounts and general power in the marketplace to negotiate lower prices.

There is also a general tendency for sales revenue per unit to reduce as volume is expanded, since to sell more units of the product or service, it will probably be necessary to lower the selling price.

Economists tend to recognise that, in real life, the relationships portrayed in the break-even chart are usually non-linear. The typical economist's view of the chart is shown in Figure 3.10.

Note, in that diagram, that the variable costs start to increase quite steeply with volume, but around point A economies of scale start to take effect and further increases in volume do not cause such a large increase, per unit of output, in variable costs. These economies of scale continue to have a benign effect on costs until a point is reached where the business will be operating towards the end of its efficient range. Here the business may have problems with finding supplies of the variable-cost elements, which will normally adversely affect their price. Also, the business may find it more difficult to produce, there may be machine breakdowns, and so on.

At low levels of output, sales may be made at a relatively high price per unit. To increase sales output beyond point B it may be necessary to lower the average sales price per unit.

Note how this 'curvilinear' representation of the break-even chart can easily lead to the existence of two break-even points.

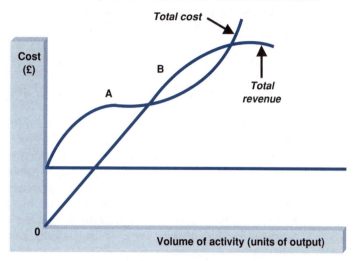

| Figure 3.10 |
|---|

**The economist's view of the break-even chart**

As volume increases, economies of scale have a favourable effect on variable costs, but this effect is reversed at still higher levels of output. At the same time, sales revenue per unit will tend to decrease at higher levels to encourage additional buyers.

Accountants justify their approach to this topic by the fact that, although the line may not in practice be perfectly straight, this defect is probably not worth taking into account in most cases. This is partly because all of the information used in the analysis is based on estimates of the future. Since this will inevitably be flawed, it seems pointless to be pedantic about minor approximations, such as treating the total cost and revenue lines as straight ones when strictly this is invalid. Only where significant economies or diseconomies of scale are involved should the non-linearity of the variable costs be taken into account. Also, in practice, for most businesses the range of possible volumes of activity at which they might operate (the **relevant range**) is pretty narrow. Over very short distances, it is perfectly reasonable to treat a curved line as being straight.

## Weaknesses of break-even analysis

As we have seen, break-even analysis can provide some useful insights to the important relationship between fixed costs, variable costs and the volume of activity. It does, however have its weaknesses. There are probably three general points:

■ *Non-linear relationships.* The normal approach to break-even analysis, in practice, assumes that the relationships between sales revenues, variable costs and volume are strictly straight-line ones. In real life this is unlikely to be true. This is probably not a major problem, since break-even analysis is normally conducted in advance of the activity actually taking place. Our ability to predict future costs, revenues and so on is somewhat limited; hence, what are probably minor variations from strict linearity are unlikely to be significant compared with other forecasting errors.

■ *Stepped fixed costs.*   Most fixed costs are not fixed over all volumes of activity. They tend to be 'stepped' in the way depicted in Figure 3.2. This means that, in practical circumstances, great care must be taken in making assumptions about fixed costs. The problem is particularly heightened because most activities will probably involve fixed costs of various types (rent, supervisory salaries, administration costs), all of which are likely to have their steps at different points.

■ *Multi-product businesses.*   Most businesses do not offer just one product or service. This is a problem for break-even analysis since it raises the question of the effect of additional sales of one product or service on sales of another of the business's products or services. There is also the problem of identifying the fixed costs of one particular activity. Fixed costs tend to relate to more than one activity; for example, two activities may be carried out in the same rented premises. There are ways of dividing fixed costs between activities, but these tend to be arbitrary, which calls the value of the break-even analysis into question.

## Marginal analysis

If you cast your mind back to Chapter 2, when we were discussing relevant costs for decision making, you will recall that we concluded that only costs varying with the decision should be included in the decision analysis. For many decisions that involve relatively small variations from existing practice and/or are for relatively limited periods of time, fixed costs are not relevant to the decision. This is because either:

■ Fixed costs tend to be impossible to alter in the short term, or
■ Managers are reluctant to alter them in the short term.

Suppose that a business occupies premises that it owns in order to carry out its activities. There is a downturn in demand for the service that the business provides and it would be possible to carry on the business from smaller, cheaper premises. Does this mean that the business will sell its old premises and move to new ones overnight? Clearly, it cannot mean this. This is partly because it is not usually possible to find a buyer for premises at very short notice, and it may be difficult to move premises quickly where there is, say, delicate equipment to be moved. Apart from external constraints on the speed of any such move, management may feel that the downturn is not permanent and would thus be reluctant to take such a dramatic step as to deny itself the opportunity to benefit from a possible revival of trade.

A business's premises may provide an example of an area of one of the more inflexible types of cost, but most fixed costs tend to be broadly similar in this context.

We shall now consider some decision-making areas where fixed costs can be regarded as irrelevant, and we shall then analyse decisions in those areas. The fact that the decisions that we are considering here are short term means that the objective of wealth enhancement will be promoted by seeking to generate as

➡ much net cash inflow as possible. In **marginal analysis**, we concern ourselves just with costs and revenues that vary with the decision. This often means that fixed costs are ignored.

## Accepting/rejecting special contracts

Cottage Industries Ltd (see Example 3.1), has spare capacity in that it has spare basket makers. An overseas retail chain has offered the business an order for 300 baskets at a price of £13 each. Without considering any wider issues, should the business accept the order? *Note:* Assume that the business does not rent the machine.

Since the fixed costs will be incurred in any case, they are not relevant to this decision. All we need to do is to see whether the price offered will yield a contribution. If it will, then the business will be better off by accepting the contract than by refusing it.

|  | £ |
|---|---|
| Additional revenue per unit | 13 |
| *Less* additional cost per unit | 12 |
| Additional contribution per unit | 1 |

For 300 units, the additional contribution will be £300. Since no fixed cost increase is involved, irrespective of whatever else may be happening to the business, it will be £300 better off by taking this contract than by refusing it.

As ever with decision making, there are other factors that are either difficult or impossible to quantify. These should be taken into account before reaching a final decision. In the case of Cottage Industries Ltd's decision on the overseas customer, these could include:

■ The possibility that spare capacity will be 'sold off' cheaply when there is another potential customer who will offer a higher price, but by which time the capacity will be fully committed. It is a matter of commercial judgement as to how likely this will be.
■ The problem that selling the same product, but at different prices, could lead to a loss of customer goodwill. The fact that a different price will be set for customers in different countries (that is, in different markets) may be sufficient to avoid this potential problem.
■ If the business is going to suffer continually from being unable to sell its full production potential at the 'regular' price, it might be better in the long run to reduce capacity and make fixed-cost savings. Using the spare capacity to produce marginal benefits may lead to the business failing to address this issue.
■ On a more positive note, the business may see this as a way of breaking into the overseas market. This is something that might be impossible to achieve if the business charges its regular price.

## The most efficient use of scarce resources

We tend to think in terms of the size of the market being the brake on output. That is to say, the ability of a business to sell is likely to limit production, rather than the ability to produce being likely to limit sales. In some cases, however, it is a limit on what can be produced that limits sales. Limited production might stem from a shortage of any factor of production – labour, raw materials, space, machinery, and so on.

The most profitable combination of products will occur where the **contribution per unit of the scarce factor** is maximised. Let us look at Example 3.2 to illustrate this point.

---

**Example 3.2**

A business provides three different services, the details of which are as follows:

| Service (codename) | AX107 | AX109 | AX220 |
|---|---|---|---|
| | £ | £ | £ |
| Selling price per unit | 50 | 40 | 65 |
| Variable cost per unit | 25 | 20 | 35 |
| Contribution per unit | 25 | 20 | 30 |
| Labour time per unit | 5 hours | 3 hours | 6 hours |

Within reason, the market will take as many units of each service as can be provided, but the ability to provide the service is limited by the availability of labour, all of which needs to be skilled. Fixed costs are not affected by the choice of service provided because provision of all three services uses the same production facilities.

The most profitable service is AX109 because it generates a contribution of £6.67 (£20/3) per hour. The other two generate only £5.00 each per hour (£25/5 and £30/6).

---

Your first reaction to Example 3.2 may have been that the business should provide only service AX220, because this is the one that yields the highest contribution per unit sold. If so, you are making the mistake of thinking of the ability to sell as being the limiting factor. If you are not convinced by the analysis, take an imaginary number of available labour hours and ask yourself what is the maximum contribution (and, therefore, profit) that could be made by providing each service exclusively. Bear in mind that there is no shortage of anything else, including market demand – just a shortage of labour.

---

**Activity 3.10**

A business makes three different products, the details of which are as follows:

| Product (codename) | B14 | B17 | B22 |
|---|---|---|---|
| Selling price per unit (£) | 25 | 20 | 23 |
| Variable cost per unit (£) | 10 | 8 | 12 |
| Weekly demand (units) | 25 | 20 | 30 |
| Machine time per unit | 4 hours | 3 hours | 4 hours |

Fixed costs are not affected by the choice of product because all three products use the same machine. Machine time is limited to 148 hours a week.

Which combination of products should be manufactured if the business is to produce the highest profit?

| Product (codename) | B14 | B17 | B22 |
|---|---|---|---|
| | £ | £ | £ |
| Selling price per unit | 25 | 20 | 23 |
| Variable cost per unit | 10 | 8 | 12 |
| Contribution per unit | 15 | 12 | 11 |
| Machine time per unit | 4 hours | 3 hours | 4 hours |
| Contribution per machine hour | 3.75 | 4.00 | 2.75 |
| Order of priority | 2nd | 1st | 3rd |

Therefore

produce   20 units of product B17 using   60 hours
22 units of product B14 using   88 hours
148 hours

This leaves unsatisfied the market demand for a further 3 units of product B14 and 30 units of product B22.

---

**Activity 3.11**

**What steps could be contemplated that could lead to a higher level of contribution for the business in Activity 3.10?**

The possibilities for improving matters might include:

■ Contemplate obtaining additional machine time. This could mean obtaining a new machine, subcontracting the machining to another business or, perhaps, squeezing a few more hours per week out of the business's own machine. Perhaps a combination of two or more of these is a possibility.
■ Redesign the products in a way that requires less time per unit on the machine.
■ Increase the price per unit of the three products. This may well have the effect of dampening demand, but the existing demand cannot be met at present and it may be more profitable, in the long run, to make a greater contribution on each unit sold than to take one of the other courses of action to overcome the problem.

---

**Activity 3.12**

**Going back to Activity 3.10, what is the maximum price that the business concerned would logically be prepared to pay to have the remaining B14s machined by a sub-contractor, assuming that no fixed or variable costs would be saved as a result of not doing the machining 'in house'? Would there be a different maximum if we were considering the B22s?**

If the remaining three B14s were subcontracted at no cost, the business would be able to earn a contribution of £15 that it would not otherwise be able to gain. Therefore it would be worth paying a subcontractor any price up to £15 per unit to undertake the machining. Naturally, the business would prefer to pay as little as possible, but anything up to £15 would still make it worthwhile subcontracting the machining.

This would not be true of the B22s because they have a different contribution per unit. £11 would be the relevant figure in their case.

## Make-or-buy decisions

Businesses are frequently confronted by the need to decide whether to produce their product or service themselves or to buy it in from some other business. Thus, a producer of electrical appliances might decide to subcontract the manufacture of one of its products to another business, perhaps because there is a shortage of production capacity in the producer's own factory, or because it believes it to be cheaper to subcontract than to make the appliance itself.

It might be just part of a product that is subcontracted. For example, the producer may have a component for the appliance made by another manufacturer. In principle, there is hardly any limit to the scope of make-or-buy decisions. Virtually any part, component or service that is required in production of the main product or service, or the main product or service itself, could be the subject of a make-or-buy decision. So, for example, the personnel function of a business, which is normally performed 'in house', could be subcontracted. At the same time, electrical power, which is typically provided by an outside electrical utility business, could be generated 'in house'.

---

**Example 3.3**

Shah Ltd needs a component for one of its products. It can subcontract production of the component to a subcontractor, who will provide the component for £20 each. The business can produce the components internally for total variable costs of £15 per component. Shah Ltd has spare capacity. Should the component be subcontracted or produced internally?

The answer is that Shah Ltd should produce the component internally since the variable cost of subcontracting is greater by £5 than the variable cost of internal manufacture.

---

**Activity 3.13**

Now assume that Shah Ltd (Example 3.3) has no spare capacity, so it can only produce the component internally by reducing its output of another of its products. While it is making each component, it will lose contributions of £12 from the other product. Should the component be subcontracted or produced internally?

The answer is to subcontract. The relevant cost of internal production of each component is:

|  | £ |
|---|---|
| Variable cost of production of the component | 15 |
| Opportunity cost of lost production of the other product | 12 |
|  | 27 |

This is clearly more costly than the £20 per component that will have to be paid to the subcontractor.

| Activity 3.14 | What factors, other than those immediately financially quantifiable, would you consider when making a make-or-buy decision? |
|---|---|

We suggest the following factors:

- *The general problems of subcontracting*, namely loss of control of quality, and the potential unreliability of supply.
- *Expertise and specialisation*. It is possible for most businesses, with sufficient determination, to do virtually everything 'in house'. This may, however, require a level of skill and facilities that most businesses neither have nor feel inclined to acquire. Though it is true that most businesses could generate their own electricity, their managements tend to take the view that this is better done by a specialist generator business.

## Closing or continuation decisions

It is quite common for businesses to account separately for each department or section to try to assess the relative effectiveness of each one.

| Example 3.4 | Goodsports Ltd is a retail shop that operates through three departments, all in the same premises. The three departments occupy roughly equal areas of the shop. The trading results for the year just ended showed the following: |
|---|---|

|  | Total | Sports equipment | Sports clothes | General clothes |
|---|---|---|---|---|
|  | £000 | £000 | £000 | £000 |
| Sales | 534 | 254 | 183 | 97 |
| Costs | 482 | 213 | 163 | 106 |
| Profit (loss) | 52 | 41 | 20 | (9) |

It would appear that if the general clothes department were to close, the business would be more profitable, by £9,000 a year, assuming last year's performance to be a reasonable indication of future performance.

When the costs are analysed between those that are variable and those that are fixed, however, the following results were obtained:

|  | Total | Sports equipment | Sports clothes | General clothes |
|---|---|---|---|---|
|  | £000 | £000 | £000 | £000 |
| Sales | 534 | 254 | 183 | 97 |
| Variable costs | 344 | 167 | 117 | 60 |
| Contribution | 190 | 87 | 66 | 37 |
| Fixed costs (rent etc.) | 138 | 46 | 46 | 46 |
| Profit (loss) | 52 | 41 | 20 | (9) |

Now it is clear that closing the general clothes department, without any other developments, would make the business worse off by £37,000 (the department's contribution). The department should not be closed, because it makes a positive contribution. The fixed costs would continue whether the department closed or not. As can be seen from analysis, distinguishing between variable and fixed costs can make the picture a great deal clearer.

**Activity 3.15**

In considering Goodsports Ltd in Example 3.4, we said is was stated that the general clothes department should not be closed 'without any other developments'. What 'other developments' could affect this decision, making continuation either more attractive or less attractive?

The things that we thought of include:

■ Expansion of the other departments or replacing the general clothes department with a completely new activity. This would make sense only if the space currently occupied by the general clothes department could generate contributions totalling at least £37,000 a year.
■ Subletting the space occupied by the general clothes department. Once again, this would need to generate a net rent of more than £37,000 a year to make it more financially beneficial than keeping the department open.
■ There may be advantages in keeping the department open even if it generated no contribution whatsoever (assuming no other use for the space). This is because customers may be attracted into the shop because it has general clothing and they may then buy something from one of the other departments. By the same token, the activity of a subtenant may attract customers into the shop. On the other hand, it may drive them away!

**?** **Self-assessment question 3.1**

Khan Ltd can make three products (A, B and C) using the same machines. Various estimates for next year have been made as follows:

|  | A £/unit | B £/unit | C £/unit |
|---|---|---|---|
| Selling price | 30 | 45 | 20 |
| Variable material cost | 15 | 18 | 10 |
| Other variable production costs | 6 | 16 | 5 |
| Share of fixed overheads | 8 | 12 | 4 |
| Time required on machines (hr/unit) | 2 | 3 | 1 |

Fixed overhead costs for next year are expected to total £40,000.

**Required:**
(a) If the business were to make only product A next year, how many units would it need to make in order to break even? (Assume for this part of the question that there is no effective limit to market size and production capacity.)
(b) If the business has maximum machine capacity for next year of 10,000 hours, in which order of preference would the three products come?
(c) The maximum market for next year for the three products is as follows:
Product A      3,000 units
Product B      2,000 units
Product C      5,000 units.
If we continue to assume a maximum machine capacity of 10,000 hours for the year, what quantities of which product should the business make next year and how much profit would this be expected to yield?

## Summary

In this chapter we have seen that costs divide broadly into those that are fixed relative to the level of activity and those that are not affected by changes in the level of activity. Knowledge of how this distinction applies to any particular activity enables us to undertake break-even analysis – that is, deducing the break-even point for the activity. We have also seen that, for short-run decisions, all fixed costs (that is, costs that do not vary with the level of activity) can be assumed to be irrelevant, and all variable costs can be assumed to be relevant. This helps us to make decisions on short-term contracts, on the use of spare capacity, on the most effective use of scarce resources, on short-term make-or-buy and on the continuance or deletion of part of a business.

 **Key terms**

| | |
|---|---|
| Fixed cost   p. 37 | Break-even point   p. 43 |
| Variable cost   p. 37 | Contribution   p. 46 |
| Stepped fixed cost   p. 39 | Marginal cost   p. 46 |
| Semi-fixed (semi-variable) cost   p. 41 | Margin of safety   p. 46 |
| Break-even analysis   p. 42 | Operating gearing   p. 48 |
| Total cost   p. 42 | Profit–volume (PV) chart   p. 49 |
| Break-even chart   p. 43 | Marginal analysis   p. 53 |

## Further reading

If you would like to explore the topics covered in this chapter in more depth, we recommend the following books:

**Management Accounting**, *Atkinson, A., Banker, R., Kaplan, R.* and *Mark Young, S.*, 3rd edn, Prentice Hall, 2001, chapter 3.

**Management and Cost Accounting**, *Drury, C.*, 5th edn, Thomson Learning, 2000, chapter 8.

**Cost Accounting: A managerial emphasis**, *Horngren, C., Foster, G.* and *Datar, S.*, 10th edn, Prentice Hall International, 2000, chapter 3.

**Cost and Management Accounting**, *Williamson, D.*, Prentice Hall International, 1996, chapters 3 and 11.

**3.1** Define the terms 'fixed cost' and 'variable cost'.

**3.2** What is meant by the 'break-even point' for some activity? How is the break-even point calculated?

**3.3** When we say that some business activity has 'high operating gearing', what do we mean?

**3.4** If there is a scarce resource that is restricting sales, how will the business maximise its profit?

Exercises 3.5–3.8 are more advanced than 3.1–3.4. Those with coloured numbers have answers at the back of the book.

**3.1** The management of your company is concerned at its inability to obtain enough fully trained labour to enable it to meet its present budget projection.

| Product: | Alpha £ | Beta £ | Gamma £ | Total £ |
|---|---|---|---|---|
| Variable costs: | | | | |
| Materials | 6,000 | 4,000 | 5,000 | 15,000 |
| Labour | 9,000 | 6,000 | 12,000 | 27,000 |
| Expenses | 3,000 | 2,000 | 2,000 | 7,000 |
| Allocated fixed costs | 13,000 | 8,000 | 12,000 | 33,000 |
| Total cost | 31,000 | 20,000 | 31,000 | 82,000 |
| Profit | 8,000 | 9,000 | 2,000 | 19,000 |
| Sales | £39,000 | £29,000 | £33,000 | £101,000 |

The amount of labour likely to be available amounts to £20,000. All of the variable labour is paid at the same hourly rate. You have been asked to prepare a statement ensuring that at least 50 per cent of the budget sales are achieved for each product and the balance of labour used to produce the greatest profit.

**Required:**
(a) Prepare a statement showing the greatest profit available from the limited amount of labour available, within the constraint stated. *Hint*: Remember that all variable labour is paid at the same rate.
(b) Provide an explanation of the method you have used.
(c) Provide an indication of any other factors that need to be considered.

**3.2** Lannion and Co. is engaged in providing and marketing a standard cleaning service. Summarised results for the past two months reveal the following:

| | October | November |
|---|---|---|
| Sales (units of the service) | 200 | 300 |
| Sales (£) | 5,000 | 7,500 |
| Operating profit (£) | 1,000 | 2,200 |

There were no price changes of any description during these two months.

**Required:**
(a) Deduce the break-even point (in units of the service) for Lannion.
(b) State why the company might find it useful to know its break-even point.

**3.3** A hotel group prepares accounts on a quarterly basis. The senior managers are reviewing the performance of one hotel and making plans for next year. They have in front of them the results for this year (based on some actual results and some forecasts to the end of this year):

| Quarter | Sales £000 | Profit (loss) £000 |
|---|---|---|
| 1 | 400 | (280) |
| 2 | 1,200 | 360 |
| 3 | 1,600 | 680 |
| 4 | 800 | 40 |
| Total | 4,000 | 800 |

The total estimated number of visitors (guest nights) for this year is 50,000. The results follow a regular pattern, there being no unexpected cost fluctuations beyond the seasonal trading pattern exhibited. The managers intend to incorporate into their plans for next year an anticipated increase in unit variable costs of 10 per cent and a profit target for the hotel of £1m.

**Required:**
(a) Determine the total variable and total fixed costs of the hotel for this year, by the use of a PV chart or by calculation. Tabulate the provisional annual results for this year in total, showing variable and fixed costs separately; show also the revenue and costs per visitor.
(b) (i) If there is no increase in visitors next year, what will be the required revenue rate per hotel visitor to meet the profit target?
(ii) If the required revenue rate per visitor is not raised above this year's level, how many visitors will be required to meet the profit target?
(c) Outline and briefly discuss the assumptions that are contained within the accountants' typical PV or break-even analysis, and assess whether they limit its usefulness.

**3.4** Motormusic Ltd makes a standard model of car radio, which it sells to car manufacturers for £60 each. Next year the company plans to make and sell 20,000 radios. The company's costs are as follows:

| | |
|---|---|
| Manufacturing | |
| Variable materials | £20 per radio |
| Variable labour | £14 per radio |
| Other variable costs | £12 per radio |
| Fixed costs | £80,000 per year |
| Administration and selling | |
| Variable | £3 per radio |
| Fixed | £60,000 per year |

**Required:**

(a) Calculate the break-even point for next year, expressed both in radios and sales value.

(b) Calculate the margin of safety for next year, expressed both in radios and sales value.

**3.5** A company makes three products, A, B and C. All three products require the use of two types of machine: cutting machines and assembling machines. Estimates for next year include the following:

|  | A | B | C |
|---|---|---|---|
| Selling price (per unit) | £25.00 | £30.00 | £18.00 |
| Sales demand (units) | 2,500 | 3,400 | 5,100 |
| Variable material cost (per unit) | £12.00 | £13.00 | £10.00 |
| Variable production cost (per unit) | £7.00 | £4.00 | £3.00 |
| Time required per unit on cutting machines | 1.0 hours | 1.0 hours | 0.5 hours |
| Time required per unit on assembling machines | 0.5 hours | 1.0 hours | 0.5 hours |

Fixed overhead costs for next year are expected to total £42,000. It is the company's policy for each unit of production to absorb these in proportion to its total variable costs. The company has cutting machine capacity of 5,000 hours a year and assembling machine capacity of 8,000 hours a year.

**Required:**

(a) State, with supporting workings, which products in which quantities the company should plan to make next year on the basis of the above information. *Hint*: First determine which machines will be a limiting factor (scarce resource).

(b) State the maximum price per product that it would be worth the company paying a subcontractor to carry out that part of the work which could not be done internally.

**3.6** Darmor Ltd has three products, A, B and C, which require the same production facilities. Information about their per-unit production costs is as follows:

|  | A<br>£ | B<br>£ | C<br>£ |
|---|---|---|---|
| Labour – skilled | 6 | 9 | 3 |
| – unskilled | 2 | 4 | 10 |
| Materials | 12 | 25 | 14 |
| Other variable costs | 3 | 7 | 7 |
| Fixed costs | 5 | 10 | 10 |

All labour and materials are variable costs. Skilled labour is paid a basic rate of £6 an hour and unskilled labour is paid a basic rate of £4 an hour. The labour costs per unit, shown above, are based on basic rates of pay. Skilled labour is scarce, which means that the business could sell more than the maximum that it is able to make of any of the three products.

Product A is sold in a regulated market and the regulators have set a price of £30 per unit for it.

**Required:**

(a) State, with supporting workings, the price that must be charged for products B and C, such that the business would find it equally profitable to make and sell any of the three products.

(b) State, with supporting workings, the maximum rate of overtime premium that the business would logically be prepared to pay its skilled workers to work beyond the basic time.

**3.7** Intermediate Products Ltd produces four types of water pump. Two of these (A and B) are sold by the business. The other two (C and D) are incorporated, as components, into other of the business's products. Neither C nor D is incorporated into A or B. Costings (per unit) for the products are as follows:

|  | A £ | B £ | C £ | D £ |
|---|---|---|---|---|
| Variable materials | 15 | 20 | 16 | 17 |
| Variable labour | 25 | 10 | 10 | 15 |
| Other variable costs | 5 | 3 | 2 | 2 |
| Other fixed costs | 20 | 8 | 8 | 12 |
|  | £65 | £41 | £36 | £46 |
| Selling price (per unit) | £70 | £45 | | |

There is an outside supplier who is prepared to supply unlimited quantities of products C and D to the business, charging £40 per unit for type C and £55 per unit for type D.

Next year's estimated demand for the products, from the market (in the case of A and B) and from other production requirements (in the case of C and D) is as follows:

|  | Units |
|---|---|
| A | 5,000 |
| B | 6,000 |
| C | 4,000 |
| D | 3,000 |

For strategic reasons, the business wishes to supply a minimum of 50 per cent of the above demand for products A and B.

Manufacture of all four products requires the use of a special machine. The products require time on this machine as follows:

|  | Hours per unit |
|---|---|
| A | 0.5 |
| B | 0.4 |
| C | 0.5 |
| D | 0.3 |

Next year there are expected to be a maximum of 6,000 special-machine hours available. There will be no shortage of any other factor of production.

**Required:**

(a) State, with supporting workings and assumptions, which products the business should plan to make next year.

(b) Explain the maximum amount that it would be worth the business paying per hour to rent a second special machine.

(c) Suggest ways, other than renting an additional special machine, that could solve the problem of the shortage of special machine time.

**3.8** Gandhi Ltd renders a promotional service to small retailing businesses. There are three levels of service: the 'basic', the 'standard' and the 'comprehensive'. On the basis of past experience, the business plans next year to work at absolute full capacity as follows:

| Service | Number of units of the service | Selling price £ | Variable cost per unit £ |
|---------|-------------------------------|-----------------|--------------------------|
| Basic | 11,000 | 50 | 25 |
| Standard | 6,000 | 80 | 65 |
| Comprehensive | 16,000 | 120 | 90 |

The business's fixed costs total £660,000 a year. Each service takes about the same length of time, irrespective of the level.

One of the accounts staff has just produced a report that seems to show that the standard service is unprofitable. The relevant extract from the report is as follows:

**Standard service cost analysis**

| | £ | |
|---|---|---|
| Selling price per unit | 80 | |
| Variable cost per unit | (65) | |
| Fixed cost per unit | (20) | (£660,000/(11,000 + 6,000 + 16,000)) |
| Net loss | (5) | |

The producer of the report suggests that the business should not offer the standard service next year. In contrast, the marketing manager believes that the market for the basic service could be expanded by dropping its price to all customers.

**Required:**

(a) Should the standard service be offered next year, assuming that the quantity of the other services could not be expanded to use the spare capacity?

(b) Should the standard service be offered next year, assuming that the released capacity could be used to render a new service, the 'nova', for which customers would be charged £75, and which would have variable costs of £50 and take twice as long as the other three services?

(c) What is the minimum price that could be accepted for the basic service, assuming that the necessary capacity to expand it will come only from not offering the standard service?

## CHAPTER 4

# Full costing

## Introduction

In this chapter we are going to look at a widely used approach for deducing the cost of a unit of output, which takes account of all of the costs. The precise approach taken tends to depend on whether each unit of output is identical to the next or whether each job has its own individual characteristics. It also tends to depend on whether or not the business accounts for overheads on a departmental basis. We shall look at how full costing is achieved and then we shall consider its usefulness for management purposes.

**OBJECTIVES**

When you have completed this chapter you should be able to:

■ Deduce the full cost of a unit of output in a single-product environment.
■ Distinguish between direct and indirect costs and use this distinction to deduce the full cost of a job in a multi-product environment.
■ Discuss the problem of charging overheads to jobs in a multi-product environment.
■ Deduce the overheads to be charged to a job in a departmental-costing environment.

## The nature of full costing

➡ With **full costing**, we are not concerned with relevant or with variable costs, but with all costs involved with achieving some objective. The logic of full costing is that all of the costs of running a particular facility, say a factory, are part of the cost of the output of that factory. For example, the rent may be a cost that will not alter merely because we make one more unit of production, but if the factory were not rented there would be nowhere for production to take place and so rent is an important element of the cost of each unit of output.

➡ **Full cost** is the total amount of resources, usually measured in monetary terms, sacrificed to achieve a particular objective. It takes account of *all* resources sacrificed to achieve the objective.

# Uses of full cost information

Why do we need to deduce full cost information? There are probably two reasons:

➡ ■ *For pricing purposes.* In some industries and circumstances, full costs are used as the basis of pricing. Here, the full cost is deduced and a percentage is added on for profit. This is known as **cost-plus pricing**. Garages carrying out vehicle repairs typically operate this way.

In many circumstances, suppliers are not in a position to set prices on a cost-plus basis. Where there is a competitive market, a supplier will usually have to accept the price that the market offers; that is, most suppliers are 'price takers' not 'price makers'. We shall take a closer look at the subject of pricing, and the place of full costs in it, in Chapter 5.

■ *For income measurement purposes.* To provide a valid means of measuring a business's income it is necessary to match expenses with the revenues realised in the same accounting period. Where manufactured stock is made or partially made in one period but sold in the next, or where a service is partially rendered in one accounting period but the revenue is realised in the next, the full cost (including an appropriate share of overheads) must be carried from one accounting period to the next. Unless we are able to identify the full cost of work done in one period, which is the subject of a sale in the next, the profit figures of the periods concerned will become meaningless. This will mean that users of accounting information will not have a reliable means of assessing the effectiveness of the business or its parts.

This second reason for needing full cost information is illustrated by Example 4.1.

| | |
|---|---|
| **Example 4.1** | During the accounting year that ended on 31 December last year, Engineers Ltd made a special machine for a customer. At the beginning of this year, after having a series of tests successfully completed by a subcontractor, the machine was delivered to the customer. The business's normal practice (typical of most businesses) is to take account of sales when the product passes to the customer. The sale price of the machine was £25,000.

Last year, the total cost of making the machine was £17,000. Testing the machine cost £1,000.

With these facts in mind:

(a) How much profit or loss did the business make on the machine last year?
(b) How much profit or loss did the business make on the machine this year?
(c) At what value must the business carry the machine in its balance sheet at the end of last year so that the correct profit will be recorded for each of the two years?

(a) No profit or loss was made last year, following the business's (and the generally accepted) approach to recognising sales revenues (the realisation convention). If the sale were not to be recognised until last year, it would be illogical (and contravene the matching convention) to treat the costs of making the machine as expenses until that time. |

(b) During this year the sale would be recognised and all of the costs, including a reasonable share of overheads, would be set against it in this year's profit and loss account, as follows:

|  | £000 | £000 |
|---|---|---|
| Sales price |  | 25,000 |
| Costs – total incurred last year | 17,000 |  |
| – testing cost | 1,000 |  |
| Total cost |  | 18,000 |
| This year's profit from the machine |  | £7,000 |

(c) The machine would have been shown as an asset of the business at £17,000 at the end of last year.

Unless all production costs are charged in the same accounting period as the sale is recognised in the profit and loss account, distortions will occur that will render the profit and loss account much less useful. Thus, it is necessary to deduce the full cost of any production undertaken completely or partially in one accounting period, but sold in a subsequent one.

Much of this chapter will be devoted to how the cost of doing something, like the £17,000 cost of making the machine in Example 4.1, is deduced in practice.

## Criticisms of full costing

Full costing is widely criticised because, in practice, it tends to use past costs and to restrict its consideration of future costs to outlay costs. In Chapter 2 we argued that past costs are irrelevant, irrespective of the purpose for which the information is to be used, and that opportunity costs can be very important. Advocates of full costing would argue that it provides a long-run relevant cost and that so-called relevant costing gives information that relates only to the narrow circumstances of the moment.

Despite the criticisms that are made of full costing, it is, according to the survey evidence that we shall consider later in this chapter, very widely practised.

## Full costs in single-product operations

The simplest case for which to deduce the full cost per unit is where the business has only one product line or service; that is, each unit of its product or service is identical. Here, it is simply a question of adding up all the costs of production incurred in the period (materials, labour, rent, fuel, power and so on) and dividing this total by the total number of units of output for the period.

**Activity 4.1**

Rustic Breweries Ltd has just one product, a bitter beer that is marketed as 'Old Rustic'. During last month the business produced 7,300 pints of the beer. The costs incurred were as follows:

|  | £ |
|---|---|
| Ingredients | 390 |
| Labour | 880 |
| Fuel | 85 |
| Rental of brewery premises | 350 |
| Depreciation of brewery equipment | 75 |

**What is the full cost per pint of producing 'Old Rustic'?**

This is found simply by taking all of the costs and dividing by the number of pints brewed, as follows:

$$\frac{£(390 + 880 + 85 + 350 + 75)}{7,300} = £0.24 \text{ per pint}$$

There can be problems in deciding exactly how much cost was incurred. In the case of Rustic Breweries Ltd, for example, how is the cost of depreciation deduced? It is certainly an estimate and so its reliability is open to question. Should we use the 'relevant' cost of the raw materials (almost certainly the replacement cost) or the actual price paid for the stock used? If it is worth calculating the cost per pint, then it must be because this information will be used for some decision-making purpose and so the replacement cost is probably more logical. In practice, however, it seems that historic costs are more often used to deduce full costs.

There can also be problems in deciding precisely how many units of output there were. Brewing beer is not a very fast process. This means that there is likely to be some beer that is in the process of being brewed at any given moment. This in turn means that part of the costs incurred last month were in respect of some beer that was work in progress at the end of the month and is not therefore included in the output quantity of 7,300 pints. Similarly, part of the 7,300 pints was started and incurred costs in the previous month, yet all of those pints were included in the 7,300 pints that we used in our calculation of the cost per pint. Work in progress is not a serious problem, but account does need to be taken of it if reliable full-cost information is to be obtained.

➔ This approach to full costing, which can be taken with identical or near-identical units of output, is usually referred to as **process costing**.

## Full costs in multi-product operations

Where the units of output of the product or service are not identical, for the purposes for which full costing is used it will not be acceptable to adopt the approach that we used with pints of 'Old Rustic' in Activity 4.1. It is clearly reasonable to ascribe an identical cost to units of output that are identical; it is *not* reasonable where the units of output are obviously different. Every pint of 'Old Rustic' will be more or less identical, but every case handled by a solicitor for a client, for example, is not identical to every other. Whether full costs are being used as a basis for pricing, as a basis for income measurement or for both purposes, treating each client's case the same will not normally be acceptable.

## Direct and indirect costs

Where the units of output are not identical, we normally separate costs into two categories. These are:

- **Direct costs**. These are costs that can be identified with specific cost units. That is to say, the effect of the cost can be measured in respect of each particular unit of output. The main examples of these are direct materials and direct labour. Collecting direct costs is a simple matter of having a cost-recording system that is capable of capturing the cost of direct material used on each job and the cost, based on the hours worked and the rate of pay, of direct workers.
- **Indirect costs** (or **overheads**). These are all other costs – that is, those that cannot be directly measured in respect of each particular unit of output.

We shall use the terms 'indirect costs' and 'overheads' interchangeably for the remainder of this book. Overheads are sometimes known as '**common costs**' because they are common to all production of the production unit (for example, factory) for the period.

---

| Exhibit 4.1 | **Direct and indirect costs in practice** |
|---|---|

A survey of 176 fairly large UK businesses conducted during 1999 revealed that, on average, total costs of businesses are in the following proportions:

- Direct costs      70 per cent
- Indirect costs    30 per cent

Perhaps surprisingly, these proportions did not vary greatly between manufacturers, retailers and service businesses. The only significant variation from the 70/30 proportions was with financial and commercial businesses, which had an average 52/48 split.

*Source*: Based on information taken from Drury and Tayles (see reference (1) at the end of the chapter).

---

## Job costing

The term **job costing** is used to describe the way in which we identify the full cost per unit of output (job) where the units of output differ. To cost (that is, deduce the full cost of) a particular unit of output (job), we usually ascribe the direct costs to the job, which, by the definition of direct costs, is capable of being done. We then seek to 'charge' each unit of output with a fair share of indirect costs. This is shown graphically in Figure 4.1.

---

Figure 4.1

### The relationship between direct costs and indirect costs

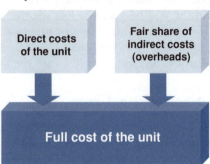

The full cost of any particular job is the sum of those costs that can be measured specifically in respect of the job (direct costs) and a share of those costs that create the environment in which production (of an object or service) can take place, but that do not relate specifically to any particular job (overheads).

---

**Activity 4.2**

Sparky Ltd is a business that employs a number of electricians. The business undertakes a range of work for its customers, from repairing fuses to installing complete wiring systems in new houses.

In respect of a particular job done by Sparky Ltd, into which category, direct or indirect, would each of the following costs fall?

(a) The wages of the electrician who did the job.
(b) Depreciation (wear and tear) of the tools used by the electrician.
(c) The salary of Sparky Ltd's accountant.
(d) The cost of cable and other materials used on the job.
(e) Rental of the premises where Sparky Ltd stores its stock of cable and other materials.

---

Only (a) and (d) are direct costs. This is because it is possible to measure how much time (and, therefore, the labour cost) was spent on the particular job and how much material was used in the job.

All of the other costs are general costs of running the business. As such, they must form part of the full cost of doing the job, but they cannot be directly measured in respect of the particular job.

---

It is important to note that whether a cost is direct or indirect depends on the item being costed (the cost objective). People tend to refer to overheads without stating what the cost objective is; this is incorrect.

---

**Activity 4.3**

Into which category, direct or indirect, would each of the costs listed in Activity 4.2 fall if we were seeking to find the cost of operating the entire business of Sparky Ltd for a month?

---

The answer is that all of them will be direct costs, since they can all be related to, and measured in respect of, running the business for a month.

Naturally, broader-reaching cost units, like operating Sparky Ltd for a month, tend to include a higher proportion of direct costs than do more limited ones, such as a particular job done by Sparky Ltd. As we shall see shortly, this makes costing broader cost units rather more straightforward than costing narrower ones, since direct costs are easier to deal with.

| Figure 4.2 | **The relationship between fixed costs, variable costs and total costs** |
| --- | --- |

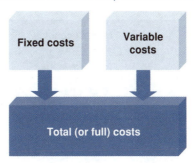

The total cost of a job is the sum of those costs that remain the same irrespective of the level of activity (fixed costs) and those that vary according to the level of activity (variable costs).

## Full costing and the behaviour of costs

We saw in Chapter 3 that the relationship between fixed and variable costs is that, between them, they make up the full cost (or total cost, as it is usually known in the context of marginal analysis). This is illustrated in Figure 4.2.

The similarity of what is shown in Figure 4.2 to that depicted in Figure 4.1, might lead us to believe that there might be some relationship between fixed, variable, direct and indirect costs. More specifically, some people seem to believe – mistakenly – that variable costs and direct costs are the same and that fixed costs and overheads are the same. This is incorrect.

The notions of 'fixed' and 'variable' are concerned entirely with **cost behaviour** in the face of changes to the volume of output. *Directness* of costs is simply concerned with collecting together the elements that make up the full cost, that is, with the extent to which costs can be measured directly in respect of particular units of output or jobs. These are entirely different concepts. Though it may be true that there is a tendency for fixed costs to be overheads and for variable costs to be direct costs, there is no link and there are many exceptions to this tendency. For example, most operations have variable overheads. Labour, a major element of direct cost in most business contexts, is usually a fixed cost, certainly over the short term.

The relationship between the reaction of costs to volume changes, on the one hand, and how costs need to be gathered to deduce the full cost, on the other, in respect of a particular job is shown in Figure 4.3.

Total cost is the sum of direct and indirect costs. It is also the sum of fixed and variable costs. These two facts are independent of one another. Thus, a particular cost may be fixed relative to the level of output, on the one hand, and be either direct or indirect on the other.

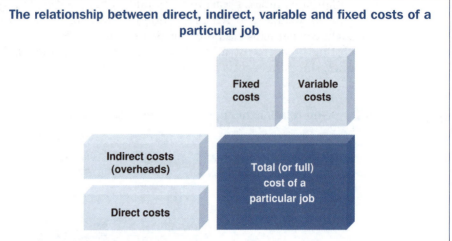

**Figure 4.3**

**The relationship between direct, indirect, variable and fixed costs of a particular job**

A particular job's full (or total) cost will be made up of some variable and some fixed element. It will also be made up of some direct and some indirect (overhead) element.

## The problem of indirect costs

The notion of distinguishing between direct and indirect costs is only related to deducing full cost in a job-costing environment. You may recall that when we were considering costing a pint of 'Old Rustic' beer in Activity 4.1, whether particular elements of cost were direct or indirect was of absolutely no consequence. This was because all costs were shared equally between the pints of beer. Where we have units of output that are not identical, we have to look more closely at the make-up of the costs to achieve a fair measure of the total cost of a particular job.

Indirect costs of any activity must form part of the cost of each unit of output. By definition, however, indirect costs cannot be directly related to individual **cost units**. This raises a major practical issue; how are indirect costs to be apportioned to individual cost units?

It is reasonable to view the overheads as rendering a service to the cost units. A manufactured product can be seen as being rendered a service by the factory in which the product is made. In this sense, it is reasonable to charge each cost unit with a share of the costs of running the factory (rent, lighting, heating, cleaning, building maintenance and so on). It also seems reasonable to relate the charge for the 'use' of the factory to the level of service that the product received from the factory.

The next step is the difficult one. How might the cost of running the factory, which is a cost of all production, be divided among individual products that are not similar in size and complexity of manufacture? One possibility is sharing this overhead cost equally among each cost unit produced in the period. Most of us would not propose this method unless the cost units were close to being identical in terms of the extent to which they had 'benefited' from the overheads. If we are not to propose equal shares, we must identify something observable and measurable about the cost units that we feel provides a reasonable basis for distinguishing between one cost unit and the next in this context.

In practice, time spent working on the cost unit by direct labour is the basis that is most popular. (Later in the chapter we shall consider survey evidence of what happens in practice.) It must be stressed that this is not the 'correct' way and it certainly is not the *only* way. We could, for example, use relative size of products as measured by weight or by relative material cost. Possibly, we could use the relative lengths of time that each unit of output was worked on by machines.

## Job costing: a worked example

To see how job costing (as is is usually called) works, let us consider Example 4.2.

| Example 4.2 | Johnson Ltd, a business that provides a television repair service to its customers, has overheads of £10,000 each month. Each month also 2,500 direct labour hours are worked and charged to units of output (repairs carried out by the business). A particular repair job undertaken by the business used direct materials costing £15. Direct labour worked on the job was 15 hours and the wage rate is £5 an hour. Overheads are charged to jobs on a direct-labour-hour basis. We need to establish what the full cost of the job is. |

 First let us establish the **overhead absorption (recovery) rate** – that is, the rate at which jobs will be charged with overheads. This is £4 (£10,000/2,500) per direct labour hour. Thus, the full cost of the job is:

|  | £ |
|---|---|
| Direct materials | 15 |
| Direct labour (15 × £5) | 75 |
|  | 90 |
| Overheads (15 × £4) | 60 |
| Full cost of the job | 150 |

Note that in Example 4.2, the number of labour hours (15) appears twice in deducing the full cost: once to deduce the direct labour cost and a second time to deduce the overheads to be charged to the job. These are really two separate issues, though they are both based on the same number of labour hours.

Note also that if all of the jobs that are undertaken during the month are assigned overheads in a similar manner, all £10,000 of overheads will be charged to the jobs between them. Jobs that involve a lot of direct labour will be assigned a large share of overhead costs and those that involve little direct labour will be assigned a small share of overheads.

| Activity 4.4 | **Can you think of reasons why direct labour hours are regarded as the most logical basis for sharing overheads among cost units?** |

The reasons that occurred to us are:

- Large jobs should logically attract large amounts of overheads because they are likely to have been rendered more 'service' by the overheads than small ones. The length of time that they are worked on by direct labour may be seen as a rough-and-ready way of measuring relative size, even though other means of doing this may be found (for example relative physical size, where the cost unit is a physical object, like a manu-factured product).

■ Most overheads are related to time. Rent, heating, lighting, fixed asset depreciation, supervisors' and managers' salaries and loan interest, which are all typical overheads, are all more or less time-based. That is to say, the overhead cost for one week tends to be about half of that for a similar two-week period. Thus, a basis of apportioning overheads to jobs that takes account of the length of time that the units of output benefited from the 'service' rendered by the overheads seems logical.

■ Direct labour hours are capable of being measured in respect of each job. They will normally be measured to deduce the direct labour element of cost in any case. Thus, a direct-labour-hour basis of dealing with overheads is practical to apply in the real world.

It cannot be emphasised enough that there is no 'correct' way to apportion overheads to jobs. Overheads (indirect costs), by definition, do not naturally relate to individual jobs. If, nevertheless, we wish to take account of the fact that overheads are part of the cost of all jobs, we must find some acceptable way of including a share of the total overheads in each job. If a particular means of doing this is accepted by those who are affected by the full cost deduced, then the method is as good as any other method. Accounting is concerned only with providing useful information to decision makers. In practice, the method that gains the most acceptability as being useful is the direct-labour-hour method.

---

**Activity 4.5**

Marine Suppliers Ltd undertakes a range of work, including making sails for small sailing boats on a made-to-measure basis. The following costs are expected to be incurred by the business during next month:

| | |
|---|---|
| Indirect labour cost | £9,000 |
| Direct labour time | 6,000 hours |
| Depreciation (wear and tear) of machinery, etc. | £3,000 |
| Rent and rates | £5,000 |
| Direct labour costs | £30,000 |
| Heating, lighting and power | £2,000 |
| Machine time | 2,000 hours |
| Indirect materials | £500 |
| Other miscellaneous indirect costs | £200 |
| Direct materials cost | £3,000 |

The business has received an enquiry about a sail and it is estimated that the sail will take 12 direct labour hours to make and will require 20 square metres of sail-cloth (which costs £2 per square metre). The business normally uses a direct-labour-hour basis of charging overheads to individual jobs.

What is the full cost of making the sail?

First it is necessary to identify which are the indirect costs and total them as follows:

|  | £ |
|---|---|
| Indirect labour | 9,000 |
| Depreciation | 3,000 |
| Rent and rates | 5,000 |
| Heating, lighting and power | 2,000 |
| Indirect materials | 500 |
| Other miscellaneous indirect costs | 200 |
| Total indirect costs | 19,700 |

(Note that this list does not include the direct costs. We shall deal with these separately.)

Since the business uses a direct-labour-hour basis of charging overheads to jobs, we need to deduce the indirect cost or overhead recovery rate per direct labour hour. This is simply:

$$\frac{£19,700}{6,000} = £3.28 \text{ per direct labout hour}$$

Thus, the full cost of the sail would be expected to be:

|  | £ |
|---|---|
| Direct materials (20 × £2) | 40.00 |
| Direct labour (12 × (£30,000/6,000)) | 60.00 |
| Indirect costs (12 × £3.28) | 39.36 |
| Total cost | £139.36 |

---

**Activity 4.6**

Suppose that Marine Suppliers Ltd (Activity 4.5) used a machine-hour basis of charging overheads to jobs. What would be the cost of the job detailed, if it is expected to take five machine hours (as well as 12 direct-labour hours)?

The total overheads will, of course, be the same irrespective of the method of charging them to jobs. Thus the overhead recovery rate, on a machine-hour basis, will be:

$$\frac{£19,700}{2,000} = £9.85 \text{ per machine hour}$$

Thus the full cost of the sail would be expected to be:

|  | £ |
|---|---|
| Direct materials (20 × £2) | 40.00 |
| Direct labour (12 × (£30,000/6,000)) | 60.00 |
| Indirect costs (5 × £9.85) | 49.25 |
| Total cost | 149.25 |

## Selecting the basis for charging overheads

A question now presents itself as to which of the two costs for this sail – that in Activity 4.5 or that in Activity 4.6 – is the correct one, or simply the better one? The answer is that neither is the correct one, as was pointed out earlier. Which is the better is a matter of judgement. This judgement is concerned entirely with usefulness of information, which in this context is probably concerned with the attitudes of those who will be affected by the figure used. Thus fairness, as it is perceived by those people, is likely to be the important issue.

Probably most people would feel that the nature of the overheads should influence the choice of the basis of charging the overhead to jobs. Where, because the operation is a capital-intensive one, the overheads are dominated by those relating to machinery (depreciation, machine maintenance, power and so on), machine hours might be favoured. Otherwise, direct-labour hours might be preferred.

It could appear that one of these bases might be preferred to the other simply because it apportions either a higher or a lower amount of overheads to a particular job. This would normally be irrational, however. Since the total overheads are the same irrespective of the method of charging the total to individual jobs, a method that gives a higher share of overheads to one particular job must give a lower share to the remaining jobs. To illustrate this point, consider Example 4.3.

---

**Example 4.3**

A business that provides a service to its customers expects to incur overheads totalling £20,000 next month. The total direct labour time worked is expected to be 1,600 hours and machines are expected to operate for a total of 1,000 hours.

During a particular month, the business expects to do just two large jobs, the outlines of which are as follows:

|  | Job 1 | Job 2 |
|---|---|---|
| Direct labour hours | 800 | 800 |
| Machine hours | 700 | 300 |

It is necessary to work out how much of the overheads will be charged to each job if overheads are to be charged on (a) a direct labour hour basis, and (b) a machine-hour basis.

(a) Direct-labour-hour basis

$$\text{Overhead recovery rate} = \frac{£20,000}{1,600}$$

$$= £12.50 \text{ per direct labour hour}$$

Job 1: £12.50 × 800 = £10,000
Job 2: £12.50 × 800 = £10,000

(b) Machine-hour basis

$$\text{Overhead recovery rate} = \frac{£20,000}{1,000}$$

$$= £20.00 \text{ per machine hour}$$

Job 1: £20.00 × 700 = £14,000
Job 2: £20.00 × 300 = £6,000

It is clear from these calculations that the total overheads charged to jobs is the same whichever method is used. So, whereas the machine-hour basis gives job 1 a higher share than does the direct-labour-hour method, the opposite is true for job 2.

It is not possible to charge overheads on one basis to one job and on the other basis to the other job. This is because either total overheads will not be fully charged to the jobs, or the jobs will be overcharged with overheads. For example, the direct-labour-hour method for job 1 (£10,000) and the machine-hour basis for job 2 (£6,000) will mean that only £16,000 of a total £20,000 of overheads will be charged to jobs. As a result, the objective of full costing, which is to charge all overheads to jobs done, will not be achieved. In this particular case, if selling prices are based on full costs, the business may not charge prices high enough to cover all of its costs.

| Activity 4.7 | The point was made above that it would normally be irrational to prefer one basis of charging overheads to jobs simply because it apportions either a higher or a lower amount of overheads to a particular job. This is because the total overheads are the same irrespective of the method of charging the total to individual jobs. Can you think of any circumstances where it would not necessarily be so irrational? |

This might apply where a customer has agreed to pay for a particular job a price based on full cost plus an agreed fixed percentage for profit. Here, it would be beneficial to the producer for the total cost of the job to be as high as possible. This would be relatively unusual, but sometimes public-sector organisations, particularly central and local government departments, have entered into contracts to have work done, with the price to be deduced, after the work has been completed, on a cost-plus basis. Such contracts are pretty rare these days, probably because they are open to abuse in the way described. Usually, contract prices are agreed in advance, typically in conjunction with competitive tendering.

Exhibit 4.2 provides some information on overhead recovery rates used in practice.

| Exhibit 4.2 | **Overhead recovery rates in practice** |

In 1993, *A Survey of Management Accounting Practices in UK Manufacturing Companies* was published by the Chartered Association of Certified Accountants (ACCA). Though this evidence is not totally up to date and it was restricted to private-sector manufacturing companies, it does provide us with some impression of management accounting practices in the real world.

The direct-labour-hour basis of charging overheads to cost units is overwhelmingly the most popular, used by 73 per cent of respondents to the ACCA survey. Where the work has a strong labour element, this seems reasonable; but the survey also showed that 68 per cent of businesses use this rate for automated activities. It is surprising that direct-labour hours should be used in an environment where machines, and machine-related costs, dominate.

*Source*: Information taken from Drury, Braund, Osborne and Tayles (see reference (2) at the end of this chapter).

## Segmenting the overheads

Though, as we have just seen, charging the same overheads to different jobs on different bases is not possible, it is possible to charge one part of the overheads on one basis and another part, or other parts, on another basis.

Segmenting the overheads in the way shown in Activity 4.8 may well be seen as providing a better basis of charging overheads to jobs. This is quite often found in practice, usually by dividing a business into separate 'areas' for costing purposes, charging overheads differently from one area to the next.

| Activity 4.8 | |
|---|---|

Consider the business in Example 4.3. On closer analysis we find that of the overheads totalling £20,000 next month, £8,000 relate to machines (depreciation, maintenance, rental of the space occupied by the machines, and so on) and the remainder to more general overheads. The other information about the business is exactly as it was before.

How much overheads will be charged to each job if the machine-related overheads are to be charged on a machine-hour basis and the remaining overheads are charged on a direct-labour-hour basis?

Direct-labour-hour basis:

$$\text{Overhead recovery rate} = \frac{£12,000}{1,600} = £7.50 \text{ per direct labour hour}$$

Machine-hour basis:

$$\text{Overhead recovery rate} = \frac{£8,000}{1,000} = £8.00 \text{ per machine hour}$$

Overheads charged to jobs:

|  | Job 1 £ | Job 2 £ |
|---|---|---|
| Direct-labour-hour basis | | |
| £7.50 × 800 | 6,000 | |
| £7.50 × 800 | | 6,000 |
| Machine-hour basis | | |
| £8.00 × 700 | 5,600 | |
| £8.00 × 300 | | 2,400 |
| Total | 11,600 | 8,400 |

We can see from this that the total expected overheads of £20,000 is charged in total.

Remember that there is no 'correct' basis of charging overheads to jobs, and so our frequent reference to the direct-labour-hour and machine-hour bases should not be taken to imply that these are the correct methods. However, it should be said that these two methods do have something to commend them and are popular in practice. As we have already discussed, a sensible method needs to identify something about each job that can be measured and that distinguishes it from other jobs. There is also a lot to be said for methods that are concerned with time, because most overheads are time-related.

## Dealing with overheads on a departmental basis

In general, all but the smallest businesses are divided into departments. Normally, each department deals with a separate activity.

The reasons for dividing a business into departments include the following:

- Many businesses are too large and complex to be run as a single unit and it is more practical to run them as a series of relatively independent units with each one having its own manager.
- Each department normally has its own area of specialism and is managed by a specialist.
- Each department can have its own accounting records that enable its performance to be assessed, which can lead to greater motivation among the staff.

Very many businesses deal with charging overheads to cost units on a department-by-department basis. They do this in the expectation that it will give rise to a fairer means of charging overheads. It is probably not an expensive exercise to apply overheads on a departmental basis. Since costs are collected department by department for other purposes (particularly for control), to apply overheads in the same way is a relatively simple matter.

An example of how the departmental approach to deriving full costs works in a manufacturing context is depicted in Figure 4.4.

The job in Figure 4.4 starts life in the preparation department, when some direct materials are taken from the stores and worked on by a direct worker. Thus, the job will be charged with direct materials, direct labour and with a share of the preparation department's overheads. The job then passes into the machining department, already valued at the costs that it picked up in the preparation department. Further direct labour and, possibly, materials are added in the machining department, plus a share of that department's overheads. The job now passes into the finishing department, valued at the cost of the materials, labour and overheads that it accumulated in the first two departments. In the finishing department, further direct labour and, perhaps, materials are added and the job picks up a share of that department's overheads. The job, now complete, passes into the finished goods store or is despatched to the customer. The basis of charging overheads to jobs (for example, direct-labour hours) might be the

**Figure 4.4**

### A cost unit passing through the production process

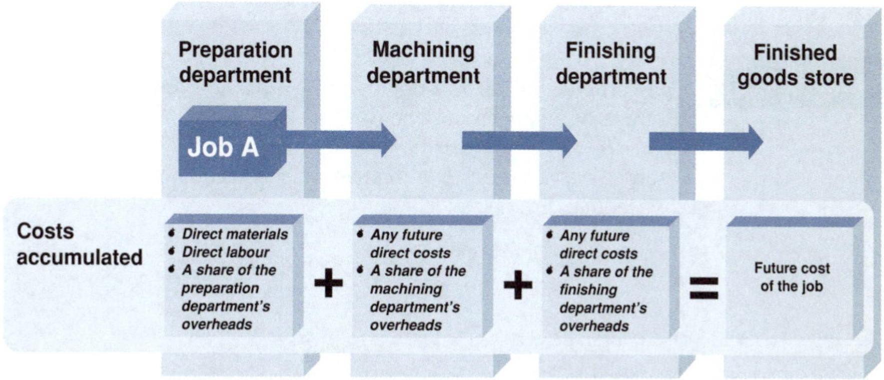

As the particular job passes through the three departments where work is carried out on it, it 'gathers' costs of various types.

same for all three departments or it may be different from one department to another. In the present example, it is quite likely that machine-related costs dominate the machining department, and so overheads might well be charged to jobs on a machine-hour basis. The other two departments may well be labour intensive so that direct labour hours may be seen as being appropriate there. The passage of the job through the departments can be compared to a snowball being rolled across snow; as it rolls, it picks up more and more snow (overheads).

Where costs are dealt with departmentally, each department is known as a **cost centre**. A cost centre can be defined as some physical area or some activity or function for which costs are separately identified.

Charging direct costs to jobs, in a departmental system, is exactly the same as where the whole business is one single cost centre. It is simply a matter of keeping a record of:

- The number of hours of direct labour worked on the particular job and the grade of labour, assuming that there are different grades with different rates of pay.
- The cost of the direct materials taken from stores and applied to the job.
- Any other direct costs – for example, some subcontracted work associated with the job.

This record keeping will normally be done departmentally with a departmental system.

It is clearly necessary to identify the production overheads of the entire organisation on a departmental basis. This means that the total overheads of the business must be divided among the departments such that the sum of the departmental overheads equals the overheads for the entire business. By charging all of their overheads to jobs, between them the departments will charge all of the overheads of the business to jobs.

For the present purposes, it is necessary to distinguish between **product cost centres** (or departments) and **service cost centres**. Product cost centres are departments through which the jobs pass and can be charged with a share of their overheads. The preparation, machining and finishing departments, in the example discussed above, are examples of product cost centres.

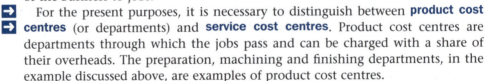

| Activity 4.9 | Can you guess what the definition of a service cost centre is? Can you think of an example of a service cost centre? |

A service cost centre is one through which jobs do not pass. It renders a service to other cost centres. Examples include:

- General administration
- Accounting
- Stores
- Maintenance
- Personnel
- Catering.

All of these render services to product cost centres.

Service cost centre costs must be charged to product cost centres, and become part of the product cost centres' overheads, so that they can be recharged to jobs. This must be done so that all of the overheads of the business find their way into the cost of the jobs done. If this is not done, the 'full' cost derived will not really be the full cost of the jobs.

Logically, the costs of a service cost centre should be charged to product cost centres on the basis of the level of service provided to the product cost centre concerned. For example, a production department that has a lot of machine maintenance carried out relative to other production departments should be charged with a larger share of the maintenance department's costs than should those other product cost centres.

The process of dividing overheads between departments is as follows:

1. **Cost allocation.** Allocate costs that are specific to the departments. These are costs that relate to, and are measurable in respect of, individual departments, that is, they are direct costs of running the department. Examples include:

   (a) Salaries of indirect workers whose activities are wholly within the department, for example the salary of the departmental manager.
   (b) Rent, where the department is housed in its own premises for which rent can be separately identified.
   (c) Electricity, where it is separately metered for each department.

2. **Cost apportionment.** Apportion the more general overheads to the departments. These are overheads that relate to more than one department, and even perhaps to them all. These would include:

   (a) Rent, where more than one department is housed in the same premises.
   (b) Electricity, where it is not separately metered.
   (c) Salaries of cleaning staff who work in a variety of departments.

   These costs would be apportioned to departments on some fair basis, such as by square metres of floor area, in the case of rent, or by level of mechanisation, for electricity used to power machinery. As with charging overheads to individual jobs, fairness is the issue; there is no correct basis of apportioning general overheads to departments.

3. Having totalled, allocated and apportioned costs to all departments, it is now necessary to apportion the total costs of service cost centres to production departments. Logically, the basis of apportionment should be the level of service rendered by the individual service department to the individual production department. With personnel department costs, for example, the basis of apportionment might be the number of staff in each production department, because it could be argued that the higher the number of staff, the more benefit the production department has derived from the personnel department. This is, of course, rather a crude approach. A particular production department may have severe personnel problems and a high staff turnover rate, which may make it a user of the personnel service that is way out of proportion to the number of staff in the production department.

The final total for each product cost centre is that cost centre's overheads. These can be charged to jobs as they pass through. We shall now go on to consider an example dealing with overheads on a departmental basis (Example 4.4).

**Example 4.4**

A business consists of four departments:

- Preparation department
- Machining department
- Finishing department
- General administration (GA) department.

The first three are product cost centres and the last renders a service to the other three. The level of service rendered is thought to be roughly in proportion to the number of employees in each production department.

Overhead costs, and other data, for next month are expected to be as follows:

|  | £000 |
|---|---|
| Rent | 5,000 |
| Electricity to power machines, etc. | 1,500 |
| Electricity for heating and lighting | 400 |
| Insurance of premises | 100 |
| Cleaning | 300 |
| Depreciation of machines | 1,000 |

Salaries of departmental managers, etc.:

|  | £000 |
|---|---|
| Preparation department | 1,000 |
| Machining department | 1,200 |
| Finishing department | 900 |
| General administration department | 900 |

The general administration department has only one employee, the manager. The other departments have a manager and direct workers. Managers never do any 'direct' work.

Each direct worker is expected to work 160 hours next month. The number of direct workers in each department is:

| | |
|---|---|
| Preparation department | 6 |
| Machining department | 9 |
| Finishing department | 5 |

Machining department direct workers are paid £5 an hour; other direct workers are paid £4 an hour.

All of the machinery is in the machining department. Machines are expected to operate for 1,200 hours next month.

The floorspace (in square metres) occupied by the departments is as follows:

|  | Sq m |
|---|---|
| Preparation department | 800 |
| Machining department | 1,000 |
| Finishing department | 500 |
| General administration department | 100 |

Deducing the overheads department by department can be done, using a schedule, as follows:

| | £000 | Total £000 | Prep'n £000 | Mach'g £000 | Fin'g £000 | GA £000 |
|---|---|---|---|---|---|---|
| Allocated costs: | | | | | | |
| Machine power | | 1,500 | | 1,500 | | |
| Machine depreciation | | 1,000 | | 1,000 | | |
| Indirect salaries | | 4,000 | 1,000 | 1,200 | 900 | 900 |
| | | | | | | |
| Apportioned costs | | | | | | |
| Rent | 5,000 | | | | | |
| Heating and lighting | 400 | | | | | |
| Insurance of premises | 100 | | | | | |
| Cleaning | 300 | | | | | |
| Apportioned by floor area | | 5,800 | 1,933 | 2,417 | 1,208 | 242 |
| Departmental overheads | | 12,300 | 2,933 | 6,117 | 2,108 | 1,142 |
| Reapportion GA costs by number of staff (including the manager) | | | 348 | 496 | 298 | (1,142) |
| | | 12,300 | 3,281 | 6,613 | 2,406 | zero |

---

**Activity 4.10**

Assume that the machining department overheads (in Example 4.4) are to be charged to jobs on a machine-hour basis, but that the direct-labour-hour basis is to be used for the other two departments. What will be the full cost of a job with the following characteristics?

| | Preparation | Machining | Finishing |
|---|---|---|---|
| Direct labour hours | 10 | 7 | 5 |
| Machine hours | – | 6 | – |
| Direct materials (£) | 85 | 13 | 6 |

*Hint*: This should be tackled as if each department were a separate business, then departmental costs added together for the job so as to arrive at the total full cost.

---

Firstly, we need to deduce the overhead recovery rates for each department:
Preparation department (direct-labour-hour-based):

$$\frac{£3,281}{6 \times 160} = £3.42$$

Machining department (machine-hour based):

$$\frac{£6,613}{1,200} = £5.51$$

Finishing department (direct-labour-hour-based):

$$\frac{£2,406}{5 \times 160} = £3.01$$

The cost of the job is as follows:

|  | £ | £ |
|---|---:|---:|
| Direct labour: | | |
| Preparation department (10 × £4) | 40.00 | |
| Machining department (7 × £5) | 35.00 | |
| Finishing department (5 × £4) | 20.00 | |
| | | 95.00 |
| Direct materials: | | |
| Preparation department | 85.00 | |
| Machining department | 13.00 | |
| Finishing department | 6.00 | |
| | | 104.00 |
| Overheads: | | |
| Preparation department (10 × £3.42) | 34.20 | |
| Machining department (6 × £5.51) | 33.06 | |
| Finishing department (5 × £3.01) | 15.05 | |
| | | 82.31 |
| Full cost of the job | | 281.31 |

---

**Activity 4.11**

The manufacturing costs for Buccaneers Ltd for 2002 are expected to be as follows:

|  | £000 |
|---|---:|
| Direct materials: | |
| Forming department | 450 |
| Machining department | 100 |
| Finishing department | 50 |
| Direct labour: | |
| Forming department | 120 |
| Machining department | 80 |
| Finishing department | 50 |
| Indirect materials: | |
| Forming department | 40 |
| Machining department | 30 |
| Finishing department | 10 |
| Administration department | 10 |
| Indirect labour: | |
| Forming department | 80 |
| Machining department | 70 |
| Finishing department | 60 |
| Administration department | 60 |
| Maintenance costs | 50 |
| Rent and rates | 100 |
| Heating and lighting | 20 |
| Building insurance | 10 |
| Machinery insurance | 10 |
| Depreciation of machinery | 120 |
| Total manufacturing costs | 1,520 |

The following additional information is available:

(i) All direct labour is paid £4 per hour for all hours worked.
(ii) The administration department renders personnel and general services to the production departments.
(iii) The area of the premises in which the business manufactures amounts to 50,000 square metres, divided as follows:

| | Sq m |
|---|---|
| Forming department | 20,000 |
| Machining department | 15,000 |
| Finishing department | 10,000 |
| Administration department | 5,000 |

(iv) The maintenance staff are expected to divide their time between the production departments as follows:

| | % |
|---|---|
| Forming department | 15 |
| Machining department | 75 |
| Finishing department | 10 |

(v) Machine hours are expected to be as follows:

| | Hours |
|---|---|
| Forming department | 5,000 |
| Machining department | 15,000 |
| Finishing department | 5,000 |

On the basis of the foregoing information:

(a) Allocate and apportion overheads to the three production departments.
(b) Deduce overhead recovery rates for each department using two different bases for each department's overheads.
(c) Calculate the full cost of a job with the following characteristics:

| Direct labour hours: | |
|---|---|
| Forming department | 4 hours |
| Machining department | 4 hours |
| Finishing department | 1 hour |

| Machine hours: | |
|---|---|
| Forming department | 1 hour |
| Machining department | 2 hours |
| Finishing department | 1 hour |

| Direct materials: | |
|---|---|
| Forming department | £40 |
| Machining department | £9 |
| Finishing department | £4 |

Use whichever of the two bases of overhead recovery, deduced in (b), that you consider more appropriate.

(d) Explain why you consider the basis used in (c) as the more appropriate.

(a)

| Cost | Basis of apport't | | Total £000 | Forming £000 | Machining £000 | Finishing £000 | Admin. £000 |
|---|---|---|---|---|---|---|---|
| Indirect materials | Specifically allocated | | 90 | 40 | 30 | 10 | 10 |
| Indirect labour | Specifically allocated | | 270 | 80 | 70 | 60 | 60 |
| Maintenance | Staff time | | 50 | 7.5 | 37.5 | 5 | – |
| Rent/rates | | 100 | | | | | |
| Heat/light | | 20 | | | | | |
| Buildings insurance | | 10 | | | | | |
| | Area | | 130 | 52 | 39 | 26 | 13 |
| Machine insurance | | 10 | | | | | |
| Machine depreciation | | 120 | | | | | |
| | Machine hours | | 130 | 26 | 78 | 26 | – |
| | | | 670 | 205.5 | 254.5 | 127 | 83 |
| Admin. | Direct labour | | | 39.84 | 26.56 | 16.6 | (83) |
| | | | 670 | 245.34 | 281.06 | 143.6 | – |

Note that direct costs are not included in the above because they are allocated *directly* to jobs.

(b)  Basis 1: direct labour hours

$$\text{Forming} = \frac{£245{,}340}{120{,}000/4} = £8.18 \text{ per direct labour hour}$$

$$\text{Machining} = \frac{£281{,}060}{80{,}000/4} = £14.05 \text{ per direct labour hour}$$

$$\text{Finishing} = \frac{£143{,}600}{50{,}000/4} = £11.49 \text{ per direct labour hour}$$

Basis 2: machine hours

$$\text{Forming} = \frac{£245{,}340}{5{,}000} = £49.07 \text{ per machine hour}$$

$$\text{Machining} = \frac{£281{,}060}{15{,}000} = £18.74 \text{ per machine hour}$$

$$\text{Finishing} = \frac{£143{,}600}{5{,}000} = £28.72 \text{ per machine hour}$$

(c)  Cost of job – on direct-labour-hour basis of overhead recovery

| | £ | £ |
|---|---|---|
| Direct labour cost (9 × £4) | | 36.00 |
| Direct materials (£40 + £9 + £4) | | 53.00 |
| Overheads: | | |
|   Forming (4 × £8.18) | 32.72 | |
|   Machining (4 × £14.05) | 56.20 | |
|   Finishing (1 × £11.49) | 11.49 | 100.41 |
| Total | | £189.41 |

(d) The reason for using the direct-labour-hour basis rather than the machine-hour basis was that labour is more important, in terms of the number of hours applied to output, than is machine time. Strong arguments could have been made for the use of the alternative basis; certainly, a machine-hour basis could have been justified for the machining department.

It would be possible, and it may be reasonable, to use one basis in respect of one department's overheads and a different one for those of another department. For example, machine hours could have been used for the machining department and a direct-labour-hours basis for the other two.

Exhibit 4.3 provides some information on 'departmentalisation' of overheads in practice.

---

**Exhibit 4.3**

### Departmentalisation of overheads in practice

The 1993 ACCA survey of manufacturing businesses revealed that 69 per cent of the businesses that responded use some form of departmental approach to deriving the overhead recovery rate to be charged to cost units. The remainder use some form of company-wide basis. Where overheads are dealt with on a departmental basis, this seems to lead to a number of different rates being applied, presumably as many rates as there are departments. Thirty-seven per cent of the respondents use more than 11 different rates, and 20 per cent use more than 20 different rates.

Where respondents took a departmental approach to charging overheads to cost units, charging service department costs to product departments was done by using some fairly arbitrary factor, such as direct labour hours, in 68 per cent of those respondents who took this approach. Only 32 per cent sought to charge service department costs to product departments on the basis of the level of service provided by the service department.

*Source*: Information taken from Drury, Braund, Osborne and Tayles (see reference (2) at the end of the chapter).

---

## Batch costing

The production of many types of goods and services (particularly goods) involves producing a batch of identical, or nearly identical, units of output yet with each batch differing from other batches. For example, a theatre may put on a production whose nature (and therefore costs) is very different from those of other productions. On the other hand, ignoring differences in the desirability of the various types of seating, all of the individual units of output (tickets to see the production) are identical.

In these circumstances, we should normally deduce the cost per ticket by using a job-costing approach (taking account of direct and indirect costs and so on) to find the cost of mounting the production, and then we should simply divide this value by the number of tickets expected to be sold, in order to find the cost per ticket. This approach is known as **batch costing**.

## Full cost as the break-even price

It may have occurred to you by now that if all goes according to plan (so that direct costs, overheads and the basis of charging overheads (for example, direct-labour hours) prove to be as expected), then selling the output for its full cost should cause the business exactly to break even. Thus, whatever profit (in total) is loaded onto full cost, to set selling prices will result in that level of profit being earned for the period.

## The forward-looking nature of full costing

Though deducing full costs can be done after the work has been completed, it is often done in advance. In other words, costs are frequently predicted. Where, for example, full costs are needed as a basis on which to set selling prices, it is usually the case that prices need to be set before the customer will enter a contract for the job to be done. Even where no particular customer has been identified, some idea of the ultimate price will need to be known before the manufacturer will be able to make a judgement as to whether potential customers will buy the product and in what quantities.

## Full costing in service industries

You should be clear that the concepts of full costing – whether it is through process costing, job costing or batch costing – apply equally to service and manufacturing businesses. The examples and activities in this chapter have reflected this fact.

With service businesses, the full cost of each unit of output is likely to include a relatively low (perhaps zero) proportion of direct material cost.

### ? Self-assessment question 4.1

Hector and Co. Ltd has been invited to tender for a contract to produce 1,000 clothes hangers. The following information relates to the contract.

- *Materials*: The clothes hangers are made of metal wire covered with a padded fabric. Each hanger requires 2 metres of wire and 0.5 square metres of fabric.
- *Direct labour*: – Skilled 10 minutes per hanger
  – Unskilled 5 minutes per hanger.

The business already has sufficient stock of each of the materials required to complete the contract. Information on the cost of the stock is as follows:

|  | Metal wire £/m | Fabric £/m² |
|---|---|---|
| Historic cost | 2.20 | 1.00 |
| Current buying-in cost | 2.50 | 1.10 |
| Scrap value | 1.70 | 0.40 |

The metal wire is in constant use by the business for a range of its products. The fabric has no other use for the business and is scheduled to be scrapped.

Unskilled labour, which is paid at the rate of £5.00 an hour, will need to be taken on specifically to undertake the contract. The business is fairly quiet at the moment, which means that a pool of skilled labour exists that will still be employed at full pay of £7.50 an hour to do nothing if the contract does not proceed. The pool of skilled labour is sufficient to complete the contract.

The business charges jobs with overheads on a direct-labour-hour basis. The production overheads of the entire business for the month in which the contract will be undertaken are estimated at £50,000. The estimated total direct-labour hours that will be worked are 12,500. The business tends not to alter the established overhead recovery rate to reflect increases or reductions to estimated total hours arising from new contracts. The total overhead cost is not expected to increase as a result of undertaking the contract.

The business normally adds 12.5 per cent profit loading to the job cost to arrive at a first estimate of the tender price.

**Required:**
(a) Price this job on a traditional job-costing basis; and
(b) indicate the minimum price at which the contract could be undertaken such that the business would be neither better nor worse off as a result of doing it.

## Summary

In this chapter we have seen that many – perhaps most – businesses seek to identify the total or full cost of pursuing some objective, typically of a unit of output.

Where all units of goods or service produced by a business are identical, this tends to be a fairly straightforward matter: a case of simply finding the total cost for a period and dividing by the number of units of output for the same period.

Where a business's output is of units that are not similar, we have seen that it is necessary to take a less straightforward approach to the problem. Normally, such businesses identify the direct costs of production – that is, those costs that can be directly measured in respect of a particular unit of output. To these is added a share of the overheads according to some formula, which, of necessity, must be to some extent arbitrary. We saw that survey evidence shows direct-labour hours to be the most popular basis of charging overheads to cost units. Costing individual cost units in this way is known as 'job costing'.

Full cost information is widely used by businesses but it is also widely criticised for not providing very helpful or relevant information.

 **Key terms**

| | |
|---|---|
| Full costing   p. 65 | Cost unit   p. 72 |
| Full cost   p. 65 | Overhead absorption (recovery) rate |
| Cost-plus pricing   p. 66 |    p. 73 |
| Process costing   p. 68 | Cost centre   p. 80 |
| Direct costs   p. 69 | Product cost centre   p. 80 |
| Indirect costs   p. 69 | Service cost centre   p. 80 |
| Overheads   p. 69 | Cost allocation   p. 81 |
| Common costs   p. 69 | Cost apportionment   p. 81 |
| Job costing   p. 69 | Batch costing   p. 87 |
| Cost behaviour   p. 71 | |

## Further reading

If you would like to explore the topics covered in this chapter in more depth, we recommend the following books:

**Management Accounting**, *Atkinson, A.*, *Barker, R.*, *Kaplan, R.* and *Mark Young, S.*, 3rd edn, Prentice Hall, 2001, chapter 4.

**Management and Cost Accounting**, *Drury, C.*, 5th edn, Thomson Learning, 2000, chapters 3, 4 and 5.

**Cost Accounting: A managerial emphasis**, *Horngren, C.*, *Foster, G.* and *Datar, S.*, 10th edn, Prentice Hall International, 2000, chapter 4.

**Cost and Management Accounting**, *Williamson, D.*, Prentice Hall International, 1996, chapters 6, 8 and 10.

## References

1. **Cost Systems Design and Profitability Analysis in UK Companies**, *Drury, C.* and *Tayles, M.*, CIMA Publishing, 2000.
2. **A Survey of Management Accounting Practices in UK Manufacturing Companies**, *Drury, C.*, *Braund, S.*, *Osborne, P.* and *Tayles, M.*, Chartered Association of Certified Accountants, 1993.

**4.1** What is the problem that the existence of work in progress causes in process costing?

**4.2** What is the point of distinguishing direct costs from indirect ones?

**4.3** Are direct costs and variable costs the same thing?

**4.4** It is sometimes claimed that the full cost of pursuing some objective represents the long-run, break-even selling price. Why is this said and what does it mean?

**? EXERCISES**

Exercises 4.6–4.8 are more advanced than 4.1–4.5. Those with coloured numbers have answers at the back of the book.

**4.1** 'In a job costing system it is necessary to divide the business up into departments. Fixed costs (or overheads) will be collected for each department. Where a particular fixed cost relates to the business as a whole, it must be divided between the departments. Usually this is done on the basis of area of floor space occupied by each department relative to the entire business. When the total fixed costs for each department have been identified, this will be divided by the number of hours that were worked in each department to deduce an overhead recovery rate. Each job that was worked on in a department will have a share of fixed costs allotted to it according to how long it was worked on. The total cost for each job will therefore be the sum of the variable costs of the job and its share of the fixed costs. It is essential that this approach is taken in order to deduce a selling price for the firm's output.'

**Required:**
Prepare a table of two columns. In the first column you should show any phrases or sentences with which you do not agree in the above statement, and in the second column you should show *briefly* your reason for disagreeing with each one.

**4.2** Distinguish between:

- Job costing
- Process costing
- Batch costing.

What tend to be the problems specifically associated with each of these?

**4.3** Bodgers Ltd, a business that provides a market research service, operates a job costing system. Towards the end of each financial year, the overhead absorption rate (the rate at which overheads will be charged to jobs) is established for the forthcoming year.

**Required:**
(a) Why does the business bother to predetermine the absorption rate in the way outlined?
(b) What steps will be involved in predetermining the rate?
(c) What problems might arise with using a predetermined rate?

**4.4** Pieman Products Ltd makes road trailers to the precise specifications of individual customers. The following are predicted to occur during the forthcoming year, which is about to start:

| | |
|---|---|
| Direct materials cost | £50,000 |
| Direct labour costs | £80,000 |
| Direct labour time | 16,000 hours |
| Indirect labour cost | £25,000 |
| Depreciation (wear and tear) of machinery, etc. | £8,000 |
| Rent and rates | £10,000 |
| Heating, lighting and power | £5,000 |
| Indirect materials | £2,000 |
| Other indirect costs | £1,000 |
| Machine time | 3,000 hours |

All direct labour is paid at the same hourly rate.

A customer has asked the business to build a trailer for transporting a racing motor cycle to races. It is estimated that this will require materials and components that will cost £1,150. It will take 250 direct-labour hours to do the job, of which 50 will involve the use of machinery.

**Required:**
Deduce a logical cost for the job, and explain the basis of dealing with overheads that you propose.

**4.5** Many businesses charge overheads to jobs on a departmental basis.

**Required:**
(a) What is the advantage that is claimed for charging overheads to jobs on a departmental basis, and why is it claimed?
(b) What circumstances need to exist to make a difference to a particular job whether overheads are charged on a business-wide basis or on a departmental basis. (Note that the answer to this part of the question is not specifically covered in the chapter. You should, nevertheless, be able to deduce the reason from what you know.)

**4.6** Promptprint Ltd, a printing business, has received an enquiry from a potential customer for the quotation of a price for a job. The pricing policy of the business is based on the plans for the next financial year shown below.

| | £ |
|---|---|
| Sales (billings to customers) | 196,000 |
| Materials (direct) | (38,000) |
| Labour (direct) | (32,000) |
| Variable overheads | (2,400) |
| Advertising (for business) | (3,000) |
| Depreciation | (27,600) |
| Administration | (36,000) |
| Interest | (8,000) |
| Profit (before tax) | 49,000 |

A first estimate of the direct costs for the job are:

|  | £ |
|---|---|
| Direct materials | 4,000 |
| Direct labour | 3,600 |

**Required:**
Based on the estimated direct costs:

(a) Prepare a recommended price for the job based on the plans, commenting on your method, ignoring the information given in the Appendix (below).
(b) Comment on the validity of using financial plans in pricing, and recommend any improvements you would consider desirable for the pricing policy used in (a).
(c) Incorporate the effects of the information shown in the Appendix (below) into your estimates of direct material costs, explaining any changes you consider it necessary to make to the above direct materials cost of £4,000.

**Appendix to Exercise 4.6**
Direct material costs were computed as follows based on historic costs:

|  | £ |
|---|---|
| Paper grade 1 | 1,200 |
| Paper grade 2 | 2,000 |
| Card (zenith grade) | 500 |
| Inks and other miscellaneous items | 300 |
|  | 4,000 |

Paper grade 1 is in stock and in regular use. Because it is imported, it is estimated that if it is used for this job, a new stock order will have to be placed shortly. Sterling has depreciated against the foreign currency by 25 per cent since the last purchase.

Paper grade 2 is purchased from the same source as grade 1. However, current stock was bought in for a special order. This order was cancelled, although the defaulting customer was required to pay £500 towards the cost of the paper. The accountant has offset this against the original cost to arrive at the figure of £2,000 shown above. This paper is rarely used, and due to its special chemical coating will be unusable if it is not used on the job in question.

The card is another specialist item currently in stock. There is no use foreseen, and it would cost £750 to replace if required. However, the stock controller had planned to spend £130 on overprinting to use the card as a substitute for other materials costing £640.

Inks and other items are in regular use in the print shop.

**4.7** Bookdon plc manufactures three products, X, Y and Z, in two production departments: a machine shop and a fitting section; it also has two service departments: a canteen and a machine maintenance section. Shown below are next year's planned production data and manufacturing costs for the business.

|  | X | Y | Z |
|---|---|---|---|
| Production | 4,200 units | 6,900 units | 1,700 units |
| Direct materials | £11/unit | £14/unit | £17/unit |
| Direct labour |  |  |  |
|     Machine shop | £6/unit | £4/unit | £2/unit |
|     Fitting section | £12/unit | £3/unit | £21/unit |
| Machine hours | 6 hrs/unit | 3 hrs/unit | 4 hrs/unit |

Planned overheads are as follows:

| | Machine shop | Fitting section | Canteen | Machine maintenance section | Total |
|---|---|---|---|---|---|
| Allocated overheads | £27,660 | £19,470 | £16,600 | £26,650 | £90,380 |
| Rent, rates, heat and light | | | | | £17,000 |
| Depreciation and insurance of equipment | | | | | £25,000 |
| Additional data: | | | | | |
| Gross book value of equipment | £150,000 | £75,000 | £30,000 | £45,000 | |
| Number of employees | 18 | 14 | 4 | 4 | |
| Floor space occupied | 3,600 m² | 1,400 m² | 1,000 m² | 800 m² | |

It has been estimated that approximately 70 per cent of the machine maintenance section's costs are incurred servicing the machine shop and the remainder servicing the fitting section.

**Required:**
(a) Calculate the following planned overhead absorption rates:
   (i) A machine-hour rate for the machine shop.
   (ii) A rate expressed as a percentage of direct wages for the fitting section.
(b) Calculate the planned full cost per unit of product X.

**4.8** Shown below is an extract from next year's plans for a business manuacturing three products, A, B and C, in three production departments.

| | A | B | C |
|---|---|---|---|
| Production | 4,000 units | 3,000 units | 6,000 units |
| Direct material cost | £7 per unit | £4 per unit | £9 per unit |
| Direct labour requirements: | | | |
| Cutting department: | | | |
| Skilled operatives | 3 hr/unit | 5 hr/unit | 2 hr/unit |
| Unskilled operatives | 6 hr/unit | 1 hr/unit | 3 hr/unit |
| Machining department | $\frac{1}{2}$ hr/unit | $\frac{1}{4}$ hr/unit | $\frac{1}{3}$ hr/unit |
| Pressing department | 2 hr/unit | 3 hr/unit | 4 hr/unit |
| Machine requirements: | | | |
| Machining department | 2 hr/unit | $1\frac{1}{2}$ hr/unit | $2\frac{1}{2}$ hr/unit |

The skilled operatives employed in the cutting department are paid £8 per hour and the unskilled operatives are paid £5 per hour. All the operatives in the machining and pressing departments are paid £6 per hour.

|  | Production departments | | | Service departments | |
|---|---|---|---|---|---|
|  | Cutting | Machining | Pressing | Engineering | Personnel |
| Planned total overheads | £154,482 | £64,316 | £58,452 | £56,000 | £34,000 |
| Service department costs incurred for the benefit of other departments, as follows: | | | | | |
| Engineering services | 20% | 45% | 35% | – | – |
| Personnel services | 55% | 10% | 20% | 15% | – |

The business operates a full absorption costing system.

**Required:**
Calculate, as equitably as possible, the total planned cost of:

(a) One completed unit of product A.
(b) One incomplete unit of product B, which has been processed by the cutting and machining departments but which has not yet been passed into the pressing department.

## CHAPTER 5

# Managing in a competitive environment

## Introduction

In recent years we have witnessed major changes in the business world. Such factors as deregulation, privatisation, the growing expectations of shareholders and the impact of new technology have led to a much faster-changing and competitive environment that has radically altered the way in which managers should manage. In this chapter we consider some of the financial techniques that are being used to manage in this new era.

We begin by considering the impact of this new, highly competitive environment on the full costing approach that we considered in the previous chapter. We shall see that activity-based costing, which is a development of the traditional full-costing approach, takes a much more enquiring, much less accepting attitude towards overheads. We shall see how, in theory and in practice, a business can use costing information to aid pricing decisions. We shall also examine some recent approaches to costing that can lower costs and, therefore, increase the ability of a business to compete on price.

**OBJECTIVES** When you have completed this chapter, you should be able to:

■ Discuss the nature of the modern costing and pricing environment.
■ Discuss the nature and practicalities of activity-based costing.
■ Explain the theoretical underpinning of pricing and discuss the issues involved in reaching a pricing decision in real-world situations.
■ Explain how new developments such as total life-cycle costing and target costing can be used to control costs.

## Costing and the changed business environment

The traditional approach to costing and pricing output developed when the notion of trying to cost industrial production first emerged, probably around the time of the UK Industrial Revolution. At that time, manufacturing industry was characterised by the following features:

■ *Direct-labour-intensive and direct-labour-paced production.* Labour was at the heart of production. To the extent that machinery was used, it was to support the efforts of direct labour, and the speed of production was dictated by direct labour.

■ *A low level of overheads relative to direct costs.* Little was spent on power, personnel services, machinery (with the resulting low depreciation charges) and other areas typical of the overheads of modern businesses.

■ *A relatively uncompetitive market.* Transport difficulties, limited industrial production worldwide and a lack of knowledge by customers of competitors' prices meant that businesses could prosper without being too scientific in costing and pricing their output.

Since overheads then represented a pretty small element of total costs, it was acceptable and practical to deal with them in a fairly arbitrary manner. Not too much effort was devoted to trying to control the cost of overheads because the rewards of better control were relatively small – certainly compared with the rewards from controlling direct labour and material costs. It was also reasonable to charge overheads to individual jobs on a direct-labour-hour basis. Most of the overheads were incurred directly in support of direct labour: providing direct workers with a place to work, heating and lighting that workplace, employing people to supervise the direct workers, and so on. At the same time, all production was done by direct workers, perhaps aided by machinery.

By now, the start of this new millennium, the world of much industrial production had fundamentally altered. Most of it is now characterised by:

■ *Capital-intensive and machine-paced production.* Machines are at the heart of production. Most labour supports the efforts of machines – for example, technically maintaining them – and the speed of production is dictated by machines.

■ *A high level of overheads relative to direct costs.* Depreciation, servicing and power costs are very high. Also, there are costs of a nature scarcely envisaged in the early days of industrial production, such as personnel and staff welfare costs; these, too, are high. At the same time, there are very low (perhaps no) direct labour costs. The proportion of total cost accounted for by direct materials has typically not altered too much, but more efficient production tends to lead to less waste and, therefore, less material cost, again tending to make overheads dominant.

■ *A highly competitive international market.* Industrial production, much of it highly sophisticated, is carried out worldwide. Transport, including fast air freight, is relatively cheap. Fax, telephone and the Internet ensure that potential customers can find out the prices of a range of suppliers quickly and cheaply. The market is, therefore, likely to be highly competitive. This means that businesses need to know their costs with a degree of accuracy that historically had been unnecessary. Businesses also need to take a considered and informed approach to pricing their output.

## Activity-based costing

In Chapter 4, we considered the traditional approach to job costing (deriving the full cost of output where one unit of output differs from another). This approach is to collect those costs for each job, which can be unequivocally linked to and measured in respect of the particular job (direct costs). All other costs (overheads) are thrown into a pool of costs and charged to individual jobs according to some formula. As we saw in Chapter 4, survey evidence indicates that this formula has usually been on the basis of the number of direct-labour hours worked on each individual job.

Whereas the traditional overhead recovery rate (that is, the rate at which overheads are absorbed by jobs) was much less per direct-labour hour than the actual rate paid to direct workers, recently there have been examples of overhead recovery rates five and ten times the hourly rate of pay. When production is dominated by direct labour paid £5 an hour, it might be reasonable to have a recovery rate of £1 an hour. When, however, direct labour plays a relatively small part in production, to have overhead recovery rates of £50 per direct-labour hour is likely to lead to very arbitrary costing. Just a small change in the amount of direct labour worked on a job could massively affect the cost deduced, not because the direct worker is massively well paid, but for no better reason than that this is the way in which it has always been done: overheads, not particularly related to labour, are charged on a direct-labour-hour basis.

The whole question of overheads, what causes them and how they are charged to jobs has been receiving closer attention recently, as a result of changes in the environment in which businesses operate. Historically, businesses have been content to accept that overheads exist and, therefore, they must be dealt with, for costing purposes, in as practical a way as possible.

In recent years there has been an increasing realisation that overheads do not just happen; they must be caused by something. To illustrate this point, let us consider Example 5.1.

| | |
|---|---|
| **Example 5.1** | Modern Producers Ltd has, like virtually all manufacturers, a storage area (known as the stores) that is set aside for finished goods. The costs of running the stores include a share of the factory rent and other establishment costs, such as heating and lighting. They also include the salaries of staff employed to look after the stock, and the cost of financing the stock held in the stores. |

The company has two product lines: A and B. Product A tends to be made in small batches, and low levels of finished stock are held. The company prides itself on its ability to supply product B in relatively large quantities instantly. As a consequence, much of the finished goods store is filled with finished product B ready to be despatched soon after an order is received.

Traditionally, the whole cost of operating the stores would have been treated as a general overhead and included in the total of overheads charged to jobs on a direct-labour-hour basis. This means that when assessing the cost of products A and B, the cost of operating the stores has fallen on them according to the number of direct-labour hours worked on each one. In fact, most of the stores cost should be charged to product B, since this product causes (and benefits from) the stores cost much more than is true of product A. Failure to account more precisely for the costs of running the stores is masking the fact that product B is not as profitable as it seems to be; it may even be making a loss as a result of the relatively high cost that it causes of operating the stores, but that so far have been charged to product A, without regard to the fact that product A causes little of the cost. In fact, traditionally, the products would absorb stores costs in proportion to their direct-labour-hour content, a factor that has nothing to do with storage.

### Cost drivers

Realisation that overheads do not just occur, but that they are caused by activities – like holding products in stores – that 'drive' the costs, is at the heart of ➡ **activity-based costing (ABC)**. The traditional approach is that direct-labour hours ➡ are a **cost driver**, which probably used to be true. It is now recognised not to be the case.

There is a basic philosophical difference between the traditional and the ABC approaches. Traditionally we tend to think of overheads as *rendering a service to cost units*, the cost of which must be charged to those units. ABC sees overheads as being *caused by cost units*, and those cost units must be charged with the costs that they cause.

| | |
|---|---|
| **Activity 5.1** | **Can you think of any other purpose that identification of the cost drivers serves, apart from deriving more accurate costs?** |

Identification of the activities that cause costs puts management in a position where it may well be able to control them.

The opaque nature of overheads has traditionally rendered them difficult to control, relative to the much more obvious direct-labour and material costs. If, however, analysis of overheads can identify the cost drivers, questions can be asked about whether the activity driving certain costs is necessary at all, and whether the cost justifies the benefit. In our example, it may be a good marketing ploy that product B can be supplied immediately from stock, but there is an associated cost and that cost should be recognised and assessed against the benefit.

Advocates of activity-based costing argue that most overheads can be analysed and cost drivers identified. If true, this means that it is possible to gain much clearer insights to the costs that are caused, activity by activity, so that fairer and more accurate product costs can be identified, and costs can be controlled more effectively.

### Cost pools

➡ Under ABC, an overhead **cost pool** is established for each type of cost that can be linked to a cost-driving activity. So the business in Example 5.1 would create a cost pool for operating the stores. All costs associated with this activity would be allocated to that cost pool. Costs in that pool would then be allocated to output (goods or services) according to the extent to which each unit of output 'drove' those costs, using the cost driver identified.

| | |
|---|---|
| **Example 5.2** | The accountant at Modern Producers Ltd (see Example 5.1) has estimated that the costs of running the finished goods stores for next year will be £90,000. This will be the amount allocated to the 'finished goods stores cost pool'. |

It is estimated that each product A will spend an average of one week in the stores before being sold. With product B, the equivalent period is four weeks. Both products are of roughly similar size and have very similar storage needs. It is felt, therefore, that the quantity of each product and the period spent in the stores are the cost drivers.

> It is estimated that, next year, 50,000 units of product A and 25,000 units of product B will pass though the stores. The total number of 'product weeks' in store will thus be:
>
> | | | |
> |---|---|---|
> | Product A | 50,000 × 1 week = | 50,000 |
> | B | 25,000 × 4 weeks = | 100,000 |
> | | | 150,000 |
>
> The stores cost per 'product week' is given by
>
> £90,000/150,000 = £0.60.
>
> Therefore each product A will be charged with £0.60 for finished stores costs, and each product B with £2.40 (that is, £0.60 × 4).

Allocating overhead costs to cost pools with ABC contrasts with the traditional approach, where the overheads are allocated to production departments, in both cases then to be charged to cost units (products – goods and services). This contrast is illustrated in Figure 5.1.

With the traditional approach, overheads are apportioned to product departments. Each department would then derive an overhead recovery rate, typically overheads per direct-labour hour. Overheads would then be applied to units of output according to how many direct-labour hours were worked on them.

With ABC, the overheads are analysed into cost pools, with one cost pool for each cost driver. The overheads are then charged to units of output, through activity cost driver rates. These rates are an attempt to represent the extent to which each particular cost unit is believed to cause the particular part of the overheads.

## ABC and service industries

Much of our discussion of ABC has concentrated on manufacturing industry, perhaps because early users of ABC were manufacturing businesses. In fact, ABC is possibly even more relevant to service industries because, in the absence of a direct materials element, a service business's total costs are likely to be particularly heavily affected by overheads. There is certainly evidence that ABC has been adopted by businesses that sell services rather than goods.

| Activity 5.2 | What is the difference in the way in which direct costs are accounted for when using ABC, relative to their treatment taking a traditional approach to full costing? |
|---|---|

The answer is no difference at all. ABC is concerned only with the way in which overheads are charged to jobs to derive the full cost.

## Criticisms of ABC

Critics of ABC argue that analysis of overheads in order to identify cost drivers is time-consuming and costly, and that the benefit of doing so, in terms of more

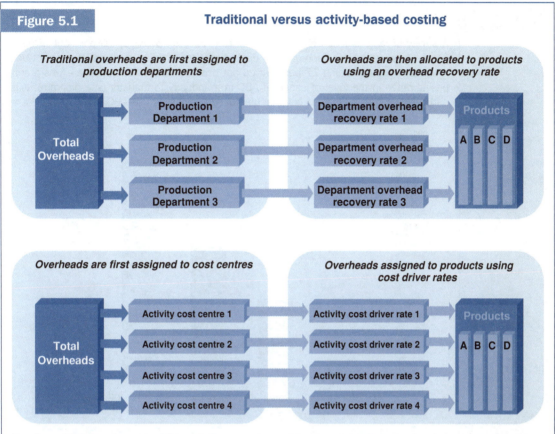

| **Figure 5.1** | **Traditional versus activity-based costing** |

**Traditional overheads are first assigned to production departments**

**Overheads are then allocated to products using an overhead recovery rate**

Total Overheads → Production Department 1 → Department overhead recovery rate 1 → Products

Production Department 2 → Department overhead recovery rate 2

Production Department 3 → Department overhead recovery rate 3

A B C D

**Overheads are first assigned to cost centres**

**Overheads assigned to products using cost driver rates**

Total Overheads → Activity cost centre 1 → Activity cost driver rate 1 → Products

Activity cost centre 2 → Activity cost driver rate 2

Activity cost centre 3 → Activity cost driver rate 3

Activity cost centre 4 → Activity cost driver rate 4

A B C D

The figure highlights the main differences between the traditional costing approach and the activity-based costing approach. With the traditional approach, overheads are first assigned to production departments and then overheads are allocated to products based on an overhead recovery rate (based on the direct-labour hours worked on the product or some other basis) for each department. With the activity-based costing approach, overheads are assigned to cost centres and then products are charged with overheads to the extent that they drive the costs of the cost centres.

*Source*: Adapted from Innes and Mitchell (see reference (1) at the end of the chapter).

accurate costing and the potential for cost control, does not justify the cost of carrying out the analysis.

ABC is also criticised for the same reason that full costing generally is criticised: because it does not provide very relevant information for decision making. The point was made in Chapter 4 that full costing tends to use past costs and to ignore opportunity costs. Since past costs are always irrelevant in decision making and opportunity costs can be very significant, full costing information is an expensive irrelevance. In contrast, advocates of full costing claim that it *is* relevant, in that it provides a long-run average cost, whereas 'relevant costing', which we considered in Chapter 2, relates only to the specific circumstances of the short term.

Despite the criticisms that are made of full costing, it is, according to survey evidence, very widely practised. Exhibit 5.1 provides some indication of the extent to which ABC is used in practice.

| Exhibit 5.1 | **ABC in practice** |

A survey of large businesses in 1999 revealed that, on average, 15 per cent of businesses fully use an ABC approach to dealing with full costing, a further 8 per cent use it partially. The remaining 77 per cent do not use ABC at all. Even so, there was a surprising range in the level of usage of ABC from industry to industry (see diagram). It is particularly surprising that so few manufacturing businesses use ABC.

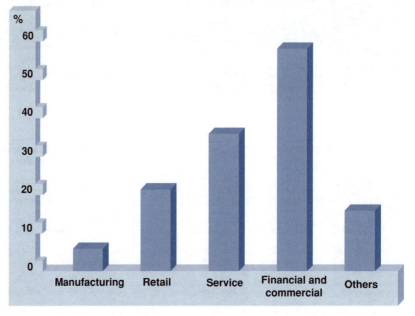

*Source*: Constructed with data from Drury and Tayles (see reference (2) at the end of the chapter).

There is no real evidence of an increase in the use of ABC, possibly the opposite. A study conducted by Drury, Braund, Osborne and Tayles in 1993 (see reference (3) at the end of the chapter) showed that 13 per cent of manufacturing businesses had adopted ABC at that time.

The Drury and Tayles (2) survey shows that it tends to be larger businesses that adopt ABC.

| ? | **Self-assessment question 5.1** |

Psilis Ltd makes a product in two qualities, called 'Basic' and 'Super'. The company had been able to sell these products at a price that gave a standard profit mark-up of 25 per cent of full cost. Management is concerned by the lack of profit.

Full cost per unit is calculated by apportioning overheads to each type of product on the basis of direct labour hours. The costs are as follows:

|  | Basic £ | Super £ |
|---|---|---|
| Direct labour (all £5/hour) | 20 | 30 |
| Direct material | 15 | 20 |

The total overheads are £1,000,000.

Based on experience over recent years, for the forthcoming year the company expects to make and sell 40,000 Basics and 10,000 Supers.

Recently, the company's management accountant has undertaken an exercise to try to identify cost drivers in an attempt to be able to deal with the overheads on a more precise basis than had been possible before. This exercise has revealed the following analysis of the annual overheads:

| Activity (and cost driver) | | Annual number of activities | | |
|---|---|---|---|---|
| | Cost £000 | Total | Basic | Super |
| Number of machine set-ups | 280 | 100 | 20 | 80 |
| Number of quality-control inspections | 220 | 2,000 | 500 | 1,500 |
| Number of sales orders processed | 240 | 5,000 | 1,500 | 3,500 |
| General production (machine hours) | 260 | 500,000 | 350,000 | 150,000 |
| Total | 1,000 | | | |

The management accountant explained the analysis of the £1,000,000 overheads as follows:

- The two products are made in relatively small batches, so that storage of finished stock is negligible. The Supers are made in very small batches because demand for them is relatively low. Each time a new batch is produced, the machines have to be reset by skilled staff. Resetting for Basic production occurs about 20 times a year and for Supers about 80 times: about 100 times in total. The costs of employing the machine-setting staff is about £280,000 a year. It is clear that the more set-ups that occur, the higher the total set-up costs; in other words, the number of set-ups is the factor that drives set-up costs.
- All production has to be inspected for quality and this costs about £220,000 a year. The higher specifications of the Supers means that there is more chance that there will be quality problems. Thus the Supers are inspected in total 1,500 times annually, whereas the Basics only need about 500 inspections. The number of inspections is the factor that drives these costs.
- Sales order processing (dealing with customers' orders from receiving the original order to despatching the products) costs about £240,000 a year. Despite the larger amount of Basic production, there are only 1,500 sales orders each year because the Basics are sold to wholesalers in relatively large-sized orders. The Supers are sold mainly direct to the public by mail order, usually in very small-sized orders. It is believed that the number of orders drives the costs of processing orders.
- The remaining general production overheads, totalling £260,000 a year, are thought to be driven by the number of hours for which the machines operate. The machine time per product is somewhat higher for Supers than for Basics.

**Required:**
(a) Deduce the full cost of each of the two products on the basis used at present and, from these, deduce the current selling price.
(b) Deduce the full cost of each product, taking account of the management accountant's recent investigations.
(c) What conclusions do you draw? What advice would you offer the management of the company?

## Pricing

As we have just seen, full costing can be used as a basis for setting prices for the business's output. We have also seen that it can be criticised in that role. In this section we are going to take a closer look at pricing. We shall begin by considering some theoretical aspects of the subject before going on to look at some more practical issues, particularly the role of management accounting information in pricing decision making.

### Economic theory

In most market conditions found in practice, the price charged by a business will determine the number of units sold. This is shown graphically in Figure 5.2.

The diagram in Figure 5.2 shows the number of units of output that the market would demand at various prices. As price increases, the less willing people are to buy the commodity (call it commodity A). At a relatively low price per unit ($P_1$), the quantity of units demanded by the market ($Q_1$) is fairly high. When the price is increased to $P_2$, the demand decreases to $Q_2$. The graph shows a linear relationship between price and demand. In practice, the relationship, though broadly similar, may not be quite so straightforward.

Not all commodities show exactly the same slope of line. Figure 5.3 shows the demand/price relationship for commodity B, a different commodity from the one depicted in Figure 5.2.

Though a rise in price of commodity B, from $P_1$ to $P_2$, causes a fall in demand, the fall in demand is much smaller than is the case for commodity A with a

| Figure 5.2 | **Graph of quantity demanded against price for a commodity** |

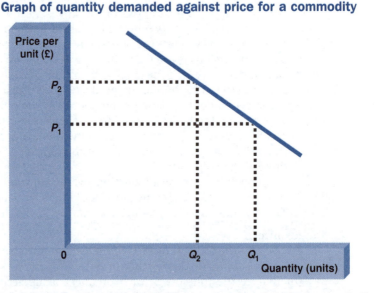

As the price of the commodity under consideration increases from $P_1$ to $P_2$, the quantity that the market will buy falls from $Q_1$ to $Q_2$.

| Figure 5.3 | **Graph of quantity demanded against price for commodity B** |

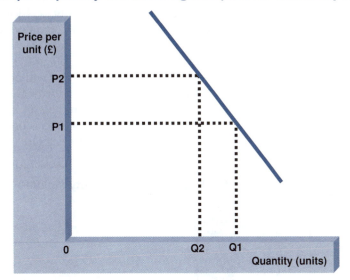

As the price of the commodity increases from $P_1$ to $P_2$, the quantity that the market will buy falls from $Q_1$ to $Q_2$. This fall in demand is less than was the case for commodity A, which has the greater elasticity of demand.

 similar rise in price. As a result, we say that commodity A has a higher **elasticity of demand** than commodity B: demand for A reacts much more dramatically (stretches more) to price changes than demand for B. Elastic demand tends to be associated with commodities that are not essential, perhaps because there is a ready substitute.

| *Activity 5.3* | **Which would be the more elastic of the following commodities?** |

■ **A particular brand of chocolate bar?**
■ **Mains electricity supply?**

A branded chocolate bar seems likely to have a fairly *elastic* demand. This is for several reasons, including the following:

■ Few buyers of the bar would feel that chocolate bars are essentials.
■ Other chocolate bars, probably quite similar to the commodity in question, will be easily available.

Mains electricity probably has a relatively *inelastic* demand. This is because:

■ Many users of electricity would find it very difficult to manage without fuel of some description.
■ For neither domestic nor commercial users of electricity is there an immediate, practical substitute. For some uses of electricity – for example powering machinery – there is probably no substitute. Even for a purpose such as heating, where there are substitutes such as gas and oil, it may be impractical to switch to the substitute because gas and oil heating appliances are not immediately available and are costly to acquire.

It is very helpful for those involved with pricing decisions to have some feel for the elasticity of demand of the commodity that will be the subject of a decision. The sensitivity of the demand to the pricing decision is obviously much greater (and the pricing decision more crucial) with commodities whose demand is elastic than with commodities whose demand is relatively inelastic.

As we saw in Chapter 1, the objective of most businesses is to enhance the wealth of their owners. Broadly speaking, this will be best achieved by seeking to maximise profits – that is, having the largest possible difference between total costs and total revenues. Thus prices should be set in a way that is likely to have this effect. To be able to do this, the price decision maker needs to have some insight to the way in which costs and prices relate to volume of output.

| Figure 5.4 | **Graph of total cost against quantity (volume) of output of product X** |

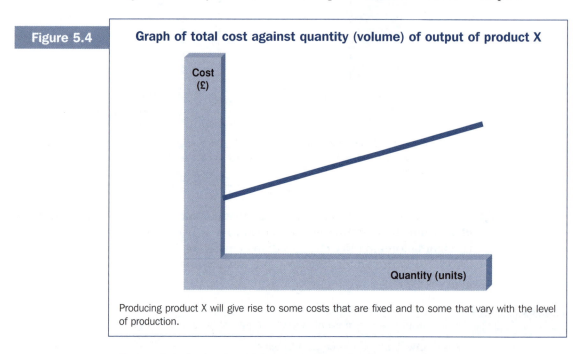

Producing product X will give rise to some costs that are fixed and to some that vary with the level of production.

Figure 5.4 shows the relationship between cost and volume of output, which we have already met in Chapter 3. The figure shows that the total cost of producing a particular commodity (product X) increases as the quantity of output increases. It is shown here as a straight line; in practice it may be curved, either curving upwards (tending to become closer to the vertical) or flattening out (tending to become closer to the horizontal). The figure assumes that the marginal cost of each unit is constant over the range shown.

| Activity 5.5 | What general effect would tend to cause the total cost line in Figure 5.4 to (a) curve towards the vertical, and (b) curve towards the horizontal? (You may recall that we considered this issue in Chapter 3.) |

(a) Curving towards the vertical would mean that the marginal cost (additional cost of making one more) of each successive unit of output would become greater. This would probably imply that increased activity would be causing a shortage of supply of some factor of production, which had the effect of increasing cost prices. This might be caused by a shortage of labour, meaning that overtime payments would need to be made to encourage people to work the hours necessary for increased production. It might also/alternatively be caused by a shortage of raw materials: perhaps normal supplies were exhausted at lower levels of output and more expensive sources had to be used to expand output.

(b) Curving towards the horizontal might be caused by the business being able to exploit the economies of scale at higher levels of output, making the marginal cost of each successive unit of output cheaper. Perhaps higher volumes of output enable division of labour or more mechanisation. Possibly, suppliers of raw materials offer better deals for larger orders.

Figure 5.5 shows the total sales revenue against quantity of product X sold.

| **Figure 5.5** | **Graph of total sales revenue against quantity (volume) sold of product X** |
| --- | --- |

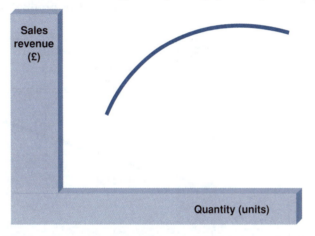

As more units of product X are sold, the total sales revenue initially increases, but at a declining rate. This is because, in order to persuade people to buy increasing quantities, the price must be reduced. Eventually the price will have to be reduced so much, to encourage additional sales, that the total sales revenue will fall as the number of units sold increases.

The total sales revenue increases as the quantity of output increases, up to a certain point.

| **Activity 5.5** | **What assumption does Figure 5.5 make about the price per unit of product X at which output can be sold as the number of units sold increases?** |
| --- | --- |

The graph suggests that, to sell more units, the price must be lowered, meaning that the average price per unit of output reduces as volume sold increases. As we discussed earlier in this section, this is true of most markets found in practice.

Figure 5.5 implies that there will come a point where, to make increased sales, prices will have to be reduced so much that total sales revenue will not increase; it may even reduce.

You may recall from Chapter 3 that, when we considered break-even analysis, we assumed a steady price per unit over the range that we were considering. Now we are saying that, in practice, it does not work like this. How can these two positions be reconciled? The answer is that, when we dealt with break-even analysis, we were only considering a relatively small range of output, namely from zero sales up to the break-even point. It may well be that over a small range, particularly at low levels of output, a constant sales price per unit is a reasonable assumption. That is to say, to the left of the curve in Figure 5.5 there may be a straight line from zero up to the start of the curve.

There is nothing in break-even analysis that demands that the assumption about steady selling prices is made, but making it does mean that the analysis is very straightforward.

| Figure 5.6 | **Graph of total sales revenue and total cost against quantity (volume) of output of product X** |

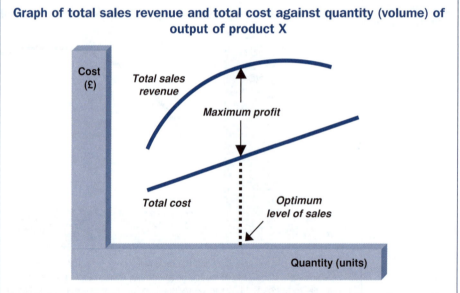

Profit is the vertical distance between the total-cost and total-sales-revenue lines. For a wealth-maximising business, the optimum level of sales will occur when this is at a maximum.

Figure 5.6 combines information about total sales revenue and total cost for product X over a range of output levels. The total sales revenue increases, but at a decreasing rate, and total cost of production increases as the quantity of output increases. The maximum profit is made where the total sales revenue and total cost lines are vertically furthest apart. At the left-hand end of the graph, we are clearly above break-even point because the total-sales-revenue line has already gone above the total-cost line. At the lower levels of volume of sales and output, the total-sales-revenue line is climbing faster than the total-cost line. The business will wish to keep expanding output as long as this continues to be the case, because profit is the vertical distance between the two lines. A point will be reached where the total-sales line flattens towards the horizontal to such an extent that further expansion will reduce profit.

The point at which profit is maximised is where the two lines stop diverging, that is, the point at which the two lines are climbing at exactly the same rate. Thus we can say that profit is maximised at the point where:

Marginal sales revenue = Marginal cost of production

that is,

$$\begin{bmatrix} \text{Increase in total sales revenue} \\ \text{from selling one more unit} \end{bmatrix} = \begin{bmatrix} \text{Increase in total costs that will} \\ \text{result from selling one more unit} \end{bmatrix}$$

To see how this approach can be applied, consider Example 5.3.

**Example 5.3**

A schedule of predicted total sales revenue and total costs at various levels of production for product Y is shown in columns (a) and (c) of the table.

| Quantity of output | Total sales revenue £ (a) | Marginal sales revenue £ (b) | Total cost £ (c) | Marginal cost £ (d) | Profit (loss) £ (e) |
|---|---|---|---|---|---|
| 0 | 0 | | 0 | | 0 |
| 1 | 1,000 | 1,000 | 2,300 | 2,300 | (1,300) |
| 2 | 1,900 | 900 | 2,600 | 300 | (700) |
| 3 | 2,700 | 800 | 2,900 | 300 | (200) |
| 4 | 3,400 | 700 | 3,200 | 300 | 200 |
| 5 | 4,000 | 600 | 3,500 | 300 | 500 |
| 6 | 4,500 | 500 | 3,800 | 300 | 700 |
| 7 | 4,900 | 400 | 4,100 | 300 | 800 |
| 8 | 5,200 | 300 | 4,400 | 300 | 800 |
| 9 | 5,400 | 200 | 4,700 | 300 | 700 |
| 10 | 5,500 | 100 | 5,000 | 300 | 500 |

Column (b) is deduced by taking the total sales revenue for one less unit sold from the total sales revenue at the sales level under consideration (column (a)). For example, the marginal sales revenue of the fifth unit sold (£600) is deduced by taking the total sales revenue for four units sold (£3,400) away from the total sales revenue for five units sold (£4,000).

Column (d) is deduced similarly, but using total cost figures from column (c). Column (e) is found by deducting column (c) from column (a).

It can be seen by looking at the profit (loss) column that the maximum profit occurs with an output of 7 or 8 units (£800). Thus the maximum output should be 8 units. This is the point where marginal cost and marginal revenue are equal (at £300).

**Activity 5.6**

Specialist Ltd makes a very specialised machine that is sold to manufacturing businesses. The business is about to commence production of a new model of machine for which facilities exist to produce a maximum of 10 machines each week. To assist management in a decision on the price to charge for the new machine, two pieces of information have been collected:

■ *Market demand*. The business's marketing staff believe that at a price of £3,000 per machine, the demand would be zero. Each £100 reduction in unit price below £3,000 would generate one additional sale per week. Thus, for example, at a price of £2,800 each, two machines could be sold each week.

■ *Manufacturing costs*. Fixed costs associated with manufacture of the machine are estimated at £3,000 per week. Since the work is highly labour-intensive and labour is short, unit variable costs are expected to be progressive. The manufacture of one machine each week is expected to have a variable cost of £1,100, but each additional machine produced will increase the variable cost for the entire output by £100. For example, if the output were three machines per week, the variable cost per machine (for all three machines) would be £1,300.

It is the policy of the business always to charge the same price for its entire output of a particular model. What is the most profitable level of output of the new machine?

| Output | Unit sales revenue £ | Total sales revenue £ | Marginal sales revenue £ | Unit variable cost £ | Total variable cost £ | Total cost £ | Marginal cost £ | Profit (loss) £ |
|---|---|---|---|---|---|---|---|---|
| 0 | 0 | 0 | 0 | 0 | 0 | 3,000 | 3,000 | (3,000) |
| 1 | 2,900 | 2,900 | 2,900 | 1,100 | 1,100 | 4,100 | 1,100 | (1,200) |
| 2 | 2,800 | 5,600 | 2,700 | 1,200 | 2,400 | 5,400 | 1,300 | 200 |
| 3 | 2,700 | 8,100 | 2,500 | 1,300 | 3,900 | 6,900 | 1,500 | 1,200 |
| 4 | 2,600 | 10,400 | 2,300 | 1,400 | 5,600 | 8,600 | 1,700 | 1,800 |
| 5 | 2,500 | 12,500 | 2,100 | 1,500 | 7,500 | 10,500 | 1,900 | 2,000 |
| 6 | 2,400 | 14,400 | 1,900 | 1,600 | 9,600 | 12,600 | 2,100 | 1,800 |
| 7 | 2,300 | 16,100 | 1,700 | 1,700 | 11,900 | 14,900 | 2,300 | 1,200 |
| 8 | 2,200 | 17,600 | 1,500 | 1,800 | 14,400 | 17,400 | 2,500 | 200 |
| 9 | 2,100 | 18,900 | 1,300 | 1,900 | 17,100 | 20,100 | 2,700 | (1,200) |
| 10 | 2,000 | 20,000 | 1,100 | 2,000 | 20,000 | 23,000 | 2,900 | (3,000) |

An output of five machines each week will maximise profit at £2,000 per week.

The additional cost of producing the fifth machine compared with the cost of producing the first four (£1,900) is just below the marginal revenue (the amount by which the total revenue from five machines exceeds that from selling four (£2,100)).

The additional cost of producing the sixth machine compared with the cost of producing the first five (£2,100) is just above the marginal revenue (the amount by which the total revenue from six machines exceeds that from selling five (£1,900)).

## Some practical considerations

Despite the analysis in Activity 5.6, in practice the answer of five machines a week may prove not to be the best answer. This might be for one or more of several reasons:

■ Demand is notoriously difficult to predict, even assuming no changes in the environment.

■ The effect of sales of the new machine on the other of the business's products may mean that the machine cannot be considered in isolation. Five machines a week may be the optimum level of output if sales were being taken from a rival firm or a new market is being created, but possibly not in other circumstances.

- Costs are difficult to estimate.
- Since labour is in short supply, the relevant labour cost should probably include an element for opportunity cost.
- The level of sales is calculated on the assumption that short-run profit maximisation is the goal of the business. Unless this is consistent with wealth enhancement in the longer term, it may not be in the company's best interests.

These points highlight some of the weaknesses of the theoretical approaches to pricing, particularly the fact that costs and demands are difficult to predict. It would be wrong, however, to dismiss the theory. The fact that the theory does not work perfectly in practice does not mean that it cannot offer helpful insights to the nature of markets, how profit relates to volume, and the notion of an optimum level of output.

## Full cost (cost-plus) pricing

Now that we have considered pricing theory, let us return to the subject of using full cost as the basis for setting prices. We saw in Chapter 4 that one of the reasons why certain businesses deduce full costs is to base selling prices on them. There is a lot of logic in this. If a business charges the full cost of its output as a selling price, the business will, in theory, break even. This is because the sales revenue will exactly cover all of the costs. Charging something above full cost will yield a profit.

➜ If a **full cost (cost-plus) pricing** approach is to be taken, the question that must be addressed is the level of profit that is required from each unit sold. This must logically be based on the total profit that is required for the period. Normally, businesses seek to enhance their wealth through trading. The extent to which they expect to do this is normally related to the amount of wealth that is invested to promote wealth enhancement. Businesses tend to seek to produce a particular percentage increase in wealth. In other words, businesses seek to generate a target return on capital employed. It seems logical, therefore, that the profit loading on full cost should reflect the business's target profit and that the target should itself be based on a target return on capital employed.

| **Activity 5.7** | A business has just completed a job whose full cost has been calculated at £112. For the current period, the total manufacturing costs (direct and indirect) are estimated at £250,000. The profit target for the period is £100,000. |
|---|---|

Suggest a selling price for the job.

If the profit is to be earned by jobs in proportion to their full cost, then the profit per pound of full cost must be £0.40 (£100,000/250,000). Thus, the profit on the job must be:

$$£0.40 \times 112 = £44.80$$

This means that the price for the job must be:

$$£112 + £44.80 = £156.80$$

Other ways could be found for apportioning a share of profit to jobs – for example, direct-labour or machine hours. Such bases may be preferred where it is believed that these factors are better representatives of effort and, therefore, profitworthiness. It is clearly a matter of judgement as to how profit is apportioned to units of output.

An obvious problem with cost-plus pricing is that the market may not agree with the price. Put another way, cost-plus pricing takes no account of the market demand function (the relationship between price and quantity demanded, which we considered above). A business may fairly deduce the full cost of some product and then add what might be regarded as a reasonable level of profit, only to find that a rival producer is offering a similar product for a much lower price, or that the market simply will not buy at the cost-plus price.

Most suppliers are not strong enough in the market to dictate pricing. Most are 'price takers' not 'price makers'. They must accept the price offered by the market or they do not sell any of their wares. Cost-plus pricing may be appropriate for price makers, but it has less relevance for price takers.

The cost-plus price is not entirely useless to price takers, however. When contemplating entering a market, knowing the cost-plus price will give useful information. It will tell the price taker whether it can profitably enter the market or not. As has been said already in this chapter, the full cost can be seen as a long-run break-even selling price. If entering a market means that this break-even price, plus an acceptable profit, cannot be achieved, then the business should probably stay out. Having a breakdown of the full cost may put the business in a position to examine where costs might be capable of being cut in order to bring the full cost, plus profit within a figure acceptable to the market.

Being a price maker does not always imply that the business dominates a particular market. Many small businesses are, to some extent, price makers. This tends to be where buyers find it difficult to make clear distinctions between the prices offered by various suppliers. An example of this might be a car repair. Though it may be possible to obtain a series of binding estimates for the work from various garages, most people would not normally do so. As a result, garages normally charge cost-plus prices for car repairs.

Exhibit 5.2 considers the extent to which cost-plus pricing seems to be used in practice.

---

| Exhibit 5.2 | **Cost-plus pricing in practice** |
| --- | --- |

The 1999 survey of fairly large UK businesses by Drury and Tayles (see reference (2) at end of chapter) revealed that cost-plus pricing is used by 60 per cent of businesses. Of that 60 per cent, not all use it to set the price of all of the business's sales, however. The 60 per cent breaks down as follows:

| % of sales accounted for by cost-plus pricing | % of businesses |
| --- | --- |
| 1 to 20 | 26 |
| 21 to 50 | 11 |
| 51 to 100 | 23 |
| | 60 |

Thus, for example, 26 per cent of all businesses responding to the survey used a cost-plus approach to pricing for between 1% and 20% of their total sales.

It is difficult to interpret these data to reach a general conclusion, but it is fair to say that cost-plus pricing is an important approach to pricing in the UK.

The 1993 survey by Drury, Braund, Osborne and Tayles (3) indicated that 39 per cent of respondents used the cost-plus approach to most of their pricing decisions. This might indicate that the cost-plus approach was more popular in 1993 than in 1999, when only 23 per cent of respondents used it for more than 50 per cent of their output.

## Relevant/marginal cost pricing

The relevant/marginal cost approach deduces the minimum price for which the business can offer the product for sale, and which will leave the business better off as a result of making the sale than it would have been if the sale were not made but the next best opportunity pursued instead. We considered the general approach to relevant cost pricing in Chapter 2. In Chapter 3, we looked at the

➔ more restricted case of relevant cost pricing: **marginal cost pricing**. Here it is assumed that fixed costs will not be affected by the decision to produce and, therefore, only the variable-cost element need be considered.

It would normally be the case that a relevant/marginal cost approach would only be used where there is no opportunity to sell at a price that will cover the full cost. The business can sell at the marginal cost-plus price and still be better off, simply because it happens to find itself in the position that certain costs will be incurred in any case.

**Activity 5.8**

A commercial aircraft is due to take off in one hour's time with 20 seats unsold. What is the minimum price at which these seats could be sold such that the airline company would be no worse off as a result?

The answer is that any price above the additional cost per passenger, caused by people occupying the previously unsold seats, would represent an acceptable minimum. If there are no such costs, the minimum price is zero.

This is not to say that the airline company will seek to charge the minimum price; it will presumably seek to charge the highest price that the market will bear. The fact that the market will not bear the full cost, plus a profit margin, should not, in principle, be sufficient for the company to refuse to sell seats.

Relevant/marginal pricing must be regarded as a short-term approach that can be adopted because a business finds itself in a particular position, for example having spare aircraft seats. Ultimately, if the business is to be profitable, all costs must be covered by sales revenue.

**Activity 5.9**

When we considered marginal costing in Chapter 3, we identified three problems with its use. Can you remember what these problems are?

The three problems are as follows:

- The possibility that spare capacity will be 'sold off' cheaply when there is another potential customer who will offer a higher price, but by which time the capacity will be

> fully committed. It is a matter of commercial judgement as to how likely this will be. With reference to Activity 5.8, would an hour before take-off be sufficiently close to be fairly confident that no 'normal' passenger will come forward to buy a seat?
> ■ The problem that selling the same product but at different prices could lead to a loss of customer goodwill. Would a 'normal' passenger be happy to be told by another passenger that the latter had bought his or her ticket very cheaply, compared with the normal price?
> ■ If the business is going to suffer continually from being unable to sell its full production potential at the 'regular' price, it might be better, in the long run, to reduce capacity and make fixed-cost savings. Using the spare capacity to produce marginal benefits may lead to the business failing to address this issue. Would it be better for the airline company to operate smaller aircraft or to have fewer flights, either of these leading to fixed-cost savings, than to sell off surplus seats at marginal prices?

## Pricing strategies

Costs and the market-demand function are not the only determinants of price. Businesses often employ pricing strategies that, in the short term, may not maximise profit. They do this in the expectation that they will gain in the long term. An example of such a strategy is **penetration pricing**. Here, the product is sold relatively cheaply in order to sell in quantity and to gain a large share of the market. This would tend to have the effect of dissuading competitors from entering the market. Subsequently, once the business has established itself as the market leader, prices would be raised to more profitable levels. By its nature, penetration pricing would tend to apply to new products.

**Price skimming** is almost the opposite of penetration pricing. It seeks to exploit the notion that the market can be stratified according to resistance to price. Here, a new product is initially priced highly and sold only to those buyers in the stratum that is fairly unconcerned by high prices. Once this stratum of the market is saturated, the price is lowered to attract the next stratum. The price is gradually lowered as each stratum is saturated. This strategy tends only to be able to be employed where there is some significant barrier to entry for other potential suppliers, such as patent protection.

Mobile telephones are an example of a price-skimming strategy.

# Recent developments in pricing and cost management

The increasingly competitive environment in which modern businesses operate is leading to increased effort being applied in trying to manage costs. Businesses need to keep costs to a minimum so that they can supply goods and services at a price that customers will be prepared to pay and, at the same time, generate a level of profit necessary to meet the businesses' objectives of enhancing shareholder wealth. We shall now outline some techniques that have recently emerged in an attempt to meet these goals of competitiveness and profitability.

Firstly, we need to appreciate that the total life-cycle of a product or service has three phases. The first is the period that precedes manufacture of the product for sale: the **preproduction phase**. During this phase, research and development – both of the product and of the market – is conducted. The product is invented/

Figure 5.7

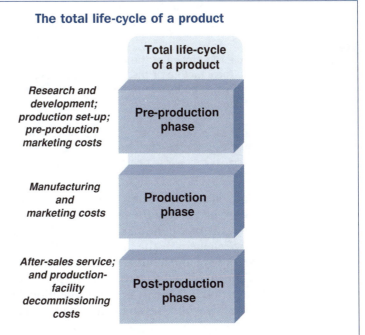

**The total life-cycle of a product**

Total life-cycle
of a product

*Research and
development;
production set-up;
pre-production
marketing costs*

**Pre-production
phase**

*Manufacturing
and
marketing costs*

**Production
phase**

*After-sales service;
and production-
facility
decommissioning
costs*

**Post-production
phase**

From the producer's viewpoint, the life of a product can be seen as having three distinct phases. During the first the product is developed and everything is prepared so that production and marketing can start. Next come production and sales. Lastly, dealing with post-production activities is undertaken.

designed and so is the means of production. The phase culminates with acquiring and setting up the necessary production facilities and with advertising and promotion. The second phase is that in which the product is made and sold to the market: the **production phase**. Lastly comes the **post-production phase**; during this phase, any costs necessary to correct faults that arose with products that have been sold (after-sales service) are incurred. There would also be the costs of closing production at the end of the product's life-cycle, such as the cost of decommissioning production facilities. Since after-sales service will tend to arise from as early as the first product being sold and, therefore, well before the last one is sold, this phase would typically overlap the manufacturing phase. The total life-cycle is shown in Figure 5.7.

## Total life-cycle costing

In some types of business, particularly those engaged in an advanced manufacturing environment, it is estimated that a very high proportion (as much as 80 per cent) of the total costs that will be incurred over the total life of a particular product are either incurred or committed at the pre-production phase. For example, a motor-car manufacturer, when designing, developing and setting up production of a new model, incurs a high proportion of the total costs that will be incurred on that model during the whole of its life. Not only are pre-production costs specifically incurred during this phase but the need to incur particular costs during the production phase is also established. This is because the design will incorporate features that will lead to particular manufacturing costs. Once the design of the car has been finalised and the manufacturing plant set up, it may be too late to 'design out' a costly feature without incurring another large cost.

**Activity 5.10**

A decision taken at the design stage could well commit the business to costs after the manufacture of the product has taken place. Can you suggest a potential cost that could be built in at the design stage that will show itself after the manufacture of the product?

After-sales service costs could be incurred as a result of some design fault. Once the manufacturing facilities have been established, it may not be economic to revise the design but merely to deal with the problem through after-sales service procedures.

➡ **Total life-cycle costing** seeks to focus management's attention on the fact that it is not just during the production phase that attention needs to be paid to cost management. By the start of the production phase it is too late to try to manage a large element of the product's total life-cycle cost. Efforts need to be made to assess the manufacturing costs of alternative designs.

There needs to be a review of the product over its entire life-cycle, which could be a period of 20 years or more. Traditional management accounting tends to be concerned with assessing performance over periods of just one year or less.

## Target costing

With the traditional cost-plus pricing, costs are totalled for a product and a percentage is added for profit to give a selling price. This, for reasons raised earlier in this chapter, is not a very practical basis on which to price output for many businesses – certainly not those operating in a price-competitive market. The cost-plus price may well be totally unacceptable to the market.

➡ **Target costing** approaches the problem from the other direction. First, with the help of market research or other means, a unit selling price and sales volume are established. From the unit selling price is taken an amount for profit. This unit profit figure must be such as to be acceptable to meet the business's profit objective. The resulting figure is the target cost. Efforts are then made to establish a way of producing the product that will enable the target cost to be met. This may involve revising the design, finding more efficient means of production or requiring raw material suppliers to supply more cheaply.

Target costing is seen as a part of a total life-cycle costing approach, in that cost savings are sought at a very early stage in the life-cycle, during the pre-production phase.

Exhibit 5.3 indicates the level of usage of target costing.

**Exhibit 5.3**

### Target costing in practice

The ACCA survey suggests that target costing is not much used by UK businesses. Twenty-two per cent of respondents never use this approach and only 26 per cent use it often or always.

By contrast, survey evidence shows that target costing is very widely used by Japanese manufacturing companies.

*Source:* Drury, Braund, Osborne and Tayles (see reference (3) at the end of the chapter).

| Activity 5.11 | Though target costing seems effective and has its enthusiasts, some people feel it has its problems. Can you suggest what these problems might be? |
|---|---|

There seem to be three main problem areas:

- It can lead to various conflicts – for example, between the business, its suppliers and its own staff.
- It can cause a great deal of stress for employees who are trying to meet target costs – sometimes ones that are extremely difficult to meet.
- Though, in the end, ways may be found to meet a target cost (through product redesign, negotiating lower prices with suppliers and so on), the whole process can be very expensive.

## *Kaizen* costing

➡ *Kaizen* **costing** is linked to total life-cycle costing and focuses on cost saving during the production phase. Since that is at a relatively late stage in the life-cycle (from a cost control point of view), and because major cost savings should already have been effected through target costing, in the production phase only relatively small cost savings can be made. The Japanese word *kaizen* implies 'small changes'.

With *kaizen* costing, efforts are made to reduce the unit manufacturing cost of the particular product under review, if possible taking it below the unit cost in the previous period. Target percentage reductions can be set. Usually, production workers are encouraged to identify ways of reducing costs – something that their 'hands on' experience may enable them to do. Even though the scope to reduce costs is limited at the manufacturing stage, significant savings can still be made.

## Benchmarking

➡ **Benchmarking** is an activity – usually a continuing one – where a business or one of its divisions seeks to emulate a successful business or division and so achieve a similar level of success. The successful business or division provides a benchmark against which the business can measure its own performance, as well as providing examples of approaches that can lead to success. Sometimes the benchmark business will help with the activity, but even where no co-operation is given, observers can still learn quite a lot about what makes that business successful.

Exhibits 5.4 and 5.5 outline the use of benchmarking in practice in the UK.

| Exhibit 5.4 | **Benchmarking in local government** |
|---|---|

The Audit Commission is a public body that has a statutory right to investigate public sector organisations and report on the extent to which those organisations provide value for money to the public.

In the context of local government, the Commission sees one way of assessing value for money as benchmarking. It has been doing this since the 1980s, and so while benchmarking may be seen as a recent innovation in the private sector, it has a fairly long history in the public sector.

Since the Commission has statutory powers, it has been able to insist that the various local government authorities provide information to enable a comprehensive benchmarking operation to take place. Contrast this with the private sector where benchmarking between businesses is difficult because there is no compulsion. Businesses are reluctant to divulge commercially sensitive information to other businesses with which they may be in competition. Often, the best that can be achieved in the private sector is for businesses to benchmark internally, with one division or department comparing itself with another part of the same business.

---

**Exhibit 5.5**

### Benchmarking on safety issues at Tate & Lyle

Tate & Lyle plc is a large, multinational food business operating through subsidiaries in many parts of the world. The annual report for 2000 describes how the business was able to reduce dramatically the record of injuries at work of its staff. This was achieved by benchmarking the divisions of the business with the best safety records. Other divisions then sought to emulate the benchmark divisions' approaches to safety.

Tate & Lyle, through its size and diversity, provides an example of a private-sector organisation able to use benchmarking successfully.

---

## Summary

In this chapter we have seen how modern production methods can mean that traditional approaches to costing and pricing may make a business unable to compete in the modern and increasingly global market. We have seen that the traditional approach of treating all overheads as part of a common pool and charging them to jobs on a direct-labour-hour basis although time-honoured, is probably inappropriate in many modern business environments. Activity-based costing (ABC) seeks to identify the activities that are driving overhead costs and to charge jobs with overheads on the basis of the extent to which each job drives costs. Identifying what drives costs is also valuable because it could well enable managers to exercise greater control over those costs.

We have considered the pricing decision in rather more detail, firstly by looking at some theoretical arguments on the subject and then by considering some practical pricing issues. We have seen that cost information, both full and marginal, can have severe limitations as an aid to deciding the best price to be charged for a product.

Lastly we looked at some modern approaches to costing that are designed to exert further downward pressure on costs. Total life-cycle costing, target costing and *kaizen* costing have all been developed to help a business survive in today's highly competitive markets.

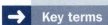

**Key terms**

Activity-based costing (ABC)   p. 99
Cost driver   p. 99
Cost pool   p. 99
Elasticity of demand   p. 105
Full cost (cost-plus) pricing   p. 111
Marginal cost pricing   p. 113

Penetration pricing   p. 114
Price skimming   p. 114
Total life-cycle costing   p. 116
Target costing   p. 116
*Kaizen* costing   p. 117
Benchmarking   p. 117

## Further reading

If you would like to explore the topics covered in this chapter in more depth, we recommend the following books:

**Management Accounting**, *Atkinson, A., Barker, R., Kaplan, R.* and *Mark Young, S.*, 3rd edn, Prentice Hall, 2001, chapters 5, 7 and 9.

**Management and Cost Accounting**, *Drury, C.*, 5th edn, Thomson Learning, 2000, chapters 10, 11 and 23.

**Cost Accounting: A managerial emphasis**, *Horngren, C., Foster, G.* and *Datar, S.*, 10th edn, Prentice Hall International, 2000, chapters 5, 12 and 13.

**Cost and Management Accounting**, *Williamson, D.*, Prentice Hall International, 1996, chapters 7, 13 and 20.

## References

1. **Activity-Based Costing – a review with case studies**, *Innes, J.* and *Mitchell, F.*, CIMA Publishing, 1990.
2. **Cost Systems Design and Profitability Analysis in UK Companies**, *Drury, C.* and *Tayles, M.*, CIMA Publishing, 2000.
3. **A Survey of Management Accounting Practices in UK Manufacturing Companies**, *Drury, C., Braund, S., Osborne, P.* and *Tayles, M.*, Chartered Association of Certified Accounts, 1993.

## ? REVIEW QUESTIONS

**5.1** How does activity-based costing differ from the traditional approach?

**5.2** The use of activity-based costing in helping to deduce full costs has been criticised. What has tended to be the basis of this criticism?

**5.3** What is meant by elasticity of demand? How does knowledge of the elasticity of demand affect pricing decisions?

**5.4** According to economic theory, at what point is profit maximised?

## ? EXERCISES

Exercises 5.6–5.8 are more advanced than 5.1–5.5. Those with coloured numbers have answers at the back of the book.

**5.1** Woodner Ltd provides a standard service. It is able to provide a maximum of 100 units of this service each week. Experience shows that at a price of £100, no unit of the service would be sold. For every £5 below this price, the company is able to sell 10 more units. For example, at a price of £95, 10 units would be sold, at £90, 20 units would be sold, and so on. The company's fixed costs total £2,500 a week. Variable costs are £20 per unit over the entire range of possible output. The market is such that it is not feasible to charge different prices to different customers.

**Required:**
What is the most profitable level of output of the service?

**5.2** It appears from research evidence that a cost-plus approach influences pricing decisions in practice. What is meant by cost-plus pricing and what are the problems of using this approach?

**5.3** Kaplan plc makes a range of suitcases of various sizes and shapes. There are ten different models of suitcase produced by the company. In order to keep stocks of finished suitcases to a minimum, each model is made in a small batch. Each batch is costed as a separate job and the cost per suitcase deduced by dividing the batch cost by the number of suitcases in the batch.

At present, the business costs the batches using a traditional job-costing approach. Recently, however, a new management accountant was appointed, who is advocating the use of activity-based costing (ABC) to deduce the cost of the batches. The management accountant claims that ABC leads to much more reliable and relevant costs and that it has other benefits.

**Required:**
(a) Explain how the business deduces the cost of each suitcase at present.
(b) Discuss the purposes to which the knowledge of the cost per suitcase, deduced on a traditional basis, can be put and how valid the cost is for the purpose concerned.
(c) Explain how ABC could be applied to costing the suitcases, highlighting the differences between ABC and the traditional approach.

(d) Explain what advantages the new management accountant probably believes ABC to have over the traditional approach.

**5.4** Comment critically on the following statements that you have overheard:

(a) 'To maximise profit you need to sell your output at the highest price.'
(b) 'Elasticity of demand deals with the extent to which costs increase as demand increases.'
(c) 'Provided that the price is large enough to cover the marginal cost of production, the sale should be made.'
(d) 'According to economic theory, profit is maximised where total cost equals total revenue.'
(e) 'Price skimming is charging low prices for the output until you have a good share of the market, and then putting up your prices.'

Explain clearly all technical terms.

**5.5** Comment critically on the following statements that you have overheard:

(a) 'Direct labour hours are the most appropriate basis to use to charge overheads to jobs in the modern manufacturing environment where people are so important.'
(b) 'Activity-based costing is a means of more accurately accounting for direct labour costs.'
(c) 'Activity-based costing cannot really be applied to the service sector because the "activities" that it seeks to analyse tend to be related to manufacturing.'
(d) '*Kaizen* costing is an approach where great efforts are made to reduce the costs of developing a new product and setting up its production processes.'
(e) 'Benchmarking is an approach to job costing where each direct worker keeps a record of the time spent by each job on his or her workbench before it is passed on to the next direct worker or into finished stock stores.'

**5.6** The GB Company manufactures a variety of electric motors. The business is currently operating at about 70 per cent of capacity and is earning a satisfactory return on investment.

The management of GB has been approached by International Industries (II) with an offer to buy 120,000 units of an electric motor. II manufactures a motor that is almost identical to GB's motor, but a fire at the II plant has shut down its manufacturing operations. II needs the 120,000 motors over the next four months to meet commitments to its regular customers; II is prepared to pay £19 each for the motors, which it will collect from the GB plant.

GB's product cost, based on current planned cost for the motor is:

|  | £ |
|---|---|
| Direct materials | 5.00 |
| Direct labour (variable) | 6.00 |
| Manufacturing overhead | 9.00 |
| Total | 20.00 |

Manufacturing overhead is applied to production at the rate of £18.00 per direct-labour hour. This overhead rate is made up of the following components:

|  | £ |
|---|---|
| Variable factory overhead | 6.00 |
| Fixed factory overhead – direct | 8.00 |
| – allocated | 4.00 |
| Applied manufacturing overhead rate | 18.00 |

Additional costs usually incurred in connection with sales of electric motors include sales commissions of 5 per cent and freight expenses of £1.00 per unit.

In determining selling prices, GB adds a 40 per cent mark-up to product costs. This provides a suggested selling price of £28 for the motor. The marketing department, however, has set the current selling price at £27.00 to maintain market share. The order would, however, require additional fixed factory overheads of £15,000 per month in the form of supervision and clerical costs. If management accepts the order, 30,000 motors will be manufactured and shipped to II each month for the next 4 months.

**Required:**
(a) Prepare a financial evaluation showing the impact of accepting the Industrial Industries' order. What is the minimum unit price that the business's management could accept without reducing its operating profit?
(b) State clearly any assumptions contained in the analysis of (a) above and discuss any other organisational or strategic factors that GB should consider.

**5.7** Sillycon Ltd is a business engaged in the development of new products in the electronics industry. Subtotals on the spreadsheet of planned overheads reveal:

|  | Electronics department | Testing department | Service department |
|---|---|---|---|
| Overheads – variable (£000) | 1,200 | 600 | 700 |
| – fixed (£000) | 2,000 | 500 | 800 |
| Planned activity: Labour hours ('000) | 800 | 600 | – |

For the purposes of reallocation of service department overheads, it is agreed that variable overheads accrue in line with the labour hours worked in each department. Fixed overheads of the service department are to be reallocated on the basis of maximum practical capacity of the two departments, which is the same for each.

It has been a long-standing company practice to mark up full manufacturing costs by between 25 and 35 per cent in order to establish selling prices.

It is hoped that one new product, which is in a final development stage, will offer some improvement over competitors' products, which are currently marketed at between £110 and £130 each. Product development engineers have determined that the direct material content is £7 per unit. The product will take four labour hours in the electronics department and three hours in testing. Hourly labour rates are £10 and £6, respectively.

Management estimates that the fixed costs that would be specifically incurred in relation to the product are: supervision £13,000, depreciation of a recently acquired machine £100,000 and advertising £37,000 per annum. These fixed costs are included in the table given above.

Market research indicates that the business could expect to obtain and hold about 25 per cent of the market or, optimistically, 30 per cent. The total market is estimated at 20,000 units.

*Note*: it may be assumed that the existing plan has been prepared to cater for a range of products and no single product decision will cause the business to amend it.

**Required:**
(a) Prepare a summary of information that would help with the pricing decision. Such information should include marginal cost and full cost implications after allocation of service department overheads.
(b) Explain and elaborate on the information prepared.

**5.8** A business manufactures refrigerators for domestic use. There are three models: Lo, Mid and Hi. The models, their quality and their price are aimed at different markets.

Product costs are computed on a blanket overhead-rate basis using a labour-hour method. Prices as a general rule are set based on cost plus 20 per cent. The following information is provided:

|  | Lo | Mid | Hi |
|---|---|---|---|
| Material cost (£/unit) | 25 | 62.5 | 105 |
| Direct labour hours (per unit) | $\frac{1}{2}$ | 1 | 1 |
| Budget production/sales (units) | 20,000 | 1,000 | 10,000 |

The budgeted overheads for the business amount to £4,410,000. Direct labour is costed at £8 per hour.

The business is currently facing increasing competition, especially from imported goods. As a result, the selling price of Lo has been reduced to a level that produces very little profit margin. To address this problem, an activity-based costing approach has been suggested. The overheads are examined and these are grouped round the main business activities of machining (£2,780,000), logistics (£590,000) and establishment (£1,040,000) costs. It is maintained that these costs could be allocated based respectively on cost drivers of machine hours, material orders and space, to reflect the use of resources in each of these areas. After analysis, the following proportionate statistics are available related to the total volume of products:

|  | Lo % | Mid % | Hi % |
|---|---|---|---|
| Machine hours | 40 | 15 | 45 |
| Material orders | 47 | 6 | 47 |
| Space | 42 | 18 | 40 |

**Required:**
(a) Calculate for each product the full cost and selling price determined by:
   (i) the original costing method
   (ii) the activity-based costing method.
(b) What are the implications of the two systems of costing in the situation given?
(c) What business/strategic options exist for the business in the light of the new information?

## CHAPTER 6

# Budgeting

## Introduction

Budgets are an important tool for management planning and control. In this chapter we consider the role and nature of budgets and we shall also see how budgets are prepared. It is important to recognise that budgets do not exist in a vacuum; they are an integral part of a planning framework that is adopted by well-run businesses. To understand fully the nature of budgets we must, therefore, understand the planning framework within which they are set. The chapter begins with a discussion of this framework and then goes on to consider detailed aspects of the budgeting process.

**OBJECTIVES**

When you have completed this chapter you should be able to:

- Define a budget and show how budgets, corporate objectives and long-term plans are related.
- Explain the interlinking of the various budgets within the business.
- Discuss the budgeting process.
- Indicate the uses of budgeting and construct various budgets, including the cash budget, from relevant data.

## Budgets, long-term plans and corporate objectives

It is vitally important that businesses develop plans for the future. Whatever a business is trying to achieve, it is unlikely to be successful unless its managers are clear what the future direction of the business is going to be.

The development of plans involves five key steps:

1. Setting the aims and objectives of the business.
2. Identifying the options available.
3. Evaluating the options and making a selection.
4. Setting detailed short-term plans or budgets.
5. Collecting information on performance and exercising control.

### Step 1: Setting the aims and objectives of the business

The aims and objectives set out what the business is basically trying to achieve. It is sometimes useful to make a distinction between aims and objectives. The aims of the business are often couched in broad terms and may be set out in the form of a **mission statement**. This statement is usually brief and will often articulate high standards or ideals for the business. An example of a mission statement is provided in Exhibit 6.1.

| Exhibit 6.1 | Cadbury Schweppes plc, the multinational food business, takes a fairly stark approach. In its 1999 annual report the company states its mission as follows: |
|---|---|
| | Cadbury Schweppes' objective is growth in shareholder value. |

The objectives of a business are more specific than its aims. They will set out more precisely what has to be achieved. The objectives will vary between businesses but may include the following aspects of operations and performance:

- The kind of market the business seeks to serve.
- The share of that market it wishes to achieve.
- The level of operating efficiency (for example, lowest-cost producer).
- The kinds of product and/or service that should be offered.
- The levels of profit and returns to shareholders (for example, return on capital employed or dividends) that are required.
- The levels of growth required (for example, increase in assets, sales).
- Technological leadership (for example, the degree of innovation).

Objectives should be quantifiable and should be consistent with the aims of the business as set out in its mission statement. An example of the objectives of a business are set out in Exhibit 6.2.

| Exhibit 6.2 | Cadbury Schweppes goes on to say in its 1999 annual report that it intends to achieve its shareholders' wealth mission by: |
|---|---|
| | ■ Focusing on core growth markets of beverages and confectionery. |
| | ■ Developing robust, sustainable market positions which are built on a platform of strong brands with supported franchises. |
| | ■ Expanding market share through innovation in products, packaging and route to market, where economically profitable. |
| | ■ Enhancing market position by acquisitions or disposals where they are in line with strategy, are value-creating and are available. |

## Step 2: Identifying the options available

In order to achieve the objectives set for a business, a number of possible options (strategies) may be available. A creative search for the various strategic options should be undertaken. This will involve collecting information – an activity that can be extremely time consuming, particularly when the business is considering entering new markets or investing in new technology.

The type of information collected should include an external analysis of the competitive environment and will relate to such matters as:

■ Market size and growth prospects
■ Level of competition within the industry
■ Bargaining power of suppliers and customers
■ Threat of new entrants to the market
■ Threat of substitute products
■ Relative power of trades unions, community interest groups and so on.

Information should also be collected that provides an *internal* analysis of the resources and expertise of the business that are available to pursue each option. Information concerning the capabilities of the business in each of the following areas may be collected:

■ Organisation culture
■ Marketing and distribution
■ Manufacturing and production operations
■ Finance and administration
■ Research and development
■ Information systems
■ Human resources.

Any deficiencies or gaps in these areas that could affect the ability of the business to pursue a particular option must be identified. This topic of identification and selection of strategic options is picked up again in the opening section of Chapter 11.

## Step 3: Evaluating the options and making a selection

When deciding on the most appropriate option(s) to choose, managers must examine information relating to each option to see whether the option fits with the objectives that have been set and to assess whether the resources to pursue the option are available. The managers must also consider the effect of pursuing each option on the financial performance and position of the business.

| Activity 6.1 | The approach described above suggests that decision makers will systematically collect information and then carefully evaluate all the options available. Do you think this is what decision makers really do? Is this how you approach decisions? |
|---|---|

In practice, decision makers may not be as rational and capable as implied in the process described. Individuals may find it difficult to handle a wealth of information relating to a wide range of options. As a result, they may restrict their range of possible options and/or discard some information in order to avoid becoming overloaded. They may also adopt rather simple approaches to evaluating the mass of information provided, and these approaches might not fit very well with the outcome they would like to achieve.

Humans have a restricted ability to process information. Too much information can be as bad as too little, as it can overload individuals and create confusion.

This, in turn, can lead to poor evaluations and poor decisions. The information provided to managers must be restricted to what is relevant to a particular decision and what is capable of being absorbed. This may mean that, in practice, information is produced in summary form and that only a restricted range of options will be considered.

The option selected will form the basis of the long-term plan for the business. This plan will usually cover a period of five years or more and will specify such things as:

- The market that the business will seek to serve.
- The products or services to be offered.
- Amounts and sources of finance to be raised by the business.
- Capital investments to be made.
- Amounts and sources of bought-in goods and services required.
- Personnel requirements.

## Step 4: Setting detailed short-term plans or budgets

A **budget** is a financial plan for the short term – typically one year. It is likely to be expressed mainly in financial terms. Its role is to convert the long-term plans into actionable blueprints for the immediate future. Budgets will define precise targets concerning:

- Cash receipts and payments
- Sales, broken down into amounts and prices for each of the products or services provided by the business
- Detailed stock requirements
- Detailed labour requirements
- Specific production requirements.

Clearly, the relationship between objectives, long-term plans and budgets is that the objectives, once set, are likely to last for quite a long time – perhaps throughout the life of the business. A series of long-term plans identifies how each objective is to be pursued, and budgets identify how the long-term plan is to be fulfilled.

An analogy might be found in terms of someone enrolling on a course of study. His or her objective might be to embark on a career that will be rewarding in various ways. He or she might have identified the course as the most effective way to work towards this objective. In working towards this, passing a particular stage of the course might be identified as the target for the forthcoming year. Here, the intention to complete the entire course is analogous to a long-term plan, and passing each stage is analogous to the budget. Having achieved the 'budget' for the first year, that for the second year becomes passing the second stage.

## Step 5: Collecting information on performance and exercising control

However well planned the activities of a business might be, they will come to nothing unless steps are taken to try to achieve them in practice. The process of making planned events actually occur is known as **control**.

Control can be defined as compelling events to conform to plan. This definition is valid in any context. For example, when we talk about controlling a motor car, we mean making the car do what we plan that it should do. In a business context, accounting is very useful in the control process. This is because it is possible to state plans in accounting terms (as budgets) and it is also possible to state *actual* outcomes in the same terms, thus making comparison between actual and planned outcomes a relatively easy matter. Where actual outcomes are at variance with budgets, this variance should be highlighted by accounting information. Managers can then take steps to get the business back on track towards the achievement of the budgets.

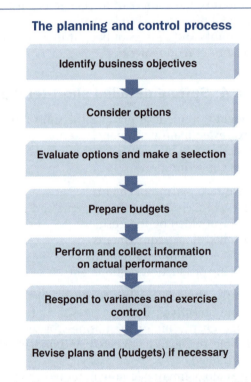

**The planning and control process**

Identify business objectives

Consider options

Evaluate options and make a selection

Prepare budgets

Perform and collect information on actual performance

Respond to variances and exercise control

Revise plans and (budgets) if necessary

The figure shows the planning and control sequence within a business. Once the objectives of the business have been determined, the various options that can fulfil these objectives must be considered and evaluated in order to derive a long-term plan. The budget is a short-term financial plan for the business that is prepared within the framework of the long-term plan. Control can be exercised through the comparison of budgeted and actual performance. Where a significant divergence emerges, some form of corrective action should be taken. If the budget figures prove to be based on incorrect assumptions about the future, it might be necessary to revise the budget.

Figure 6.1 shows the planning and control process in diagrammatic form.

It should be emphasised that planning is the role of managers rather than accountants. Traditionally, the role of the management accountant has been simply to provide technical advice and assistance to managers to help them plan. However, things are changing. Increasingly, the management accountant is seen as a member of the management team and, in this management role, is expected to contribute towards the planning process.

## Time horizon of plans and budgets

The setting of plans is typically performed as a major exercise every five years, and budgets are usually set annually. It need not necessarily be the case that long-term plans are set for five years and that budgets are set for twelve months: it is up to the management of the business concerned. Businesses involved in certain industries – say information technology – may feel that five years is too long a planning period since new developments can, and do, occur virtually overnight. Nor need it be the case that a budget is set for one year. However, this appears to be a widely used time horizon.

| Activity 6.2 | Can you think of any reason why most businesses prepare detailed budgets for the forthcoming year, rather than for a shorter or longer period? |
|---|---|

The reason is probably that a year represents a long enough time for the budget preparation exercise to be worthwhile, yet short enough into the future for detailed plans to be capable of being made. As we shall see later in this chapter, the process of formulating budgets can be a time-consuming exercise, but there are economies of scale – for example, preparing the budget for the next twelve months would not normally take twice as much time and effort as preparing the budget for the next six months.

An annual budget sets targets for the forthcoming year for all levels of the business. It is usually broken down into monthly budgets, which define monthly targets. Indeed, in many instances, the annual budget will be built up from monthly figures. For example, where sales are the key factor determining the level of activity, the sales staff will be required to make sales targets for each month of the budget period. Other budgets will be set, for each month of the budget period, as we shall explain below.

## Budgets and forecasts

A budget may be defined as a **financial plan** for a future period of time. *Financial* because the budget is, to a great extent, expressed in financial terms. Note also, particularly, that a budget is a *plan*, not a forecast. To talk of a plan suggests an intention or determination to achieve planned targets; **forecasts** tend to be predictions of the future state of the environment.

Clearly, forecasts are very helpful to the planner/budget setter. If, for example, a reputable forecaster has forecast the number of new cars to be purchased in the UK during next year, it will be valuable for a manager in a car manufacturing business to obtain and take account of this forecast figure when setting sales budgets. However, a forecast and a budget are distinctly different.

## Periodic and continual budgets

Budgeting can be undertaken on a periodic or a continual basis. A **periodic budget** is prepared for a particular period (usually one year). Managers will agree the budget for the year and then allow the budget to run its course. Although it may be necessary to revise the budget on occasions, preparing the budget is in essence a one-off exercise during a financial year. A **continual budget**, as the name suggests, is continually updated. We have seen that an annual budget will normally be broken down into smaller time intervals (usually monthly periods) to help control the activities of a business. A continual budget will add a new month to replace the month that has just passed, thereby ensuring that, at all times, there will be a budget for a full planning period. Continual budgets are also referred to as **rolling budgets**.

| *Activity 6.3* | **What do you think are the advantages and disadvantages of each form of budgeting?** |
| --- | --- |

Periodic budgeting will usually take less time and effort to prepare and will therefore be less costly. However, as time passes, the budget period shortens and toward the end of the financial year managers will be working to a very short planning period indeed. Continual budgeting, on the other hand, will ensure that managers always have a full year's budget to help them make decisions. It is claimed that continual budgeting ensures that managers plan throughout the year rather than just once each year. However, there is a danger that budgeting will become a mechanical exercise as managers may not have time to step back from their other tasks each month and consider the future carefully.

# The interrelationship of various budgets

For a particular business for a particular period, there is more than one budget. Each one will relate to a specific aspect of the business. It is generally considered that the ideal situation is that there should be a separate budget for each person who is in a managerial position, no matter how junior. The contents of all of the individual budgets will be summarised in **master budgets** consisting usually of a budgeted income statement (profit and loss account) and balance sheet. However, the cash flow statement (in summarised form) may also be considered part of the master budget.

Figure 6.2 illustrates the interrelationship and interlinking of individual budgets, in this particular case using a manufacturing business as an example.

Starting at the top of Figure 6.2, the sales budget is usually the first budget to be prepared, as this will determine the overall level of activity for the forthcoming period. The finished stock requirement would be dictated largely by the level of sales, although it would also be dictated by the policy of the business on finished stockholding. The requirement for finished stock would define the required production levels, which would, in turn, dictate the requirements of the individual production departments or sections. The demands of manufacturing, in conjunction with the business's policy on raw materials stock, define the raw materials stock budget. The purchases budget will be dictated by the materials stock budget which will, in conjunction with the policy of the business on creditor payment, dictate the trade creditors budget. One of the determinants of the cash budget will be the trade creditors budget; another will be the trade debtors budget, which itself derives, through the debtor policy of the business, from the sales budget. Cash will also be affected by overheads and direct labour costs (themselves linked to production) and by capital expenditure. The factors that

Figure 6.2

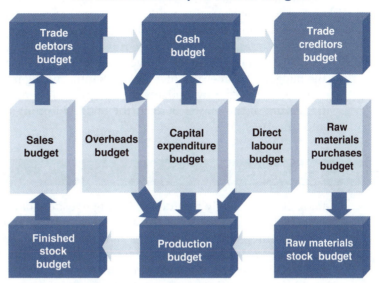

**The interrelationship of various budgets**

The figure shows the interrelationship of budgets for a manufacturing business. The starting point is usually the sales budget. The expected level of sales normally defines the overall level of activity for the business, and the other budgets will be drawn up in accordance with this. Thus, the sales budget will largely define the finished stock requirements, and from this we can define the production requirements and so on.

affect policies on matters such as stockholding and debtor and creditor collection periods will be discussed in some detail in Chapter 9.

Assuming that the budgeting process takes the order just described, it might be found in practice that there is some constraint to achieving the sales target. For example, the production capacity of the business may be incapable of meeting the necessary levels of output to match the sales budget for one or more months. In this case, it might be reasonable to look at ways of overcoming the problem. As a last resort, it might be necessary to revise the sales budget to a lower level to enable production to meet the target.

Activity 6.4

**Can you think of any ways in which a short-term shortage of production facilities might be overcome?**

We thought of the following:

■ Higher production in previous months and stockpiling to meet the higher demand period(s).
■ Increasing production capacity, perhaps by working overtime and/or acquiring (buying or leasing) additional plant.
■ Subcontracting some production.
■ Encouraging potential customers to change the timing of their buying by offering discounts or other special terms during the months that have been identified as quiet.

You might well have thought of other approaches.

There will be the horizontal relationships between budgets, which we have just looked at; but there will usually be vertical ones as well. For example, the sales budget may be broken down into a number of subsidiary budgets, perhaps one for each regional sales manager. The overall sales budget will be a summary of the subsidiary ones. The same may be true of virtually all of the other budgets, most particularly the production budget. Figure 6.2 gives a very simplified outline of the budgetary framework of a typical manufacturing business.

All of the operating budgets that we have just reviewed are set within the framework of the master budget (the budgeted profit and loss account and balance sheet).

## The uses of budgets

Budgets are generally regarded as having five areas of usefulness, which we shall describe below. Figure 6.3 shows those areas in diagrammatic form.

Firstly, they tend to *promote forward thinking and the possible identification of short-term problems*. We saw (above) that a shortage of production capacity might be identified during the budgeting process. Making this discovery in good time could leave a number of means of overcoming the problem open to exploration. Take, for example, the problem of a shortage of production at a particular part of the year. If the potential problem is picked up early enough, all of the suggestions in the answer to Activity 6.4 and, possibly, other ways of overcoming the problem can be explored and considered rationally. Budgeting should help to achieve this.

The second area of usefulness is in their *helping to co-ordinate the various sections of the business*. It is crucially important that the activities of the various departments and sections of the business are linked so that the activities of one are complementary to those of another. For example, the activities of the purchasing/procurement department of a manufacturing business should dovetail with the

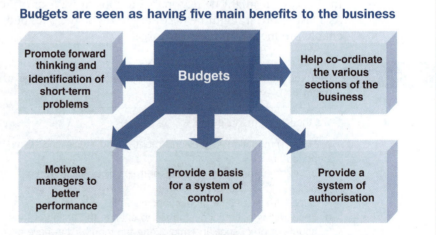

| Figure 6.3 | **Budgets are seen as having five main benefits to the business** |

The figure sets out the main benefits that budgets are traditionally seen as providing. These benefits are discussed in the chapter.

raw materials needs of the production departments. If this is not the case, production could run out of stock, leading to expensive production stoppages. Alternatively, excessive stocks could be bought, leading to large and unnecessary stockholding costs.

Budgets' third area of usefulness is in their *ability to motivate managers to better performance*. Having a stated task can motivate managers and staff in their performance. It is a well-established view that to tell a manager to do his or her best is not very motivating, but to define a required level of achievement is likely to be. It is felt that managers will be better motivated by being able to relate their particular role in the business to the overall objectives of the business. Since budgets are directly derived from corporate objectives, budgeting makes this possible.

| Activity 6.5 | Do you think there is a danger that requiring managers to work towards predetermined targets will stifle their skill, flair and enthusiasm? |
|---|---|
| | There is this danger if targets are badly set. If, however, the budgets are set in such a way as to offer challenging yet achievable targets, the manager is still required to show skill, flair and enthusiasm. |

It is clearly not possible to allow managers to operate in an unconstrained environment. Having to operate in a way that matches the goals of the business is a price of working in an effective business.

Fourthly, budgets can *provide a basis for a system of control*. As stated earlier in the chapter, control is concerned with ensuring that events conform to plans. If senior management wishes to control and to monitor the performance of more junior staff, it needs some yardstick against which the performance can be measured and assessed. It is possible to compare current performance with past performance or perhaps with what happens in another business. However, the most logical yardstick is usually planned performance.

| Activity 6.6 | What is wrong with comparing actual performance with past performance or the performance of others in an effort to exercise control? |
|---|---|
| | There is no automatic reason to believe that what happened in the past, or is happening elsewhere, represents a sensible target for this year in this business. Considering what happened last year, and in other businesses, may help in the formulation of plans, but past events and the performance of others should not automatically be seen as the target. |

If there are data available concerning the actual performance for a period, and this can be compared with the planned performance, then a basis for control will have been established. Such a basis will enable the use of **management by exception**, a technique where senior managers can spend most of their time dealing with those staff or activities that have failed to achieve the budget and not having to spend too much time on those that are performing well. It also allows junior managers to exercise self-control, since by knowing what is expected of them and what they have actually achieved, they can assess how well they are performing and take steps to correct matters where they are failing to achieve.

We shall consider the effect of making plans and being held accountable for their achievement later in this chapter and in Chapter 7.

The fifth and final recognised area of usefulness lies in the ability of budgets to *provide a system of authorisation* for managers to spend up to a particular limit. A good example of this is where there are certain activities (for example, staff development and research expenditure) that are allocated a fixed amount of funds at the discretion of senior management.

| **Activity 6.7** | Could the five identified uses of budgets conflict with one another on occasions? For example, can you think of a possible conflict: |
|---|---|

(a) between the budget as a motivational device and the budget as a means of control?

(b) between the budget as a means of control and the budget as a system of authorisation?

It is quite possible for the uses identified to be in conflict with one another.

(a) Where the budget is being used as a motivational device, the budget targets may be set at a more difficult level than is expected to be achieved. This may be valuable as a means of getting managers to strive to reach their targets; however, for control purposes, the budget becomes less meaningful as a benchmark against which to compare actual performance.

(b) Where a budget is being used as a system of authorisation, managers may be motivated to spend to the limit of their budget, even though this may be wasteful. This may occur where the managers are not allowed to carry over unused funds to the next budget period or if they believe that the budget for the next period will be reduced because not all the funds for the current period were spent. The wasting of resources in this way conflicts with the role of budgets as a means of exercising control.

Conflict between the different uses will mean that managers must decide which particular uses for budgets should be given priority; managers must be prepared, if necessary, to trade off the benefits resulting from one particular use for the benefits of another.

## The budget-setting process

Budgeting is such an important area for businesses and other organisations that it tends to be approached in a fairly methodical and formal way. This usually involves a number of steps, described below and shown in diagrammatic form in Figure 6.4.

Steps in the budget-setting process

The figure shows the sequence of events in the preparation of the budgets. Once the budgets are prepared, they are communicated to all interested parties and, over time, actual performance is monitored in relation to the targets set out in the budgets.

## Step 1: Establish who will take responsibility

It is usually seen as crucial that those responsible for the budget-setting process have real authority within the organisation.

---

**Activity 6.8**

Why is it crucial that those responsible for the budget-setting process have real authority in the organisation?

One of the crucial aspects of the process is establishing co-ordination between budgets so that the plans of one department match and are complementary to those of other departments. This usually requires compromise where adjustment of initial budgets must be undertaken. This in turn means that someone on the board of directors (or its equivalent) has to be closely involved; only people of this rank are likely to have the necessary moral and, in the final analysis, formal managerial authority to force departmental managers to compromise.

---

➡ Quite commonly, a **budget committee** is formed to supervise and take resposibility for the budget-setting process. This committee usually comprises a senior representative of most of the functional areas of the business – marketing, produc-
➡ tion, personnel and so on. Often, a **budget officer** is appointed to carry out, or to take immediate responsibility for others carrying out, the tasks of the committee. Not surprisingly, given their technical expertise in the activity, accountants are often required to take budget officer roles.

## Step 2: Communicate budget guidelines to relevant managers

Budgets are intended to be the short-term plans that seek to work towards the achievement of long-term plans and to the overall objectives of the business. It is therefore important that, in drawing up budgets, managers are well aware of what the long-term plans are and how the forthcoming budget period is intended to work towards them. Managers also need to be made well aware of the commercial/economic environment in which they will be operating. It is the responsibility of the budget committee to see that managers have all the necessary information.

## Step 3: Identify the key, or limiting, factor

There will always be some aspect of the business that will stop it achieving its objectives to the maximum extent. This is often a limited ability of the business to sell its products; sometimes, it is some production shortage (labour, materials, plant) that is the **limiting factor**, or, linked to these, a shortage of funds. Often, production shortages can be overcome by an increase in funds – for example, more plant can be bought or leased – but not always, because no amount of money will buy certain labour skills or increase the world supply of some raw material.

As has been pointed out earlier in this chapter, it is sometimes possible to ease an initial limiting factor; for example, a plant capacity problem can be eliminated by subcontracting. This means that some other factor, perhaps sales, will replace the production problem, though at a higher level of output. Ultimately, however, the business will hit a ceiling; some limiting factor will prove impossible to ease.

For entirely practical reasons, it is important that the limiting factor is identified. Ultimately, most, if not all, budgets will be affected by the limiting factor, and so if it can be identified at the outset, all managers can be informed of the restriction early in the process.

## Step 4: Prepare the budget for the area of the limiting factor

The limiting-factor budget will quite often be the sales budget since the ability to sell is frequently the limiting factor that simply cannot be eased. It is the limiting factor that will determine the overall level of activity for the business. (When discussing the interrelationship of budgets earlier in the chapter, we started with the sales budget for this reason.)

Exhibit 6.3 looks at the methods favoured by businesses of different sizes to determine their sales budgets.

| Exhibit 6.3 | Determining the future level of sales can be a difficult problem. In practice, a business may rely on the judgements of sales staff, statistical techniques or market surveys (or some combination of these) to arrive at a sales budget. A 1993 survey of UK manufacturing businesses provides the following insights concerning the use of such techniques and methods. |
| --- | --- |

| | All respondents | Small businesses | Large businesses |
|---|---|---|---|
| | % | % | % |
| **Technique** | | | |
| Statistical forecasting | 31 | 19 | 29 |
| Market research | 36 | 13 | 54 |
| Subjective estimates based on sales staff experience | 85 | 97 | 80 |

We can see that the most popular approach by far is the opinion of sales staff. We can also see that there are differences between large and small businesses, particularly concerning the use of market surveys.

*Source:* Drury, Braund, Osborne and Tayles (see reference (1) at the end of the chapter).

## Step 5: Prepare draft budgets for all other areas

The other budgets are prepared, complementing the budget for the area of the limiting factor. In all budget preparation, the computer has become an almost indispensable tool. Much of the work of preparing budgets is repetitive and tedious, yet the resultant budget has to represent reliably the actual plans made. Computers are ideally suited to such tasks and human beings are not. It is often the case that budgets have to be redrafted several times because of some minor alteration and, again, computers do this without complaint.

There are two broad approaches to setting individual budgets. The **top-down approach** is where the senior management of each budget area originates the budget targets, perhaps discussing them with lower levels of management and, as a result, refining them before the final version is produced. With the **bottom-up approach**, the targets are fed upwards from the lowest level. For example, junior sales managers will be asked to set their own sales targets, which then become incorporated into the budgets of higher levels of management until the overall sales budget emerges.

Where the bottom-up approach is adopted, it is usually necessary to haggle and negotiate at different levels of authority to achieve agreement. This may be because the plans of some departments do not fit in with those of others or because the targets set by junior managers are not acceptable to their superiors. This approach is rarely found in practice.

| Activity 6.9 | What are the advantages and disadvantages of each type of budgeting approach? |
|---|---|

The bottom-up approach allows greater involvement among managers in the budgeting process and this, in turn, may increase the level of commitment to the targets set. It also allows the business to draw more fully on the local knowledge and expertise of its managers. However, this approach can be time consuming and may result in some managers setting undemanding targets for themselves in order to have an easy life.

> The top-down approach enables senior management to communicate plans to employees and to co-ordinate the activities of the business more easily. It may also help in establishing more demanding targets for managers. However, the level of commitment to the budget may be lower, as many of those responsible for achieving the budgets will have been excluded from the budget-setting process.

There will be a brief discussion of the benefits of participation in target setting in Chapter 7.

### Step 6: Review and co-ordinate budgets

A business's budget committee must at this stage review the various budgets and satisfy itself that the budgets complement one another. Where there is a lack of co-ordination, steps must be taken to ensure that the budgets mesh. Since this will require that at least one budget must be revised, this activity normally benefits from a diplomatic approach. Ultimately, however, the committee may be forced to assert its authority and insist that alterations are made.

### Step 7: Prepare the master budgets

The master budgets are the budgeted profit and loss account and budgeted balance sheet (and perhaps a summarised, budgeted cash flow statement). All of the information required to prepare these statements should be available from the individual budgets that have already been prepared. The task of preparing the master budgets is usually undertaken by the budget committee.

### Step 8: Communicate the budgets to all interested parties

The formally agreed budgets are now passed to the individual managers who will be responsible for their implementation. This is, in effect, senior management formally communicating to the other managers the targets that they must achieve.

### Step 9: Monitor performance relative to the budget

Much of the budget-setting activity will have been pointless unless each manager's actual performance is compared with planned performance, which is embodied in the budget. This issue is examined in detail in Chapter 7.

## Incremental and zero-base budgeting

Traditionally, much setting of budgets has tended to be on the basis of what happened last year, with some adjustment for any changes in factors that are expected to affect the forthcoming budget period (for example, inflation). This approach is sometimes known as **incremental budgeting**; it is often used for 'discretionary' budgets, such as research and development and staff training, where the **budget holder** (the manager responsible for the budget) is allocated a sum

of money to be spent in the area of activity concerned. They are referred to as
➜ **discretionary budgets** because the sum allocated is normally at the discretion of
senior management. These budgets are very common in local and central government (and in other public bodies) but are also used in commercial businesses
to cover certain types of activity.

A feature of the types of activity for which discretionary budgets exist is the
lack of a clear relationship between inputs (resources applied) and outputs
(benefits). Compare this with, say, a raw materials usage budget in a manufacturing company, where the amount of material used and, therefore, the amount of
funds taken by it are clearly related to the level of production and, ultimately, to
sales. It is easy for discretionary budgets to eat up funds with no clear benefit
being derived. It is often only proposed increases in these budgets that are closely
scrutinised.

➜ **Zero-base budgeting (ZBB)** rests on the philosophy that all spending needs to
be justified. Thus, when establishing the training budget each year, it is not automatically accepted that training courses should be financed in the future simply
because they were undertaken this year. The training budget will start from a zero
base and will only be increased if a good case can be made for the scarce resources
of the business to be allocated to this form of activity. Top management will need
to be convinced that the proposed activities represent 'value for money'.

ZBB encourages managers to adopt a more questioning approach to their areas
of responsibility. To justify the allocation of resources, they are often forced to
think carefully about the particular activities and the ways in which they are
undertaken. This questioning approach should result in a more efficient use of
business resources. With an increasing portion of the total costs of most businesses being in areas where the link between outputs and inputs is not always
clear, and where commitment of resources is discretionary rather than demonstrably essential to production, ZBB is increasingly relevant.

---

**Activity 6.10**

Can you think of any disadvantages of using ZBB? How might any disadvantages be
partially overcome?

The principal problems with ZBB are:

- It is time consuming and therefore expensive to undertake.
- Managers, whose sphere of responsibility is subjected to ZBB, can feel threatened by it.

The benefits of a ZBB approach can be gained to some extent – perhaps at not too great
a cost – by using the approach on a selective basis. For example, a particular budget area
could be subjected to a ZBB-type scrutiny only every third or fourth year. If ZBB is used
more frequently, there is, in any case, the danger that managers will use the same arguments each year to justify their activities. The process will simply become a mechanical
exercise and the benefits will be lost. For a typical business, some areas are likely to
benefit from ZBB more than others. ZBB could, in these circumstances, be applied only
to those areas that will benefit from it, and not to others. The areas that are most likely
to benefit from ZBB are discretionary spending ones, such as training, advertising, and
research and development.

If senior management is aware of the potentially threatening nature of this form of budgeting, care can be taken to apply ZBB with sensitivity. However, in the quest for value
for money, the application of ZBB can result in some tough decisions being made.

# An example of a budget: the cash budget

We shall now look in some detail at one particular budget, the cash budget. We shall use this because:

- It is a key budget; most economic aspects of a business are reflected in cash sooner or later, so that for a typical business the cash budget reflects the whole business more than any other single budget.
- Very small, unsophisticated businesses (for example, a corner shop) may feel that full-scale budgeting is not appropriate to their needs, but almost certainly they should prepare a cash budget as a minimum.

We shall consider other budgets later in the chapter.

Since budgets are documents that are to be used only internally by a business, their style and format is a question of management choice and will therefore vary from one business to the next. However, since managers, irrespective of the business, are likely to be using budgets for similar purposes, there is a tendency for some consistency of approach to exist. We can probably say that, in most businesses, the cash budget would possess the following features:

1. The budget period would be broken down into subperiods, typically months.
2. The budget would be in columnar form, with one column for each month.
3. Receipts of cash would be identified under various headings and a total for each month's receipts shown.
4. Payments of cash would be identified under various headings and a total for each month's payments shown.
5. The surplus of total cash receipts over payments or of payments over receipts for each month would be identified.
6. The running cash balance would be identified. This would be achieved by taking the balance at the end of the previous month and adjusting it for the surplus or deficit of receipts over payments for the current month.

Typically, all of the pieces of information in (3) to (6) in the above list would be useful to management for one reason or another.

The best way to deal with this topic is through an example (Example 6.1).

---

**Example 6.1**

Vierra Popova Ltd is a wholesale business. The budgeted profit and loss account for the next six months is as follows:

|  | Jan £000 | Feb £000 | Mar £000 | Apr £000 | May £000 | June £000 |
|---|---|---|---|---|---|---|
| Sales | 52 | 55 | 55 | 60 | 55 | 53 |
| Cost of goods sold | 30 | 31 | 31 | 35 | 31 | 32 |
| Salaries and wages | 10 | 10 | 10 | 10 | 10 | 10 |
| Electricity | 5 | 5 | 4 | 3 | 3 | 3 |
| Depreciation | 3 | 3 | 3 | 3 | 3 | 3 |
| Other overheads | 2 | 2 | 2 | 2 | 2 | 2 |
| Total expenses | 50 | 51 | 50 | 53 | 49 | 50 |
| Net profit | 2 | 4 | 5 | 7 | 6 | 3 |

The business allows all of its customers one month's credit (this means, for example, that cash from January sales will be received in February). Sales during December were £60,000.

The business plans to maintain stocks at their existing level until some time in March, when they are to be reduced by £5,000. Stocks will remain at this lower level indefinitely. Stock purchases are made on one month's credit (the December purchases having been £30,000). Salaries, wages and 'other overheads' are paid in the month concerned. Electricity is paid quarterly in arrears in March and June. The business plans to buy and pay for a new delivery van in March. This will cost a total of £15,000, but an existing van will be traded in for £4,000 as part of the deal.

The business expects to have £12,000 in cash at the beginning of January.

Let us show how the cash budget for the six months ending in June will look.

|  | Jan £000 | Feb £000 | Mar £000 | Apr £000 | May £000 | June £000 |
|---|---|---|---|---|---|---|
| **Receipts** | | | | | | |
| Debtors (note 1) | 60 | 52 | 55 | 55 | 60 | 55 |
| **Payments** | | | | | | |
| Creditors (note 2) | 30 | 30 | 31 | 26 | 35 | 31 |
| Salaries and wages | 10 | 10 | 10 | 10 | 10 | 10 |
| Electricity | | | 14 | | | 9 |
| Other overheads | 2 | 2 | 2 | 2 | 2 | 2 |
| Van purchase | | | 11 | | | |
| Total payments | 42 | 42 | 68 | 38 | 47 | 52 |
| Cash surplus | 18 | 10 | (13) | 17 | 13 | 3 |
| Opening balance (note 3) | 12 | 30 | 40 | 27 | 44 | 57 |
| Closing balance | 30 | 40 | 27 | 44 | 57 | 60 |

*Notes*
1. The cash receipts lag a month behind sales because customers are given a month in which to pay for their purchases.
2. In most months, the purchases of stock will equal the cost of goods sold. This is because the business maintains a constant level of stock. For stock to remain constant at the end of each month, the business must replace exactly the amount which has been used. During March, however, the business plans to reduce its stock by £5,000. This means that stock purchases will be lower than stock usage in that month. The payments for stock purchases lag a month behind purchases because the business expects to be allowed a month to pay for what it buys.
3. Each month's cash balance is the previous month's figure plus the cash surplus (or minus the cash deficit) for the current month. The balance at the start of January is £12,000 according to the information provided earlier.
4. Depreciation does not give rise to a cash payment.

**Activity 6.11**

Looking at the cash budget of Vierra Popova Ltd, what conclusions do you draw and what possible course of action do you recommend regarding the cash balance over the period concerned?

There appears to be a fairly large cash balance, given the size of the business, and it seems to be increasing. Management might give consideration to putting some of the cash into an income-yielding deposit. Alternatively, it could be used to expand the trading activities of the business by, for example, increasing the investment in fixed assets.

**Activity 6.12**

Vierra Popova Ltd (see Example 6.1) now wishes to prepare its cash budget for the second six months of the year. The budgeted profit and loss account for the second six months is as follows:

|  | July £000 | Aug £000 | Sept £000 | Oct £000 | Nov £000 | Dec £000 |
|---|---|---|---|---|---|---|
| Sales | 57 | 59 | 62 | 57 | 53 | 51 |
| Cost of goods sold | 32 | 33 | 35 | 32 | 30 | 29 |
| Salaries and wages | 10 | 10 | 10 | 10 | 10 | 10 |
| Electricity | 3 | 3 | 4 | 5 | 6 | 6 |
| Depreciation | 3 | 3 | 3 | 3 | 3 | 3 |
| Other overheads | 2 | 2 | 2 | 2 | 2 | 2 |
| Total expenses | 50 | 51 | 54 | 52 | 51 | 50 |
| Net profit | 7 | 8 | 8 | 5 | 2 | 1 |

The business will continue to allow all of its customers one month's credit.

The business plans to increase stocks from the 30 June level by £1,000 each month until, and including, September. During the following three months, stock levels will be decreased by £1,000 each month.

Stock purchases, which had been made on one month's credit until the June payment, will, starting with the purchases made in June, be made on two months' credit.

Salaries, wages and 'other overheads' will continue to be paid in the month concerned. Electricity is paid quarterly in arrears in September and December.

At the end of December the business intends to pay off part of a loan. This payment is to be such that it will leave the business with a cash balance of £5,000 with which to start next year.

**Required:**
Prepare the cash budget for the six months ending in December. (Remember that any information you need that relates to the first six months of the year, including the cash balance that is expected to be brought forward on 1 July, is given in Example 6.1.)

The cash budget for the six months ended 31 December is:

|  | July £000 | Aug £000 | Sept £000 | Oct £000 | Nov £000 | Dec £000 |
|---|---|---|---|---|---|---|
| **Receipts** | | | | | | |
| Debtors | 53 | 57 | 59 | 62 | 57 | 53 |
| **Payments** | | | | | | |
| Creditors (note 1) | – | 32 | 33 | 34 | 36 | 31 |
| Salaries and wages | 10 | 10 | 10 | 10 | 10 | 10 |
| Electricity | | | 10 | | | 17 |
| Other overheads | 2 | 2 | 2 | 2 | 2 | 2 |

| | July £000 | Aug £000 | Sept £000 | Oct £000 | Nov £000 | Dec £000 |
|---|---|---|---|---|---|---|
| Loan repayment (note 2) | – | – | – | – | – | 131 |
| Total payments | 12 | 44 | 55 | 46 | 48 | 191 |
| Cash surplus | 41 | 13 | 4 | 16 | 9 | (138) |
| Cash balance | 60 | 101 | 114 | 118 | 134 | 143 |
| Closing balance | 101 | 114 | 118 | 134 | 143 | 5 |

*Notes:*
1. There will be no payment to creditors in July because the June purchases will be made on two months' credit and will therefore be paid in August. The July purchases, which will equal the July cost of sales figure plus the increase in stock made in July, will be paid for in September, and so on.
2. The repayment is simply the amount that will cause the balance at 31 December to be £5,000.

# Preparing other budgets

Though each one will have its own idiosyncrasies, other budgets will tend to follow the same sort of pattern as the cash budget. Take the debtors budget for example. This would normally show the planned amount owing from credit sales to the business at the beginning and at the end of each month, the planned total sales for each month and the planned total cash receipts from debtors. The layout would be something like the following:

| | Month 1 £ | Month 2 £ | . . . |
|---|---|---|---|
| Opening balance | X | X | |
| *Add* Sales | X | X | |
| | X | X | |
| *Less* Cash receipts | X | X | |
| Closing balance | X | X | |

A raw materials stock budget (for a manufacturing business) would follow a similar pattern, as follows:

| | Month 1 £ (or physical units) | Month 2 £ (or physical units) | . . . |
|---|---|---|---|
| Opening balance | X | X | |
| *Add* Purchases | X | X | |
| | X | X | |
| *Less* Issues to production | X | X | |
| Closing balance | X | X | |

The stock budget will normally be expressed in financial terms, but may well be expressed in physical terms (for example, kilograms or metres) too for individual stock items.

A study of budgeting practice in small and medium-sized enterprises (SMEs) revealed that the most frequently prepared budget is the sales budget, followed by the budgeted profit and loss account and the overheads budget. Relevant data are given in Exhibit 6.4.

**Exhibit 6.4**

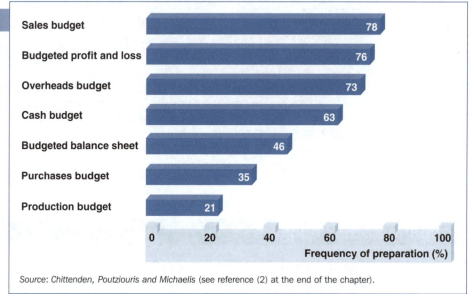

*Source: Chittenden, Poutziouris and Michaelis (see reference (2) at the end of the chapter).*

**Activity 6.13**

**Have a go at preparing the debtors budget for Vierra Popova Ltd for the six months July to December (see Activity 6.12).**

The debtors budget for the six months ended 31 December is:

|  | July £000 | Aug £000 | Sept £000 | Oct £000 | Nov £000 | Dec £000 |
|---|---|---|---|---|---|---|
| Opening balance (Note 1) | 53 | 57 | 59 | 62 | 57 | 53 |
| *Add* Sales (Note 2) | 57 | 59 | 62 | 57 | 53 | 51 |
|  | 110 | 116 | 121 | 119 | 110 | 104 |
| *Less* Cash receipts (Note 3) | 53 | 57 | 59 | 62 | 57 | 53 |
| Closing balance (Note 4) | 57 | 59 | 62 | 57 | 53 | 51 |

*Notes:*
1. The opening debtors figure is the previous month's sales figure (sales are on one month's credit).
2. The sales are the current month's figure.
3. The cash received each month is equal to the previous month's sales figure.
4. The closing balance is equal to the current month's sales figure.

Note that if we knew three of the four figures each month, we could deduce the fourth.

This budget could, of course, be set out in any manner that would have given the sort of information that management would require in respect of planned levels of debtors and associated transactions.

Note how the debtors budget in Activity 6.13 links to the cash budget: the cash receipts row of figures is the same in both. The debtors budget would link to the sales budget in a similar way. This is how the linking, which was discussed earlier in this chapter, is achieved.

| Activity 6.14 | Have a go at preparing the creditors budget for Vierra Popova Ltd for the six months of July to December (see Activity 6.12). *Hint*: Remember that the creditors' payment period alters from the June purchases onwards. |
| --- | --- |

The creditors budget for the six months ended 31 December is:

|  | July £000 | Aug £000 | Sept £000 | Oct £000 | Nov £000 | Dec £000 |
| --- | --- | --- | --- | --- | --- | --- |
| Opening balance | 32 | 65 | 67 | 70 | 67 | 60 |
| *Add* purchases | 33 | 34 | 36 | 31 | 29 | 28 |
|  | 65 | 99 | 103 | 101 | 96 | 88 |
| *Less* cash payments | – | 32 | 33 | 34 | 36 | 31 |
| Closing balance | 65 | 67 | 70 | 67 | 60 | 57 |

This, again, could be set out in any manner that would have given the sort of information that management would require in respect of planned levels of creditors and associated transactions.

# Activity-based budgeting

→ **Activity-based budgeting (ABB)** applies the philosophy of activity-based costing (ABC), which we discussed in Chapter 5, to planning and control through budgets. You may recall that ABC recognises that it is activities that cause or 'drive' costs. If the cost-driving activities can be identified, ascertaining the cost of the output of a business can be achieved with greater accuracy. Not only this, but costs become easier to control simply because their cause is known.

It is a central feature of budgeting that those who are responsible for meeting a particular budget (budget holders) should have control over the events that affect performance in their area. A typical problem in this regard is illustrated by the manager whose costs are increased beyond the budgeted costs as a result of increased volume of activity, which is outside of that manager's control. In other words, the costs are driven by activities not controlled by the manager who is being held accountable for those costs.

ABB seeks to generate budgets in such a way that the manager who has control over the cost drivers is accountable for the costs that are caused.

# Non-financial measures in budgeting

The efficiency of internal operations and customer satisfaction has become of critical importance to businesses striving to survive in an increasingly competitive environment. Non-financial measures have an important role to play in assessing performance in such key areas as customer/supplier delivery times, set-up times, defect levels and customer satisfaction levels. There is no reason why management accounting need be confined to reporting only financial targets and measures. Non-financial measures can also be used as the basis for targets and can be incorporated into the budgeting process and reported alongside the financial targets for the business (see Exhibit 6.5).

| | | | | | | |
|---|---|---|---|---|---|---|

**Exhibit 6.5**

A 1993 survey of manufacturing businesses revealed that non-financial measures are widely used by businesses. The following table is taken from this study.

| | Never/rarely | | Sometimes | | Often/always | |
|---|---|---|---|---|---|---|
| | Smaller firms % | Larger firms % | Smaller firms % | Larger firms % | Smaller firms % | Larger firms % |
| Customer satisfaction/ product quality | 22 | 2 | 11 | 7 | 67 | 91 |
| Customer delivery efficiency | 16 | 2 | 22 | 7 | 62 | 91 |
| Supplier quality/delivery | 16 | 4 | 32 | 15 | 52 | 81 |
| Throughput times | 33 | 6 | 24 | 20 | 43 | 74 |
| Set-up times | 59 | 32 | 19 | 22 | 22 | 46 |

*Extent to which performance is measured*

We can see that customer-based measures are the most widely used form of non-financial performance measures. There are also clear differences between the smaller firms and larger firms in the extent to which non-financial measures are used.

*Source: Drury, Braund, Osborne and Tayles (see reference (1) at end of chapter).*

**? Self-assessment question 6.1**

Antonio Ltd has planned production and sales for the next nine months as follows:

| | Production (units) | Sales (units) |
|---|---|---|
| May | 350 | 350 |
| June | 400 | 400 |
| July | 500 | 400 |
| August | 600 | 500 |
| September | 600 | 600 |
| October | 700 | 650 |
| November | 750 | 700 |
| December | 750 | 800 |
| January | 750 | 750 |

During the period, the business plans to advertise heavily to generate these increases in sales. Payments for advertising of £1,000 and £1,500 will be made in July and October respectively.

The selling price per unit will be £20 throughout the period. Forty per cent of sales are normally made on two months' credit. The other 60 per cent are settled within the month of the sale.

Raw materials will be held in stock for one month before they are taken into production. Purchases of raw materials will be on one month's credit (buy one month, pay the next). The cost of raw materials is £8 per unit of production.

Other direct production expenses, including labour, are £6 per unit of production. These will be paid in the month concerned.

Various production overheads, which during the period to 30 June had run at £1,800 per month, are expected to rise to £2,000 each month from 1 July to 31 October. These are expected to rise again from 1 November to £2,400 per month and to remain at that level for the foreseeable future. These overheads include a steady £400 each month for depreciation. Overheads are planned to be paid 80 per cent in the month of production and 20 per cent in the following month.

To help to meet the planned increased production, a new item of plant will be bought and will be delivered in August. The cost of this item is £6,600; the contract with the supplier will specify that this will be paid in three equal amounts in September, October and November.

Raw materials stock is planned to be 500 units on 1 July. The balance at the bank the same day is planned to be £7,500.

**Required:**

(a) Draw up the following for the six months ending 31 December:
   (i)   a raw materials budget, showing both physical quantities and financial values
   (ii)  a creditors budget
   (iii) a cash budget.

(b) The cash budget reveals a potential cash deficiency during October and November. Can you suggest any ways in which a modification of plans could overcome this problem?

## Who needs budgets?

Until recently it would have been a heresy to suggest that budgeting was not of central importance to any business. The benefits of budgeting mentioned earlier in the chapter have been widely recognised and, indeed, the vast majority of businesses still continue to prepare annual budgets. However, there is increasing concern that, in today's highly dynamic and competitive environment, budgets may actually be harmful to the achievement of business objectives. This has led a small but growing number of businesses to abandon budgets as a tool of planning and control.

Various charges have been levelled against the conventional budgeting process (see Exhibit 6.6 for one example). It is claimed that budgets:

■ Cannot deal with a fast-changing environment and that budgets are often out of date before the commencement of the budget period.

- Focus too much management attention on the achievement of short-term financial targets. Instead, managers should focus on the things that create value for the business (for example, innovation, building brand loyalty, responding quickly to competitive threats, and so on).
- Reinforce a 'command and control' structure that prevents managers from exercising autonomy. This may be particularly true where a 'top-down' approach that allocates budgets to managers is being used. Where managers feel constrained, attempts to retain and recruit able managers can be difficult.
- Take up an enormous amount of management time that could be better utilised. In practice, budgeting can be a lengthy process that may involve much negotiation, reworking and updating. However, this may add little to the achievement of business objectives.
- Are based around business functions (sales, marketing, production and so on). However, to achieve the business's objectives, the focus should be on business processes that cut across functional boundaries and reflect the needs of the customer.
- Encourage incremental thinking by employing a 'last year plus $x$ per cent' approach to planning. This can inhibit the development of 'break out' strategies that may be necessary in a fast-changing environment.

Although some believe that many of the problems identified can be solved by better budgeting systems such as activity-based budgeting and zero-base budgeting, others believe that a more radical solution is required.

Those businesses that have abandoned budgets still recognise the need for forward planning. There is still general agreement that there must be appropriate systems in place to steer a business towards its objectives. However, the systems adopted reflect a broader, more integrated approach to planning. The new systems are often based around a 'leaner' financial planning process that is more closely linked to other measurement and reward systems. Emphasis is placed on the use of rolling forecasts, key performance indicators (such as market share, customer satisfaction and innovations) and/or 'scorecards' that identify both monetary and non-monetary targets to be achieved over the long term and short term.

It is too early to predict whether or not the trickle of businesses that are now seeking an alternative to budgets will turn into a flood. However, it is clear that in today's highly competitive environment a business must be flexible and responsive to changing conditions. Management systems that in any way hinder these attributes will not survive.

| Exhibit 6.6 | Jeremy Hope and Robin Fraser are at the forefront of those who argue that budgeting systems have an adverse effect on the ability of businesses to compete effectively. Below we reproduce a short case study of Volvo Cars that they have written. |
| --- | --- |

**New steering mechanisms at Volvo Cars**

Following losses in 1990–92 and a small profit in 1993, Volvo Cars decided to make a number of important changes, one of which was to adopt a radically different approach to managing the business. But senior managers were quick to realise that such an approach was unlikely to be successful in the longer term unless they tackled the problems of the budgeting and planning process that encouraged the old mindset of compliance and control. As Ole Johannesson, VP finance, explains, 'the budget and long-range planning systems are no longer efficient when the business environment is changing more and more rapidly. Today we need a process that enables us to react not only immediately but even beforehand.' In 1994 there was no budget requested by the Group company, AB Volvo, from operating units for the forthcoming year, 1995. As Johannesson notes, 'we recognised the extent of the cultural change needed. We wanted less and less of order giving, victims of circumstance, administration, checking, reactive positions, functional ties and hierarchical thinking, and more and more of creating opportunities, communication, development, confidence-building, proactive positions, network ties, and process thinking. Since that time Volvo Cars has built a highly advanced management model that has helped it face the intense competitive pressures that are endemic to the world car market.

Volvo reckoned that its previous planning, budgeting and control processes absorbed around 20% of total management time. By abandoning these processes and managing in a different way, managers have not only saved significant costs but they now have more time to focus on strategy, action planning and beating the competition. This is a battle not tied to an annual cycle, but is waged continuously month by month and quarter by quarter. Strategy and forecasts are reviewed and updated several times a year with four distinct cycles apparent. Each month a 'flash' forecast is prepared covering the next three months; each quarter a two-year rolling forecast is updated; and each year sees a revised four-year and ten-year strategic plan. While targets are broad-brush and comprise a number of key performance indicators, there is more time spent on developing action plans to support them. Monthly reports to the board include financial information (actual month, actual year-to-date, forecast remainder of year, revised forecast for total years, and last year-to-date) and a number of key performance indicators such as market share, order intake, customer satisfaction, product costs, dealer profitability, warranty costs, fault frequency, and total ownership cost (all where possible compared with the competition). Four years after dismantling the budgeting process there is now a strong 'responsibility' and 'no blame' culture at Volvo Cars.

According to Ole Johannesson, 'managers now know that they mustn't come to meetings with problems, but with explanations about what they've done to solve them'. The management accountants now spend more time collecting a whole range of measurement data but, more importantly, they see their role as one of analysing and interpreting the data so that operating managers can take the appropriate action. Indeed the whole emphasis is on 'actions' rather than 'problems'. Volvo has transformed itself into an action-orientated company in which decisions are made by people at the appropriate level to meet changing conditions. This has contributed to Volvo's remarkable turnaround. It now ranks as the 16th largest motor vehicle manufacturer in the world, but in terms of profitability it is second only to Ford on profits on sales and assets.

*Source*: Hope and Fraser (see reference (3) at the end of the chapter).

## Summary

We began this chapter by considering the relationship between business objectives, long-term plans and budgets. We have seen that budgets are set within the framework of the long-term plans and represent one step towards the realisation of the business objectives. They are concerned with the short term and provide precise targets to be achieved in key business areas. We have considered the potential uses for budgets and have seen that these uses may conflict with one another. Where this occurs, managers must decide which uses are most important for the business and must prepare the budgets accordingly.

We have examined the key steps in the budget-setting process and have seen how budgets for different facets of the business are interlinked. The various budgets of the business are summarised in the form of master budgets, which are the budgeted income statement and balance sheet (and, perhaps, a budgeted cash flow statement in summarised form). We have considered the basic principles of budget preparation and have examined a practical example of how budgets are prepared.

Finally, we considered the case against budgeting. We saw that some believe that budgets are unable to cope with a fast-changing environment and should be abandoned in favour of more flexible and more integrated methods of planning. However, it would be premature to consign budgets to the dustbin of history. For most businesses, budgets still remain a key tool for planning purposes.

Budgeting is an important topic that requires further consideration. In the next chapter, we discuss in more detail the role of budgets in controlling the business.

➡ **Key terms**

| | |
|---|---|
| Mission statement  p. 125 | Budget committee  p. 135 |
| Budget  p. 127 | Budget officer  p. 135 |
| Control  p. 127 | Limiting factor  p. 136 |
| Forecast  p. 129 | Incremental budgeting  p. 138 |
| Periodic budget  p. 129 | Budget holder  p. 138 |
| Continual budget  p. 130 | Discretionary budget  p. 139 |
| Master budgets  p. 130 | Zero-base budgeting (ZBB)  p. 139 |
| Management by exception  p. 133 | Activity-based budgeting (ABB)  p. 145 |

## Further reading

If you would like to explore the topics covered in this chapter in more depth, we recommend the following books:

**Management Accounting**, *Atkinson, A., Banker, R., Kaplan, R.* and *Mark Young, S.*, 3rd edn, Prentice Hall International, 2001, chapter 11.
**Management and Cost Accounting**, *Drury, C.*, 5th edn, Thomson Learning, 2000, chapter 15.
**Accounting for Management Control**, *Emmanuel, C.* and *Otley, D.*, 2nd edn, Chapman and Hall, 1990, chapter 7.
**Cost Accounting: A managerial emphasis**, *Horngren, C., Foster, G.* and *Datar, S.*, 10th edn, Prentice Hall International, 2000, chapter 6.

## References

1. **A Survey of Management Accounting Practices in UK Manufacturing Companies**, *Drury, C., Braund, S., Osborne, P.* and *Tayles, M.*, Chartered Association of Certified Accountants, 1993.
2. **Financial Management and Working Capital Practices in UK SMEs**, *Chittenden, F., Poutziouris, P.* and *Michaelis, N.*, Manchester Business School, 1998.
3. **Beyond Budgeting**, *Hope, J.* and *Fraser, R.*, Management Accounting, January 1999, p. 17.

## ? REVIEW QUESTIONS

**6.1** Define a budget. How is a budget different from a forecast?

**6.2** What were the five uses of budgets which were identified in the chapter?

**6.3** What do budgets have to do with control?

**6.4** What is a budget committee? What purpose does it serve?

## ? EXERCISES

Exercises 6.5–6.8 are more advanced than 6.1–6.4. Those with coloured numbers have answers at the back of the book.

**6.1** Daniel Chu Ltd, a new business, started production on 1 April. Planned sales for the next nine months are as follows:

|  | Sales units |
|---|---|
| May | 500 |
| June | 600 |
| July | 700 |
| August | 800 |
| September | 900 |
| October | 900 |
| November | 900 |
| December | 800 |
| January | 700 |

The selling price per unit will be a consistent £100, and all sales will be made on one month's credit. It is planned that sufficient finished goods stock for each month's sales should be available at the end of the previous month.

Raw materials purchases will be such that there will be sufficient raw materials stock available at the end of each month precisely to meet the following month's planned production. This planned policy will operate from the end of April. Purchases of raw materials will be on one month's credit. The cost of raw material is £40 per unit of finished product.

The direct labour cost, which is variable with the level of production, is planned to be £20 per unit of finished production. Production overheads are planned to be £20,000 each month, including £3,000 for depreciation. Non-production overheads are planned to be £11,000 per month, of which £1,000 will be depreciation.

Various fixed assets costing £250,000 will be bought and paid for during April.

Except where specified, assume that all payments take place in the same month as the cost is incurred.

The business will raise £300,000 in cash from a share issue in April.

**Required:**
Draw up the following for the six months ending 30 September:

(a) A finished stock budget, showing just physical quantities.
(b) A raw materials stock budget showing both physical quantities and financial values.
(c) A trade creditors budget.
(d) A trade debtors budget.
(e) A cash budget.

6.2 You have overheard the following statements:

(a) 'A budget is a forecast of what is expected to happen in a business during the next year.'
(b) 'Monthly budgets must be prepared with a column for each month so that you can see the whole year at a glance, month by month.'
(c) 'Budgets are ok but they stifle all initiative. No manager worth employing would work for a business that seeks to control through budgets.'
(d) 'Activity-based budgeting is an approach that takes account of the planned volume of activity in order to deduce the figures to go into the budget.'
(e) 'Any sensible person would start with the sales budget and build up the other budgets from there.'

**Required:**
Critically discuss these statements, explaining any technical terms.

6.3 A nursing home, which is linked to a large hospital, has been examining its budgetary control procedures, with particular reference to overhead costs.

The level of activity in the facility is measured by the number of patients treated in the budget period. For the current year, the budget stands at 6,000 patients and this is expected to be met.

For months 1 to 6 of this year (assume 12 months of equal length) 2,700 patients were treated. The actual variable overhead costs incurred during this six-month period are as follows:

| Expense | £ |
|---|---|
| Staffing | 59,400 |
| Power | 27,000 |
| Supplies | 54,000 |
| Other | 8,100 |
| Total | 148,500 |

The hospital accountant believes that the variable overhead costs will be incurred at the same rate during months 7 to 12 of the year.

Fixed overhead costs are budgeted for the whole year as follows:

| Expense | £ |
|---|---|
| Supervision | 120,000 |
| Depreciation/financing | 187,200 |
| Other | 64,800 |
| Total | 372,000 |

**Required:**

(a) Present an overheads budget for months 7 to 12 of the year. You should show each expense, but should not separate individual months. What is the total overhead cost per patient that would be incorporated into any statistics?

(b) The home actually treated 3,800 patients during months 7 to 12, the actual variable overhead was £203,300, and the fixed overhead was £190,000. In summary form, examine how well the home exercised control over its overheads.

(c) Interpret your analysis and point out any limitations or assumptions.

**6.4**  Linpet is to be incorporated on 1 June. The opening balance sheet of the business will then be as follows:

| Assets | £ |
|---|---|
| Cash at bank | 60,000 |
| | |
| Share capital | |
| £1 ordinary shares | 60,000 |

During June, the business intends to make payments of £40,000 for a freehold property, £10,000 for equipment and £6,000 for a motor vehicle. The business will also purchase initial trading stock costing £22,000 on credit.

The business has produced the following estimates:

(i)     Sales for June will be £8,000 and will increase at the rate of £3,000 per month until September. In October, sales will rise to £22,000 and in subsequent months sales will be maintained at this figure.

(ii)    The gross profit percentage on goods sold will be 25 per cent.

(iii)   There is a risk that supplies of trading stock will be interrupted towards the end of the accounting year. The business therefore intends to build up its initial level of stock (£22,000) by purchasing £1,000 of stock each month in addition to the monthly purchases necessary to satisfy monthly sales. All purchases of stock (including the initial stock) will be on one month's credit.

(iv)    Sales will be divided equally between cash and credit sales. Credit customers are expected to pay two months after the sale is agreed.

(v)     Wages and salaries will be £900 per month. Other overheads will be £500 per month for the first four months and £650 thereafter. Both types of expense will be payable when incurred.

(vi)    80 per cent of sales will be generated by salespeople, who will receive 5 per cent commission on sales. The commission is payable one month after the sale is agreed.

(vii)   The business intends to purchase further equipment in November for £7,000 cash.

(viii)  Depreciation is to be provided at the rate of 5 per cent a year on freehold property and 20 per cent a year on equipment. (Depreciation has not been included in the overheads mentioned in (v) above.)

**Required:**

(a) State why a cash budget is required for a business.

(b) Prepare a cash budget for Linpet Ltd for the six-month period to 30 November.

**6.5** Lewisham Ltd manufactures one product line – the Zenith. Sales of Zeniths over the next few months are planned to be as follows:

1. *Demand*

|  | Units |
|---|---|
| July | 180,000 |
| August | 240,000 |
| September | 200,000 |
| October | 180,000 |

Each Zenith sells for £3.

2. *Debtor receipts*   Debtors are expected to pay as follows:
   - 70 per cent during the month of sale
   - 28 per cent during the following month.

   The remainder of debtors are expected to go bad (that is, to be uncollectable). Debtors who pay in the month of sale are entitled to deduct a 2 per cent discount from the invoice price.

3. *Finished goods stocks*   Stocks of finished goods are expected to be 40,000 units at 1 July. The business's policy is that, in future, the stock at the end of each month should equal 20 per cent of the following month's planned sales requirements.

4. *Raw materials stock*   Stocks of raw materials are expected to be 40,000 kg on 1 July. The business's policy is that, in future, the stock at the end of each month should equal 50 per cent of the following month's planned production requirements. Each Zenith requires 0.5 kg of the raw material, which costs £1.50/kg. Raw materials purchases are paid in the month after purchase.

5. *Labour and overheads*   The direct labour cost of each Zenith is £0.50. The variable overhead element of each Zenith is £0.30. Fixed overheads, including depreciation of £25,000, total £47,000 per month. All labour and overheads are paid during the month in which they arose.

6. *Cash in hand*   At 1 August the business plans to have a bank balance (in funds) of £20,000.

**Required:**
Prepare the following budgets:

(a) Finished stock budget (expressed in units of Zenith) for each of the three months July, August and September.
(b) Raw materials budget (expressed in kilograms of the raw material) for the two months July and August.
(c) Cash budget for August and September.

**6.6** Newtake Records Ltd owns a chain of 14 shops selling cassette tapes and compact discs. At the beginning of June the business had an overdraft of £35,000 and the bank had asked for this to be eliminated by the end of November. As a result, the directors have recently decided to review their plans for the next six months in order to comply with this requirement.

The following forecast information was prepared for the business some months earlier:

| | May £000 | June £000 | July £000 | August £000 | Sept £000 | Oct £000 | Nov £000 |
|---|---|---|---|---|---|---|---|
| Expected sales | 180 | 230 | 320 | 250 | 140 | 120 | 110 |
| Purchases | 135 | 180 | 142 | 94 | 75 | 66 | 57 |
| Administration expenses | 52 | 55 | 56 | 53 | 48 | 46 | 45 |
| Selling expenses | 22 | 24 | 28 | 26 | 21 | 19 | 18 |
| Taxation payment | | | | 22 | | | |
| Finance payments | 5 | 5 | 5 | 5 | 5 | 5 | 5 |
| Shop refurbishment | – | – | 14 | 18 | 6 | – | – |

**Notes:**
(i) Stock held at 1 June was £112,000. The business believes it is preferable to maintain a minimum stock level of £40,000 of goods over the period to 30 November.
(ii) Suppliers allow one month's credit. The first three months' purchases are subject to a contractual agreement, which must be honoured.
(iii) The gross profit margin is 40 per cent.
(iv) All sales income is received in the month of sale. However, 50 per cent of customers pay with a credit card. The charge made by the credit card company to Newtake Records Ltd is 3 per cent of the sales value. These charges are in addition to the selling expenses identified above. The credit card company pays Newtake Records Ltd in the month of sale.
(v) The business has a bank loan, which it is paying off in monthly instalments of £5,000 per month. The interest element represents 20 per cent of each instalment.
(vi) Administration expenses are paid when incurred. This item includes a charge of £15,000 each month in respect of depreciation.
(vii) Selling expenses are payable in the following month.

**Required (working to the nearest £1,000):**
(a) Prepare a cash budget for the six months ended 30 November which shows the cash balance at the end of each month.
(b) Compute the stock levels at the end of each month for the six months to 30 November.
(c) Prepare a budgeted profit and loss account for the six months ended 30 November. (A monthly breakdown of profit is *not* required.)
(d) What problems is Newtake Records Ltd likely to face in the next six months? Can you suggest how the business might deal with these problems?

**6.7** Prolog Ltd is a small wholesaler of personal computers. It has in recent months been selling 50 machines a month at a price of £2,000 each. These machines cost £1,600 each. A new model has just been launched and this is expected to offer greatly enhanced performance. Its selling price and cost will be the same as for the old model. From the beginning of January, sales are expected to increase at a rate of 20 machines each month until the end of June, when sales will amount to 170 units per month. They are expected to continue at that level thereafter. Operating costs including depreciation of £2,000 a month, are forecast as follows:

| | January | February | March | April | May | June |
|---|---|---|---|---|---|---|
| Operating costs (£000) | 6 | 8 | 10 | 12 | 12 | 12 |

Prolog expects to receive no credit for operating costs. Additional shelving for storage will be bought, installed and paid for in April, costing £12,000. Corporation tax of £25,000 is due at the end of March. Prolog anticipates that debtors will amount to two months' sales. To give their customers a good level of service, Prolog plans to hold enough stock at the end of each period to fulfil anticipated demand from customers in the following month. The computer manufacturer, however, grants one month's credit to Prolog. Prolog Ltd's balance sheet appears below.

**Balance sheet at 31 December**

| | £000 | £000 |
|---|---|---|
| Fixed assets | | 80 |
| **Current assets** | | |
| Stock | 112 | |
| Debtors | 200 | |
| Cash | – | |
| | 312 | |
| | | |
| **Creditors: amounts due within one year** | | |
| Trade creditors | 112 | |
| Taxation | 25 | |
| Overdraft | 68 | |
| | 205 | |
| Net current assets | | 107 |
| Total assets less current liabilities | | 187 |
| | | |
| **Capital and reserves** | | |
| Share capital (25p ordinary shares) | | 10 |
| Profit and loss account | | 177 |
| | | 187 |

**Required:**

(a) Prepare a cash budget for Prolog Ltd showing the cash balance or required overdraft for the six months ending 30 June.

(b) State briefly what further information a banker would require from Prolog before granting additional overdraft facilities for the anticipated expansion of sales.

**6.8** Brown and Jeffreys, a West Midlands business, makes one standard product for use in the motor trade. The product, known as the Fuel Miser, for which the business holds the patent, when fitted to the fuel system of production model cars has the effect of reducing petrol consumption.

Part of the production is sold direct to a local car manufacturer, which fits the Fuel Miser as an optional extra to several of its models and the rest of the production is sold through various retail outlets, garages and so on.

The Fuel Miser is assembled by Brown and Jeffreys but all three components are manufactured by local engineering businesses. The three components are codenamed A, B and C. One Fuel Miser consists of one of each component.

The planned sales for the first seven months of the forthcoming accounting period, by channels of distribution and in terms of Fuel Miser units, are as follows:

| | Jan | Feb | Mar | Apr | May | June | July |
|---|---|---|---|---|---|---|---|
| Manufacturers | 4,000 | 4,000 | 4,500 | 4,500 | 4,500 | 4,500 | 4,500 |
| Retail, etc. | 2,000 | 2,700 | 3,200 | 3,000 | 2,700 | 2,500 | 2,400 |
| | 6,000 | 6,700 | 7,700 | 7,500 | 7,200 | 7,000 | 6,900 |

The following further information is available:

(i)   There will be a stock of finished units at 1 January of 7,000 Fuel Misers.
(ii)  The stocks of raw materials at 1 January will be:
      A 10,000 units
      B 16,500 units
      C 7,200 units
(iii) The selling price of Fuel Misers is to be £10 each to the motor manufacturer and £12 each to retail outlets.
(iv)  The maximum production capacity of the company is 7,000 units per month. There is no possibility of increasing this output.
(v)   Assembly of each Fuel Miser will take 15 minutes of direct labour. Direct labour is paid at the rate of £4.80 per hour during the month of production.
(vi)  The components are each expected to cost the following:
      A £2.50
      B £1.30
      C £0.80
(vii) Indirect costs are to be paid at a regular rate of £32,000 each month.
(viii) The cash at the bank at 1 January will be £2,620.

The business plans to follow the following policies for as many months as possible and in a manner consistent with the planned sales:

■ Finished stocks at the end of each month are to equal the following month's total sales to retail outlets, and half the total of the following month's sales to the motor manufacturer.
■ Raw materials at the end of each month are to be sufficient to cover production requirements for the following month. The production for July will be 6,800 units.
■ Creditors for raw materials are to be paid during the month following purchase. The creditors payment for January will be £21,250.
■ Debtors will pay in the month of sale in the case of sales to the motor manufacturer and the month after sale in the case of retail sales. Retail sales during December were 2,000 units at £12 each.

**Required:**
Prepare the following budgets in monthly columnar form, both in terms of money and units (where relevant), for the six months of January to June inclusive:

(a) Sales budget.[†]
(b) Finished stock budget (valued at direct cost).[‡]
(c) Raw materials stock budget.[‡]
(d) Production budget (direct costs only).[†]
(e) Debtors' budget.[‡]
(f) Creditors' budget.[‡]
(g) Cash budget.[‡]

† The sales and production budgets should merely state each month's sales or production in units and in money terms.
‡ The other budgets should all seek to reconcile the opening balance of stocks, debtors, creditors or cash with the closing balance through movements of the relevant factors over the month.

## CHAPTER 7

# Accounting for control

## Introduction

This chapter deals with the role of accounting in management control. We shall consider how a budget can be used in helping to control a business. We shall see that, by collecting information on actual performance and comparing it with the revised budget, it is possible to identify fairly precisely which activities are in control and which seem to be out of control.

**OBJECTIVES**

When you have completed this chapter you should be able to:

- Discuss the role and limitations of using budgets to help to exercise control.
- Carry out a complete analysis of variances.
- Explain the nature and role of standard costs.
- Discuss possible reasons for key variances and other practical matters surrounding control through budgets.

## Using budgets for control – flexible budgets

In Chapter 6 we saw that budgets can provide a useful basis for exercising control over a business. This is because control is usually seen as making events conform to a plan. Since the budget represents the plan, making events conform to it is the obvious way to try to control the business. Using budgets in this way is popular in practice. As we saw in Chapter 6, for most businesses the routine is as shown in Figure 7.1.

The steps in the control process are fairly easy to understand. The point is that if plans are drawn up sensibly, we have a basis for exercising control over a business. This also requires that we have the means of measuring actual performance in the same terms as those in which the budget is stated. If they are not in the same terms, comparison will not usually be possible.

Taking steps to exercise control means finding out where and why things did not go according to plan and seeking ways to put things right for the future. One of the reasons why things may have gone wrong is that the plans may, in reality, prove to be unachievable. In this case, if budgets are to be a useful basis for exercising control in the future, it may be necessary to revise them for future periods to bring targets into the realms of achievability.

| Figure 7.1 | |
|---|---|

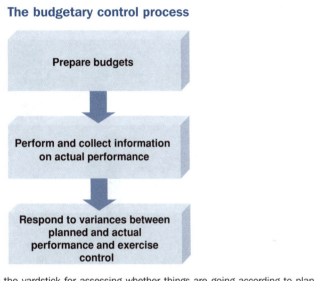

**The budgetary control process**

Prepare budgets

↓

Perform and collect information on actual performance

↓

Respond to variances between planned and actual performance and exercise control

Budgets, once set, provide the yardstick for assessing whether things are going according to plan. Variances between budgeted and actual performances can be identified and reacted to.

This last point should not be taken to mean that budget targets can simply be ignored if the going gets tough; rather, they should be flexible. Budgets may prove to be totally unrealistic targets for a variety of reasons, including unexpected changes in the commercial environment (for example, an unexpected collapse in demand for services of the type that the business supplies). In this case, nothing whatsoever will be achieved by pretending that the targets can be met.

➡ By having a system of budgetary control through **flexible budgets**, a position can be established where decision making and responsibility can be delegated to junior management, yet control can still be retained by senior management. This is because senior managers can use the budgetary control system to ascertain which junior managers are meeting targets and, therefore, working towards the objectives of the business. This enables a management-by-exception environment to be created. Here, senior management concentrates its energy on areas where things are not going according to plan (the exceptions – it is to be hoped). Junior managers who are performing to budget can be left to get on with their jobs.

## Feedback and feedforward controls

➡ The control process that we have just outlined is known as **feedback control**. Its main feature is that steps are taken to get operations back on track as soon as there is a signal that they have gone wrong. This is similar to the thermostatic control that is a feature of most central heating systems. The thermostat senses when the temperature has fallen below a preset level (analogous to the budget), and takes action to correct matters by activating the heating device that restores

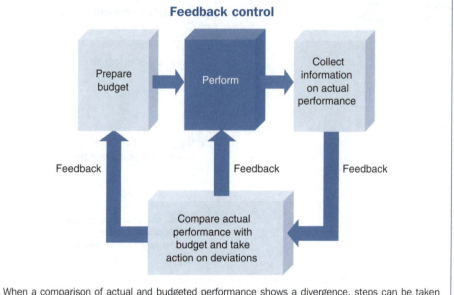

**Figure 7.2**

## Feedback control

Prepare budget → Perform → Collect information on actual performance

Feedback    Feedback    Feedback

Compare actual performance with budget and take action on deviations

When a comparison of actual and budgeted performance shows a divergence, steps can be taken to get performance back to plan. If the plans need revising, this can be done.

the required minimum temperature. Figure 7.2 depicts the stages in a feedback control system using budgets.

There is an alternative type of control, known as **feedforward control**. Here, predictions are made as to what can go wrong and steps taken to avoid that outcome. The preparation of budgets, which we discussed in Chapter 6, provides an example of this type of control. When preparing a particular budget it would normally be obvious that a problem will arise unless the business changes its plans. For example, the cash budget may reveal that if the original plans are followed there will be a negative cash balance for some part of the budget period. By recognising this, the plans may be able to be revised so as to eliminate the problem.

Feedforward controls are probably better than feedback controls since, with the former, things should never go wrong because steps are taken to ensure that they cannot go wrong. Feedback controls react to a loss of control. In many situations, however, feedforward controls are not possible to install.

## Comparison of actual performance with the budget

Since the principal objective of most private-sector businesses is to enhance their shareholders' wealth, and remembering that profit is the net increase in wealth as a result of trading, the most important budget target to meet is the profit target. In view of this, we shall begin with that aspect in our consideration of making the comparison between actuals and budgets. Example 7.1 shows the budgeted and actual profit and loss account for Baxter Ltd for the month of May.

**Example 7.1**

Baxter Ltd, month of May

|  | Budget | | Actual | |
|---|---|---|---|---|
| Output | 1,000 units | | 900 units | |
| (production and sales) | | | | |
|  | £ | | £ | |
| Sales | 100,000 | | 92,000 | |
| Raw materials | (40,000) | (40,000 m) | (36,900) | (37,000 m) |
| Labour | (20,000) | (5,000 hr) | (17,500) | (4,375 hr) |
| Fixed overheads | (20,000) | | (20,700) | |
| Operating profit | 20,000 | | 16,900 | |

From Example 7.1 it is clear that the budgeted profit was not achieved. As far as May is concerned, this is a matter of history. However, the business, or at least one aspect of it, is out of control. Senior management must discover where things went wrong and try to ensure that they are not repeated in later months. Thus, it is not enough to know that, overall, things went wrong; we need to know where and why. The approach that is taken is to compare the budgeted and actual figures for the various items (sales, raw materials and so on) in the above statement.

**Activity 7.1**

**Can you see any problems in comparing the various items (sales, raw materials and so on) for the budget and the actual performance of Baxter Ltd in order to draw conclusions as to which aspects were out of control?**

The problem is that the actual level of output was not as budgeted. The actual level of output was 900 units, whereas the budgeted level was 1,000. This means that we cannot, for example, say that there was a labour cost saving of £2,500 (£20,000 – £17,500) and conclude that all is well in that area.

## Flexing the budget

➡ One practical way to overcome our difficulty is to **'flex' the budget** to what it would have been had the planned level of output been 900 units rather than 1,000 units. Flexing the budget simply means revising it to what it would have been had the planned level of output been some different figure.

In the context of control, the budget is usually flexed to reflect the volume that actually occurred. To be able to do this, we need to know which items are fixed and which are variable, relative to the level of output. Once we have this knowledge, flexing is a simple operation. We shall assume that sales revenue, materials cost and labour cost vary strictly with volume. Fixed overheads, by definition, will not. (Whether, in real life, labour cost really does vary with the level of output is not so certain, but it will serve well enough as an assumption for our purposes.)

On the basis of the assumptions regarding the behaviour of costs, the flexed budget would be as follows:

| | Flexed budget |
| --- | --- |
| Output<br>(production and sales) | 900 units |
| | £ |
| Sales | 90,000 |
| Raw materials | (36,000)   (36,000 m) |
| Labour | (18,000)   (4,500 hr) |
| Fixed overheads | (20,000) |
| Operating profit | 16,000 |

Putting the original budget, the flexed budget and the actual for May together, we obtain the following:

| | Original budget | Flexed budget | | Actual | |
| --- | --- | --- | --- | --- | --- |
| Output<br>(production and sales) | 1,000 units | 900 units | | 900 units | |
| | £ | £ | | £ | |
| Sales | 100,000 | 90,000 | | 92,000 | |
| Raw materials | (40,000) | (36,000) | (36,000 m) | (36,900) | (37,000 m) |
| Labour | (20,000) | (18,000) | (4,500 hr) | (17,500) | (4,375 hr) |
| Fixed overheads | (20,000) | (20,000) | | (20,700) | |
| Operating profit | 20,000 | 16,000 | | 16,900 | |

We can now make a more valid comparison between budget (using the flexed figures) and actual. We can now also see that there was a genuine labour-cost saving, even after allowing for the output shortfall.

## Sales volume variance

It may occur to you that we seem to be saying that it does not matter if there are volume shortfalls, because we just revise the budget and carry on as if nothing adverse has happened. This must be an invalid approach, because losing sales means losing profit. The first point we must pick up, therefore, is the loss of profit arising from the loss of sales of 100 units of the product.

| | |
| --- | --- |
| **Activity 7.2** | **What will be the loss of profit as a result of the sales shortfall, assuming that everything except sales volume was as planned?** |

The answer is simply the difference between the original and the flexed budget profit figures. The only difference between these two profit figures is the assumed volume of sales; everything else was the same. Thus, the figure is £4,000 (that is, £20,000 – £16,000).

You will remember from Chapter 3, where we considered the relationship between cost, volume and profit, that selling one unit less will result in one less contribution to profit. The contribution is sales revenue per unit less variable cost per unit. We can see from the original budget that the sales revenue per unit is £100 (that is, £100,000/1,000), raw material cost per unit is £40 (that is, £40,000/1,000), and labour cost per unit is £20 (that is, £20,000/1,000). Thus the contribution per unit is £40 (that is, £100 − (40 + 20)).

If, therefore, 100 units of sales are lost, £4,000 (that is 100 × £40) of contributions, and, therefore profit, are forgone. This would be an alternative means of finding the sales volume variance, instead of taking the difference between the original and the flexed budget profit figures; nevertheless once we have produced the flexed budget, it is generally easier simply to compare the two profit figures.

→ The difference between the original and the flexed budget profit figures is called the **sales volume variance**. It is an **adverse variance** because, taken alone, it has the effect of making the actual profit lower than that which was budgeted. A variance that has the effect of increasing profit above that which was budgeted
→ is known as a **favourable variance**.
→ We can, therefore, say that a **variance** is the effect of that factor on the budgeted profit. When looking at some particular aspect, such as sales volume, we assume that all other factors went according to plan. This is shown in Figure 7.3.

| **Figure 7.3** | **Relationship between the budgeted and the actual profit** |

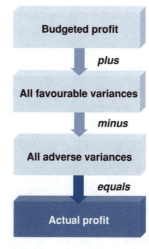

The variances represent the differences between budgeted and actual profit and can be used to reconcile the two profit figures.

| **Activity 7.3** | **What else does the senior management of Baxter Ltd need to know about the May sales volume variance?** |

It needs to know why the volume of sales fell below the budgeted figure, and so enquiries must be made to find out. Only by discovering this information will management be in any position to try to see that it does not occur again.

> **Sales volume variance**
> The difference between the profit as shown in the original budget and the profit as shown in the flexed budget for the period.

Who should be asked about this sales volume variance? The answer would probably be the sales manager. This person should know precisely why the departure from budget has occurred. This is not the same as saying that it was the sales manager's fault. The reason for the problem could easily have been that production was at fault in not having produced the budgeted quantities, meaning that there were not sufficient items to sell. What is not in doubt is that, in the first instance, it is the sales manager who should know the reason for the problem.

The budget and actual figures for Baxter Ltd for June are given in Activity 7.4 below. They will be used as the basis for a series of activities that you should work through as we look at variance analysis. Note that the business had budgeted for a higher level of output for June than it did for May.

---

**Activity 7.4**

| | Budget | | Actual | |
|---|---|---|---|---|
| Output (production and sales) | 1,100 units | | 1,150 units | |
| | £ | | £ | |
| Sales | 110,000 | | 113,500 | |
| Raw materials | (44,000) | (44,000 m) | (46,300) | (46,300 m) |
| Labour | (22,000) | (5,500 hr) | (23,200) | (5,920 hr) |
| Fixed overheads | (20,000) | | (19,300) | |
| Operating profit | 24,000 | | 24,700 | |

**Try flexing the June budget, comparing it with the original June budget, and so find the sales volume variance.**

| | Flexed budget | |
|---|---|---|
| Output (production and sales) | 1,150 units | |
| | £ | |
| Sales | 115,000 | |
| Raw materials | (46,000) | (46,000 m) |
| Labour | (23,000) | (5,750 hr) |
| Fixed overheads | (20,000) | |
| Operating profit | 26,000 | |

The sales volume variance is £2,000 (£26,000 – £24,000). This is favourable because the original budget profit was lower than the the flexed budget profit, because more sales were actually made than were budgeted.

---

Having dealt with the sales volume variance, we have picked up the profit difference caused by any variation between the budgeted and the actual volumes of sales. This means that, for the remainder of the analysis of the difference between the actual and budgeted profits, we can ignore the original budget and concentrate exclusively on the differences between the figures in the flexed budget and the actual figures.

## Sales price variance

Going back to May, it is now a matter of comparing the actual figures with those in the flexed budget so as to find out the other causes of the £3,100 (£20,000 – £16,900) profit shortfall.

Starting with the sales revenue figure, we can see that there is a difference of £2,000 (favourable) between the flexed budget and the actual figures. This can only arise from higher prices being charged than were envisaged in the original budget, because any variance arising from the volume difference has already been 'stripped out' in the flexing process. This is known as the **sales price variance.** Higher sales prices, all other things being equal, mean more profit. Hence a favourable variance.

---

**Sales price variance**
The difference between the actual sales figure for the period and the sales figure as shown in the flexed budget.

---

**Activity 7.5**  **Using the figures in Activity 7.4, what is the sales price variance for June?**

The sales price variance for June is £1,500 (adverse) (£115,000 – £113,500). Actual sales prices, on average, must have been lower than those budgeted. The actual price averaged £98.70 (that is £113,500/1,150) whereas the budgeted price was £100. Selling output at a lower price than budget must tend to reduce profit.

We shall now move on to look at the expenses.

## Materials variances

In May there was an overall or **total direct material variance** of £900 adverse (that is, £36,900 – £36,000). It is adverse because the actual material cost was higher that the budgeted one, which has an adverse effect on profit. Who should be held accountable for this variance? The answer depends on whether the difference arises from excess usage of the raw materials, in which case it is the production manager, or whether it is a higher than budgeted price per metre being paid, in which case it is the responsibility of the buying manager.

---

**Total direct material variance**
The difference between the actual direct material cost and the direct material cost as per the flexed budget (standard usage for the actual output).

---

Fortunately, we have the means available to go beyond this total variance. We can see from the figures that there was a 1,000-metre excess usage of the raw materials (that is, 37,000 m – 36,000 m). All other things being equal, this alone would have led to a profit shortfall of £1,000, since clearly the budgeted price per metre is £1. The £1,000 (adverse) variance is known as the **direct material usage variance**. Normally, this variance would be the responsibility of the production manager.

---

**Direct material usage variance**
The difference between the actual quantity of direct material used and the quantity of direct material as per the flexed budget (standard usage for the actual output). This quantity is multiplied by the standard direct material cost per unit.

---

| **Activity 7.6** | Using the figures in Activity 7.4, what was the direct materials usage variance for June? |
| --- | --- |

The direct materials usage variance for June was £300 (adverse) [(46,300 – 46,000) × £1]. It is adverse because more material was used than budgeted for an output of 11,500 units. Excess usage of material will tend to reduce profit.

The other aspect of direct materials is the **direct materials price variance**. Here, we simply take the actual cost of materials used and compare it with the cost that was allowed, given the quantity used. In May, the actual cost of direct materials used was £36,900, whereas the budgeted (or allowed) cost of the 37,000 metres was £37,000. Paying less than the budgeted price will tend to increase profit; hence a favourable variance. Thus we have a favourable variance of £100.

---

**Direct material price variance**
The difference between the actual cost of the direct material used and the direct material cost allowed (actual quantity of material used at the standard direct material cost).

---

| **Activity 7.7** | Using the figures in Activity 7.4, what was the direct materials price variance for June? |
| --- | --- |

The direct materials price variance for June was zero [(46,300 – 46,300) × £1].

As we have just seen, the total direct materials variance is the sum of the usage variance and the price variance. This is illustrated in Figure 7.4.

| Figure 7.4 | **Relationship between the total, usage and price variances of direct materials** |

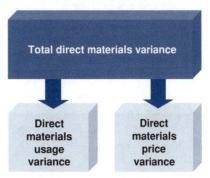

The total direct materials variance is the sum of the direct materials usage variance and the price variance, and can be analysed into those two.

## Labour variances

Direct labour variances are similar in form to those for raw materials. The **total direct labour variance** for May was £500 favourable (£18,000 – £17,500). It was favourable because £500 less was spent on labour than was budgeted, for the actual level of output achieved. Again, this information is not particularly helpful since the responsibility for the rate of pay lies primarily with the personnel manager, and so that person should be able to explain the variance. The number of hours taken to complete a particular quantity of output is, however, the responsibility of the production manager.

---

**Total direct labour variance**
The difference between the actual direct labour cost and the direct labour cost as per the flexed budget (standard direct labour hours for the actual output).

---

The **direct labour efficiency variance** compares the number of hours that would be allowed for the level of production achieved with the actual number of hours and then costs the difference at the allowed hourly rate. Thus, for May, it was $(4,500 - 4,375) \times £4 = £500$ (favourable). We know that the budgeted hourly rate is £4 because the original budget shows that 5,000 hours cost £20,000. The variance is favourable because fewer hours were used than would have been allowed for the actual level of output. Working more quickly would tend to lead to higher profit.

---

**Direct labour efficiency variance**
The difference between the actual direct labour hours worked and the number of direct labour hours as per the flexed budget (standard direct labour hours for the actual output). This figure is multiplied by the standard direct labour rate per hour.

---

| Activity 7.8 | Using the figures in Activity 7.4, what was the direct labour efficiency variance for June? |
|---|---|

The direct labour efficiency variance for June was £680 (adverse) [(5,920 – 5,750) × £4]. It is adverse because the work took longer than the budget allowed. This would tend to lead to less profit.

The **direct labour rate variance** compares the actual cost of the hours worked with the allowed cost. For 4,375 hours worked in May the allowed cost would be £17,500 (4,375 × £4). Since this is exactly the amount that was paid, there is no rate variance.

> **Direct labour rate variance**
> The difference between the actual cost of the direct labour hours worked and the direct labour cost allowed (actual direct labour hours worked at the standard labour rate).

| Activity 7.9 | Using the figures in Activity 7.4, what was the direct labour rate variance for June? |
|---|---|

The direct labour rate variance for June was £480 (favourable) [(5,920 × £4) – 23,200]. It is favourable because a lower rate was paid than the budgeted one. Paying a lower wage rate will, of itself, tend to increase profit.

## Fixed overheads variance

The remaining area is that of fixed overheads. Here the **fixed overhead spending variance** is simply the difference between the flexed budget and the actual figures. For May, this was £700 (adverse) (that is, £20,700 – £20,000). It is adverse because more overhead cost was actually incurred than was budgeted, which would tend to lead to less profit. In theory, this is the responsibility of whoever controls overheads expenditure. In practice, this tends to be a very slippery area and one which is notoriously difficult to control.

> **Fixed overhead spending variance**
> The difference between the actual fixed overhead cost and the fixed overhead cost as per the flexed (and the original) budget.

| Activity 7.10 | Using the figures in Activity 7.4, what was the fixed overhead spending variance for June? |
|---|---|

The fixed overhead spending variance for June was £700 (favourable) (£20,000 – £19,300). It was favourable because less was spent on overheads than was budgeted, tending to increase profit.

We are now in a position to reconcile the original May budget profit with the actual one, as follows:

|  |  | £ | £ |
|---|---|---:|---:|
|  | **Budgeted profit** |  | 20,000 |
| *Add* | **Favourable variances:** |  |  |
|  | Sales price variance | 2,000 |  |
|  | Direct materials price | 100 |  |
|  | Direct labour efficiency | 500 | 2,600 |
|  |  |  | 22,600 |
| *Less* | **Adverse variances:** |  |  |
|  | Sales volume | 4,000 |  |
|  | Direct material usage | 1,000 |  |
|  | Fixed overhead spending | 700 | 5,700 |
|  | **Actual profit** |  | 16,900 |

---

**Activity 7.11**

Using the figures in Activity 7.4, try reconciling the original profit figure for June with the actual June figure.

|  |  | £ | £ |
|---|---|---:|---:|
|  | **Budgeted profit** |  | 24,000 |
| *Add* | **Favourable variances** |  |  |
|  | Sales volume | 2,000 |  |
|  | Fixed overhead spending | 700 |  |
|  | Direct labour rate | 480 |  |
|  |  |  | 3,180 |
|  |  |  | 27,180 |
| *Less* | **Adverse variances** |  |  |
|  | Sales price | 1,500 |  |
|  | Direct material usage | 300 |  |
|  | Direct labour efficiency | 680 |  |
|  |  |  | 2,480 |
|  | **Actual profit** |  | 24,700 |

---

**Activity 7.12**

The following are the budgeted and actual profit and loss accounts for Baxter Ltd for the month of July:

|  | Budget |  | Actual |  |
|---|---|---|---|---|
| Output | 1,000 units |  | 1,050 units |  |
| (production and sales) |  |  |  |  |
|  | £ |  | £ |  |
| Sales | 100,000 |  | 104,300 |  |
| Raw materials | (40,000) | (40,000 m) | (41,200) | (40,500 m) |
| Labour | (20,000) | (5,000 hr) | (21,300) | (5,200 hr) |
| Fixed overheads | (20,000) |  | (19,400) |  |
| Operating profit | 20,000 |  | 22,400 |  |

Produce a reconciliation of the budgeted and actual operating profit, going into as much detail as possible with the variance analysis.

The original, flexed and actual budgets are as follows:

| | Original 1,000 units | Flexed 1,050 units | Actual 1,050 units |
|---|---|---|---|
| Output (production and sales) | | | |
| | £ | £ | £ |
| Sales | 100,000 | 105,000 | 104,300 |
| Raw materials | (40,000) | (42,000) | (41,200) |
| Labour | (20,000) | (21,000) | (21,300) |
| Fixed overheads | (20,000) | (20,000) | (19,400) |
| Operating profit | 20,000 | 22,000 | 22,400 |

Reconciliation of the budgeted and actual operating profits for June is as follows:

| | £ | £ |
|---|---|---|
| Budgeted profit | | 20,000 |
| *Add* **Favourable variances** | | |
| Sales volume (22,000 – 20,000) | 2,000 | |
| Direct material usage {[(1,050 × 40) – 40,500] × £1} | 1,500 | |
| Direct labour efficiency {[(1,050 × 5) – 5,200] × £4} | 200 | |
| Fixed overhead spending (20,000 – 19,400) | 600 | 4,300 |
| | | 24,300 |
| *Less* **Adverse variances** | | |
| Sales price variance (104,300 – 105,000) | 700 | |
| Direct materials price [(40,500 × £1) – 41,200] | 700 | |
| Direct labour rate [(5,200 × £4) – 21,300] | 500 | 1,900 |
| Actual profit | | 22,400 |

➡ Exhibit 7.1 gives some indication of the extent of use of **variance analysis in practice**.

---

**Exhibit 7.1**  **Accounting for control in practice**

A 1993 survey of UK manufacturing businesses showed variance analysis to be very widely used: 76 per cent of all the survey respondents used it, with 83 per cent of larger businesses using it. Interestingly, 11 per cent of businesses had abandoned using variance analysis during the ten years preceding the date of the survey. Does this imply that there is a significant shift away from its use?

The variances that are widely used, and regarded as important, are those that we have looked at in some detail in this chapter.

*Source:* Taken from information appearing in Drury, Braund, Osborne and Tayles (see reference (1) at the end of the chapter).

---

# Standard quantities and costs

The budget is a financial plan for a future period of time. It is built up from stand-
➡ ards. **Standard quantities and costs** (or revenues) are those planned for individual units of input or output. Thus, standards are the building blocks of the budget.

We can say about Baxter Ltd's operations that:

- The standard selling price is £100 per unit of output.
- The standard raw material cost is £4 per unit of output.
- The standard raw material usage is 4 metres per unit of output.
- The standard raw material price is £1 per metre (that is, per unit of input).
- The standard labour cost is £20 per unit of output.
- The standard labour time is 5 hours per unit of output.
- The standard labour rate is £4 per hour (that is, per unit of input).

The standards, like the budgets to which they are linked, represent targets and, therefore, yardsticks by which actual performance is measured. They are derived from experience of what is a reasonable quantity of input (for labour time and materials usage) and from assessments of the market for the product (standard selling price) and the market for the inputs (labour rate and materials price). These should be subject to frequent review and, where necessary, revision. It is vital, if they are to be used as part of the control process, that they represent realistic targets.

Calculation of most variances is, in effect, based on standards. For example, the materials usage variance is the difference between the standard materials usage for the level of output and the actual usage, costed at the standard materials price.

Standards can have uses other than in the context of budgetary control. The existence of a set of information of costs, usages, selling prices and so on, that are known to be broadly realistic, provides decision makers with a ready set of information for decision making and income measurement purposes.

Exhibit 7.2 provides some information on the use of standard costs in practice.

| Exhibit 7.2 | **Standard costing in practice** |

The Drury, Braund, Osborne and Tayles survey from 1993 showed that the respondent businesses found standard costs important to them for the following purposes:

|  | Percentage of respondents |
| --- | --- |
| Cost control and performance evaluation | 72 |
| Valuing stock and work in progress | 80 |
| Deducing costs for decision-making purposes | 62 |
| To help in constructing budgets | 69 |

Thus standards are seen as very important in the context of the subject of this chapter (cost control and performance evaluation); but they also seem to be widely used for other financial and management accounting purposes.

The conventional wisdom on the level of standards is that they should be demanding but achievable. Thus if the standard direct-labour time for some activity is five minutes, this should be capable of being achieved, yet require staff to be working efficiently to achieve it. The survey showed that 44 per cent of respondents deliberately set standards of this type; 46 per cent, however, set standards based on past performance. Perhaps this was because the businesses' managements felt that past performance represents an achievable (obviously) yet demanding level of achievement. Only 5 per cent of respondents set standards at a level that could be achieved if everything went perfectly all of the time. Many people believe that such standards are not helpful because they *do* not represent a realistic target in a world where things *do* go wrong from time to time.

Standards are formally reviewed annually or more frequently by 91 per cent of the respondent businesses. This would amount to considering whether the existing standards are set at an appropriate level and amending them where necessary.

*Source*: Drury, Braund, Osborne, and Tayles (see reference (1) at the end of chapter).

## Labour cost standards and the learning-curve effect

Where a particular activity undertaken by direct workers has been unchanged in nature for some time, and the workers are experienced at performing it, normally an established standard labour time will be unchanged over time. Where a new activity is introduced, or new people are involved with performing an existing task, a **learning-curve** effect will normally occur. This is shown in Figure 7.5.

The first unit of output takes a long time to produce. As experience is gained, the person takes less time to produce each unit of output. The rate of reduction in the time taken will, however, decrease as experience is gained. Thus, for example, the reduction in time taken between the first and second unit produced will be much bigger than the reduction between the ninth and the tenth. Eventually, the rate of reduction in time taken will reduce to zero so that each unit will take as long as the preceding one. At this point, the point where the curve in Figure 7.5 becomes horizontal (the bottom right of the graph), the learning-curve effect will have been eliminated and a steady, long-term standard time for the activity will have been established.

The learning-curve effect seems to have little to do with whether workers are skilled or unskilled; if they are unfamiliar with the task, the learning-curve effect

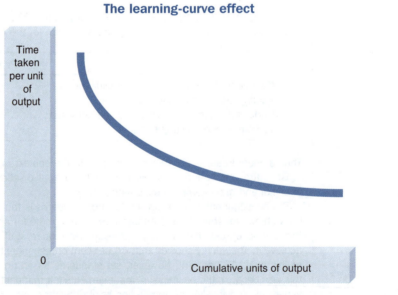

**Figure 7.5**

**The learning-curve effect**

Time taken per unit of output

0

Cumulative units of output

Each time a particular task is performed, people become quicker at it. This learning-curve effect becomes less and less significant until, after the task has been performed a number of times, no further learning occurs.

will occur. Practical experience shows that learning curves show remarkable regularity and, therefore, predictability from one activity to the next.

Clearly, the learning-curve effect must be taken into account when setting standards, and when interpreting any adverse labour efficiency variances, where a new process and/or new personnel are involved.

## Reasons for adverse variances

One reason why variances might occur is that the standards against which performance is being measured are not reasonable targets. This is certainly not to say that the immediate reaction to an adverse variance should be that the standard is unreasonably harsh. On the other hand, standards that are not achievable are useless.

| *Activity 7.13* | The variances that we have considered are:

- Sales volume
- Sales price
- Direct materials usage
- Direct materials price
- Direct labour efficiency
- Direct labour rate
- Fixed overhead spending.

Ignoring the possibility that standards may be unreasonable, jot down any ideas which occur to you as possible practical reasons for adverse variances in each case.

---

The reasons that we thought of included the following:

Sales volume
- Poor performance by sales personnel.
- Deterioration in market conditions between the setting of the budget and the actual event.
- Lack of stock to sell as a result of some production problem.

Sales price
- Poor performance by sales personnel.
- Deterioration in market conditions between the setting of the budget and the actual event.

Direct materials usage
- Poor performance by production department staff leading to high rates of scrap.
- Substandard materials leading to high rates of scrap.
- Faulty machinery causing high rates of scrap.

Direct materials price
- Poor performance by buying department staff.
- Change in market conditions between setting the standard and the actual event.

Labour efficiency
- Poor supervision.
- A low-skilled grade of worker taking longer to do the work than was envisaged for the correct skill grade.

- Low-grade materials leading to high levels of scrap and wasted labour time.
- Problems with machinery leading to labour time being wasted.
- Dislocation of material supply leading to workers being unable to proceed with production.

Labour rate
- Poor performance by the personnel function.
- Using a higher grade of worker than was planned.
- Change in labour-market conditions between the setting of the standard and the actual event.

Fixed overheads
- Poor supervision of overheads.
- General increase in costs of overheads not taken into account in the budget.

It is possible to calculate a very large number of variances, given the range of operations found in practice. We have considered just the more basic of them. For example, in the examples and activities above, we have ignored the possible existence of variable overheads, and we have done this simply to restrict the amount of detailed explantion. All variance analysis is, however, based on similar principles.

Though we have tended to use the example of a manufacturing business to explain variance analysis, this should not be taken to imply that the technique is not equally applicable and useful in a service-sector business.

## Non-operating profit variances

There are many areas of business that have a budget but where a failure to meet the budget does not have a direct effect on profit. Frequently, however, it has an indirect effect on profit, and sometimes a profound effect. For example, the cash budget sets out the planned receipts, payments and resultant cash balance for the period. If the person responsible for the cash budget gets things wrong, or is forced to make unplanned expenditures, this could lead to unplanned cash shortages and accompanying costs. These costs might be limited to lost interest on possible investments, which could otherwise have been made, or to the need to pay overdraft interest. If the cash shortage cannot be covered by some form of borrowing, the consequences could be more profound, such as the loss of profits on business that was not able to be undertaken because of the lack of funds.

It is clearly necessary that control is exercised over areas such as cash management as well as over areas such as production and sales in order to avoid adverse ➔ **non-operating profit variances**.

## Investigating variances

It is unreasonable to expect budget targets to be met precisely each month. Whatever the reason for a variance, finding it will take time, and time is costly. ➔ Given that small variances are almost inevitable and that **investigating variances** can be expensive, management needs to establish a policy on which variances to investigate and which to accept. For example, for Baxter Ltd (see Example 7.1) the budgeted usage of materials during May was 40,000 metres at a cost of £1 per metre. Suppose that actual production had been the same as the budgeted quantity of output, but that 40,005 metres of material, costing £1 per metre, had actually been used. Would this adverse variance of £5 be investigated? Probably not. What, though, if the variance were £50 or £500 or £5,000?

| Activity 7.14 | **What broad approach do you feel should be taken on whether to spend money investigating a particular variance?** |
|---|---|

The general approach to this policy must be concerned with cost and benefit. What benefit there is likely to be from knowing why a variance exists needs to be balanced against the cost of obtaining that knowledge. The issue of balancing the benefit of having information with the cost of having it was discussed in Chapter 1.

Knowing the reason for a variance can only have value when it might provide management with the means to bring things back under control, so that future targets can be met. It should be borne in mind here that variances should normally either be zero or very close to zero. This is to say that achieving targets, give or take small variances, should be normal.

Broadly, we suggest the following:

■ Significant adverse variances should be investigated because continuation of the fault that they represent could be very costly. Management must decide what 'significant' means. A certain amount of science (in the form of statistical models) can be brought to bear in making this decision, but ultimately it must be a matter of judgement as to what is significant. Perhaps a variance of 5 per cent from the budgeted figure would be deemed to be significant.

■ Significant *favourable* variances should probably also be investigated. Though such variances would not cause such immediate concern as adverse ones, they still represent things not going according to plan. If actual performance is significantly better than target, it may well mean that the target is unrealistically low.

■ Insignificant variances, though not triggering immediate investigation, should be kept under review. For each aspect of operations, the cumulative sum of variances over a series of control periods should be zero, with small adverse variances in some periods being compensated for by small favourable ones in others. This should be the case with variances that are caused by chance factors, which will not necessarily repeat themselves.

Where a variance is caused by a more systematic factor that will repeat itself, the cumulative sum of the periodic variances will not be zero but an increasing figure. Where the increasing figure represents a set of adverse variances, it may well be worth investigating the situation, even though the individual variances might be insignificant. Even where the direction of the cumulative total points to favourable variances, investigation may still be considered to be valuable.

To illustrate this last point, let us consider Example 7.2.

| Example 7.2 | A business finds that the variances for materials usage for a special plastic, used in the manufacture of a product codenamed XLS 234, since the product was first manufactured at the beginning of the year, have been as follows: |

|  | £ |  | £ |
| --- | --- | --- | --- |
| January | 25 (adverse) | July | 20 (adverse) |
| February | 15 (favourable) | August | 15 (favourable) |
| March | 5 (favourable) | September | 23 (adverse) |
| April | 20 (adverse) | October | 15 (favourable) |
| May | 22 (adverse) | November | 5 (favourable) |
| June | 8 (favourable) | December | 26 (adverse) |

The average cost of XLS 234 used each month is about £1,200. Management believes that none of these variances, taken alone, is significant given the total cost of plastic used each month. The question is, are they significant when taken together? If we add them together, taking account of the signs, we find that we have a net adverse variance for the year of £73. Of itself this, too, is probably not significant, but we should expect the cumulative total to be close to zero, were the variances random. We might feel that a pattern is developing and, given long enough, a net adverse variance of significant size might build up.

Investigating the plastic usage might be worth doing. (We should note that 12 periods are probably not enough to reach a statistically sound conclusion on whether the variances are random or not, but it provides an illustration of the point.)

Exhibit 7.3 indicates the attitude of businesses to investigating variances in practice.

| Exhibit 7.3 | **Investigating variances in practice** |

The 1993 survey by Drury, Braund, Osbourne and Tayles showed that a very high proportion of respondent businesses used no formal approach to investigating variances but based a decision as to whether to investigate a particular variance on managerial judgement. Quite a lot of businesses seemed to operate systems where variances were investigated when they exceeded a specific monetary amount. Relatively few businesses were found to operate systems where variances exceeding a predetermined percentage of the standard were followed up.

*Source*: Taken from information appearing in Drury, Braund, Osborne, and Tayles (see reference (1) at the end of chapter).

## Compensating variances

➡ There is superficial appeal in the idea of **compensating variances**, that is, the act of trading off linked favourable and adverse variances against each other without further consideration. For example, a sales manager believes that she could sell more of a product if prices were lowered and that this would feed through to increased net operating profit. This would lead to a favourable sales volume variance, but also an adverse sales price variance. On the face of it, provided the former is at least equal to the latter, all would be well.

| Activity 7.15 | What possible reason is there why the sales manager mentioned above should not go ahead with the price reduction? |
|---|---|

The change in policy will have ramifications for other areas of the business, including the following:

- The need for more goods to be available to sell. Production may not be able to supply them, and it may not be possible to buy the stock in from elsewhere.
- Increased sales will involve an increased need for finance to pay for increased production.

Thus, trading off variances is not automatically acceptable without a more far-reaching consultation and revision of plans.

## Necessary conditions for effective budgetary control

➡ It is obvious from what we have seen of **budgetary control** that if it is to be successful, a system, or a set of routines, must be established to enable the potential benefits to be gained.

| Activity 7.16 | Jot down the points that you think would need to be included in any system that will enable control through budgets to be effective. (We have not specifically covered these points, but your common sense, and perhaps your background knowledge, should enable you to think of a few points.) |
|---|---|

There is no unequivocally correct answer to this activity. However, most businesses that operate successful budgetary control systems tend to show some common factors. These include:

- A serious attitude taken to the system by all levels of management, right from the very top.
- Clear demarcation between areas of managerial responsibility, so that accountability can more easily be ascribed for any area that seems to be going out of control.
- Budget targets being reasonable, so that they represent a rigorous yet achievable target. This may be promoted by managers being involved in setting their own targets. It is argued that this can promote the managers' commitment and motivation.
- Established data collection, analysis and dissemination routines that take the actual results and the budget figures, then go on to calculate and report the variances.
- Reports aimed at individual managers, rather than general-purpose documents. This avoids managers having to wade through reams of reports to find the part that is relevant to them.
- Fairly short reporting periods – typically a month – so that things cannot go too far wrong before they are picked up.
- Variance reports being produced and disseminated shortly after the end of the relevant reporting period.
- Action being taken to get operations back under control if they are shown to be out of control.

# Limitations of the traditional approach to control through variances and standards

Budgetary control of the type that we have reviewed in this chapter has obvious appeal. As we have seen through Exhibit 7.1, it is widely used in practice, which suggests that managers believe it has value. It is somewhat limited at times, however. Some of its limitations are:

- Vast areas of most business and commercial activities simply do not have the same direct relationship between inputs and outputs as is the case with, say, level of output and the amount of raw materials used. Many of the expenses of the modern business are in areas such as training and advertising, where the expense is discretionary and not linked to the level of output in a direct way.
- Standards can quickly become out of date as a result of both technological change and price changes. This does not pose insuperable problems, but it does require that the potential problem is systematically addressed. Standards that are unrealistic are, at best, useless. At worst, they could have adverse effects on performance. A buyer who knows that it is impossible to meet price targets, because of price rises, has a reduced incentive to minimise costs.
- Sometimes factors that are outside the control of the manager concerned can affect the calculation of the variance for which that manager is held accountable. This is likely to have an adverse effect on the manager's performance. The situation can often be overcome by a more considered approach to the calculation of the variance, resulting in the factors that are controllable by the manager being separated from those that are not.
- In practice, creating clear lines of demarcation between the areas of responsibility of various managers may be difficult. Thus, one of the prerequisites of good budgetary control is lost.

# Behavioural aspects of budgetary control

Budgets, perhaps more than any other accounting statement, are prepared with the objective of affecting the attitudes and behaviour of managers. The point was made in Chapter 6 that budgets are intended to motivate managers, and research evidence generally shows this to be true. More specifically, the research shows:

- The existence of budgets generally tends to improve performance.
- Demanding, yet achievable, budget targets tend to motivate better than less demanding targets. It seems that setting the most demanding targets that will be accepted by managers is a very effective way to motivate them.
- Unrealistically demanding targets tend to have an adverse effect on managers' performance.
- The participation of managers in setting their targets tends to improve motivation and performance. This is probably because those managers feel a sense of commitment to the targets and a moral obligation to achieve them.

It has been suggested that allowing managers to set their own targets will lead to slack being introduced, so making achievement of the target that much easier. On the other hand, in a effort to impress, a manager may select a target that is not really achievable. These points imply that care must be taken in the extent to which managers have unfettered choice of their own targets.

There has been a great deal of literature published on the way in which managers use information generated by the budgeting system and the impact of its use on the attitudes and behaviour of subordinates. A pioneering study by Hopwood (see reference (2) at the end of the chapter) examined the way in which managers working within a manufacturing environment used budget information to evaluate the performance of subordinates. He argued that three distinct styles of management could be observed. These are:

- *Budget-constrained style.* This management style focuses rigidly on the ability of subordinates to meet the budget. Other factors relating to the performance of subordinates are not given serious consideration.
- *Profit-conscious style.* This management style uses budget information in a more flexible way and often in conjunction with other data. The main focus is on the ability of each subordinate to improve the long-term effectiveness of the area for which he/she has responsibility.
- *Non-accounting style.* In this case, budget information plays no significant role in the evaluation of a subordinate's performance.

---

**Activity 7.17**

How might a manager respond to budget information that indicates a subordinate has not met the budget targets for the period, assuming the manager to operate with:

(a) A budget-constrained style?
(b) A profit-conscious style?
(c) A non-accounting style?

---

(a) A manager adopting a budget-constrained style is likely to take the budget information very seriously. This may result in criticism of the subordinate and, perhaps, some form of punishment.
(b) A manager adopting a profit-conscious style is likely to take a broader view when examining the budget information and so will take other factors into consideration (for example, factors that could not have been anticipated at the time of preparing the budgets), before deciding whether criticism or punishment is justified.
(c) A manager adopting a non-accounting style will regard the failure to meet the budget as being relatively unimportant and so no action is likely to be taken.

---

Hopwood found that subordinates working for a manager adopting a budget-constrained style suffered higher levels of job-related stress and had poorer working relationships with both their colleagues and their manager than those subordinates whose manager adopted one of the other two styles. He also found that the subordinates of a budget-constrained style of manager were more likely to manipulate the budget figures or to take undesirable actions to ensure the budgets were met.

Although these findings are interesting, subsequent studies have cast doubt on their universal applicability. Later studies confirm that human attitudes and behaviour are complex and can vary according to the particular situation. For example, it has been found that the impact of different management styles on such factors as job-related stress and the manipulation of budget figures is likely to vary according to such factors as the level of independence enjoyed by the subordinates and the level of uncertainty associated with the tasks to be undertaken.

It seems that where there is a high level of interdependence between business divisions, subordinate managers are more likely to feel that they have less control over their performance. This is because the performance of staff in other divisions could be an important influence on the final outcome. In such a situation, rigid application of the budget could be viewed as being unfair and may lead to undesirable behaviour. However, where managers have a high degree of independence, the application of budgets as a measure of performance is likely to be more acceptable. In this case, the managers are likely to feel that the final outcome is much less dependent on the performance of others.

Later studies have also shown that where a subordinate is undertaking a task that has a high degree of uncertainty concerning the outcome (for example developing a new product for the market), budget targets are unlikely to be an adequate measure of performance. In such a situation, other factors and measures should be taken into account in order to derive a more complete assessment of performance. However, where a task has a low degree of uncertainty concerning the outcome (for example, producing a standard product using standard equipment and an experienced workforce) budget measures may be regarded as more reliable indicators of performance (see reference (3) at the end of the chapter). Thus, it appears that a budget-constrained style is more likely to work where subordinates enjoy a fair amount of independence and where the tasks set have a low level of uncertainty concerning their outcomes.

Where a manager fails to meet a budget, care must be taken by that manager's senior in dealing with the failure. A harsh, critical approach may demotivate the manager. Adverse variances may imply that the manager needs help from the senior.

The existence of budgets gives senior managers a ready means to assess the performance of their subordinates. Where promotion or bonuses depend on the absence of variances, senior management must be very cautious.

➡ Exhibit 7.4 gives some indication of the effects of the **behavioural aspects of budgetary control** in practice.

---

| Exhibit 7.4 | **Behavioural aspects of budgetary control in practice** |
|---|---|

The 1993 survey by Drury, Braund, Osborne and Tayles indicates that there is a large degree of participation in setting budgets by those who will be expected to perform to the budget standard (the budget holders). It also indicates that senior management has greater influence in setting the targets than the budget holders.

Where there is a conflict between the cost estimates submitted by the budget holders and their managers, in 40 per cent of respondent businesses the senior manager's view would prevail without negotiation, but in nearly 60 per cent of cases there would be reduction, but it would be negotiated between the budget holder and the senior manager.

The general philosophy of the respondent businesses, regarding budget holders influencing the setting of their own budgets, is, in 23 per cent of cases, that they should not have too much influence since they will seek to obtain easy budgets if they do. The opposite view was taken by 69 per cent of respondents.

Almost half (46 per cent) of respondent businesses thought that senior managers should judge junior managers mainly on their ability to achieve the budget; 40 per cent thought otherwise.

*Source*: Taken from information appearing in Drury, Braund, Osborne and Tayles (see reference (1) at the end of chapter).

### ? Self-assessment question 7.1

Toscanini Ltd makes a standard product, which is budgeted to sell at £4.00 per unit, in a competitive market. It is made by taking a budgeted 0.4 kg of material, budgeted to cost £2.40 per kg, and working on it by hand by an employee, paid a budgeted £4.00 per hour, for a budgeted 12 minutes. Monthly fixed overheads are budgeted at £4,800. The output for May was budgeted at 4,000 units.

The actual results for May were as follows:

|  | £ |
|---|---|
| Sales (3,500 units) | 13,820 |
| Materials (1,425 kg) | (3,420) |
| Labour (690 hours) | (2,690) |
| Fixed overheads | (4,900) |
| Actual operating profit | 2,810 |

No stocks of any description existed at the beginning and end of the month.

**Required:**
(a) Deduce the budgeted profit for May and reconcile it with the actual profit in as much detail as the information provided will allow.
(b) State which manager should be held accountable, in the first instance, for each variance calculated.
(c) Assuming that the standards were all well set in terms of labour times and rates and materials usage and prices, suggest at least one feasible reason for each of the variances which you identified in (a), given what you know about the company's performance for May.
(d) If it were discovered that the actual world-market demand for the company's product was 10 per cent lower than estimated when the May budget was set, state how and why the variances that you identified in (a) could be revised to provide information which would be potentially more useful.

## Summary

We began this chapter by reviewing how budgeting itself can be a form of feed-forward control, while budgetary control is a form of feedback control. Next we considered how, by flexing the budget, it is possible to make direct and valid comparisons between budget and actual results and so be in a position to exercise control over operations. We considered how variances reconcile the budgeted profit with the actual profit, because each variance explains any divergence, between budgeted and actual profit, that was caused by the particular factor under review. We considered possible reasons for adverse variances and some general guidelines for the circumstances under which resources should be devoted to finding the precise reason for each adverse variance.

Next we looked at the type of infrastructure that a business needs to enable an effective system of budgetary control to exist. Lastly, we reviewed some of the behavioural issues concerned with trying to exercise control through budgets and variances.

 **Key terms**

| | |
|---|---|
| Flexible budget   p. 159 | Standard quantities and costs   p. 170 |
| Feedback control   p. 159 | Learning curve   p. 172 |
| Feedforward control   p. 160 | Non-operating profit variances   p. 174 |
| Flex the budget   p. 161 | Investigating variances   p. 174 |
| Adverse variance   p. 163 | Compensating variances   p. 176 |
| Favourable variance   p. 163 | Budgetary control   p. 177 |
| Variance   p. 163 | Behavioural aspects of budgetary |
| Variance analysis   p. 170 | control   p. 180 |

## Further reading

If you would like to explore the topics covered in this chapter in more depth, we recommend the following books:

**Management Accounting**, *Atkinson, A., Banker, R., Kaplan, R.* and *Mark Young, S.*, 3rd edn, Prentice Hall, 2001, chapter 12.

**Management and Cost Accounting**, *Drury, C.*, 5th edn, Thomson Learning, 2000, chapters 16, 18 and 19.

**Cost Accounting: A managerial emphasis**, *Horngren, C., Foster, G.* and *Datar, S.*, 10th edn, Prentice Hall International, 2000, chapters 7 and 8.

**Cost and Management Accounting**, *Williamson, D.*, Prentice Hall International, 1996, chapter 15.

## References

1. **A Survey of Managment Accounting Practices in UK Manufacturing Companies**, *Drury, C., Braund, S., Osborne, P.* and *Tayles, M.*, Chartered Association of Certified Accountants, 1993.
2. 'An empirical study of the role of accounting data in performance evaluation', *Hopwood, A. G.*, **Empirical Research in Accounting**, a supplement to the Journal of Accounting Research, 1972, pp. 156–82.
3. **Accounting for Management Control**, *Emmanual, C., Otley, D.* and *Merchant, K.*, 2nd edn, Chapman & Hall, 1990.

## ? REVIEW QUESTIONS

**7.1** Explain what is meant by feedforward control and distinguish it from feedback control.

**7.2** What is meant by a variance?

**7.3** What is the point in flexing the budget in the context of variance analysis? Does flexing imply that differences between budget and actual in the volume of output are ignored in variance analysis?

**7.4** Should all variances be investigated to find their cause? Explain your answer.

## ? EXERCISES

Exercises 7.4–7.8 are more advanced than 7.1–7.3. Those with coloured numbers have answers at the back of the book.

**7.1** You have recently overheard the following remarks:

(a) 'A favourable direct-labour rate variance can only be caused by staff working more efficiently than budgeted.'
(b) 'Selling more units than budgeted, because the units were sold at less than standard price, automatically leads to a favourable sales volume variance.'
(c) 'Using below standard materials will tend to lead to adverse materials usage variances but cannot affect labour variances.'
(d) 'Higher than budgeted sales could not possibly affect the labour rate variance.'
(e) 'An adverse sales price variance can only arise from selling a product at less than standard price.'

**Required:**
Critically assess these remarks, explaining any technical terms.

**7.2** Pilot Ltd makes a standard product, which is budgeted to sell at £5.00 per unit. It is made by taking a budgeted 0.5 kg of material, budgeted to cost £3.00 per kg, and working on it by hand by an employee, paid a budgeted £5.00 per hour, for a budgeted 15 minutes. Monthly fixed overheads are budgeted at £6,000. The output for March was budgeted at 5,000 units.

The actual results for March were as follows:

|  | £ |
|---|---|
| Sales (5,400 units) | 26,460 |
| Materials (2,830 kg) | (8,770) |
| Labour (1,300 hours) | (6,885) |
| Fixed overheads | (6,350) |
| Actual operating profit | 4,455 |

No stocks existed at the start or end of March.

**Required:**

(a) Deduce the budgeted profit for March and reconcile it with the actual profit in as much detail as the information provided will allow.

(b) State which manager should be held accountable, in the first instance, for each variance calculated.

**7.3** Antonio plc makes product X, the standard costs of which are:

|  | £ |
|---|---|
| Sales revenue | 31 |
| Direct labour (2 hours) | (11) |
| Direct materials (1 kg) | (10) |
| Fixed overheads | (3) |
| Standard profit | 7 |

The budgeted output for March was 1,000 units of product X; the actual output was 1,100 units, which was sold for £34,950. There were no stocks at the start or end of March.

The actual production costs were:

|  | £ |
|---|---|
| Direct labour (2,150 hours) | 12,210 |
| Direct materials (1,170 kg) | 11,630 |
| Fixed overheads | 3,200 |

**Required:**

Calculate the variances for March as fully as you are able from the available information, and use them to reconcile the budgeted and actual profit figures.

**7.4** You have recently overheard the following remarks:

(a) 'When calculating variances, we in effect ignore differences of volume of output, between original budget and actual, by flexing the budget. If there were a volume difference, it is water under the bridge by the time that the variances come to be calculated.'

(b) 'It is very valuable to calculate variances because they will tell you what went wrong.'

(c) 'All variances should be investigated to find their cause.'

(d) 'Research evidence shows that the more demanding the target, the more motivated the manager.'

(e) 'Most businesses do not have feedforward controls of any type, just feedback controls through budgets.'

**Required:**

Critically assess these remarks, explaining any technical terms.

**7.5** Bradley-Allen Ltd makes one standard product. Its budgeted operating statement for May is as follows:

| | | £ | £ |
|---|---|---|---|
| Sales: | 800 units | | 64,000 |
| Direct materials: | Type A | 12,000 | |
| | Type B | 16,000 | |
| Direct labour: | Skilled | 4,000 | |
| | Unskilled | 10,000 | |
| Overheads: | (All fixed) | 12,000 | |
| | | | 54,000 |
| Budgeted operating profit | | | 10,000 |

The standard costs were as follows:

- Direct materials: Type A £50/kg
  Type B £20/m
- Direct labour: Skilled £5/hour
  Unskilled £4/hour

During May, the following occurred:

(i)   950 units were sold for a total of £73,000.
(ii)  310 kilos (costing £15,200) of type A material were used in production.
(iii) 920 metres (costing £18,900) of type B material were used in production.
(iv)  Skilled workers were paid £4,628 for 890 hours.
(v)   Unskilled workers were paid £11,275 for 2,750 hours.
(vi)  Fixed overheads cost £11,960.

There was no stock of finished production or of work in progress at either end of May.

**Required:**

(a) Prepare a statement that reconciles the budgeted to the actual profit of the company for May. Your statement should analyse the difference between the two profit figures in as much detail as you are able.
(b) Explain how the statement in (a) might be helpful to managers.

7.6 Mowbray Ltd makes and sells one product, the standard costs of which are as follows:

| | £ |
|---|---|
| Direct materials (3 kg at £2.50/kg) | 7.50 |
| Direct labour: (30 minutes at £4.50/hr) | 2.25 |
| Fixed overheads | 3.60 |
| | 13.35 |
| Selling price | 20.00 |
| Standard profit margin | 6.65 |

The planned monthly production and sales are 1,200 units.
   The actual results for May were as follows:

| | | £ | |
|---|---|---|---|
| | Sales | 18,000 | |
| Less | Direct materials | (7,400) | (2,800 kg) |
| | Direct labour | (2,300) | (510 hr) |
| | Fixed overheads | (4,100) | |
| | Operating profit | 4,200 | |

There were no stocks at the start or end of May. As a result of poor sales demand during May, the company reduced the price of all sales by 10 per cent.

**Required:**
Calculate the budgeted profit for May and reconcile it to the actual profit through variances, going into as much detail as possible from the information available.

**7.7** Varne Chemprocessors is a business that specialises in plastics. It uses a standard costing system to monitor and report its purchases and usage of materials. During the most recent month, accounting period 6, the purchase and usage of chemical UK 194 were as follows:

> Purchases/usage: 28,100 litres
> Total price: £51,704

Because of fire risk and the danger to health, no stocks are held by the business.

UK194 is used solely in the manufacture of a product called Varnelyne. The standard cost specification shows that, for the production of 5,000 litres of Varnelyne, 200 litres of UK194 are needed at a total standard cost of £392. During period 6, 637,500 litres of Varnelyne were produced.

**Required:**
(a) Calculate the purchase price and usage variances for UK 194 for period 6.
(b) The following comment was made by the production manager:

> I knew at the beginning of period 6 that UK194 would be cheaper than the standard cost specification, so I used rather more of it than normal; this saved £4,900 on other chemicals.

> What changes do you need to make in your analysis for (a) as a result of this comment?

(c) Calculate, for each material below, the cumulative variances and comment briefly on the results.

| Variances: periods 1–6 | | |
|---|---|---|
| Period | UK500 | UK800 |
| | £ | £ |
| 1 | 301 F | 298 F |
| 2 | 251 A | 203 F |
| 3 | 102 F | 52 A |
| 4 | 202 A | 98 A |
| 5 | 153 F | 150 A |
| 6 | 103 A | 201 A |

where F = cost saving and A = cost overrun.

**7.8** Brive plc has the following standards for its only product:

> Selling price: £110/unit
> Direct labour: 2 hours at £5.25/hour
> Direct material: 3 kg at £14.00 kg
> Fixed overheads: £27.00, based on a budgeted output of 800 units/month

During May, there was an actual output of 850 units and the operating statement for the month was as follows:

|  | £ |
|---|---|
| Sales | 92,930 |
| Direct labour (1,780 hours) | (9,665) |
| Direct materials (2,410 kg) | (33,258) |
| Fixed overheads | (21,365) |
| Operating profit | 28,642 |

There was no stock of any description at the beginning and end of May.

**Required:**
Prepare the original budget and a budget flexed to the actual volume. Use these to compare the budgeted and actual profits of the company for the month, going into as much detail with your analysis as the information given will allow.

## CHAPTER 8

# Making capital investment decisions

## Introduction

In this chapter we shall look at how businesses can make decisions involving investments in new plant, machinery, buildings and similar long-term assets. The general principles that we shall consider can equally well be applied to investments in any long-term asset, including the shares of companies, irrespective of whether the investment is being considered by a business or by a private individual. We shall also look at the research evidence relating to the use of the various appraisal techniques in practice. We shall see that there are important differences between the theoretical appeal of particular techniques and their popularity in practice. We shall also consider the problems of risk and uncertainty and examine various ways in which risk can be incorporated into capital investment appraisal.

Once a decision has been made to implement a capital investment proposal, proper review and control procedures must be in place. We shall discuss the ways in which managers can oversee capital investment projects and how control may be exercised throughout the life of the project.

**OBJECTIVES**  When you have completed this chapter you should be able to:

■ Explain the nature and importance of investment decision making.
■ Identify and discuss the four main investment-appraisal methods used in practice.
■ Discuss the strengths and weaknesses of various techniques for dealing with risk in investment appraisal.
■ Explain the methods used to review and control capital expenditure projects.

## The nature of investment decisions

The essential feature of investment decisions is **time**. Investment involves making an outlay of something of economic value, usually cash, at one point in time that is expected to yield economic benefits to the investor at some other point in time. Usually, the outlay precedes the benefits. Also, the outlay is typically a single large amount and the benefits arrive in a stream of smaller amounts over a fairly protracted period.

Investment decisions tend to be of crucial importance to the business because:

- *Large amounts of resources are often involved.* Many investments made by a business involve committing a significant proportion of its total resources. If the wrong decision is made, the effects on the business could be significant, if not catastrophic.
- *It is often difficult and/or expensive to 'bail out' of an investment once it has been undertaken.* It is often the case that investments made by a business are specific to its needs. For example, a business may have premises built that are designed to provide its particular service. This may make the premises of much less value to other potential users with different needs. If the business finds, after having made the investment, that the service is not selling as well as expected, the only course of action might be to close down the activity and sell the premises at a significant loss.

---

**Activity 8.1**

When managers are making decisions involving capital investments, what should their decisions seek to achieve?

---

Investment decisions must be consistent with the objectives of the business. For a private-sector business, maximising shareholder wealth is usually assumed to be the key objective.

---

# Methods of investment appraisal

Given the importance of investment decisions to investors, it is vital that proper screening of investment proposals takes place. An important part of this screening process is to ensure that the business uses appropriate methods of evaluation. Research shows that there are basically four methods used in practice by businesses throughout the world to evaluate investment opportunities. They are:

- Accounting rate of return (ARR)
- Payback period (PP)
- Net present value (NPV)
- Internal rate of return (IRR)

It is possible to find businesses that use variants of these four methods. It is also possible to find businesses, particularly smaller ones, that do not use *any* formal appraisal method but rely more on the 'gut feeling' of their managers. Most businesses, however, seem to use one (or more) of the four, that we have listed above and that we shall now review in greater depth.

To help us examine each of the four methods, it is useful to see how each would deal with a particular investment opportunity. Consider the following example.

**Example 8.1**

Billingsgate Battery Company has carried out some market research showing that it is possible to manufacture and sell a product that has recently been developed.

The decision to manufacture would require an investment in a machine costing £100,000, payable immediately. Production and sales of the product would take place throughout the next five years, at the end of which time the machine is expected to be sold for £20,000. Production and sales of the product are expected to occur as follows:

|  | Number of units |
| --- | --- |
| Next year | 5,000 |
| Second year | 10,000 |
| Third year | 15,000 |
| Fourth year | 15,000 |
| Fifth year | 5,000 |

It is estimated that the new product can be sold for £12 a unit and that the relevant material and labour costs will total £8 a unit. To simplify matters, we shall assume that cash from sales and payments for production costs are received and paid, respectively, at the end of each year. In practice, these cash flows will tend to occur throughout the year.

Bearing in mind that each product sold will give rise to a net cash inflow of £4 (that is £12–£8), the cash flows (receipts and payments) over the life of the product will be as follows:

|  |  | £000 |
| --- | --- | --- |
| Immediately | Cost of machine | (100) |
| 1 year's time | Net profit before depreciation (£4 × 5,000) | 20 |
| 2 years' time | Net profit before depreciation (£4 × 10,000) | 40 |
| 3 years' time | Net profit before depreciation (£4 × 15,000) | 60 |
| 4 years' time | Net profit before depreciation (£4 × 15,000) | 60 |
| 5 years' time | Net profit before depreciation (£4 × 5,000) | 20 |
| 5 years' time | Disposal proceeds from the machine | 20 |

Note that, broadly speaking, the net profit before deducting depreciation equals the net amount of cash flowing into the business. Apart from depreciation, all expenses cause cash to flow out of the business, and sales revenues lead to cash flowing in.

We shall now go on to consider how each investment appraisal method works.

# Accounting rate of return (ARR)

➡ The **accounting rate of return (ARR)** method takes the average accounting profit that the investment will generate and expresses it as a percentage of the average investment over the life of the project. Thus:

$$\text{ARR} = \frac{\text{Average annual profit}}{\text{Average investment to earn that profit}} \times 100 \text{ per cent}$$

We can see from the equation that, to calculate ARR, we need to deduce two pieces of information:

- the annual average profit
- the average investment for the particular project

In our example, average annual profit *before depreciation* over the five years is £40,000 [(£20,000 + £40,000 + £60,000 + £60,000 + £20,000)/5]. Assuming 'straight-line' depreciation (that is, equal amounts), the annual depreciation charge will be £16,000 [(Cost £100,000 − Disposal value £20,000)/5]. Thus, the average annual profit *after depreciation* is £24,000 (£40,000 − £16,000).

The average investment over the five years can be calculated as follows:

$$\text{Average investment} = \frac{\text{Cost of machine} + \text{disposal value}}{2}$$

$$= \frac{£100,000 + £20,000}{2}$$

$$= £60,000$$

Thus, the ARR of the investment is:

$$\text{ARR} = \frac{£24,000}{£60,000} \times 100 \text{ per cent}$$

$$= 40 \text{ per cent}$$

In order to decide whether the 40 per cent return is acceptable, we need to compare this percentage return with a minimum required rate set by the business.

| Activity 8.2 | Chaotic Industries is considering an investment in a fleet of ten delivery vans to distribute its products to customers. The vans will cost £15,000 each to buy, payable immediately. The annual running costs are expected to total £20,000 for each van (including the driver's salary). The vans are expected to operate successfully for six years, at the end of which they will all have to be scrapped with disposal proceeds expected to be about £3,000 per van. At present, the business uses a commercial carrier for all of its deliveries. It is expected that this carrier will charge a total of £230,000 each year for the next six years to undertake the deliveries.

What is the ARR of buying the vans? (Note that cost savings are as relevant a benefit from an investment as are actual net cash inflows.)

The vans will save the business £30,000 a year [£230,000 − (£20,000 × 10)], before depreciation, in total. Thus the inflows and outflows will be:

|  |  | £000 |
|---|---|---|
| Immediately | Cost of vans | (150) |
| 1 year's time | Net saving before depreciation | 30 |
| 2 years' time | Net saving before depreciation | 30 |
| 3 years' time | Net saving before depreciation | 30 |
| 4 years' time | Net saving before depreciation | 30 |
| 5 years' time | Net saving before depreciation | 30 |
| 6 years' time | Net saving before depreciation | 30 |
| 6 years' time | Disposal proceeds from the vans | 30 |

The total annual depreciation expense (assuming a straight-line approach) will be £20,000 [(£150,000 − £30,000)/6] Thus, the average annual saving, after depreciation, is £10,000 (£30,000 − £20,000).

The average investment will be:

$$\text{Average investment} = \frac{£150,000 + £30,000}{2}$$

$$= £90,000$$

Thus, the ARR of the investment is:

$$\text{ARR} = \frac{£10,000}{£90,000} \times 100 \text{ per cent}$$

$$= 11.1 \text{ per cent}$$

It may have struck you that ARR and the return on capital employed (ROCE) ratio adopt the same approach to performance measurement. ROCE is a popular means of assessing the performance of a business *as a whole*, after the period has passed. In theory, if all investments made by Chaotic Industries (Activity 8.2) actually proved to have an ARR of 11.1 per cent, then the ROCE for that business as a whole should be 11.1 per cent. Many businesses use ROCE as a key performance measure and so, where a preset ROCE is adopted, it may seem logical to use ARR when appraising new investments. We saw earlier that a business using ARR would compare the returns achieved with a minimum required rate of return. This minimum rate may be determined in various ways. For example, it may reflect the rate that previous investments had achieved (as measured by ROCE), or the industry average ROCE. Where there are competing projects that all seem capable of exceeding the minimum rate, the one with the highest ARR would normally be selected.

ARR is said to have a number of advantages as a method of investment appraisal. It was mentioned earlier that ROCE is a widely used measure of business performance and it may, therefore, seem sensible to use a method of investment appraisal that is consistent with this overall approach to measuring business performance. ARR is also a measure of profitability that many believe is the correct way to evaluate investments. Finally, ARR produces a percentage return that managers understand. Percentages are often used when setting targets for a business, and managers seem to feel comfortable with investment appraisal methods that adopt this form of measurement.

**Activity 8.3**

ARR suffers from a very major defect as a means of assessing investment opportunities. What do you think this is? *Hint*: the defect is not concerned with the ability of the decision maker to forecast future events, though this too can be a problem. Try to remember what was the essential feature of investment decisions that we identified at the beginning of the chapter.

The problem with ARR is that it almost completely ignores the time factor. In the Billingsgate Battery Company example (Example 8.1), exactly the same ARR would have been computed under each of the following three scenarios:

|  |  | Original scenario £000 | Scenario 2 £000 | Scenario 3 £000 |
|---|---|---|---|---|
| Immediately | Cost of machine | (100) | (100) | (100) |
| 1 year's time | Net profit before depreciation | 20 | 10 | 160 |
| 2 years' time | Net profit before depreciation | 40 | 10 | 10 |
| 3 years' time | Net profit before depreciation | 60 | 10 | 10 |
| 4 years' time | Net profit before depreciation | 60 | 10 | 10 |
| 5 years' time | Net profit before depreciation | 20 | 160 | 10 |
| 5 years' time | Disposal proceeds | 20 | 20 | 20 |

Since the same total profit *before* depreciation over the five years arises in all three of these cases (that is, £200,000), the average net profit *after* depreciation must be the same in each case (that is £24,000). This means that each case will give rise to the same ARR of 40 per cent (£24,000/£60,000). We can see, however, that the pattern of profit inflows will vary under each scenario.

Given a financial objective of maximising the wealth of the owners of the business, a manager facing the three possible scenarios set out in Activity 8.3 would strongly prefer scenario 3. This is because most of the benefits from the investment arise within one year of the initial investment. The original scenario would rank second and scenario 2 would come a poor third in the rankings. Any appraisal technique not capable of distinguishing between these three situations is seriously flawed. We shall look in more detail at why time is such an important factor later in the chapter.

There are other defects associated with the ARR method. When measuring performance over the whole life of a project, it is cash flow rather than accounting profit that is important. Cash is the ultimate measure of the economic wealth generated by an investment. This is because it is cash that is used to acquire resources and for distribution to shareholders. Accounting profit, on the other hand, is more appropriate for periodic reporting: it is a useful measure of productive effort for a particular reporting period such as a year or half-year. Thus, it is really a question of 'horses for courses'. Accounting profit is fine for measuring performance over short periods, but cash is the appropriate measure when considering performance over the life of a project.

The ARR method can also create problems when considering competing investments of different size.

---

**Activity 8.4**

Joanna Sinclair (Wholesalers) plc is considering opening a new sales outlet in Coventry. Two possible sites have been identified. Site A has a capacity of 30,000 m². It will require an average investment of £6 million and will produce an average profit of £600,000 a year. Site B has a capacity of 20,000 m². It will require an average investment of £4 million and will produce an average profit of £500,000 a year.

What is the ARR of each investment opportunity? Which site would you select and why?

The ARR of site A is:

$$\frac{£600,000}{£6,000,000} = 10 \text{ per cent}$$

The ARR of site B is:

$$\frac{£500,000}{£4,000,000} = 12.5 \text{ per cent}$$

Thus, site B has the higher ARR. However, in terms of the absolute profit generated, site A is the more attractive. If the ultimate objective is to maximise the wealth of the shareholders, it might be better to choose site A even though the percentage return is lower. It is the absolute size of the return rather than the relative (percentage) size that is important.

## Payback period (PP)

→ The **payback period (PP)** is the length of time it takes for an initial investment to be repaid out of the net cash inflows from a project. Since it takes time into account, the PP method seems to go some way to overcoming the timing problem of ARR – or at least at first glance it does. Let us consider PP in the context of the Billingsgate Battery Company (Example 8.1). You will recall that the project's costs and benefits can be summarised as follows:

|  |  | £000 |
|---|---|---|
| Immediately | Cost of machine | (100) |
| 1 year's time | Net profit before depreciation | 20 |
| 2 years' time | Net profit before depreciation | 40 |
| 3 years' time | Net profit before depreciation | 60 |
| 4 years' time | Net profit before depreciation | 60 |
| 5 years' time | Net profit before depreciation | 20 |
| 5 years' time | Disposal proceeds | 20 |

Note that all of these figures are amounts of cash to be paid or received. (We saw earlier that net profit before depreciation is a rough measure of the cash flows from the project.)

Given our earlier assumption that cash flows will arise at year ends, the payback period for this investment project is three years; that is, it will be three years before the £100,000 outlay is covered by the inflows. The payback period can be derived by calculating the cumulative cash flows as follows:

|  |  | Net cash flows £000 | Cumulative net cash flows £000 |  |
|---|---|---|---|---|
| Immediately | Cost of machine | (100) | (100) |  |
| 1 year's time | Net profit before depreciation | 20 | (80) | (−100 + 20) |
| 2 years' time | Net profit before depreciation | 40 | (40) | (−80 + 40) |
| 3 years' time | Net profit before depreciation | 60 | 20 | (−40 + 60) |
| 4 years' time | Net profit before depreciation | 60 | 80 | (+20 + 60) |
| 5 years' time | Net profit before depreciation | 20 | 100 | (+80 + 20) |
| 5 years' time | Disposal proceeds | 20 | 120 | (+100 + 20) |

We can see that the cumulative cash flows become positive at the end of the third year. Had we assumed that the cash flows arise evenly over the year, the precise payback period would be:

$$2 \text{ years} + \frac{40}{60} = 2\frac{2}{3} \text{ years}$$

(where 40 represents the cash flow still required at the beginning of the third year to pay back the initial outlay and 60 represents the cash flows during the year). Again, we must ask how to decide whether this measure is acceptable. A manager using PP would need to have a minimum payback period in mind. If, for example, the Billingsgate Battery Company had a minimum PP of three years, the project would be acceptable. If there were two competing projects that both met the minimum PP criterion, the manager should select the project with the shorter payback period.

| Activity 8.5 | What is the payback period of the Chaotic Industries project from Activity 8.2? |
|---|---|

The inflows and outflows are expected to be:

| | | Net cash flows £000 | Cumulative net cash flows £000 |
|---|---|---|---|
| Immediately | Cost of vans | (150) | (150) |
| 1 year's time | Net saving before depreciation | 30 | (120) |
| 2 years' time | Net saving before depreciation | 30 | (90) |
| 3 years' time | Net saving before depreciation | 30 | (60) |
| 4 years' time | Net saving before depreciation | 30 | (30) |
| 5 years' time | Net saving before depreciation | 30 | 0 |
| 6 years' time | Net saving before depreciation | 30 | 30 |
| 6 years' time | Disposal proceeds from the vans | 30 | 60 |

The payback period is five years, that is, it is not until the end of the fifth year that the vans will pay for themselves out of the savings that they are expected to generate.

The PP approach has certain advantages. It is quick and easy to calculate and can be easily understood by managers. The logic of PP is that projects that can recoup their cost quickly are economically more attractive than those with longer payback periods. However, this method does not provide us with the *whole* answer to the problem.

| Activity 8.6 | In what respect is PP not the whole answer as a means of assessing investment opportunities? Consider the cash flows arising from three competing projects: |
|---|---|

| | | Project 1 £000 | Project 2 £000 | Project 3 £000 |
|---|---|---|---|---|
| Immediately | Cost of machine | (200) | (200) | (200) |
| 1 year's time | Net profit before depreciation | 40 | 10 | 80 |
| 2 years' time | Net profit before depreciation | 80 | 20 | 100 |

|  | | Project 1 £000 | Project 2 £000 | Project 3 £000 |
|---|---|---|---|---|
| 3 years' time | Net profit before depreciation | 80 | 170 | 20 |
| 4 years' time | Net profit before depreciation | 60 | 20 | 200 |
| 5 years' time | Net profit before depreciation | 40 | 10 | 500 |
| 5 years' time | Disposal proceeds | 40 | 10 | 20 |

*Hint*: Once again, the defects are not concerned with the ability of the decision maker to forecast future events. This is a problem whatever approach we take.

The PP for each project is three years and so the PP approach would regard the projects as being equally acceptable. The PP method cannot distinguish between those projects that pay back a significant amount at an early stage and those that do not.

In addition, this method ignores cash flows after the payback period. A decision maker concerned with maximising shareholder wealth would prefer project 3 in the table above because the cash flows come in earlier and they are greater in total. The cumulative cash flows of each project are set out in Figure 8.1.

 **Figure 8.1**

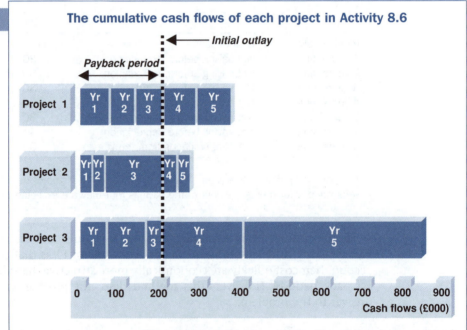

**The cumulative cash flows of each project in Activity 8.6**

The payback period cannot differentiate between the three projects. They all have the same payback period and are therefore equally acceptable (even though project 3 generated a larger amount of cash at an earlier point within the three-year payback and the cumulative cash flows of project 3 are much greater than those of the other two projects.)

We can see that the PP method is not concerned with the profitability of projects; it is concerned simply with their payback periods. Thus, cash flows arising beyond the payback period are ignored. Whilst this neatly avoids the practical problems of forecasting cash flows over a longer period, it means that relevant information will be ignored. You may feel that, by favouring projects with a short payback period, the PP approach does at least provide a means of dealing with the problems of risk and uncertainty. However, this is a fairly crude approach to the problem. We shall see later that there are more systematic approaches to dealing with risk.

## Net present value (NPV)

What we really need to help us make sensible investment decisions is a method of appraisal that takes account of *all* of the costs and benefits of each investment opportunity and that also makes a logical allowance for the *timing* of those costs and benefits. The **net present value (NPV)** method provides us with this.

Consider the Billingsgate Battery Company decision of Example 8.1, whose cash flows you will recall can be summarised as follows:

|  |  | £000 |
|---|---|---|
| Immediately | Cost of machine | (100) |
| 1 year's time | Net profit before depreciation | 20 |
| 2 years' time | Net profit before depreciation | 40 |
| 3 years' time | Net profit before depreciation | 60 |
| 4 years' time | Net profit before depreciation | 60 |
| 5 years' time | Net profit before depreciation | 20 |
| 5 years' time | Disposal proceeds | 20 |

Given that the principal financial objective of the business is probably to increase wealth, it would be very easy to assess this investment if all the cash inflows and outflows were to occur at the same time. All that we should need to do is to add up the cash inflows (total £220,000) and compare the result with the outflows (£100,000). This would lead us to the conclusion that the project should go ahead, because the business would be better off by £120,000 as a result. Of course, it is not as easy as this because time is involved. The cash outflow (payment) will occur immediately if the project is undertaken. The inflows (receipts) will arise at a range of later times.

The time factor is an important issue because people do not see £100 paid out now as equivalent in value to £100 receivable in a year's time.

---

| Activity 8.7 | Why would you see £100 to be received in a year's time as unequal in value to £100 to be paid immediately? (There are basically three reasons.) |
|---|---|

The three reasons are:

- Interest lost
- Risk
- Effects of inflation

We shall now take a closer look at the three reasons listed in the answer to Activity 8.7.

## Interest lost

If you are to be deprived of the opportunity to spend your money for a year, you could equally well be deprived of its use by placing it on deposit in a bank or building society. In this case, at the end of the year you could have your money back and have interest as well. Thus, unless the opportunity to invest offers similar returns, you will be incurring an opportunity cost. An opportunity cost occurs where one course of action deprives you of the opportunity to derive some benefit from an alternative action – for example, putting the money in the bank.

Any investment opportunity must, if it is to make you more wealthy, do better than the returns that are available from the next-best opportunity. Thus, if Billingsgate Battery Company sees putting the money in the bank on deposit as the alternative to investment in the machine, the returns from investing in the machine must be better than those from investing in the bank. If the bank offered better returns, the business would become more wealthy by putting the money on deposit.

## Risk

Buying a machine to manufacture a product that is to be sold in the market is often a risky venture. Things may not turn out as expected.

---

**Activity 8.8**

Can you suggest why things may not turn out as expected for the Billingsgate Battery Company?

You may have came up with the following:

- The machine might not work as well as expected; it might break down, leading to loss of production and loss of sales.
- Sales of the product may not be as buoyant as expected.
- The life of the product may be shorter than expected.
- Labour costs may prove to be higher than was expected.
- The sales proceeds of the machine could prove to be less than was estimated.

---

It is important to remember that the decision whether or not to invest in the machine must be taken *before* any of the potential problems listed in Activity 8.8 are solved. It is only after the machine has been purchased that we may discover that the estimated level of sales is not going to be achieved. We can study reports and analyses of the market. We can commission sophisticated market surveys and these may give us more confidence in the likely outcome. We can advertise strongly and try to promote sales. Ultimately, however, we have to jump into the dark and accept the **risk**, if we want the opportunity to make beneficial investments.

Normally, people expect to receive greater returns where they perceive risk to be a factor. Examples of this in real life are not difficult to find. One is that banks tend to charge higher rates of interest to borrowers whom the bank perceives as more risky, than to those who can offer good security for a loan and can point to a regular source of income.

Going back to Billingsgate Battery Company's investment opportunity, it is not enough to say that we should not advise making the investment unless the returns from it are higher than those from investing in a bank deposit. Clearly, we should want returns *above* the level of bank deposit interest rates because the logical equivalent to investing in the machine is not putting the money on deposit – it is making an alternative investment that seems to have a risk similar to that of the investment in the machine.

We tend to expect a higher rate of return from investment projects where the risk is perceived as being higher. How risky a particular project is, and thus how large this *risk premium* should be, are matters that are difficult to handle. It is usually necessary to make some judgement on these questions, and we shall consider this point in more detail later in the chapter.

## Inflation

If you are to be deprived of £100 for a year, when you come eventually to spend that money it will not buy as many goods and services as it would have done a year earlier. Generally, you will not be able to buy as many loaves of bread, tickets for the cinema or bus tickets for a particular journey for £100, as you could have done a year earlier. This is **inflation**. Clearly, the investor needs to be compensated for this loss of purchasing power if the investment is to be made. This is on top of a return that takes into account the returns that could have been gained from an alternative investment of similar risk.

## Actions of a logical investor

To summarise, we can say that the logical investor, who is seeking to increase his or her wealth, will only be prepared to make investments that will compensate for the loss of interest and purchasing power of the money invested and for the fact that the returns expected may not materialise (risk). This is usually assessed by seeing whether the proposed investment will yield a return that is greater than the basic rate of interest (which would include an allowance for inflation) *plus* a risk premium.

The elements of the opportunity finance cost rate are shown in Figure 8.2.

Let us now return to the Billingsgate Battery Company example. Let us assume that, instead of making this investment, the business could make an alternative investment, with similar risk, and obtain a return of 20 per cent a year. We have already seen that it is not sufficient just to compare the basic cash inflows and outflows for the investment. It would be useful if we could express each of these cash flows in similar terms so that we could make a direct comparison between the sum of the inflows and the immediate £100,000 investment. In fact, we *can* do this.

| Figure 8.2 | **The factors influencing the discount rate to be applied to a project** |

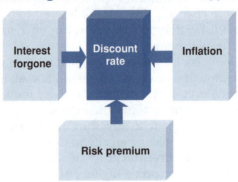

The figure shows the three factors influencing the opportunity cost of finance which were discussed earlier.

| Activity 8.9 | If we know that Billingsgate Battery Company could alternatively invest its money at a rate of 20 per cent a year, how much do you judge the present (immediate) value of the expected first-year receipt of £20,000 to be? In other words, if instead of having to wait a year for the £20,000 and being deprived of the opportunity to invest it at 20 per cent, you could have a sum of money now, what sum would you regard as exactly equivalent to getting £20,000 in a year's time? |

We should obviously be happy to accept a lower amount, if we could get it immediately than if we had to wait a year. This is because we could invest it at 20 per cent (in the alternative project) and it would grow to a larger amount in one year's time. Logically, we should be prepared to accept the amount which with a year's income will grow to £20,000. If we call this amount the present value (PV), we can say:

$$PV + (PV \times 20\%) = £20,000$$

that is, the amount plus income from investing the amount for the year equals £20,000. We can restate this equation as:

$$PV \times (1 + 0.2) = £20,000$$

(Note that 0.2 is the same as 20 per cent, but expressed as a decimal.) This equation can be rearranged as:

$$PV = \frac{£20,000}{1 + 0.2} = £16,667$$

Thus, rational investors who have the opportunity to invest at 20 per cent a year would not mind whether they have £16,667 now or £20,000 in a year's time. In this sense we can say that, given a 20 per cent investment opportunity, £20,000 to be received in one year's time has a present value of £16,667.

If we could derive the present value (PV) of each of the cash flows associated with Billingsgate's machine investment, we could easily make the direct comparison between the cost of making the investment (£100,000) and the various benefits that will derive from it in years 1 to 5. Fortunately, we can do precisely this.

We can make a more general statement about the PV of a particular cash flow. It is:

$$\text{PV of the cash flow of year } n = \frac{\text{Actual cash flow of year } n}{(1 + r)^n}$$

where $n$ is the year of the cash flow (that is, how many years into the future) and $r$ is the opportunity investing rate expressed as a decimal (instead of as a percentage).

We have already seen how this works for the £20,000 inflow for year 1. For year 2, with a cash inflow of £40,000, the calculation would be:

$$PV = \frac{£40,000}{(1 + 0.2)^2} = \frac{£40,000}{(1.2)^2} = \frac{£40,000}{1.44} = £27,778$$

Thus, the present value of the £40,000 to be received in two years' time is £27,778.

| **Activity 8.10** | See if you can show that an investor would be indifferent to £27,778 receivable now, or £40,000 receivable in two years' time, assuming that there is a 20 per cent investment opportunity. |
|---|---|

The reasoning goes like this:

|  | £ |
|---|---|
| Amount available for immediate investment | 27,778 |
| *Add* Interest for year 1 (20% × £27,778) | 5,556 |
|  | 33,334 |
| *Add* Interest for year 2 (20% × £33,334) | 6,667 |
|  | 40,001 |

(The extra £1 is only a rounding error)

Thus, because the investor can turn £27,778 into £40,000 in two years, these amounts are equivalent and we can say that £27,778 is the present value of £40,000 receivable after two years (given a 20 per cent rate of return).

Now let us calculate the present values of all of the cash flows associated with the Billingsgate machine project and hence the net present value (NPV) of the project as a whole. The relevant cash flows and calculations are as follows [note that $(1 + 0.2)^0 = 1$]:

|  | Cash flow<br>£000 | Calculation of PV | PV<br>£000 |
|---|---|---|---|
| Immediately (time 0) | (100) | $(100)/(1 + 0.2)^0$ | (100.00) |
| 1 year's time | 20 | $20/(1 + 0.2)^1$ | 16.67 |
| 2 years' time | 40 | $40/(1 + 0.2)^2$ | 27.78 |
| 3 years' time | 60 | $60/(1 + 0.2)^3$ | 34.72 |
| 4 years' time | 60 | $60/(1 + 0.2)^4$ | 28.94 |
| 5 years' time | 20 | $20/(1 + 0.2)^5$ | 8.04 |
| 5 years' time | 20 | $20/(1 + 0.2)^5$ | 8.04 |
| Net present value |  |  | 24.19 |

Once again we must ask how we can decide whether the return is acceptable to the business. In fact, the decision rule is simple. If the NPV is positive, we accept the project; if it is negative, we reject the project. In this case, the NPV is positive and so we should accept the project and buy the machine.

The reasoning behind this decision rule is quite straightforward. Given the investment opportunities available to the business, investing in the machine will make the owners of the business £24,190 better off. In other words, the gross benefits from investing in this machine are worth a total of £124,190 today, and since the business can 'buy' these benefits for just £100,000 today, the investment should be made. If, however, the gross benefits were below £100,000, they would be less than the cost of 'buying' these benefits.

| Activity 8.11 | What is the *maximum* the Billingsgate Battery Company would be prepared to pay for the machine, given the potential benefit of owning it? |
|---|---|

The business would be prepared to pay up to £124,190 since the wealth of the owners of the business would be increased up to this point, though the business would rather pay less.

### Using discount tables

Deducing the present values of the various cash flows was a little laborious using the approach that we have just taken. To deduce each PV we took the relevant cash flow and multiplied it by $1/(1 + r)^n$. Fortunately, there is a quicker way.

→ Tables exist that show values of this **discount factor** for a range of values of $r$ and $n$. Such a table appears in the appendix to this chapter. Take a look at it now.

Look at the column for 20 per cent and the row for 1 year. We find that the factor is 0.833. Thus, the PV of a cash flow of £1 receivable in one year is £0.833. So a cash flow of £20,000 receivable in one year's time is £16,667 (that is, 0.833 × £20,000) – the same result as we found working it out in full.

| Activity 8.12 | What is the NPV of the Chaotic Industries project from Activity 8.2, assuming a 15 per cent opportunity cost of finance (discount rate)? Remember that the inflows and outflow are expected to be: |
|---|---|

|  |  | £000 |
|---|---|---|
| Immediately | Cost of vans | (150) |
| 1 year's time | Net saving before depreciation | 30 |
| 2 years' time | Net saving before depreciation | 30 |
| 3 years' time | Net saving before depreciation | 30 |
| 4 years' time | Net saving before depreciation | 30 |
| 5 years' time | Net saving before depreciation | 30 |
| 6 years' time | Net saving before depreciation | 30 |
| 6 years' time | Disposal proceeds from the vans | 30 |

You should use the discount table at the end of this chapter.

The calculation of the NPV of the project is as follows:

| | Cash flows £000 | Discount factor (from the table) | Present value £000 |
|---|---|---|---|
| Immediately | (150) | 1.000 | (150.00) |
| 1 year's time | 30 | 0.870 | 26.10 |
| 2 years' time | 30 | 0.756 | 22.68 |
| 3 years' time | 30 | 0.658 | 19.74 |
| 4 years' time | 30 | 0.572 | 17.16 |
| 5 years' time | 30 | 0.497 | 14.91 |
| 6 years' time | 30 | 0.432 | 12.96 |
| 6 years' time | 30 | 0.432 | 12.96 |
| Net present value | | | (23.49) |

**Activity 8.13**

How would you interpret your result in Activity 8.12?

The fact that the project has a negative NPV means that the present value of the benefits from the investment are worth less than the cost of entering into it. Any cost up to £126,510 (the present value of the benefits) would be worth paying, but not £150,000.

The discount tables reveal clearly how the value of £1 diminishes as its receipt goes further into the future. Assuming an opportunity cost of finance of 20 per cent a year, £1 to be received immediately has, obviously, a present value of £1. However, as the time before it is to be received increases, its present value diminishes significantly, as Figure 8.3 illustrates.

**Figure 8.3**

**Present value of £1 receivable at various times in the future, assuming an annual financing cost of 20 per cent**

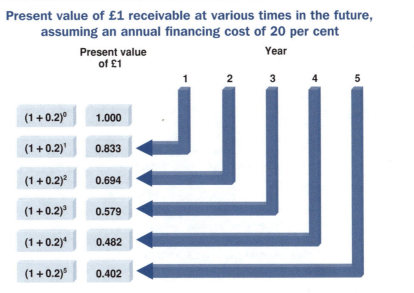

The figure shows how the present value of £1 reduces over time. Thus, the further into the future the £1 is received, the lower will be its present value.

## Why NPV is superior to ARR and PP

NPV is a better method of appraising investment opportunities than either ARR or PP because it fully addresses each of the following:

■ *The timing of the cash flows.* By discounting the various cash flows associated with each project according to when they are expected to arise, NPV takes account of the time value of money. The discount factor is based on the opportunity cost of finance (that is, the return that the next-best alternative opportunity would generate) and so the net benefit after financing costs have been met is identified (as the NPV of the project).

■ *The whole of the relevant cash flows.* NPV includes all of the relevant cash flows irrespective of when they are expected to occur. It treats them differently according to their date of occurrence, but they are all taken into account in the NPV and they all have an influence on the decision.

■ *The objectives of the business.* The output of the NPV analysis has a direct bearing on the wealth of the shareholders of a business. (Positive NPVs enhance wealth, negative ones reduce it.) Since we assume that private-sector businesses seek to maximise shareholder wealth, NPV is superior to the methods previously discussed.

We saw earlier that a business should take on all projects with positive NPVs, when they are discounted at the opportunity cost of finance. Where a choice has to be made between projects, a business should normally select the one with the largest NPV.

## Internal rate of return (IRR)

This is the last of the four major methods of investment appraisal. It is quite closely related to the NPV method as it also involves discounting future cash flows. The **internal rate of return (IRR)** of a particular investment opportunity is the discount rate that, when applied to its future cash flows, will produce an NPV of precisely zero. In essence, it represents the yield from an investment opportunity.

| Activity 8.14 | You will recall that when we discounted the cash flows of the Billingsgate Battery Company investment project at 20 per cent, we found that the NPV was a positive figure of £24,190. |
| --- | --- |

What does the NPV of the machine project tell us about the rate of return that the investment will yield for the Billingsgate Battery Company?

The fact that the NPV is positive, when discounting at 20 per cent, implies that the rate of return that the project generates is more than 20 per cent. The fact that the NPV is a pretty large figure implies that the actual rate of return is quite a lot above 20 per cent. Increasing the size of the discount rate will reduce NPV because a higher discount rate gives lower discounted cash inflows.

We have seen that the IRR can be defined as the discount rate that equates the discounted cash inflows with the cash outflows. To put it another way, the IRR

| Figure 8.4 | **Relationship between the NPV and IRR methods** |

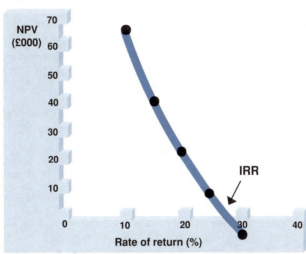

Where the discount rate is zero, the NPV will be the sum of the net cash flows. In other words, no account is taken of the time value of money. However, as the discount rate increases, there is a corresponding decrease in the NPV of the project. When the NPV line crosses the horizontal axis there will be a zero NPV and that will also represent the IRR.

is the discount rate that will have the effect of producing an NPV of precisely zero. Figure 8.4 illustrates this relation diagrammatically for the Billingsgate company.

It is somewhat laborious to deduce the IRR by hand, since it cannot usually be calculated directly. Iteration (trial and error) is the approach that must usually be adopted. Let us try a higher rate for the Billingsgate Battery Company and see what happens – say on 30 per cent:

|  | Cash flow £000 | Discount factor 30% | PV £000 |
| --- | --- | --- | --- |
| Immediately (time 0) | (100) | 1.000 | (100.00) |
| 1 year's time | 20 | 0.769 | 15.38 |
| 2 years' time | 40 | 0.592 | 23.68 |
| 3 years' time | 60 | 0.455 | 27.30 |
| 4 years' time | 60 | 0.350 | 21.00 |
| 5 years' time | 20 | 0.269 | 5.38 |
| 5 years' time | 20 | 0.269 | 5.38 |
|  |  |  | (1.88) |

In increasing the discount rate from 20 per cent to 30 per cent, we have reduced the NPV from £52,600 (positive) to £1,880 (negative). Since the IRR is the discount rate that will give us an NPV of exactly zero, we can conclude that the IRR of Billingsgate Battery Company's machine project is very slightly under 30 per cent. Further trials could lead us to the exact rate, but there is probably not much point given the likely inaccuracy of the cash flow estimates. It is probably good enough, for practical purposes, to say that the IRR is about 30 per cent.

---

**Activity 8.15**

What is the internal rate of return of the Chaotic Industries project from Activity 8.2? You should use the discount table in the appendix at the end of this chapter.
Hint: Remember that you already know the NPV of this project at 15 per cent. Try 10 per cent as your next trial.

---

Since we know that, at a 15 per cent discount rate, the NPV is a relatively large negative figure, our next trial should use a lower discount rate, say 10 per cent.

| | Cash flows £000 | Discount factor (from the table) 10% | Present value £000 |
|---|---|---|---|
| Immediately | (150) | 1.000 | (150.00) |
| 1 year's time | 30 | 0.909 | 27.27 |
| 2 years' time | 30 | 0.826 | 24.78 |
| 3 years' time | 30 | 0.751 | 22.53 |
| 4 years' time | 30 | 0.683 | 20.49 |
| 5 years' time | 30 | 0.621 | 18.63 |
| 6 years' time | 30 | 0.565 | 16.95 |
| 6 years' time | 30 | 0.565 | 16.95 |
| Net present value | | | (2.40) |

We can see that NPV rose about £21,000 (that is £23,490 – £2,400) for a 5 per cent drop in the discount rate – that is, about £4,200 for each 1 per cent. We need to know the rate for a zero NPV. (This represents an increase of a further £2,400 in the NPV where the discount rate used is 10 per cent.) As a 1 per cent change in the rate results in a £4,200 change in NPV, the required change in the rate will be roughly 0.6 per cent (£2,400/£4,200). Thus, the IRR is close to 9.4 per cent (10 – 0.6 per cent). However, to say that the IRR is about 9 per cent is near enough for most purposes.

Users of the IRR approach should apply the following decision rules:

- For any project to be acceptable, the project must meet a minimum IRR requirement. Logically, this minimum should be the opportunity cost of finance.
- Where there are competing projects (for example, the business can choose only one of several viable projects), the one with the highest IRR should be selected.

IRR has certain attributes in common with NPV. All cash flows are taken into account and the timing of them is handled logically. The main disadvantage with IRR is that it does not address the question of wealth generation. It could therefore, lead to a wrong decision being made. IRR will always see a return of 25 per cent being preferable to a 20 per cent return (assuming an opportunity cost of finance of, say, 15 per cent). Though accepting the project with the higher percentage return will often generate the most wealth, this may not always be the case. This is because the scale of investment has been ignored. With a 15 per cent cost of finance, £1.5 million invested at 20 per cent would make you richer than £0.5 million invested at 25 per cent. IRR does not recognise this.

The problem nevertheless tends to be rare; normally, competing projects involve similar-sized investments. Typically, IRR will give the same signal as NPV, but it must be better to use a method (NPV) that is always reliable than to use IRR.

## Some practical points

When carrying out an investment appraisal, there are several practical points you should bear in mind:

- *Relevant costs.*   We should only take account of cash flows that vary according to the decision in our analysis. Thus, cash flows that will be the same, irrespective of the decision under review, should be ignored. For example, overheads that will be incurred in equal amount whether or not the investment is made should be ignored, despite the fact that the investment could not be made without the infrastructure that the overhead costs create. Similarly, past costs should be ignored as they are not affected by, and do not vary with, a decision on future projects. (See Chapter 2 for a full discussion of these points.)
- *Opportunity costs.*   Opportunity costs arising from benefits forgone must be taken into account. Thus, for example, when considering whether to continue to use a machine (already owned by the business) for producing a new product, the realisable value of the machine may be an important opportunity cost.
- *Taxation.*   Tax will usually be an important consideration when making an investment decision. The profits from the investment will be taxed and the capital investment may attract tax relief. This means that, in practice, unless tax is formally taken into account, the wrong decision could be made.
- *Cash flow not profit flow.*   We have seen that for the NPV, IRR and PP methods, it is cash flows rather than profit flows that are relevant to the evaluation of investment projects. In a problem requiring the application of any of these methods, you may be given details of the profit for the investment period and so will be required to adjust these in order to derive the cash flow. Remember, the net profit *before* depreciation is an approximation to the cash flow for the period, and so you should work back to this figure.

  When the data are expressed in profit rather than cash-flow terms, an adjustment in respect of working capital may also be necessary. Some adjustment to take account of changes in the net cash investment (or disinvestment) in trade debtors, stock and creditors should be made. For example, launching a new product may give rise to an increase in working capital, requiring an immediate outlay of cash. This outlay for additional working capital should be shown in your NPV calculations as part of the initial cost. However, the additional working capital would normally be released at the end of the life of the product, so the resulting inflow of cash at the end of the project should also be taken into account.
- *Year-end assumption.*   In the examples above, we have assumed that cash flows arise at the end of the relevant year. This is a simplifying assumption that is used to make the calculations easier. (However, it is perfectly possible to deal more precisely with the cash flows.) The assumption is clearly unrealistic as money will have to be paid to employees on a weekly or a monthly basis, and customers will pay within a month or two of buying a product. It is probably

not a serious distortion. Even so, you should be clear that there is nothing about any of the appraisal methods that demands that this assumption is made.

■ *Interest payments.* When using discounted cash flow techniques, interest payments should not be taken into account in deriving the cash flow for the period. The discount factor already takes account of the costs of financing, and so to take account of interest charges in deriving cash flow for the period would be double counting.

■ *Other factors.* Investment decision making must not be viewed as a mechanical exercise. The results derived from a particular investment appraisal method will be only one input to the decision-making process. There may be broader issues that have to be taken into account but that might be difficult to quantify. For example, a regional bus company may be considering an investment in a new bus to serve a particular route that local residents would like to see operated. Although the NPV calculations may reveal that a loss will be made on the investment, it may be that, by not investing in the new bus and not operating the route, the renewal of the company's licence to operate will be put at risk. In such a situation and before a final decision is made the size of the expected loss, as revealed by the calculations made, must be weighed against the prospect of losing the right to operate. Thus, non-quantifiable factors that may have a significant economic impact must be considered.

The reliability of the forecasts and the validity of the assumptions used in the evaluation will also have a bearing on a final decision. We shall see later in the chapter that various techniques may be applied to the information concerning the proposed investment to take account of risk and to assess sensitivity to any inaccuracies in the figures used.

---

**Activity 8.16**

The directors of Manuff (Steel) Ltd have decided to close one of its factories. There has been a reduction in the demand for the products made at the factory in recent years and the directors are not optimistic about the long-term prospects for these products. The factory is situated in the north of England where unemployment is high.

The factory is leased and there are four years of the lease remaining. The directors are uncertain as to whether the factory should be closed immediately or at the end of the period of the lease. Another company has offered to sublease the premises from Manuff (Steel) Ltd at a rental of £40,000 per year for the remainder of the lease period.

The machinery and equipment at the factory cost £1.5 million and have a balance sheet value of £400,000. In the event of immediate closure, the machinery and equipment could be sold for £220,000. The working capital at the factory is £420,000 and could be liquidated for that amount immediately if required. Alternatively, the working capital can be liquidated in full at the end of the lease period. Immediate closure would result in redundancy payments to employees of £180,000 (£150,000 when closure is at the end of the lease period).

If the factory continues in operation until the end of the lease period, the following operating profits (losses) are expected:

| Year | 1 £000 | 2 £000 | 3 £000 | 4 £000 |
|---|---|---|---|---|
| Operating profit (loss) | 160 | (40) | 30 | 20 |

These figures include a charge of £90,000 per year for depreciation of machinery and equipment. The residual value of the machinery and equipment at the end of the lease period is estimated at £40,000.

The company has a cost of capital of 12 per cent. Ignore taxation.

(a) Calculate the relevant cash flows arising from a decision to continue operations until the end of the lease period rather than to close immediately.
(b) Calculate the net present value of continuing operations until the end of the lease period rather than closing immediately.
(c) What other factors might the directors of the company take into account before making a final decision on the timing of the factory closure?
(d) State, with reasons, whether or not the company should continue to operate the factory until the end of the lease period.

(a) Relevant cash flows:

| | Year | | | | |
|---|---|---|---|---|---|
| | 0 | 1 | 2 | 3 | 4 |
| | £000 | £000 | £000 | £000 | £000 |
| Operating cash flows (note 1) | | 250 | 50 | 120 | 110 |
| Sale of machinery (note 2) | (220) | | | | 40 |
| Redundancy costs (note 3) | 180 | | | | (150) |
| Sublease rentals (note 4) | | (40) | (40) | (40) | (40) |
| Working capital invested (note 5) | (420) | | | | 420 |
| | (460) | 210 | 10 | 80 | 380 |

(b)

| | | | | | |
|---|---|---|---|---|---|
| Discount rate 12%: | 1.000 | 0.893 | 0.797 | 0.712 | 0.636 |
| Present value | (460) | 187.5 | 8.0 | 57.0 | 241.7 |
| Net present value | 34.2 | | | | |

*Notes:*
1. The operating cash flows are calculated by adding back the depreciation charge for the year to the operating profit for the year. In the case of an operating loss, the depreciation charge is deducted.
2. In the event of closure, machinery could be sold immediately. Thus, an opportunity cost of £220,000 is incurred if operations continue.
3. By continuing operations, there will be a saving in immediate redundancy costs of £180,000. However, redundancy costs of £150,000 will be paid in four years' time.
4. By continuing operations, the opportunity to sublease the factory will be forgone.
5. Immediate closure would mean that working capital could be liquidated. By continuing operations this opportunity is forgone. However, working capital can be liquidated in four years' time.

(c) Other factors that may influence the decision include:

■ *The overall strategy of the company.*    The company may need to set the decision within a broader context. It may be necessary to manufacture the products made at the factory because they are an integral part of the company's product range. The company may wish to avoid redundancies in an area of high unemployment for as long as possible.

- *Flexibility*. A decision to close the factory is probably irreversible. If the factory continues, however, there may be a chance that the prospects for the factory will brighten in the future.
- *Creditworthiness of sublessee*. The company should investigate the creditworthiness of the sublessee. Failing to receive the expected sublease payments would make the closure option far less attractive.
- *Accuracy of forecasts*. The forecasts made by the company should be examined carefully. Inaccuracies in the forecasts or any underlying assumptions may change the expected outcomes.

(d) The NPV of the decision to continue operations rather than close immediately is positive. Hence, shareholders would be better off if the directors took this course of action. The factory should, therefore, continue in operation rather than close down. This decision is likely to be welcomed by employees as unemployment is high in the area.

# Investment decision making in practice

As a footnote to our examination of investment appraisal techniques, it is interesting to consider their practical significance. In recent years, there have been numerous studies concerning the use of investment appraisal techniques by businesses.

These studies have shown a trend over the past 25 years towards increasing use of the 'discounting' methods: NPV and IRR. Surprisingly, both PP and ARR remain as popular as ever. Exhibit 8.1 shows the results of one of the most recent of these studies, a survey of large UK businesses conducted in 1997.

| Exhibit 8.1 | **Use of different investment appraisal methods by large UK businesses** |
| --- | --- |

|  | % of businesses using the technique |
| --- | --- |
| Net present value | 80 |
| Internal rate of return | 81 |
| Payback period | 70 |
| Accounting rate of return | 56 |
|  | 287 |

*Note*: the percentages sum to more than 100 per cent because the businesses in the survey used more than one technique (see text following)

*Source*: Information taken from Arnold and Hatzopoulos (see reference (1) at the end of the chapter).

Exhibit 8.1 shows that the two discounting methods are clearly each more popular than either PP or ARR. This is a relatively recent development; earlier studies suggest that it was only in the 1990s that the discounting methods overtook PP.

| Activity 8.17 | How do you explain the popularity of PP, given the several theoretical limitations discussed earlier in this chapter? |
|---|---|

A number of possible reasons may explain this finding:

- PP is easy to understand and use.
- It can avoid the problems of forecasting far into the future.
- It gives emphasis to the early cash flows, when there is greater certainty concerning their accuracy.
- It emphasises the importance of liquidity. Where a business has liquidity problems, a short payback period for a project is likely to appear attractive.

The importance of payback may suggest a lack of sophistication among managers concerning investment appraisal. This criticism is most often made against managers of smaller businesses. In fact, survey evidence tends to show that smaller businesses are much less likely to use discounted cash flow methods than larger ones.

The sum of percentage usage for each appraisal method is 287 per cent (see Exhibit 8.1), which indicates that many businesses use more than one method to appraise investments. Indeed, it seems that few businesses use any one method alone. It is, therefore, possible that payback is used by some businesses as an initial screening device and that projects passing successfully through this stage are then subject to a more sophisticated discounted cash flow analysis. Exhibit 8.1 suggests that most businesses use one or both of the two discounted cash flow methods.

IRR may be as popular as NPV, despite its shortcomings, because it expresses outcomes in percentage terms rather than absolute terms. This form of expression appears to be more acceptable to managers. This may be because managers are used to using percentage figures as targets (for example, return on capital employed).

## ? Self-assessment question 8.1

Beacon Chemicals plc is considering buying some new equipment to produce a chemical named X14. The new equipment's capital cost is estimated at £100,000 and if its purchase is approved now, the equipment can be purchased and commence production by the beginning of Year 1. The company has already spent £50,000 on research and development work. Estimates of revenues and costs arising from the operation of the new plant are as follows:

|  | Year 1 | Year 2 | Year 3 | Year 4 | Year 5 |
|---|---|---|---|---|---|
| Sales price (£/unit) | 100 | 120 | 120 | 100 | 80 |
| Sales volume (units) | 800 | 1,000 | 1,200 | 1,000 | 800 |
| Variable costs (£/unit) | 50 | 50 | 40 | 30 | 40 |
| Fixed costs (£000s) | 30 | 30 | 30 | 30 | 30 |

If the new equipment is bought, sales of some existing products will be lost, resulting in a loss of contribution of £15,000 a year over its life.

The accountant has informed you that the fixed costs include depreciation of £20,000 a year on new equipment. They also include an allocation of £10,000 for fixed overheads. A separate study has indicated that if the new equipment is bought, additional overheads, excluding depreciation, arising from its use will be £8,000 a year.

The equipment would require additional working capital of £30,000. For the purposes of your initial calculations ignore taxation.

**Required:**
(a) Deduce the relevant annual cash flows associated with buying the equipment.
(b) Deduce the payback period.
(c) Calculate the net present value using a discount rate of 8 per cent.

*Hint*: you should deal with the investment in working capital by treating it as a cash outflow at the start of the project and an inflow at the end.

# Dealing with risk in investment appraisal

We have already considered the fact that risk – the likelihood that what is projected to occur will not actually happen – is an important aspect of financial decision making. It is a particularly important issue in the context of investment decisions. This is because of (1) the relatively long timescales involved (there is more time for things to go wrong between the decision being made and the end of the project), and (2) the size of the investment. If things go wrong, the impact can be both significant and lasting.

Various approaches to dealing with risk have been proposed. These fall into two categories: assessing the level of risk and reacting to the level of risk. We now consider formal methods of dealing with risk that fall within each category.

## Assessing the level of risk

One popular way of attempting to assess the level of risk is to carry out a **sensitivity analysis** on the proposed project. This involves an examination of the key input values affecting the project to see how changes in each input might influence the viability of the project.

If the result of the investment appraisal, using the best estimates, is positive, each input value is then examined to see how far the estimated figure could be changed before the project becomes unviable for that reason alone. Let us suppose that the NPV for an investment in a machine, to produce a particular product, is a positive value of £50,000. If we were to carry out a sensitivity analysis on this project, we should consider in turn each of the key input factors – cost of the machine, sales volume and price, individual manufacturing costs, length of the project, and discount rate. We should seek to find the value that each of them could have before the NPV figure would become negative (that is, the value for the factor at which NPV would be zero). The difference between the value for that factor at which the NPV would equal zero and the estimated value represents the margin of safety for that particular input. The process is set out in Figure 8.5.

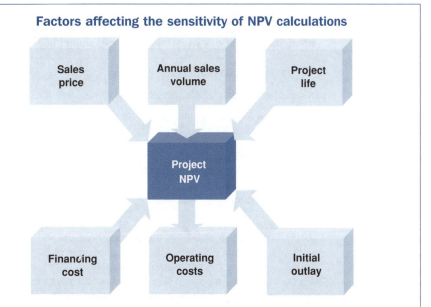

**Figure 8.5**

### Factors affecting the sensitivity of NPV calculations

Sensitivity analysis involves identifying the key factors that affect the project. In the figure, six factors have been identified for the particular project. (In practice, the key factors are likely to vary between projects.) Once identified, each factor will be examined in turn to find the value it should have for the project to have a zero NPV.

A spreadsheet model of the project can be extremely valuable for this exercise because it then becomes a very simple matter to try various values for the input data and see the effect of each. As a result of carrying out a sensitivity analysis, the decision maker is able to get a 'feel' for the project, which otherwise might not be possible. The following activity can be undertaken without recourse to a spreadsheet.

**Activity 8.18**

S. Saluja (Property Developers) Ltd intends to bid at an auction, to be held today, for a manor house that has fallen into disrepair. The auctioneer believes that the house will be sold for about £450,000. The company wishes to renovate the property and to divide it into luxury flats to be sold for £150,000 each. The renovation will be in two stages and will cover a two-year period. Stage 1 will cover the first year of the project. It will cost £500,000 and the six flats completed during this stage are expected to be sold for a total of £900,000 at the end of the first year. Stage 2 will cover the second year of the project. It will cost £300,000 and the three remaining flats are expected to be sold at the end of the second year for a total of £450,000. The cost of renovation is subject to an agreed figure with local builders; however, there is some uncertainty over the remaining input values. The company has a cost of capital of 12 per cent.

(a) What is the NPV of the proposed project?
(b) Assuming none of the other inputs deviates from the best estimates provided:

(i) What auction price would have to be paid for the manor house to cause the project to have a zero NPV?

(ii) What cost of capital would cause the project to have a zero NPV?

(iii) What is the sale price of each of the flats that would cause the project to have a zero NPV? (Each flat will be sold for the same price.)

(c) Is the level of risk associated with the project high or low? Discuss your findings.

(a) The NPV of the proposed project is as follows:

| | Cash flows £ | Discount factor 12% | Present value £ |
|---|---|---|---|
| Year 1 (£900,000 − £500,000) | 400,000 | 0.893 | 357,200 |
| Year 2 (£450,000 − £300,000) | 150,000 | 0.797 | 119,550 |
| *Less* Initial outlay | | | (450,000) |
| Net present value | | | 26,750 |

(b) (i) To obtain a zero NPV, the auction price would have to be £26,750 higher than the current estimate – that is, a total price of £476,750. This is about 6 per cent above the current estimated price.

(ii) As there is a positive NPV, the cost of capital that would cause the project to have a zero NPV must be higher than 12 per cent. Let us try 20 per cent.

| | Cash flows £ | Discount factor 20% | Present value £ |
|---|---|---|---|
| Year 1 (£900,000 − £500,000) | 400,000 | 0.833 | 333,200 |
| Year 2 (£450,000 − £300,000) | 150,000 | 0.694 | 104,100 |
| *Less* Initial outlay | | | (450,000) |
| Net present value | | | (12,700) |

The cost of capital lies somewhere between 12 per cent and 20 per cent. Increasing the discount rate by 8 percentage points (from 12 per cent to 20 per cent) causes the NPV to reduce by £39,450 (from £26,750 (positive) to £12,700 (negative)). This means £4,931 (that is £39,450/8) per 1 percentage point shift in the discount rate. At 12 per cent the NPV is £26,750 (above zero), so a discount rate of 12 per cent + [(26,750/4,931) × 1 per cent] = 17.4 per cent applies.

This approach is, of course, the same as that used when calculating the IRR of the project; in other words, 17.4 per cent is the IRR of the project.

(iii) To obtain a zero NPV, the sale price of each flat must be reduced so that the NPV is reduced by £26,750. In year 1, six flats are sold (and in year 2, three flats are sold). The discount factor at the 12 per cent rate for year 1 is 0.893 and for year 2 is 0.797. We can derive the fall in value per flat (Y) to give a zero NPV by using the equation:

$$(6Y \times 0.893) + (3Y \times 0.797) = £26,750$$
$$Y = £3,452$$

The sale price of each flat necessary to obtain a zero NPV is therefore:

£150,000 − £3,452 = £146,548

This represents a fall in the estimated price of 2.3 per cent.

(c) These calculations indicate that the auction price would have to be about 6 per cent above the estimated price before a zero NPV is obtained. The margin of safety is, therefore, not very high for this factor. The calculations also reveal that the price of the flats would only have to fall by 2.3 per cent from the estimated price before the NPV is reduced to zero. Hence, the margin of safety for this factor is even smaller. However, the cost of capital is less sensitive to changes and there would have to be an increase from 12 per cent to 17.4 per cent before the project produced a zero NPV. It seems from the calculations that the sale price of the flats is the most sensitive factor to consider. A careful re-examination of the market value of the flats seems appropriate before a final decision is made.

There are two major drawbacks with the use of sensitivity analysis:

■ It does not give managers clear decision rules concerning acceptance or rejection of the project and so they must rely on their own judgement.
■ It is a static form of analysis. Only one input is considered at a time, while the rest are held constant. In practice, however, it is likely that more than one input value will differ from the best estimates provided. Even so it would be possible to deal with changes in various inputs simultaneously, were the project data put onto a spreadsheet model.

Another means of assessing risk is through the use of statistical probabilities. It may be possible to identify a range of feasible values for each of the items of input data and to assign a probability of occurrence to each of these values. Using this information, we can derive an **expected net present value (ENPV)** that is, in effect, a weighted average of the possible outcomes where the probabilities are used as weights. To illustrate this method, let us consider Example 8.2.

| Example 8.2 | C. Piperis (Properties) Ltd has the opportunity to acquire a lease on a block of flats that has only two years remaining before it expires. The cost of the lease would be £100,000. The occupancy rate of the block of flats is currently around 70 per cent and the flats are let almost exclusively to naval personnel. There is a large naval base located nearby, and there is little other demand for the flats. The occupancy rate of the flats will change in the remaining two years of the lease, depending on the outcome of a defence review. The navy is currently considering three options for the naval base. These are: |

■ *Option 1.* Increase the size of the base by closing down a base in another region and transferring the personnel to the one located near the flats.
■ *Option 2.* Close down the naval base near to the flats and leave only a skeleton staff there for maintenance purposes. The personnel would be moved to a base in another region.
■ *Option 3.* Leave the base open but reduce staffing levels by 20 per cent.

The directors of Piperis have estimated the following net cash flows for each of the two years under each option and the probability of their occurrence:

|  | £ | Probability |
|---|---|---|
| Option 1 | 80,000 | 0.6 |
| Option 2 | 12,000 | 0.1 |
| Option 3 | 40,000 | 0.3 |
|  |  | 1.0 |

Note that the sum of the probabilities is 1.0 (in other words it is certain that one of the possible options will arise). The company has a cost of capital of 10 per cent.

Should the company purchase the lease on the block of flats?

To calculate the expected NPV of the proposed investment, we must first calculate the weighted average of the expected outcomes for each year where the probabilities are used as weights, by multiplying each cash flow by its probability of occurrence. Thus, the expected annual net cash flows will be:

|  | Cash flows £ (a) | Probability (b) | Expected cash flows £ (a × b) |
|---|---|---|---|
| Option 1 | 80,000 | 0.6 | 48,000 |
| Option 2 | 12,000 | 0.1 | 1,200 |
| Option 3 | 40,000 | 0.3 | 12,000 |
| Expected cash flows in each year |  |  | 61,200 |

Having derived the expected annual cash flows, we can now discount these using a rate of 10 per cent to reflect the cost of capital:

| Year | Expected cash flows £ | Discount rate 10% | Expected present value £ |
|---|---|---|---|
| 1 | 61,200 | 0.909 | 55,631 |
| 2 | 61,200 | 0.826 | 50,551 |
|  |  |  | 106,182 |
| Less initial investment |  |  | 100,000 |
| Expected NPV |  |  | 6,182 |

We can see that the expected NPV is positive. Hence, the wealth of shareholders is expected to increase by purchasing the lease.

The expected NPV approach has the advantage of producing a single numerical outcome and of having a clear decision rule to apply, namely; if the expected NPV is positive, we should invest; if it is negative, we should not.

However, the approach produces an average figure that may not be capable of occurring. This point was illustrated in the example above where the expected NPV does not correspond to any of the stated options. Using an average figure can also obscure the underlying risk associated with the project. This point is illustrated in Activity 8.19.

Qingdao Manufacturing Ltd is considering two competing projects. Details are as follows:

■ Project A has a 0.9 probability of producing a negative NPV of £200,000 and a 0.1 probability of producing a positive NPV of £3.8 million.
■ Project B has a 0.6 probability of producing a positive NPV of £100,000 and a 0.4 probability of producing a positive NPV of £350,000.

What is the expected net present value of each project?

The expected NPV of project A is:

$$[(0.1 \times £3.8 \text{ m}) - (0.9 \times £200,000)] = £200,000$$

The expected NPV of project B is:

$$[(0.6 \times £100,000) + (0.4 \times £350,000)] = £200,000$$

Although the expected NPV of each project in Activity 8.19 is identical, this does not mean that the business will be indifferent about which project to undertake. We can see from the information provided that project A has a high probability of making a loss whereas project B is not expected to make a loss under either possible outcome. If we assume that the shareholders of the company dislike risk – which is usually the case – they will prefer the managers of the company to take on project B as this provides the same level of expected return as project A but for a lower level of risk.

It can be argued that the problem identified above may not be significant where the business is engaged in several similar projects as it will be lost in the averaging process. However, in practice, investment projects may be unique events and this argument will not then apply. Also, where the project is large in relation to other projects undertaken, the argument loses its force.

Where the expected NPV approach is being used, it is probably a good idea to make known to managers the different possible outcomes and the probability attached to each outcome. By so doing, the managers will be able to gain an insight to the **downside risk** attached to the project. The information relating to each outcome can be presented in the form of a diagram if required. The construction of such a diagram is illustrated in Example 8.3.

Zeta Computing Services Ltd has recently produced some software for a client organisation. The software has a life of two years and will then become obsolete. The cost of producing the software was £10,000. The client has agreed to pay a licence fee of £8,000 per year for the software if it is used in only one of its two divisions, and £12,000 per year if it is used in both of its divisions. The client may use the software for either one or two years in either division but will definitely use it in at least one division in each of the two years.

Zeta Computing Services believes there is a 0.6 chance that the licence fee received in any one year will be £8,000 and a 0.4 chance that it will be £12,000. There are four possible outcomes attached to this project (where *p* denotes probability):

■ *Outcome 1.* Year 1 cash flow £8,000 ($p = 0.6$) and year 2 cash flow £8,000 ($p = 0.6$). The probability of both years having cash flows of £8,000 will be:

$$0.6 \times 0.6 = 0.36$$

■ *Outcome 2.* Year 1 cash flow £12,000 ($p = 0.4$) and year 2 cash flow £12,000 ($p = 0.4$). The probability of both years having cash flows of £12,000 will be:

$$0.4 \times 0.4 = 0.16$$

■ *Outcome 3.* Year 1 cash flow £12,000 ($p = 0.4$) and year 2 cash flow £8,000 ($p = 0.6$). The probability of this sequence of cash flows occurring will be:

$$0.4 \times 0.6 = 0.24$$

■ *Outcome 4.* Year 1 cash flow £8,000 ($p = 0.6$) and year 2 cash flow £12,000 ($p = 0.4$). The probability of this sequence of cash flows occurring will be:

$$0.6 \times 0.4 = 0.24$$

| Figure 8.6 | The different possible project outcomes for Example 8.3 |
|---|---|

| | | Cash flow £ | Probability |
|---|---|---|---|
| Outcome 1 | Year 1 (0.6) | 8,000 | 0.6 x 0.6 = 0.36 |
| | Year 2 (0.6) | 8,000 | |
| Outcome 2 | Year 1 (0.4) | 12,000 | 0.4 x 0.4 = 0.16 |
| | Year 2 (0.4) | 12,000 | |
| Outcome 3 | Year 1 (0.4) | 12,000 | 0.4 x 0.6 = 0.24 |
| | Year 2 (0.6) | 8,000 | |
| Outcome 4 | Year 1 (0.6) | 8,000 | 0.6 x 0.4 = 0.24 |
| | Year 2 (0.4) | 12,000 | Total 1.00 |

A decision tree sets out the different possible outcomes associated with a particular project and the probability of each outcome. The sum of the probabilities attached to each outcome must equal 1.00, in other words it is certain that one of the possible outcomes will occur. For example, outcome 1 would occur where only one division uses the software in each year.

The information in Example 8.3 can be displayed in the form of a diagram (Figure 8.6).

As you might expect, assigning probabilities to possible outcomes can often be a problem. There may be many possible outcomes arising from a particular investment project, and to identify each outcome and then assign a probability to it may prove to be an impossible task. When assigning probabilities to possible outcomes, either an objective or a subjective approach may be used. **Objective probabilities** are based on information gathered from past experience. Thus, for example, the transport manager of a company operating a fleet of motor vans may be able to provide information concerning the possible life of a new motor van purchased based on the record of similar vans acquired in the past. From the information available, probabilities may be developed for different possible life-spans. However, the past may not always be a reliable guide to the future, particularly during a period of rapid change. In the case of the motor vans, for example, changes in design and technology or changes in the purpose for which

➡ the vans are being used may undermine the validity of past data. **Subjective probabilities** are based on opinion and will be used where past data are either inappropriate or unavailable. The opinions of independent experts may provide a useful basis for developing subjective probabilities, although even these may contain bias, which will affect the reliability of the judgements made.

Despite these problems, we should not be dismissive of the use of probabilities. Assigning probabilities can help to make explicit some of the risks associated with a project and should help decision makers to appreciate the uncertainties that have to be faced.

---

**Activity 8.20**

Devonia (Laboratories) Ltd has recently carried out successful clinical trials on a new type of skin cream that has been developed to reduce the effects of ageing. Research and development costs incurred by the company in relation to the new product amount to £160,000. In order to gauge the market potential of the new product, independent market research consultants were hired at a cost of £15,000. The market research report submitted by the consultants indicates that the skin cream is likely to have a product life of four years and could be sold to retail chemists and large department stores at a price of £20 per 100 ml container. For each of the four years of the new product's life, sales demand has been estimated as follows:

| Number of 100 ml containers sold | Probability of occurrence |
|---|---|
| 11,000 | 0.3 |
| 14,000 | 0.6 |
| 16,000 | 0.1 |

If the company decides to launch the new product, it is possible for production to begin at once. The equipment necessary to produce the skin cream is already owned by the company and originally cost £150,000. At the end of the new product's life, it is estimated that the equipment could be sold for £35,000. If the company decides against launching the new product, the equipment will be sold immediately for £85,000 as it will be of no further use to the company.

The new skin cream will require two hours' labour for each 100 ml container produced. The cost of labour for the new product is £4.00 per hour. Additional workers will have to be recruited to produce the new product. At the end of the product's life, the workers are unlikely to be offered further work with the company and redundancy costs of £10,000 are expected. The cost of the ingredients for each 100 ml container is £6.00. Additional overheads arising from production of the new product are expected to be £15,000 per year.

The new skin cream has attracted the interest of the company's competitors. If the company decides not to produce and sell the skin cream, it can sell the patent rights to a major competitor immediately for £125,000.

Devonia has a cost of capital of 12 per cent. Ignore taxation.

(a) Calculate the expected net present value (ENPV) of the new product.
(b) State, with reasons, whether or not Devonia should launch the new product.

Your answer should be as follows:

(a) Expected sales volume per year = $(11,000 \times 0.3) + (14,000 \times 0.6)$
$+ (16,000 \times 0.1)$
= 13,300 units

Expected annual sales revenue = $13,300 \times £20$
= £266,000

Annual labour = $13,300 \times £8$
= £106,400

Annual ingredient costs = $13,300 \times £6$
= £79,800

Incremental cash flows:

| | | | Years | | |
|---|---|---|---|---|---|
| | 0 £000 | 1 £000 | 2 £000 | 3 £000 | 4 £000 |
| Sale of patent rights | (125.0) | | | | |
| Sale of equipment | (85.0) | | | | 35.0 |
| Sales | | 266.0 | 266.0 | 266.0 | 266.0 |
| Cost of ingredients | | (79.8) | (79.8) | (79.8) | (79.8) |
| Labour costs | | (106.4) | (106.4) | (106.4) | (106.4) |
| Redundancy | | | | | (10.0) |
| Additional overheads | | (15.0) | (15.0) | (15.0) | (15.0) |
| | (210.0) | 64.8 | 64.8 | 64.8 | 89.8 |
| Discount factor (12%) | 1.0 | 0.893 | 0.797 | 0.712 | 0.636 |
| | (210.0) | 57.9 | 51.6 | 46.1 | 57.1 |
| ENPV | 2.7 | | | | |

(b) As the ENPV of the project is positive, the wealth of shareholders would be increased by accepting the project. However, the ENPV is very low in relation to the size of the project and careful checking of the key estimates and assumptions would be advisable. A relatively small downward revision of sales or upward revision of costs could make the project ENPV negative.

## Reacting to the level of risk

The logical reaction to a risky project is to demand a higher rate of return. Both theory and observable evidence show that there is a relationship between risk and the return required by investors. It was mentioned earlier, for example, that a bank would normally ask for a higher rate of interest on a loan where it perceives the lender to be less likely to be able to repay the amount borrowed.

When evaluating investment projects, it is normal to increase the NPV discount rate in the face of increased risk – that is, to demand a risk premium. The higher the level of risk, therefore, the higher the risk premium that will be demanded. The risk premium is usually added to a 'risk-free' rate of return to derive the total return required. The risk-free rate is normally taken to be equivalent to the rate of return from government loan stock. In practice, a business may divide projects into low-, medium- and high-risk categories and then assign a risk premium to each category. The cash flows from a particular project will then be discounted using a rate based on the risk-free rate plus the appropriate risk premium. This relationship between risk and return is illustrated in Figure 8.7.

**Figure 8.7**

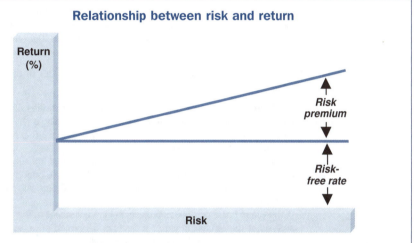

**Relationship between risk and return**

It is possible to take account of the riskiness of projects by changing the discount rate. A risk premium is added to the risk-free rate to derive the appropriate discount rate. A higher return will normally be expected from projects where the risks are higher. Thus, the riskier the project, the higher the risk premium.

→    The use of a **risk-adjusted discount rate** provides managers with a single numerical outcome, which can be used when making a decision either to accept or reject a project. Moreover, managers are likely to have an intuitive grasp of the relationship between risk and return and may well feel comfortable with this technique. However, there are practical difficulties with implementing this approach.

**Activity 8.21**

Can you think of any practical problems with the use of risk-adjusted discount rates?

Subjective judgement is required when assigning an investment project to a particular risk category and then in assigning a risk premium to each category. The choices made will reflect the personal views of the managers responsible and this may differ from the views of the shareholders they represent. The choices made can, nevertheless, make the difference between accepting or rejecting a particular project.

As we saw with Exhibit 8.1 it seems that most larger UK businesses use NPV as a technique for assessing investments. Some businesses mention their approach to using the technique, in their annual report. Exhibit 8.2 gives some examples.

| Exhibit 8.2 | **The use of NPV in practice** |
|---|---|

In its 2000 annual report, the high-street retailer Marks & Spencer plc said:

> All investment decisions are made using discounted cashflow analysis, applying a hurdle rate determined by assessing the business risk appropriate to the specific operating division.

The report also said that the business's average financing cost is 10 per cent a year.

The Boots Company plc, the high-street pharmacy that also owns the Halfords chain of motoring requisites shops, said in its 2000 annual report:

> We determine the level of investment in our businesses not by sales growth or operating profit but by 'economic profit'. This is the present value return we expect to make for shareholders after charging an appropriate amount for the capital invested. Currently, this cost of capital for most of the group is 8.5%, after tax and after discounting separately for specific risk.

In its 1999 annual report, Rolls-Royce plc, the builder of aircraft and other engines, said the following:

> The Group looks to create shareholder value in all activities undertaken. A feature of the company's business is very long product life-cycles. Typically, a gas turbine engine family will sell for over 20 years, followed by long-term aftermarket support. This provides long-term predictability of sales and hence requires extended business plans.
>
> Potential new products, acquisitions and investments are subjected to rigorous examination of risks and future cash flows. The net present value of the opportunity is calculated using a 10 per cent cost of capital to establish its value to the Group. All major investments require Board approval.
>
> The Group has a portfolio of projects at different stages of their life cycles. Discounted cash flow analysis of the remaining life of projects is performed on a regular basis to compute the value which underlies the Group's market capitalisation.

The three businesses in Exhibit 8.2 seem broadly consistent in using a discount rate around 10 per cent (Boots's 8.5 per cent rate is after having reduced the cash flows to take account of risk, so its effective discount rate is above that value). Ten per cent seems to be the rate that is currently popular in practice, according to research and to comments that appear in the financial press.

Note that all three of the businesses refer specifically to risk in the context of investment appraisal.

Rolls-Royce says that it not only assesses new projects but also re-assesses existing projects. This must be a sensible commercial approach. Businesses should not continue with existing projects unless those projects have a positive NPV based on future cash flows. Just because a project seemed to have a positive NPV before it started does not mean that this will persist, in the light of changing circumstances.

## Management of the investment project

So far, we have been concerned with the process of carrying out the necessary calculations that enable managers to select between already identified investment opportunities. This topic is given a great deal of emphasis in the literature on investment appraisal. Although the evaluation of projects is undoubtedly important, we must bear in mind that it is only *part* of the process of investment decision making. There are other important aspects that managers must also consider.

It is possible to see the investment process as a sequence of five stages, each of which managers must consider. The five stages are set out in Figure 8.8 and described below.

Figure 8.8

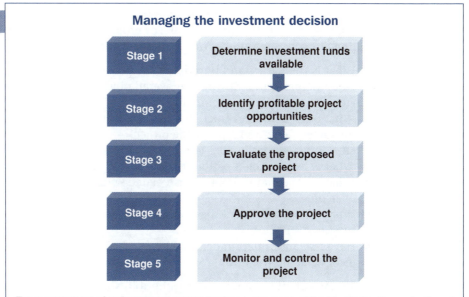

**Managing the investment decision**

| Stage 1 | Determine investment funds available |
| Stage 2 | Identify profitable project opportunities |
| Stage 3 | Evaluate the proposed project |
| Stage 4 | Approve the project |
| Stage 5 | Monitor and control the project |

The management of an investment project involves a sequence of five key stages. The evaluation of projects using the appraisal techniques discussed earlier represents only one of these stages.

## Stage 1: Determine investment funds available

The amount of funds available for investment may be determined by the external market for funds or by internal management. In practice, it is often the latter that has the greater influence on the amount available. In either case, it may be that the funds will not be sufficient to finance the profitable investment opportunities available. When this occurs, some form of **capital rationing** has to be undertaken. This means that managers are faced with the task of deciding on the most profitable use of the investment funds available. Various approaches may be used; however, these are beyond the scope of this book.

## Stage 2: Identify profitable project opportunities

A vitally important part of the investment process is the search for profitable investment opportunities. A business should carry out methodical routines for identifying feasible projects. This may be done through a research and development department or by some other means. Failure to do so will inevitably lead to the business losing its competitive position regarding product development, production methods or market penetration. To help identify good investment opportunities, some businesses provide financial incentives to staff who have good ideas. The search process will, however, usually involve looking outside the business to identify changes in technology, customer demand, market conditions and so on. Information will need to be gathered and this may take some time, particularly for unusual or non-routine investment opportunities.

## Stage 3: Evaluate the proposed project

If management is to agree to the investment of funds in a project, there must be a proper screening of each proposal. For projects of any size, this will involve providing answers to a number of questions, including:

- What is the nature and purpose of the project?
- Does the project align with the overall objectives of the business?
- How much finance is required?
- What other resources (such as expertise, factory space and so on) are required for successful completion of the project?
- How long will the project last and what are its key stages?
- What is the expected pattern of cash flows?
- What are the major problems associated with the project and how can they be overcome?
- What is the NPV/IRR of the project? How does this compare with other opportunities available?
- Have risk and inflation been taken into account in the appraisal process and, if so, what are the results?

It is important to appreciate that the ability and commitment of those responsible for proposing and managing the project will be vital to the success of the investment. Hence, when evaluating a new project, those proposing it will be judged by its success. In some cases, senior managers may decide not to support a project that appears profitable on paper if they lack confidence in the ability of key managers to see it through to completion.

## Stage 4: Approve the project

Once the managers responsible for investment decision making are satisfied that the project should be undertaken, formal approval can be given. However, a decision on a project may be postponed if senior managers need more information from those proposing the project, or if revisions are required to the proposal. In some cases, the project proposal may be rejected if it is considered unprofitable or likely to fail. Before rejecting a proposal, however, the implications of not pursuing the project for such areas as market share, staff morale and existing business operations must be carefully considered.

## Stage 5: Monitor and control the project

Making a decision to invest in, say, the plant needed to go into production of a new product does not automatically cause the investment to be made and production to go smoothly ahead. Managers will need to manage the project actively through to completion. This, in turn, will require further information-gathering exercises.

Management should receive progress reports at regular intervals concerning the project. These reports should provide information relating to the actual cash flows for each stage of the project, which can then be compared against the forecast figures provided when the proposal was submitted for approval. The reasons for significant variations should be ascertained and corrective action taken where possible. Any changes in the expected completion date of the project or any expected variations in future cash flows from budget should be reported immediately; in extreme cases, managers may even abandon the project if circumstances appear to have changed dramatically for the worse. We saw in Exhibit 8.2 that Rolls-Royce undertakes this kind of re-assessment of existing projects. No doubt most other well-managed businesses do this too.

Project management techniques (for example, critical path analysis) should be employed wherever possible and their effectiveness reported to senior management.

➡ An important part of the control process is a **post-completion audit** of the project. This is, in essence, a review of the project performance in order to see whether it lived up to expectations and whether any lessons can be learned from the way that the investment process was carried out. In addition to an evaluation of financial costs and benefits, non-financial measures of performance such as the ability to meet deadlines and levels of quality achieved should also be reported. (See Chapter 5 for a discussion of total life-cycle costing, which is based on similar principles.)

The fact that a post-completion audit is an integral part of the management of the project should also encourage those who submit projects to use realistic estimates. Where over-optimistic estimates are used in an attempt to secure project approval, the managers responsible will find themselves accountable at the post-completion audit stage. Such audits, however, can be difficult and time-consuming to carry out, and so the likely benefits must be weighed against the costs involved. Senior management may feel, therefore, that only projects above a certain size should be subject to a post-completion audit.

## Summary

In this chapter we have considered how managers might approach the problem of assessing investment opportunities. We have seen that there are basically four methods that are used to any significant extent in practice. These are:

- Accounting rate of return
- Payback period
- Net present value
- Internal rate of return.

The first two of these are seriously flawed by their failure to take full account of the time dimension of investments. Assuming that the objective of making investments is to maximise the wealth of shareholders, the NPV method is, theoretically, far superior to the other three methods in that it rationally and fully takes account of all relevant information. Since IRR is similar to NPV, it tends to give similar signals to those provided by NPV. However, IRR suffers from a fundamental theoretical flaw that can lead to it giving misleading signals on some occasions.

We have also looked at evidence concerning the use of appraisal techniques in practice. The discounting methods (NPV and IRR) are now the most popular, among large businesses at least. Despite its theoretical limitations, the payback method remains popular.

We went on to consider the problem of risk in investment appraisal and examined various techniques for incorporating risk into the decision-making process. We saw that none of the techniques discussed were perfect, but that this does not mean they should be dismissed. Any attempt to take account of risk is probably preferable to relying on intuition.

Finally, we considered the procedures for managing the investment process. We saw that investment appraisal techniques are only one aspect of the investment process and that other aspects such as the search for suitable projects and the monitoring and control of projects, are important for successful investment.

→ **Key terms**

Accounting rate of return (ARR)   p. 190
Payback period (PP)   p. 194
Net present value (NPV)   p. 197
Risk   p. 198
Inflation   p. 199
Discount factor   p. 202
Internal rate of return (IRR)   p. 204

Sensitivity analysis   p. 212
Expected net present value (ENPV)   p. 215
Objective probabilities   p. 218
Subjective probabilities   p. 219
Risk-adjusted discount rate   p. 221
Post-completion audit   p. 225

## Further reading

If you would like to explore the topics covered in this chapter in more depth, we recommend the following books:

**Corporate Financial Management**, *Arnold, G.*, Financial Times Prentice Hall, 1998, chapters 2, 3 and 4.

**Investment Appraisal and Financial Decisions**, *Lumby, S.* and *Jones, C.*, 6th edn, International Thomson Business Press, 1999, chapters 3, 5 and 6.

**Business Finance: Theory and Practice**, *McLaney, E.*, 5th edn, Financial Times Prentice Hall, 2000, chapters 4–6.

**Corporate Finance and Investment**, *Pike, R.* and *Neale, B.*, 3rd edn, Prentice Hall International, 1999, chapters 5 and 7.

## References

1. 'Investment and finance decision making in large, medium and small UK companies', *Arnold, G. C.* and *Hatzopoulos, P.*, unpublished but cited in Arnold, G. C. Corporate Financial Management, FT Pearson, 1998.

## ? REVIEW QUESTIONS

**8.1**  Why is the net present value method of investment appraisal considered to be theoretically superior to other methods found in the literature?

**8.2**  The payback method has been criticised for not taking into account the time value of money. Could this limitation be overcome? If so, would this method then be preferable to the NPV method?

**8.3**  Research indicates that the IRR method is a more popular method of investment appraisal than the NPV method. Why might this be?

**8.4**  Why are cash flows rather than profit flows used in the IRR, NPV and PP methods of investment appraisal?

## ? EXERCISES

Questions 8.5–8.8 are more advanced that 8.1–8.4. Those with coloured numbers have answers at the back of the book.

**8.1**  The directors of Mylo Ltd are currently considering two mutually exclusive investment projects. Both projects are concerned with the purchase of new plant. The following data are available for the projects:

|  | Project 1 £ | Project 2 £ |
|---|---|---|
| Cost (immediate outlay) | 100,000 | 60,000 |
| Expected annual net profit (loss): |  |  |
| Year 1 | 29,000 | 18,000 |
| Year 2 | (1,000) | (2,000) |
| Year 3 | 2,000 | 4,000 |
| Estimated residual value | 7,000 | 6,000 |

The company has an estimated cost of capital of 10 per cent and uses the straight-line method of depreciation for all fixed assets when calculating net profit. Neither project would increase the working capital of the company. The company has sufficient funds to meet all capital expenditure requirements.

**Required:**
(a) Calculate for each project:
  (i)   The net present value
  (ii)  The approximate internal rate of return
  (iii) The payback period.
(b) State which, if any, of the two investment projects the directors of Mylo Ltd should accept, and why.
(c) State, in general terms, which method of investment appraisal you consider to be most appropriate for evaluating investment projects, and why.

**8.2** Myers Software plc is a major distributor of computer software to small and medium-sized businesses. Although the company develops some software products itself, most are purchased from various software houses. The board of directors is currently considering the investment potential of three new tax-accounting software products that have been developed by different software houses and offered for sale to the company. The financial director of Myers Software plc has prepared the following financial estimates concerning the products:

| Software name | Initial outlay | Cash flows | | |
|---|---|---|---|---|
| | | Year 1 | Year 2 | Year 3 |
| | £ | £ | £ | £ |
| Taxmate | (60,000) | 25,000 | 30,000 | 32,000 |
| Easytax | (120,000) | 50,000 | 70,000 | 40,000 |
| Supertax | (180,000) | 95,000 | 80,000 | 58,000 |

The company has a cost of capital of 10 per cent. Ignore taxation.

**Required:**
(a) Using each of the following appraisal methods, rank the products in order of investment potential:
  (i)   Net present value (NPV)
  (ii)  Approximate internal rate of return (IRR)
  (iii) Payback.
(b) If the products were mutually exclusive, which product, if any, would you select and why?

**8.3** Haverhill Engineers Limited manufactures components for the car industry. It is considering automating its line for producing crankshaft bearings. The automated equipment will cost £700,000. It will replace equipment with a scrap value of £50,000 and a balance sheet value of £180,000.

At present, the existing ('old') line has a capacity of 1.25 million units a year but typically it has only been run at 80 per cent of capacity because of the lack of demand for its output. The new line has a capacity of 1.4 million units a year. Its life is expected to be five years and its scrap value at that time £100,000.

The accountant has prepared the following cost estimates based on output of 1,000,000 units a year:

| | Old line (per unit) £ | New line (per unit) £ |
|---|---|---|
| Materials | 0.40 | 0.36 |
| Labour | 0.22 | 0.10 |
| Variable overheads | 0.14 | 0.14 |
| Fixed overheads | 0.44 | 0.20 |
| | 1.20 | 0.80 |
| Selling price | 1.50 | 1.50 |
| Profit per unit | 0.30 | 0.70 |

Fixed overheads include depreciation on the old machine of £40,000 a year and £120,000 for the new machine. It is considered that, for the company overall, fixed overheads are unlikely to change.

The introduction of the new machine will enable stocks to be reduced by £160,000. The company uses 10 per cent as its cost of capital. You should ignore taxation.

**Required:**
(a) Prepare a statement of the incremental cash flows arising from the project.
(b) Calculate the project's net present value.
(c) Calculate the project's approximate internal rate of return.
(d) Explain the terms 'net present value' and 'internal rate of return'. State which method you consider to be preferable, giving reasons for your choice.

**8.4** Lansdown Engineers Limited is considering replacing its existing heating system. A firm of heating engineers has recommended two schemes, each of which will give a similar heating performance. Details of these and of the cost of the existing system appear below:

|  | Year | Existing system £000 | System A £000 | System B £000 |
|---|---|---|---|---|
| Capital cost | 0 |  | 70 | 150 |
| Annual running cost | 1 to 10 | 145 | 140 | 120 |
| Scrap value | 10 | 10 | 14 | 30 |

The existing heating system at present has a balance sheet value of £50,000 and a scrap value of £5,000. To keep the existing system working, an overhaul costing £20,000 would be required immediately. For your calculations you should ignore inflation and taxation. The company has a 12 per cent cost of capital.

**Required:**
(a) Calculate the net present value (to the nearest £1,000) of each of the two new schemes. You should consider each in isolation and ignore the existing system.
(b) Calculate the incremental cash flows (to the nearest £1,000) of system B over the existing system.
(c) Estimate the internal rate of return on the cash flow calculated in part (b).
(d) On the basis of your answers to (a), (b) and (c), give briefly your recommendations with reasons.

**8.5** Chesterfield Wanderers is a professional football club that has enjoyed considerable success in both national and European competitions in recent years. As a result, the club has accumulated £1 million to spend on its further development. The board of directors is currently considering two mutually exclusive options for spending the funds available.

The first option is to acquire another player. The team manager has expressed a keen interest in acquiring Basil ('Bazza') Ramsey, a central defender, who currently plays for a rival club. The rival club has agreed to release the player immediately for £1 million if required. A decision to acquire 'Bazza' Ramsey would mean that the existing central defender, Vinnie Smith, could be sold to another club. Chesterfield Wanderers has recently received an offer of £220,000 for this player. This offer is still open but will only be accepted if 'Bazza' Ramsey joins Chesterfield Wanderers. If this does not happen, Vinnie Smith will be expected to stay on with the club until the end of his playing career in five years' time. During this period, Vinnie will receive an annual salary of £40,000 and a loyalty bonus of £20,000 at the end of his five-year period with the club.

Assuming 'Bazza' Ramsey is acquired, the team manager estimates that gate receipts will increase by £250,000 in the first year and £130,000 in each of the four following years. There will also be an increase in advertising and sponsorship revenues of £120,000 for each of the next five years if the player is acquired. At the end of five years, the player can be sold to a club in a lower division and Chesterfield Wanderers will expect to receive £100,000 as a transfer fee. During his period at the club, 'Bazza' will receive an annual salary of £80,000 and a loyalty bonus of £40,000 after five years.

The second option is for the club to improve its ground facilities. The west stand could be converted into an all-seater area and executive boxes could be built for businesses wishing to offer corporate hospitality to clients. These improvements would also cost £1 million and would take one year to complete. During this period, the west stand would be closed, resulting in a reduction of gate receipts of £180,000. However, gate receipts for each of the following four years would be £440,000 higher than current receipts. In five years' time, the club has plans to sell the existing grounds and to move to a new stadium nearby. Payment for the improvements will be made when the work has been completed at the end of the first year. Whichever option is chosen, the board of directors has decided to take on additional ground staff. The additional wages bill is expected to be £35,000 a year over the next five years.

The club has a cost of capital of 10 per cent. Ignore taxation.

**Required:**

(a) Calculate the incremental cash flows arising from each of the options available to the club.

(b) Calculate the net present value of each of the options.

(c) On the basis of the calculations made in (b) above, which of the two options would you choose and why?

(d) Discuss the validity of using the net present value method in making investment decisions for a professional football club.

**8.6** Newton Electronics Ltd has incurred expenditure of £5 million over the past three years researching and developing a miniature hearing aid. The hearing aid is now fully developed and the directors are considering which of three mutually exclusive options should be taken to exploit the potential of the new product. The options are as follows:

1. The business could manufacture the hearing aid itself. This would be a new departure for the business, which has so far concentrated on research and development projects only. However, the business has manufacturing space available that it currently rents to another business for £100,000 a year. The business would have to purchase plant and equipment costing £9 million and invest £3 million in working capital immediately for production to begin.

   A market research report, for which the business paid £50,000, indicates that the new product has an expected life of five years. Sales of the product during this period are predicted as follows:

|  | Predicted sales for the year ended 30 November | | | | |
|---|---|---|---|---|---|
|  | Year 1 | Year 2 | Year 3 | Year 4 | Year 5 |
| Number of units ('000) | 800 | 1,400 | 1,800 | 1,200 | 500 |

The selling price per unit will be £30 in the first year but will fall to £22 in the following three years. In the final year of the product's life, the selling price will fall to £20. Variable production costs are predicted to be £14 per unit and fixed production costs (including depreciation) will be £2.4 million a year. Marketing costs will be £2 million a year.

The business intends to depreciate the plant and equipment using the straight-line method based on an estimated residual value at the end of the five years of £1 million. The business has a cost of capital of 10 per cent.

2. Newton Electronics Ltd could agree to another business manufacturing and marketing the product under licence. A multinational business, Faraday Electricals plc, has offered to undertake the manufacture and marketing of the product and, in return, will make a royalty payment to Newton Electronics of £5 per unit. It has been estimated that the annual number of sales of the hearing aid will be 10 per cent higher if the multinational business, rather than Newton Electronics, manufactures and markets the product.

3. Newton Electronics could sell the patent rights to Faraday Electricals for £24 million, payable in two equal instalments. The first instalment would be payable immediately and the second at the end of two years. This option would give Faraday Electricals the exclusive right to manufacture and market the new product.

Ignore taxation.

**Required:**
(a) Calculate the net present value of each of the options available to Newton Electronics Ltd.
(b) Identify and discuss any other factors that Newton Electronics Ltd should consider before arriving at a decision.
(c) What do you consider to be the most suitable option, and why?

**8.7** Simtex Ltd has invested £120,000 to date in developing a new type of shaving foam. The shaving foam is now ready for production and it has been estimated that the new product will sell 160,000 bottles per year over the next four years. At the end of four years, the product will be discontinued and replaced by a new product.

The shaving foam is expected to sell at £6 per can and variable costs are estimated at £4 per can. Fixed costs (excluding depreciation) are expected to be £300,000 per year. (This figure includes £130,000 in fixed costs incurred by the existing business which will be apportioned to this new product.)

To manufacture and package the new product, equipment costing £480,000 must be acquired immediately. The estimated value of this equipment in four years' time is £100,000. The business calculates depreciation using the straight-line method, and has an estimated cost of capital of 12 per cent.

**Required:**
(a) Deduce the net present value of the new product.
(b) Calculate by how much each of the following must change before the new product is no longer profitable:

  (i) the discount rate
  (ii) the initial outlay on new equipment
  (iii) the net operating cash flows
  (iv) the residual value of the equipment.
 (c) Should the business produce the new product?

**8.8** Kernow Cleaning Services Ltd provides street-cleaning services for local councils in the far south west of England. The work is currently labour intensive and few machines are employed. However, the business has recently been considering the purchase of a fleet of street-cleaning vehicles at a total cost of £540,000. The vehicles have a life of four years and are likely to result in a considerable saving of labour costs. Estimates of the likely labour savings and their probability of occurrence are set out below:

| | Estimated savings £ | Probability of occurrence |
|---|---|---|
| Year 1 | 80,000 | 0.3 |
| | 160,000 | 0.5 |
| | 200,000 | 0.2 |
| Year 2 | 140,000 | 0.4 |
| | 220,000 | 0.4 |
| | 250,000 | 0.2 |
| Year 3 | 140,000 | 0.4 |
| | 200,000 | 0.3 |
| | 230,000 | 0.3 |
| Year 4 | 100,000 | 0.3 |
| | 170,000 | 0.6 |
| | 200,000 | 0.1 |

Estimates for each year are independent of other years. The business has a cost of capital of 10 per cent.

**Required:**
(a) Calculate the expected net present value (ENPV) of the street-cleaning machines.
(b) Calculate the net present value (NPV) of the worst possible outcome and the probability of its occurrence.

## Present value table

Present value of 1, that is $1/(1 + r)^n$ where $r$ = discount rate and $n$ = number of periods until the cash flow occurs.

| Period (n) | 1% | 2% | 3% | 4% | 5% | 6% | 7% | 8% | 9% | 10% | |
|---|---|---|---|---|---|---|---|---|---|---|---|
| 1 | 0.990 | 0.980 | 0.971 | 0.962 | 0.952 | 0.943 | 0.935 | 0.926 | 0.917 | 0.909 | 1 |
| 2 | 0.980 | 0.961 | 0.943 | 0.925 | 0.907 | 0.890 | 0.873 | 0.857 | 0.842 | 0.826 | 2 |
| 3 | 0.971 | 0.942 | 0.915 | 0.889 | 0.864 | 0.840 | 0.816 | 0.794 | 0.772 | 0.751 | 3 |
| 4 | 0.961 | 0.924 | 0.888 | 0.855 | 0.823 | 0.792 | 0.763 | 0.735 | 0.708 | 0.683 | 4 |
| 5 | 0.951 | 0.906 | 0.863 | 0.822 | 0.784 | 0.747 | 0.713 | 0.681 | 0.650 | 0.621 | 5 |
| 6 | 0.942 | 0.888 | 0.837 | 0.790 | 0.746 | 0.705 | 0.666 | 0.630 | 0.596 | 0.565 | 6 |
| 7 | 0.933 | 0.871 | 0.813 | 0.760 | 0.711 | 0.665 | 0.623 | 0.583 | 0.547 | 0.513 | 7 |
| 8 | 0.923 | 0.853 | 0.789 | 0.731 | 0.677 | 0.627 | 0.582 | 0.540 | 0.502 | 0.467 | 8 |
| 9 | 0.914 | 0.837 | 0.766 | 0.703 | 0.645 | 0.592 | 0.544 | 0.500 | 0.460 | 0.424 | 9 |
| 10 | 0.905 | 0.820 | 0.744 | 0.676 | 0.614 | 0.558 | 0.508 | 0.463 | 0.422 | 0.386 | 10 |
| 11 | 0.896 | 0.804 | 0.722 | 0.650 | 0.585 | 0.527 | 0.475 | 0.429 | 0.388 | 0.350 | 11 |
| 12 | 0.887 | 0.788 | 0.701 | 0.625 | 0.557 | 0.497 | 0.444 | 0.397 | 0.356 | 0.319 | 12 |
| 13 | 0.879 | 0.773 | 0.681 | 0.601 | 0.530 | 0.469 | 0.415 | 0.368 | 0.326 | 0.290 | 13 |
| 14 | 0.870 | 0.758 | 0.661 | 0.577 | 0.505 | 0.442 | 0.388 | 0.340 | 0.299 | 0.263 | 14 |
| 15 | 0.861 | 0.743 | 0.642 | 0.555 | 0.481 | 0.417 | 0.362 | 0.315 | 0.275 | 0.239 | 15 |

| | 11% | 12% | 13% | 14% | 15% | 16% | 17% | 18% | 19% | 20% | |
|---|---|---|---|---|---|---|---|---|---|---|---|
| 1 | 0.901 | 0.893 | 0.885 | 0.877 | 0.870 | 0.862 | 0.855 | 0.847 | 0.840 | 0.833 | 1 |
| 2 | 0.812 | 0.797 | 0.783 | 0.769 | 0.756 | 0.743 | 0.731 | 0.718 | 0.706 | 0.694 | 2 |
| 3 | 0.731 | 0.712 | 0.693 | 0.675 | 0.658 | 0.641 | 0.624 | 0.609 | 0.593 | 0.579 | 3 |
| 4 | 0.659 | 0.636 | 0.613 | 0.592 | 0.572 | 0.552 | 0.534 | 0.516 | 0.499 | 0.482 | 4 |
| 5 | 0.593 | 0.567 | 0.543 | 0.519 | 0.497 | 0.476 | 0.456 | 0.437 | 0.419 | 0.402 | 5 |
| 6 | 0.535 | 0.507 | 0.480 | 0.456 | 0.432 | 0.410 | 0.390 | 0.370 | 0.352 | 0.335 | 6 |
| 7 | 0.482 | 0.452 | 0.425 | 0.400 | 0.376 | 0.354 | 0.333 | 0.314 | 0.296 | 0.279 | 7 |
| 8 | 0.434 | 0.404 | 0.376 | 0.351 | 0.327 | 0.305 | 0.285 | 0.266 | 0.249 | 0.233 | 8 |
| 9 | 0.391 | 0.361 | 0.333 | 0.308 | 0.284 | 0.263 | 0.243 | 0.225 | 0.209 | 0.194 | 9 |
| 10 | 0.352 | 0.322 | 0.295 | 0.270 | 0.247 | 0.227 | 0.208 | 0.191 | 0.176 | 0.162 | 10 |
| 11 | 0.317 | 0.287 | 0.261 | 0.237 | 0.215 | 0.195 | 0.178 | 0.162 | 0.148 | 0.135 | 11 |
| 12 | 0.286 | 0.257 | 0.231 | 0.208 | 0.187 | 0.168 | 0.152 | 0.137 | 0.124 | 0.112 | 12 |
| 13 | 0.258 | 0.229 | 0.204 | 0.182 | 0.163 | 0.145 | 0.130 | 0.116 | 0.104 | 0.093 | 13 |
| 14 | 0.232 | 0.205 | 0.181 | 0.160 | 0.141 | 0.125 | 0.111 | 0.099 | 0.088 | 0.078 | 14 |
| 15 | 0.209 | 0.183 | 0.160 | 0.140 | 0.123 | 0.108 | 0.095 | 0.084 | 0.074 | 0.065 | 15 |

# Managing working capital

## Introduction

In this chapter we consider the factors that must be taken into account when managing the working capital of a business. Each element of working capital will be identified, and the major issues surrounding the elements will be discussed.

**OBJECTIVES**

When you have completed this chapter you should be able to:

■ Identify the main elements of working capital.
■ Discuss the purpose of working capital and the nature of the working capital cycle.
■ Explain the importance of establishing policies for the control of working capital.
■ Explain the factors that have to be taken into account when managing each element of working capital.

## The nature and purpose of working capital

➡ **Working capital** is usually defined as:

> Current assets *less* Current liabilities (that is, creditors due within one year)

The major elements of current assets are:

■ Stocks
■ Trade debtors
■ Cash (in hand and at bank)

The major elements of current liabilities are:

■ Trade creditors
■ Bank overdrafts

The size and composition of working capital can vary between industries. For some types of business, the investment in working capital can be substantial. For example, a manufacturing company will typically invest heavily in raw materials, work in progress, and finished goods; and it will often sell its goods on credit thereby generating trade debtors. A retailer, on the other hand, will hold only one form of stock (finished goods) and will usually sell goods for cash.

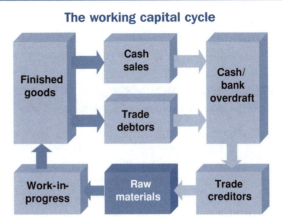

**Figure 9.1**

## The working capital cycle

The diagram shows the working capital cycle for a manufacturing business. Raw materials are acquired and converted into work in progress and, finally, into finished goods. The finished goods are sold to customers for either cash or credit. In the case of credit customers, there will be a delay before the cash is received from the sales. Cash generated from sales can then be used to pay suppliers, who will normally supply goods on credit.

Working capital represents a net investment in short-term assets. These assets are continually flowing into and out of a business and are essential for day-to-day operations. The various elements of working capital are interrelated and can be seen as part of a short-term cycle. Figure 9.1 depicts the working capital cycle for a manufacturing business.

The management of working capital is an essential part of a business's short-term planning process. It is necessary for management to decide how much of each element should be held. As we shall see later, there are costs associated with holding both too much and too little of each element. Management must be aware of these costs in order to manage effectively. Management must also be aware that there may be other, more profitable, uses for the funds of the business. Hence the potential benefits must be weighed against the likely costs in order to achieve the optimum investment.

The working capital needs of a particular business are likely to change over time, as a result of changes in the commercial environment. This means that working capital decisions are rarely one-off decisions. Managers must try to identify changes, in an attempt to ensure that the level of investment in working capital is appropriate.

**Activity 9.1**

What kinds of change in the commercial environment might lead to a decision to change the level of investment in working capital? Try to identify four possible changes.

In answering this activity, you may have thought of the following:

- Changes in interest rates
- Changes in market demand
- Changes in the seasons
- Changes in the state of the economy

You may have thought of others.

In addition to changes in the external environment, changes arising within the business – such as changes in production methods (resulting, perhaps, in a need to hold less stock) and changes in the level of risk that managers are prepared to take – could alter the required level of investment in working capital.

# The scale of working capital

It is tempting to form the impression that, compared with the scale of investment in fixed assets by a typical business, the amounts involved with working capital are pretty trivial. This would be a false assessment of reality – the scale of working capital for most businesses is vast. Exhibit 9.1 gives some impression of the working capital involvement for five UK businesses that are either very well known by name or whose products are everyday commodities for most of us.

**Exhibit 9.1**

**A summary of the balance sheets of five UK businesses**

| Business | The Boots Company plc | Rolls-Royce plc | The Go-Ahead Group plc | Fuller Smith and Turner plc | Anglia Water plc |
|---|---|---|---|---|---|
| Balance sheet date | 31.3.00 | 31.12.99 | 1.7.00 | 25.3.00 | 31.3.00 |
|  | % | % | % | % | % |
| Fixed assets | 84 | 73 | 114 | 96 | 99 |
| **Current assets** |  |  |  |  |  |
| Stock | 29 | 33 | 2 | 3 | – |
| Trade debtors | 12 | 23 | 14 | 4 | 4 |
| Other debtors | 6 | 21 | 23 | 3 | 2 |
| Cash and near cash | 18 | 25 | 26 | 8 | 4 |
|  | 65 | 102 | 65 | 18 | 10 |
| **Current liabilities** |  |  |  |  |  |
| Trade creditors | 15 | 17 | 17 | 5 | 3 |
| Tax and dividends | 14 | 8 | 13 | 5 | – |
| Other short-term liabilities | 11 | 39 | 46 | 4 | 4 |
| Overdrafts and short-term loans | 9 | 11 | 3 | – | 2 |
|  | 49 | 75 | 79 | 14 | 9 |
| Working capital | 16 | 27 | (14) | 4 | 1 |
| **Total long-term investment** | 100 | 100 | 100 | 100 | 100 |

The fixed assets, current assets and current liabilities (the last being creditors: amounts falling due within one year) expressed as a percentage of the total net investment of the business concerned. The businesses were randomly selected, except that they were deliberately taken from different industries. Boots (the high-street chemist) is a manufacturer and retailer of health and personal care products. Rolls-Royce manufactures engines and electrical generating equipment. Go-Ahead provides urban public train and bus services, including Thames Trains. Fuller Smith and Turner manages pubs and hotels in and around London, also brewing (perhaps most famously) London Pride bitter. Anglia Water supplies water and collects and treats waste water.

The totals for current assets are generally pretty large when compared with the total long-term investment. The amounts vary considerably from one type of business to the next. Rolls-Royce is the only one of the five businesses that is solely a manufacturer. Boots is the only other one that holds a significant amount of stock. Go-Ahead and Anglia provide a service and so hold little or no stock. Most of Anglia's sales are paid for in advance (water rates), so it has low trade debtors. Rolls-Royce makes most of its sales on credit and so has relatively high trade debtors.

These types of variation in the amounts and types of working capital elements are typical of other businesses.

In the sections that follow, we shall consider each element of working capital separately, examining the factors that must be considered to ensure their proper management.

## Management of stocks

A business may hold stocks for various reasons, the most common of which is to meet the immediate day-to-day requirements of customers and production. However, a business may hold more than is necessary for this purpose if it believes that future supplies may be interrupted or scarce. Similarly, if the business believes that the cost of stocks will rise in the future, it may decide to stockpile.

For some types of business, the stock held may represent a substantial proportion of the total assets held. For example, a car dealership that rents its premises may have nearly all of its total assets in the form of stock. As we have seen, manufacturing businesses' stock levels tend to be higher than in many other types of business. For some types, for example firework manufacturers, the level of stock held may vary substantially over the year owing to the seasonal nature of the industry, whereas, for other businesses, stock levels may remain fairly stable throughout the year.

Where a business holds stock simply to meet the day-to-day requirements of its customers and production, it will normally seek to minimise the amount of stock held. This is because there are significant costs associated with holding stocks. These include storage and handling costs, financing costs, the risks of pilferage and obsolescence, and the opportunities forgone in tying up funds in this form of asset. However, a business must also recognise that, if the levels of stocks held are too low, there will also be associated costs.

| Activity 9.2 | **What costs might a business incur as a result of holding too low a level of stocks? Try to identify at least three types of cost.** |

You may have thought of the following costs:

- Loss of sales, from being unable to provide the goods required immediately.
- Loss of goodwill from customers, for being unable to satisfy customer demand.
- High transport costs incurred to ensure stocks are replenished quickly.
- Lost production owing to shortage of raw materials.
- Inefficient production scheduling due to shortages of raw materials.
- Purchasing stocks at a higher price than might otherwise have been necessary in order to replenish stocks quickly.

In order to try to ensure that the stocks are properly managed, a number of procedures and techniques can be used. These are reviewed below.

## Budgets of future demand

One of the best ways a business can ensure that there is stock available to meet future sales is to produce appropriate budgets. These budgets should deal with each product that the business sells. It is important that every attempt is made to ensure the accuracy of these budgets as they will determine future ordering and production levels.

The budgets may be derived in various ways. They may be developed using statistical techniques such as time-series analysis, or may be based on the judgement of the sales and marketing staff. We considered stock budgets in Chapter 6.

## Financial ratios

➡ One ratio that can be used to help monitor stock levels is the **average stock turnover period**. This ratio is calculated as follows:

$$\text{Stock turnover period} = \frac{\text{Average stock held}}{\text{Cost of sales}} \times 365 \text{ days}$$

This will provide a picture of the average period for which stocks are held and can be useful as a basis for comparison. It is possible to calculate the stock turnover period for individual product lines as well as for stocks as a whole.

## Recording and reordering systems

The management of stocks in a business of any size requires a sound system of recording stock movements. There must be proper procedures for recording stock purchases and sales. Periodic stock checks may be required to ensure that the amount of physical stocks held is consistent with what the stock records indicate is held.

There should also be clear procedures for the reordering of stocks. Authorisation for both the purchase and issue of stocks should be confined to a few senior staff if problems of duplication and lack of co-ordination are to be avoided. To determine the point at which stock should be reordered, information concerning the lead time (the time between the placing of an order and the receipt of the goods) and the likely level of demand will be required.

| Activity 9.3 | P. Marinov Ltd is an electrical retailer that keeps a particular type of light switch in stock. The annual demand for the light switch is 10,400 units and the lead time for orders is four weeks. Demand for the stock is steady throughout the year. At what level of stock should the business reorder, assuming that it is confident of the figures mentioned above? |

The average weekly demand for the stock item is:

$$\frac{10,400}{52} = 200 \text{ units}$$

During the time between ordering the stock and receiving the goods, the stock sold will be:

$$4 \times 200 = 800 \text{ units}$$

So the business should reorder no later than when the stock level reaches 800 units in order to avoid a 'stockout'.

In most businesses, there will be some uncertainty surrounding the above factors and so a buffer or safety stock level may be maintained in case problems occur. The amount of safety stock to be held is a matter of judgement and will depend on the degree of uncertainty concerning the factors. However, the likely costs of running out of stock must also be taken into account.

## Levels of control

Management must make a commitment to the management of stocks. However, the cost of controlling stocks must be weighed against the potential benefits. It may be possible to have different levels of control according to the nature of the stocks held. The **ABC system of stock control** (see Figure 9.2) is based on the idea of selective levels of control.

**Figure 9.2**

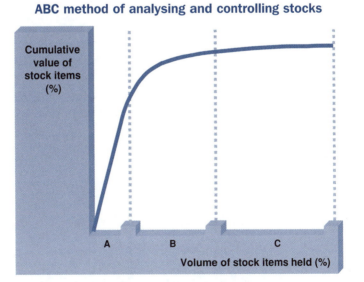

**ABC method of analysing and controlling stocks**

*Cumulative value of stock items (%)*

A    B    C

*Volume of stock items held (%)*

The graph shows that it is possible to divide stocks into three broad categories. Category A stocks are high-value items representing a high proportion of the total value of stocks held. However, they are a relatively low proportion of the total volume of stocks held. Category B stock represents less in terms of total value but account for a higher proportion of the total volume of stocks held. Category C stocks represent an even smaller proportion in terms of total value of stocks held but account for an even higher proportion of the total volume of stocks held.

A business may find that it is possible to divide its stock into three broad categories: A, B and C (see Figure 9.2). Each category will be based on the value of stock held. Category A stocks will represent the high-value items. It may be the case, however, that although the items are high in *value* and represent a high proportion of the total value of stocks held, they are a relatively small proportion of the total *volume* of stocks held. For example, 10 per cent of the physical stocks held may account for 65 per cent of the total value. For these stocks, management may decide to implement sophisticated recording procedures, exert tight control over stock movements and have a high level of security at the stock's location. Category B stocks will represent less valuable items held. Perhaps 30 per cent of the total volume of stocks may account for 25 per cent of the total value of stocks held. For these stocks, a lower level of recording and management control would be appropriate. Category C stocks will represent the least valuable items. Say 60 per cent of the volume of stocks may account for 10 per cent of the total value of stocks held. For these stocks, the level of recording and management control would be lower still.

Categorising stocks in this way can help to ensure that management effort is directed to the most important areas and that the costs of controlling stocks are appropriate to their importance.

## Stock management models

→ It is possible to use decision models to help manage stocks. The **economic order quantity (EOQ)** model is concerned with answering the question: how much stock should be ordered? In its simplest form, the EOQ model assumes that demand is constant, so that stocks will be depleted evenly over time and will be replenished just at the point that the stock runs out. These assumptions lead to the 'saw-tooth' representation of stock movements within a business, as shown in Figure 9.3.

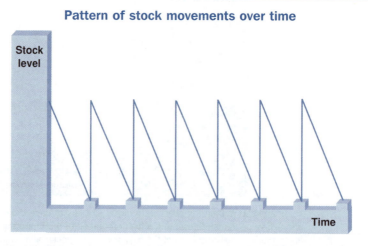

| Figure 9.3 | **Pattern of stock movements over time** |

Stock level

Time

The figure depicts a 'saw-tooth' pattern for stock movements over time. The pattern is based on the assumption that stocks are depleted evenly over time and will be replenished just at the point when the existing stocks run out.

Figure 9.4

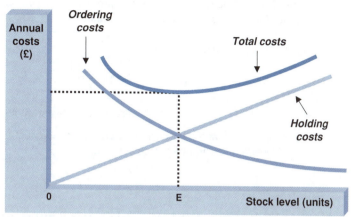

### Stockholding and stock order costs

The graph shows how the costs of ordering will decrease as the stock level increases because fewer orders are placed. However, the costs of holding stocks will increase as the stock levels increase. The total costs are made up of the holding costs and ordering costs. Point E represents the point at which total costs are minimised.

The EOQ model assumes that the key costs associated with stock are the costs of holding it and ordering it. The model can be used to calculate the optimum size of a purchase order by taking account of both of these cost elements. The cost of holding stock can be substantial and so management may try to minimise the average amount of stock held. However, by reducing the level of stock held, and therefore the holding costs, there will be a need to increase the number of orders during the period and so ordering costs will rise.

Figure 9.4 shows how, as the level of stock and the size of stock orders increase, the annual costs of placing orders will decrease because fewer orders will be placed. However, the cost of holding stock will increase as there will be higher stock levels. The total costs curve, which represents the sum of the holding costs and ordering costs, will fall until the point E, which represents the minimum total cost, is reached. Thereafter, total costs begin to rise. The EOQ model seeks to identify the point E at which total costs are minimised.

This will represent half the optimum amount that should be ordered on each occasion. Assuming – as we are doing – that stock is used evenly over time and that stock falls to zero before being replaced, the average stock level equals half of the order size.

The EOQ model, which can be used to derive the most economic order quantity, is given by:

$$EOQ = \sqrt{\frac{2DC}{H}}$$

where $D$ is the annual demand for the item of stock, $C$ is the cost of placing an order, and $H$ is the cost of holding one unit of stock for one year.

| Activity 9.4 | Louise Simon Ltd sells 2,000 units of product X each year. It has been estimated that the cost of holding one unit of the product for a year is £4. The cost of placing an order for stock is estimated at £25. Calculate the EOQ for the product. |
|---|---|

Your answer should be as follows:

$$EOQ = \sqrt{\frac{2 \times 2,000 \times 25}{4}}$$

$$= 158 \text{ units (to the nearest whole number)}$$

This will mean that the business will have to order product X about 13 times (2,000/158) each year in order to meet sales demand.

The basic EOQ model has a number of limiting assumptions. It assumes that demand for the product can be predicted with accuracy and that this demand is even over the period. It also assumes that no 'buffer' stock is required and that the amount can be purchased in single units that correspond exactly to the economic order quantity – for example, 158 units – and not in multiples of 50 or 100 units. Finally, it assumes that no discounts are available for bulk purchases. However, these limiting assumptions do not mean we should dismiss the model as being of little value. The model can be refined to accommodate the problems of uncertainty and uneven demand. Many businesses use this model (or a development of it) to help in the management of stocks.

### Materials requirements planning (MRP) system

→ A **materials requirement planning (MRP) system** takes forecasts of sales demand as its starting point. It then uses computer technology to help schedule the timing of deliveries of bought-in parts and materials to coincide with production requirements. MRP is a co-ordinated approach that links material and parts deliveries to their scheduled input to the production process. By ordering only those items that are necessary to ensure the flow of production, stock levels may be reduced. MRP is a 'top-down' approach to stock management that recognises that stock-ordering decisions cannot be viewed as being independent from production decisions. In recent years, this approach has been extended to provide a fully integrated approach to production planning. This approach also takes into account other manufacturing resources such as labour and machine capacity.

### Just-in-time (JIT) stock management

In recent years, some manufacturing businesses have tried to eliminate the need
→ to hold stocks by adopting **just-in-time (JIT) stock management**. This method was first used in the US defence industry during World War II and, in more recent times, it has been widely used by Japanese businesses. The essence of JIT is, as the name suggests, to have supplies delivered to a business just in time for them to be used in the production process. By adopting this approach, the stockholding problem rests with the suppliers rather than the business itself.

For this approach to be successful, it is important that the business informs suppliers of its production plans and requirements in advance, and that the suppliers in their turn deliver materials of the right quality at the agreed times. Failure to do so could lead to a dislocation of production and could be very costly. Thus, a close relationship between a business and its suppliers is required.

Though a business will not have to hold stocks, there may be certain costs associated with a JIT approach. As the suppliers will be required to hold stocks for the business, they may try to recoup this additional cost through increased prices. The price of stocks purchased may also be increased if JIT requires a large number of small deliveries to be made. Finally, the close relationship necessary between the business and its suppliers may prevent the business from taking advantage of cheaper sources of supply if they become available.

Many people view JIT as more than simply a stock control system. The philosophy underpinning this method is concerned with eliminating waste and striving for excellence. There is an expectation that suppliers will always deliver parts on time and that there will be no defects in the parts supplied. There is also an expectation that the production process will operate at maximum efficiency. This means that there will be no production breakdowns and the queueing and storage times of products manufactured will be eliminated as only that time spent directly on processing the products is seen as adding value. Whilst these expectations may be impossible to achieve, they do help to create a management culture that is dedicated to quality and to the pursuit of excellence (see Exhibit 9.2).

| Exhibit 9.2 | Tesco plc is one of the leading supermarket chains in the UK. To gain an advantage in this intensely competitive market, the company invested heavily in technology to support its JIT system and other stock-management systems. Laser technology is used to improve its distribution flow and to replenish stocks quickly. As a result, Tesco plc now holds less than two weeks' stock, and almost half of the goods received from suppliers are sent immediately to the stores rather than to the warehouse.

The improvement in distribution procedures has allowed stores to reduce the amount of each line of stock held, which in turn has made it possible to increase the number of lines of stock held by each store. It has also made it possible to convert storage space at the supermarkets into selling space.

*Source:* Information taken from an article appearing in The **Economist**, 1995.

## Management of debtors

Selling goods or services on credit results in costs being incurred by a business. These costs include credit administration costs, bad debts and opportunities forgone in using the funds for more profitable purposes. However, the costs must be weighed against the benefits of increased sales resulting from the opportunity for customers to delay payment.

Selling on credit is very widespread and appears to be the norm outside the retail trade. When a business offers to sell its goods or services on credit, it must have clear policies concerning:

- Which customers it is prepared to offer credit to.
- What length of credit it is prepared to offer.
- Whether discounts will be offered for prompt payment.
- What collection policies should be adopted.

Each of these considerations is discussed further below.

## Which customers should receive credit?

A business offering credit runs the risk of not receiving payment for goods or services supplied. Thus, care must be taken over the type of customer to whom credit facilities are offered. When considering a proposal from a customer for the supply of goods or services on credit, the business must take a number of factors into account.

The following '**five Cs of credit**' provide a useful checklist when considering a request from a customer for credit:

- *Capital.*  The customer must appear to be financially sound before any credit is extended. Where the customer is a business, its accounts should be examined. Particular attention should be taken of the profitability and liquidity of the customer. In addition, any major financial commitments (for example, capital expenditure, contracts with suppliers) must be taken into account.
- *Capacity.*  The customer must appear to have the capacity to pay amounts owing. Where possible, the payment record of the customer should be examined. If the customer is a business, the type of business operated and the physical resources of the business will be relevant. The value of goods that the customer wishes to buy on credit must be related to the total financial resources of the customer.
- *Collateral.*  On occasions, it may be necessary to ask for some kind of security for goods supplied on credit. When this occurs, the business must be convinced that the customer is able to offer a satisfactory form of security.
- *Conditions.*  The state of the industry in which the customer operates and the general economic conditions of the particular region or country may have an important influence on the ability of a customer to pay the amounts outstanding on the due date.
- *Character.*  It is important for a business to make some assessment of the character of the customer. The willingness to pay will depend on the honesty and integrity of the individual with whom the business is dealing. Where the customer is a limited company, this will mean assessing the characters of its directors. The business must feel satisfied that the customer will make every effort to pay any amounts owing.

Once a customer is considered creditworthy, credit limits for the customer should be established and procedures laid down to ensure that these limits are adhered to.

**Activity 9.5**

Assume that you are the credit manager of a business and that a limited company approached you with a view to buying goods on credit. What sources of information might you decide to use to help assess the financial health of the potential customer?

There are various possibilities; you may have thought of some of the following:

■ *Trade references.*  Some businesses ask for a potential customer to supply references from other businesses that have made sales on credit to the customer. This may be extremely useful, provided that the references are truly representative of the opinions of the customer's suppliers. There is a danger that a potential customer will attempt to be highly selective when giving details of other suppliers in order to gain a more favourable impression than is deserved.

■ *Bank references.*  It is possible to ask the potential customer for a bank reference. Although banks are usually prepared to supply references, the contents of a reference are not always very informative. If customers are in financial difficulties, the bank will usually be unwilling to add to their problems by supplying poor references.

■ *Published accounts.*  A limited company is obliged by law to file a copy of its annual accounts with the Registrar of Companies. The accounts are available for public inspection and provide a useful source of information.

■ *The customer.*  You may wish to interview the directors of the company and visit its premises in an attempt to gain some impression of the way that the company conducts its business. Where a significant amount of credit is required, you may ask the company for access to internal budgets and other unpublished financial information to help assess the level of risk involved.

■ *Credit agencies.*  Specialist agencies exist to provide information that can be used to assess the creditworthiness of a potential customer. The information that a credit agency supplies may be gleaned from various sources, including the accounts of the customer, court judgements and news items relating to the customer from both published and unpublished sources.

## Length of credit period

A business must determine what credit terms it is prepared to offer its customers. The length of credit offered can vary significantly between businesses and is influenced by such factors as:

■ The typical credit terms operating within the industry.
■ The degree of competition within the industry.
■ The bargaining power of particular customers.
■ The risk of non-payment.
■ The capacity of the business to offer credit.
■ The marketing strategy of the business.

The last point may require some explanation. The marketing strategy of a business may have an important influence on the length of credit allowed. For example, if a business wishes to increase its market share it may decide to liberalise its credit policy so as to try to stimulate sales. Potential customers may be attracted by the offer of a longer credit period. However, any such change in policy must take account of the likely costs and benefits arising. To illustrate this point, consider Example 9.1.

| | |
|---|---|
| **Example 9.1** | Torrance Ltd produces a new type of golf putter. The business sells the putter to wholesalers and retailers and has an annual turnover of £600,000. The following data relate to each putter produced: |

|  | £ | £ |
|---|---|---|
| Selling price |  | 36 |
| Variable costs | 18 |  |
| Fixed cost apportionment | 6 | (24) |
| Net profit |  | 12 |

The cost of capital of Torrance Ltd is estimated at 15 per cent.

The business wishes to expand sales of this new putter and believes that this can be done by offering a longer period in which to pay. The average collection period of the business is currently 30 days. The business is considering three options, in an attempt to increase sales. These are as follows:

|  | Option | | |
|---|---|---|---|
|  | 1 | 2 | 3 |
| Increase in average collection period | 10 days | 20 days | 30 days |
| Increase in sales | £30,000 | £45,000 | £50,000 |

To enable the business to decide on the best option, it must weigh the benefits of the options against their respective costs. The benefits arising will be represented by the increase in profit from the sale of additional putters. From the cost data supplied, we can see that the contribution (sales less variable costs) is £18 per putter. This represents 50 per cent of the selling price. The fixed costs can be ignored as they will remain the same whichever option is chosen.

The increase in contribution under each option will therefore be:

|  | Option | | |
|---|---|---|---|
|  | 1 | 2 | 3 |
| 50% of increase in sales | £15,000 | £22,500 | £25,000 |

The increase in debtors under each option will be as follows:

|  | Option | | |
|---|---|---|---|
|  | 1 | 2 | 3 |
|  | £ | £ | £ |
| Planned level of debtors |  |  |  |
| 630,000 × 40/365 | 69,041 |  |  |
| 645,000 × 50/365 |  | 88,356 |  |
| 650,000 × 60/365 |  |  | 106,849 |
| *Less* Current level of debtors |  |  |  |
| 600,000 × 30/365 | (49,315) | (49,315) | (49,315) |
| Increase in debtors | 19,726 | 39,041 | 57,534 |

The increase in debtors that results from each option will mean an additional cost to the company. We are told that the company has an estimated cost of capital of 15 per cent. Thus, the increase in the additional investment in debtors will be:

|  | Option | | |
|---|---|---|---|
|  | 1 | 2 | 3 |
| Cost of additional investment | | | |
| (15 per cent of increase in debtors) | £(2,959) | £(5,856) | £(8,630) |

The net increase in profits will be:

|  | Option | | |
|---|---|---|---|
|  | 1 | 2 | 3 |
|  | £ | £ | £ |
| Cost of additional investment | | | |
| (15 per cent of increase in debtors) | (2,959) | (5,856) | (8,630) |
| Increase in contribution (see above) | 15,000 | 22,500 | 25,000 |
| Net increase in profits | 12,041 | 16,644 | 16,370 |

The calculations show that option 2 will be the most profitable for the company. However, there is little to choose between options 2 and 3.

Example 9.1 illustrates the way in which a business should assess changes in credit terms. However, if there is a risk that, by extending the length of credit, there will be an increase in bad debts, this should also be taken into account in the calculations, as should any additional collection costs that will be incurred.

## Cash discounts

➜ A business may decide to offer a **cash discount** as a means of encouraging prompt payment from its credit customers. The size of any discount will be an important influence on whether a customer decides to pay promptly.

From the business's viewpoint, the cost of offering discounts must be weighed against the likely benefits in the form of a reduction in both the cost of financing debtors and the amount of bad debts.

In practice, there is always the danger that a customer may be slow to pay and yet may still take the discount offered. Where the customer is important to the business, it may be difficult to insist on full payment. Some businesses may charge interest on overdue accounts as a means of encouraging prompt payment. However, this is only possible if the business is in a strong bargaining position with its customers. For example, the business may be the only supplier of a particular product in the area.

## Collection policies

A business offering credit must ensure that amounts owing are collected as quickly as possible. An efficient collection policy requires an efficient accounting system.

---

**?** **Self-assessment question 9.1**

Williams Wholesalers Ltd at present requires payment from its customers by the end of the month after the month of delivery. On average, it takes customers 70 days to pay. Sales amount to £4 million a year and bad debts to £20,000 a year.

It is planned to offer customers a cash discount of 2 per cent for payment within 30 days. Williams estimates that 50 per cent of customers will accept this facility but that the remaining customers, who tend to be slow payers, will not pay until 80 days after the sale. At present the business has an overdraft facility at an interest rate of 13 per cent a year. If the plan goes ahead, bad debts will be reduced to £10,000 a year and there will be savings in credit administration expenses of £6,000 a year.

**Required:**
Should Williams Wholesalers Ltd offer the new credit terms to customers? You should support your answer with any calculations and explanations that you consider necessary.

---

Invoices must be sent out promptly along with regular monthly statements. Reminders must also be despatched promptly where necessary.

When a business is faced with customers who do not pay, there should be agreed procedures for dealing with those customers. However, the cost of any action to be taken against delinquent debtors must be weighed against the likely returns. For example, there is little point in taking legal action against a customer and incurring large legal expenses if there is evidence that the customer does not have the necessary resources to pay. Where possible, the cost of bad debts should be taken into account when setting prices for products or services.

➡ Management can monitor the effectiveness of collection policies in a number of ways. One method is to calculate the **average settlement period for debtors**. This ratio is calculated as follows:

$$\text{Average settlement period for debtors} = \frac{\text{Trade debtors}}{\text{Credit sales}} \times 365 \text{ days}$$

Although this ratio can be useful, it is important to remember that it produces an *average* figure for the number of days that debts are outstanding. This average may be badly distorted by a few large customers who are also very slow or very fast payers.

➡ A more detailed and informative approach to monitoring debtors is to produce an **ageing schedule of debtors**. Debts are divided into categories according to the length of time the debt has been outstanding. An ageing schedule can be produced for managers on a regular basis in order to help them see the pattern of outstanding debts. An example of an ageing schedule is set out in Example 9.2. This example shows a business's trade debtors figure at 31 December 2001, which totals £111,000. Each customer's balance is analysed according to how long the debt has been outstanding. We can see that A Ltd has £20,000 of debt that is less than 30 days old (that is, arising from sales during December 2001) and £10,000

**Example 9.2**

**Ageing schedule of debtors at 31 December 2001**

| | Days outstanding | | | | |
| Customer | 1–30 days £ | 31–60 days £ | 61–90 days £ | More than 90 days £ | Total £ |
|---|---|---|---|---|---|
| A Ltd | 20,000 | 10,000 | – | – | 30,000 |
| B Ltd | – | 24,000 | – | – | 24,000 |
| C Ltd | 12,000 | 13,000 | 14,000 | 18,000 | 57,000 |
| Total | 32,000 | 47,000 | 14,000 | 18,000 | 111,000 |

that is between 31 and 60 days old (arising from November 2001 sales). This information can be very useful for credit-control purposes.

Many accounting software packages now include this ageing schedule as one of the routine reports available. Such packages often have the facility to put customers 'on hold' when they reach their credit limit.

A slightly different approach to exercising control over debtors is to identify the pattern of receipts from credit sales on a monthly basis. This involves monitoring the percentage of trade debtors that pay (and the percentage of debts that remain unpaid) in the month of sale and the percentage that pay in subsequent months. To do this, credit sales for each month must be examined separately. To illustrate how a pattern of credit sales receipts is produced, consider a business that made credit sales of £250,000 in June and received 30 per cent of the amount owing in the same month, 40 per cent in July, 20 per cent in August and 10 per cent in September. The pattern of credit sales receipts and amounts owing is shown in Example 9.3.

**Example 9.3**

**Pattern of credit sales receipts**

| Month | Receipts from June credit sales £ | Received % | Amount outstanding from June sales at month end £ | Outstanding % |
|---|---|---|---|---|
| June | 75,000 | 30 | 175,000 | 70 |
| July | 100,000 | 40 | 75,000 | 30 |
| August | 50,000 | 20 | 25,000 | 10 |
| September | 25,000 | 10 | – | – |

Example 9.3 shows how sales made in June were received over time. This information can be used as a basis for control. The actual pattern of receipts can be compared with the expected (budgeted) pattern of receipts in order to see if there was any significant deviation (see Figure 9.5). If this comparison shows that debtors are paying more slowly than expected, management may decide to take corrective action.

Figure 9.5

**Comparison of actual and budgeted receipts over time for Example 9.3**

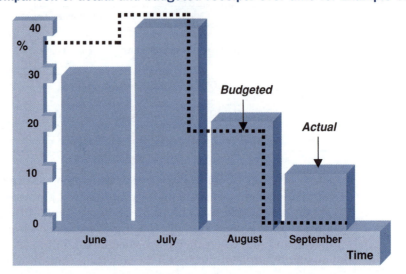

The graph shows the actual pattern of cash receipts from credit sales made in June. It can be seen that 30 per cent of the sales income for June is received in that month, and the remainder is received in the three following months. The assumed budget pattern of cash receipts for June sales is also depicted. By comparing the actual and budgeted pattern of receipts, it is possible to see whether credit sales are being properly controlled and to decide whether corrective action is required.

**Activity 9.6**

What kinds of corrective action might the managers decide to take if they found that debtors were paying more slowly than anticipated?

Managers might decide to do one or more of the following:

■ Offer cash discounts to encourage prompt payment.
■ Change the collection period.
■ Improve the accounting system to ensure that customers are billed more promptly, reminders are sent out promptly, and so on.
■ Change the eligibility criteria for customers who receive credit.

## Credit management and the small business

Credit management may be a particular problem for small businesses. Often, these businesses lack the resources to manage their trade debtors effectively. Sometimes a small business will not have a separate credit-control department, which will mean that both the expertise and the information required to make sound judgements concerning terms of sale and so on may not be available. A small business may also lack proper debt-collection procedures, such as prompt invoicing and the sending out of regular statements. This will increase the risks of late payment and defaulting debtors.

These risks may also increase through an excessive concern for growth. In order to increase sales, small businesses may be too willing to extend credit to customers that are poor credit risks. Whilst this kind of problem can occur in businesses of all sizes, small businesses seem particularly susceptible.

Another problem faced by small businesses is their lack of market power. They will often find themselves in a weak position when negotiating credit terms with larger businesses. Moreover, when a large customer exceeds the terms of credit, the small supplier may feel inhibited from pressing the customer for payment in case future sales are lost.

Surveys indicate that small businesses have a much greater proportion of overdue debts than large businesses. In the UK, the government has intervened to help deal with this problem and the law now permits small businesses to charge interest on overdue accounts.

In addition, large companies are now required to disclose in their published accounts the payment policy adopted towards suppliers. There are some signs that these changes in the law have led to a speeding-up of payments to small businesses.

# Management of cash

## Why hold cash?

Most businesses will hold a certain amount of cash. However, the amount of cash held varies considerably between businesses.

---

**Activity 9.7**

**Why do you think a business may decide to hold at least some of its assets in the form of cash?**

According to economic theory, there are three motives for holding cash. They are:

- *Transactionary motive.* To meet day-to-day commitments, a business requires a certain amount of cash. Payments for wages, overheads, goods purchased and so on must be made at the due dates. Cash has been described as the life-blood of a business; unless it circulates through the business and is available for the payment of maturing obligations, the survival of the business will be put at risk. Profitability alone is not enough: a business must have sufficient cash to pay its debts when they fall due.
- *Precautionary motive.* If future cash flows are uncertain for any reason, it would be prudent to hold a balance of cash. For example, a major customer that owes a large sum to the business may be in financial difficulties. Given this situation, the business can retain its capacity to meet its obligations by holding a cash balance. Similarly, if there is some uncertainty concerning future outlays, a cash balance will be required.
- *Speculative motive.* A business may decide to hold cash in order to be in a position to exploit profitable opportunities as and when they arise. For example, by holding cash, a business may be able to acquire a competitor business that suddenly becomes available at an attractive price. Holding cash has an opportunity cost for the business that must be taken into account. Thus, when evaluating the potential returns from holding cash for speculative purposes, the cost of forgone investment opportunities must be considered.

## How much cash should be held?

Although cash can be held for each of the reasons identified in Activity 9.7, this may not always be necessary. If a business is able to borrow quickly at a favourable rate, then the amount of cash it needs to hold can be reduced. Similarly, if the business holds assets that can easily be converted to cash (for example, marketable securities such as shares in Stock Exchange listed companies or government bonds) the amount of cash held can be reduced.

The decision as to how much cash a particular business should hold is a difficult one. Different businesses will have different views on the subject.

| Activity 9.8 | What do you think are the major factors that influence how much cash a business will hold? See if you can think of five possible factors. |

You may have thought of some of the following:

■ *The nature of the business.* Some businesses, such as utilities (water, electricity and gas suppliers) may have cash flows that are both predictable and reasonably certain. This will enable them to hold lower cash balances. For some businesses, cash balances vary greatly according to the time of year. A seasonal business may accumulate cash during the high season to enable it to meet commitments during the low season.

■ *The opportunity cost of holding cash.* Where there are profitable opportunities, it may be wiser to invest in those opportunities than to hold a large cash balance.

■ *The level of inflation.* Holding cash during a period of rising prices will lead to a loss of purchasing power. The higher the level of inflation, the greater will be this loss.

■ *The availability of near-liquid assets.* If a business has marketable securities or stocks that may easily be liquidated, the amount of cash held may be reduced.

■ *The availability of borrowing.* If a business can borrow easily (and quickly), there is less need to hold cash.

■ *The cost of borrowing.* When interest rates are high, the option of borrowing becomes less attractive.

■ *Economic conditions.* When the economy is in recession, businesses may prefer to hold cash in order to be well placed to invest when the economy improves. In addition, during a recession, businesses may experience difficulties in collecting debts. They may, therefore, hold higher cash balances than usual in order to meet commitments.

■ *Relationships with suppliers.* Too little cash may hinder the ability of a business to pay suppliers promptly. This can lead to a loss of goodwill. It might also mean that cash discounts will not be claimable.

## Controlling the cash balance

Several models have been proposed to help control the cash balance of a business. One such model proposes the use of upper and lower control limits for cash balances and the use of a target cash balance. The model assumes that the business will invest in marketable investments that can easily be liquidated. These investments will be purchased or sold, as necessary, to keep the cash balance within the control limits.

The model proposes two upper and two lower control limits (see Figure 9.6). If the business exceeds an *outer* limit, the managers must decide whether or not the cash balance is likely to return, over the following few days, to a point within the

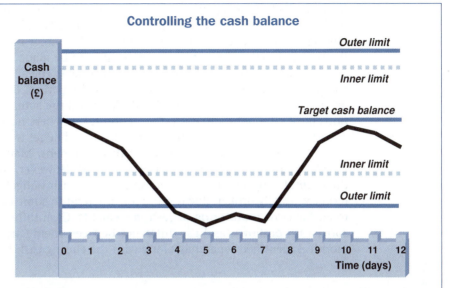

**Figure 9.6**

The graph depicts a model for controlling the cash balance that relies on the use of inner and outer control limits. Where outer control limits are breached, and there is no prospect of an early return to a point within these limits, management must take action. A breach of the higher limit will involve buying marketable securities (to ensure cash is not lying idle) and a breach of the lower limit will involve selling marketable securities (to ensure there is sufficient cash available to meet obligations).

*inner* control limits set. If this seems likely, then no action is required. If, on the other hand, this seems unlikely, management must change the cash position of the business by buying or selling marketable securities, or simply by borrowing or lending.

In Figure 9.6 we can see that the lower outer control limit has been breached for four days (days 4 to 7 inclusive). If a four-day period is unacceptable, managers must sell marketable securities to replenish the cash balance.

The model relies heavily on management judgement to determine where the control limits are set and the time period within which breaches of the limits are acceptable. Past experience may be useful in helping managers decide on these issues. There are other models, however, that do not rely on management judgement and, instead, use quantitative techniques to determine an optimal cash policy. One model proposed, for example, is the cash equivalent of the stock economic order quantity model discussed earlier.

## Cash budgets and the management of cash

In managing cash effectively, it is useful for a business to prepare a cash budget. This is a very important tool for both planning and control purposes. Cash budgets were considered in Chapter 6 and so we shall not consider them in detail again here. However, it is worth repeating the point that budgets enable managers to see the expected outcome of planned events on the cash balance. The cash budgets will identify periods when cash surpluses and deficits are expected.

When a cash surplus is expected to arise, managers must decide on the best use of the surplus funds. When a cash deficit is expected, they must make adequate provision by borrowing, liquidating assets or rescheduling cash payments/receipts to deal with this. Planning borrowing requirements beforehand can allow the business to use a cheap source of finance; such sources may not be available at the time a deficit arises, when decisions have to be made quickly. Cash budgets are also useful in helping to control the cash held. The actual cash flows can be compared with the projected cash flows for the period. If there is a significant divergence between the projected cash flows and the actual cash flows, explanations must be sought and corrective action taken where necessary.

To refresh your memory, an example of a cash budget is given in Example 9.4. Remember, there is no set format for this statement. Managers can determine how best the information should be presented. However, the format set out in the example appears to be in widespread use. Cash budgets covering the short term are usually broken down into monthly (and in some cases, weekly) periods to enable close monitoring of cash movements. Cash inflows are usually shown above cash outflows, and the difference between them (the net cash flow) for a month is identified separately along with the closing cash balance.

**Example 9.4**

**Cash budget for the six months to 30 November**

| | June £ | July £ | August £ | September £ | October £ | November £ |
|---|---|---|---|---|---|---|
| **Cash inflows** | | | | | | |
| Credit sales | – | – | 4,000 | 5,500 | 7,000 | 8,500 |
| Cash sales | 4,000 | 5,500 | 7,000 | 8,500 | 11,000 | 11,000 |
| | 4,000 | 5,500 | 11,000 | 14,000 | 18,000 | 19,500 |
| **Cash outflows** | | | | | | |
| Motor vehicles | 6,000 | | | | | |
| Equipment | 10,000 | | | | | 7,200 |
| Freehold premises | 40,000 | | | | | |
| Purchases | – | 29,000 | 9,250 | 11,500 | 13,750 | 17,500 |
| Wages/salaries | 900 | 900 | 900 | 900 | 900 | 900 |
| Commission | – | 320 | 440 | 560 | 680 | 680 |
| Overheads | 500 | 500 | 500 | 500 | 650 | 650 |
| | 57,400 | 30,720 | 11,090 | 13,460 | 15,980 | 26,930 |
| **Net cash flow** | (53,400) | (25,220) | (90) | 540 | 2,020 | (7,430) |
| Opening balance | 60,000 | 6,600 | (18,620) | (18,710) | (18,170) | (16,150) |
| Closing balance | 6,600 | (18,620) | (18,710) | (18,170) | (16,150) | (23,580) |

Although cash budgets are prepared primarily for internal management purposes, they are sometimes required by prospective lenders when a loan to a business is being considered.

## Operating cash cycle

➡ When managing cash, it is important to be aware of the **operating cash cycle** of the business. This may be defined as the time period between the outlay of cash

**Figure 9.7**

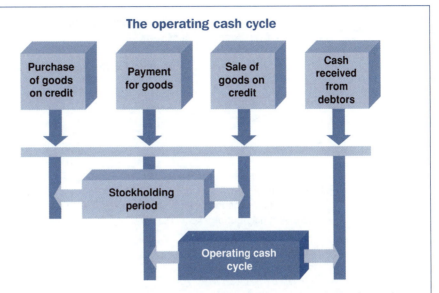

The operating cash cycle

The diagram shows that goods purchased on credit will be paid for at a later date and so no immediate cash outflow will occur. Similarly, credit sales will not lead to an immediate inflow of cash. The operating cash cycle is the time period between the payment made to the supplier and the cash received from the customer.

necessary for the purchase of stocks and the ultimate receipt of cash from the sale of the goods. The operating cash cycle of a business that purchases goods on credit, for subsequent resale on credit, is shown diagrammatically in Figure 9.7.

The diagram shows that payment for goods acquired on credit occurs some time after the goods have been purchased and, therefore, no immediate cash outflow arises from the purchase. Similarly, cash receipts from debtors will occur some time after the sale is made and so there will be no immediate cash inflow as a result of the sale. The operating cash cycle is the time period between the payment made to the creditor for goods supplied, and the receipt of cash from the debtor.

The operating cash cycle is important because it has a significant influence on the financing requirements of the business. The longer the cash cycle, the greater the financing requirements of the business and the greater the financial risks. For this reason, a business is likely to want to reduce the operating cash cycle to the minimum possible period.

For the type of business, mentioned above, that buys and sells on credit, the operating cash cycle can be calculated from the financial statements by the use of certain ratios, as follows:

**Average stockholding period**
+
**Average settlement period for debtors**
−
**Average payment period for creditors**
=
**Operating cash cycle**

**Activity 9.9**

The accounts of Freezeqwik Ltd, a distributor of frozen foods, is set out below for the year ended 31 December last year.

### Profit and loss account for the year ended 31 December

|  | £000 | £000 |
|---|---:|---:|
| Sales |  | 820 |
| Less Cost of sales |  |  |
| Opening stock | 142 |  |
| Purchases | 568 |  |
|  | 710 |  |
| Less Closing stock | 166 | 544 |
| **Gross profit** |  | 276 |
| Administration expenses | (120) |  |
| Selling and distribution expenses | (95) |  |
| Financial expenses | (32) | (247) |
| **Net profit** |  | 29 |
| Corporation tax |  | (7) |
| Retained profit for the year |  | 22 |

### Balance sheet as at 31 December

|  | £000 | £000 | £000 |
|---|---:|---:|---:|
| **Fixed assets at written down value** |  |  |  |
| Freehold premises |  |  | 180 |
| Fixtures and fittings |  |  | 82 |
| Motor vans |  |  | 102 |
|  |  |  | 364 |
| **Current assets** |  |  |  |
| Stock |  | 166 |  |
| Trade debtors |  | 264 |  |
| Cash |  | 24 |  |
|  |  | 454 |  |
| Less **Creditors: amounts falling** |  |  |  |
| **due within one year** |  |  |  |
| Trade creditors | 159 |  |  |
| Corporation tax | 7 | 166 | 288 |
|  |  |  | 652 |
| **Capital and reserves** |  |  |  |
| Ordinary share capital |  |  | 300 |
| Preference share capital |  |  | 200 |
| Retained profit |  |  | 152 |
|  |  |  | 652 |

All purchases and sales are on credit.

Calculate the operating cash cycle for the business and go on to suggest how the business may seek to reduce the cash cycle.

The operating cash cycle may be calculated as follows:

Number of days

Average stockholding period:

$$\frac{(\text{Opening stock} + \text{closing stock})/2}{\text{Cost of sales}} \times 365 = \frac{(142 + 166)/2}{544} \times 365 = 103$$

*Add* Average settlement period for debtors:

$$\frac{\text{Trade debtors}}{\text{Credit sales}} \times 365 = \frac{264}{820} \times 365 = 118$$

*Less* Average settlement period for creditors

$$\frac{\text{Trade creditors}}{\text{Credit purchases}} \times 365 = \frac{159}{568} \times 365 = (102)$$

Operating cash cycle:                                                                119

The company can reduce the operating cash cycle in a number of ways. The average stockholding period seems quite long. At present, average stocks held represent more than three months' sales. This may be reduced by reducing the level of stocks held. Similarly, the average settlement period for debtors seems long at nearly four months' sales. This may be reduced by imposing tighter credit control, offering discounts or charging interest on overdue accounts. However, any policy decisions concerning stocks and debtors must take account of current trading conditions.

The operating cash cycle could also be reduced by extending the period of credit taken to pay suppliers. However, for reasons that will be explained later, this option must be given careful consideration.

## Cash transmission

A business will normally wish to benefit from receipts from customers at the earliest opportunity. The benefit is immediate where payment is made in cash; when payment is by cheque, there is normally a delay of three to four working days before the cheque is cleared through the banking system, and the business must therefore wait for this period before it can benefit from the amount paid in. In the case of a business that receives large amounts in the form of cheques, the opportunity cost of this delay can be very significant.

To avoid this delay, a business could require payments to be made in cash. This is not usually practical for a number of reasons. Another option is to ask for payment to be made by standing order or by direct debit from the customer's bank account. This should ensure that the amount owing is always transferred on the day that has been agreed.

It is also possible for funds to be directly transferred to a business bank account. As a result of developments in computer technology, customers can pay for items by using debit cards which results in the appropriate accounts being instantly debited and sellers' bank accounts being instantly credited with the specified amounts. This method of payment is widely used by large retail businesses and may well extend to other types of business.

# Management of trade creditors

Trade credit is regarded as an important source of finance by many businesses. It has been described as a 'spontaneous' source as it tends to increase in line with the level of sales achieved by a business. Trade credit is widely regarded as a 'free' source of finance and, therefore, a good thing for a business to use. There may be real costs associated with taking trade credit, however.

Firstly, customers who take credit may not be as well favoured as those who pay immediately. For example, when goods are in short supply, credit customers may receive lower priority when allocating the stock available. In addition, credit customers may be less favoured in terms of delivery dates or the provision of technical support services. Sometimes, the goods or services provided may be more costly if credit is required. However, in most industries, trade credit is the norm and, as a result, the costs listed above will not apply unless, perhaps, the credit facilities are abused by the customer. A business purchasing supplies on credit may also have to incur additional administration and accounting costs in dealing with the scrutiny and payment of invoices, maintaining and updating creditors' accounts, and so on.

Where a supplier offers discount for prompt payment, a buyer should give careful consideration to paying within the discount period. Example 9.5 usefully illustrates the cost of forgoing possible discounts.

| | |
|---|---|
| **Example 9.5** | A. Hassam Ltd takes 70 days to pay for goods supplied by its supplier. To encourage prompt payment, the supplier has offered the company a 2 per cent discount if payment for goods is made within 30 days. Hassam is not sure whether it is worth taking the discount offered. The annual percentage cost to the company of forgoing the discount can be deduced as follows. |

If the discount is taken, payment could be made on the last day of the period (the 30th day). However, if it is not taken, payment will be made after 70 days. This means that by not taking the discount the business will receive an extra 40 (that is, 70 – 30) days' credit. The cost of this extra credit to the company will be the 2 per cent discount forgone. If we annualise the cost of this discount forgone, we have:

$$\frac{365}{40} \times 2\% = 18.3\%$$

We can see the annual cost of forgoing the discount is very high and it may be profitable for the business to pay the supplier within the discount period even if it means that the company will have to borrow to enable it to do so.

(*Note*: This is an approximate annual rate. For the more mathematically minded, the precise rate is $[(1 + (2/98)^{9.125}) - 1] \times 100\% = 20.2\%$.)

The above points are not meant to imply that taking credit is a burden to a business. There are, of course, real benefits that can accrue. Provided that trade credit is not abused, it can represent a form of interest-free loan. It can be a much more convenient method of paying for goods and services than paying by cash and, during a period of inflation, there will be an economic gain by paying later rather than sooner for goods and services purchased. For most businesses, these benefits will exceed the costs involved.

### Controlling trade creditors

To help monitor the level of trade credit taken, management can calculate the ➡️ **average settlement period for creditors** which is as follows:

$$\text{Average settlement period for creditors} = \frac{\text{Trade creditors}}{\text{Credit purchases}} \times 365 \text{ days}$$

Once again, this provides an average figure, which could be misleading. A more informative approach would be to produce an ageing schedule for creditors. This would look much the same as the ageing schedule for debtors described earlier.

## Management of bank overdrafts

➡️ A **bank overdraft** is a flexible form of borrowing and is cheap relative to other sources of finance. For this reason, the majority of UK businesses use bank overdrafts, to a greater or lesser extent, for finance. Although, in theory, bank overdrafts are a short-term source of finance, in practice they can extend over a long period of time for many businesses continually renew their overdraft facility with their bank. Though renewal may not usually be a problem, there is always a danger that the bank will demand repayment at short notice, as it has the right to do. If the business is highly dependent on borrowing and alternative sources of borrowing are difficult to find, this could raise severe problems.

When considering whether or not to have a bank overdraft, the business should first consider the purpose of the borrowing. Overdrafts are most suitable for overcoming short-term funding problems (for example, increases in stockholding requirements owing to seasonal fluctuations) and should be self-liquidating. For longer-term funding problems, or borrowings that are not self-liquidating, other sources of finance might be suitable.

It is important to agree the correct facility with the bank as borrowings in excess of the overdraft limit may incur high charges. To determine the amount of the overdraft facility, the business should produce cash budgets. There should also be regular reporting of cash flows over time to try to ensure that the overdraft limit is not exceeded.

### Summary

In this chapter we have identified and examined the main elements of working capital. We have seen that the management of working capital requires an evaluation of both the costs and benefits associated with each element. Some of these costs and benefits may be hard to quantify in practice. Nevertheless, an assessment must be made in order to try to optimise the use of funds within a business. We have examined various techniques for the management of working capital. These techniques vary in their level of sophistication: some rely heavily on management judgement whilst others adopt a more objective, quantitative approach.

→ **Key terms**

Working capital   p. 234
Average stock turnover period   p. 238
ABC system of stock control   p. 239
Economic order quantity (EOQ)   p. 240
Materials requirement planning (MRP)
  system   p. 242
Just-in-time (JIT) stock management
  p. 242
Five Cs of credit   p. 244

Cash discount   p. 247
Average settlement period for debtors
  p. 248
Ageing schedule of debtors   p. 248
Operating cash cycle   p. 254
Average settlement period for creditors
  p. 259
Bank overdraft   p. 259

## Further reading

If you would like to explore the topics covered in this chapter in more depth, we recommend the following books:

**Corporate Financial Management**, *Arnold, G.*, Financial Times Prentice Hall, 1998, chapter 13.
**Business Finance: Theory and Practice**, *McLaney, E.*, 5th edn, Financial Times Prentice Hall, 2000, chapter 13.
**Corporate Finance and Investment**, *Pike, R.* and *Neale, B.*, 3rd edn, Prentice Hall International, 1999, chapters 14 and 15.
**Financial Management and Decision Making**, *Samuels, J., Wilkes, F.* and *Brayshaw, R.*, International Thomson Business Press, 1999, chapter 18.

## ? REVIEW QUESTIONS

**9.1**  Tariq is the credit manager of Heltex plc. He is concerned that the pattern of monthly sales receipts shows that credit collection is poor compared with budget. The sales director believes that Tariq is to blame for this situation but Tariq insists that he is not. Why might Tariq *not* be to blame for the deterioration in the credit collection period?

**9.2**  How might each of the following affect the level of stocks held by a business?
(a)  An increase in the number of production bottlenecks experienced by the business.
(b)  A rise in the level of interest rates.
(c)  A decision to offer customers a narrower range of products in the future.
(d)  A switch of suppliers from an overseas business to a local one.
(e)  A deterioration in the quality and reliability of bought-in components.

**9.3**  What are the reasons for holding stocks? Are these reasons different from the reasons for holding cash?

**9.4**  Identify the costs of holding: (a) too little cash, and (b) too much cash?

## ? EXERCISES

Exercises 9.5–9.8 are more advanced than 9.1–9.4. Those with coloured numbers have answers at the back of the book.

**9.1**  Hercules Wholesalers Ltd has been particularly concerned with its liquidity position in recent months. The most recent profit and loss account and balance sheet of the company are as follows:

### Profit and loss account for the year ended 31 May last year

|  | £000 | £000 |
|---|---|---|
| Sales |  | 452 |
| Less Cost of sales |  |  |
| Opening stock | 125 |  |
| Add Purchases | 341 |  |
|  | 466 |  |
| Less Closing stock | 143 | 323 |
| Gross profit |  | 129 |
| Expenses |  | (132) |
| Net loss for the period |  | (3) |

### Balance sheet as at 31 May last year

|  | £000 | £000 | £000 |
|---|---|---|---|
| **Fixed assets** |  |  |  |
| Freehold premises at valuation |  |  | 280 |
| Fixtures and fittings at cost less depreciation |  |  | 25 |
| Motor vehicles at cost less depreciation |  |  | 52 |
|  |  |  | 357 |

|  | £000 | £000 | £000 |
|---|---|---|---|
| **Current assets** | | | |
| Stock | | 143 | |
| Debtors | | <u>163</u> | |
| | | 306 | |
| _Less_ **Creditors due within one year** | | | |
| Trade creditors | 145 | | |
| Bank overdraft | <u>140</u> | 285 | <u>21</u> |
| | | | 378 |
| _Less_ **Creditors due after more than one year** | | | |
| Loans | | | <u>120</u> |
| | | | <u>258</u> |
| **Capital and reserves** | | | |
| Ordinary share capital | | | 100 |
| Retained profit | | | <u>158</u> |
| | | | <u>258</u> |

The debtors and creditors were maintained at a constant level throughout the year.

**Required:**

(a) Explain why Hercules is concerned about its liquidity position.

(b) Calculate the operating cash cycle for Hercules based on the information above. (Assume a 360-day year.)

(c) State what steps may be taken to improve the operating cash cycle of the company.

**9.2** International Electric plc at present offers its customers 30 days credit. Half the customers, by value, pay on time. The other half take an average of 70 days to pay. The firm is considering offering a cash discount of 2 per cent to its customers for payment within 30 days.

It anticipates that half of the customers who now take an average of 70 days to pay (that is, a quarter of all customers) will pay in 30 days. The other half (the final quarter) will still take an average of 70 days to pay. The scheme will also reduce bad debts by £300,000 per year.

Annual sales of £365 million are made evenly throughout the year. At present the company has a large overdraft (£60 million) with its bank at 12 per cent a year.

**Required:**

(a) Calculate the approximate equivalent annual percentage cost of a discount of 2 per cent that reduces the time taken by debtors to pay from 70 days to 30 days. _Hint_: This part can be answered without reference to the narrative above.

(b) Calculate debtors outstanding under both the old and new schemes.

(c) How much will the scheme cost the company in discounts?

(d) Should the company go ahead with the scheme? State what other factors, if any, should be taken into account.

(e) Outline the controls and procedures that a company should adopt to manage the level of its debtors.

**9.3** The managing director of Sparkrite Ltd, a trading company, has just received summary sets of accounts for last year and this year, as set out below.

### Profit and loss account for years ended 30 September

| | last year £000 | last year £000 | this year £000 | this year £000 |
|---|---|---|---|---|
| Sales | | 1,800 | | 1,920 |
| Less Cost of sales | | | | |
| Opening stock | 160 | | 200 | |
| Purchases | 1,120 | | 1,175 | |
| | 1,280 | | 1,375 | |
| Less Closing stocks | 200 | | 250 | |
| | | 1,080 | | 1,125 |
| Gross profit | | 720 | | 795 |
| Less Expenses | | 680 | | 750 |
| Net profit | | 40 | | 45 |

### Balance sheet as at 30 September

| | last year £000 | last year £000 | this year £000 | this year £000 |
|---|---|---|---|---|
| Fixed assets | | 950 | | 930 |
| Current assets: | | | | |
| Stock | 200 | | 250 | |
| Debtors | 375 | | 480 | |
| Bank | 4 | | 2 | |
| | 579 | | 732 | |
| Less Creditors due within one year | 195 | | 225 | |
| | | 384 | | 507 |
| | | 1,334 | | 1,437 |
| **Financed by:** | | | | |
| Fully paid £1 ordinary shares | | 825 | | 883 |
| Reserves | | 509 | | 554 |
| | | 1,334 | | 1,437 |

The finance director has expressed concern at the deterioration in stock and debtors levels.

**Required:**
(a) Show by using the data given how you would calculate ratios that could be used to measure stock and debtor levels for both years.
(b) Discuss the ways in which the management of Sparkrite Ltd could exercise control over (i) stock levels and (ii) debtor levels.

**9.4** Dylan Ltd operates an advertising agency. It has an annual turnover of £20 million before taking into account bad debts of £0.1 million. All sales are on credit and, on average, the settlement period for trade debtors is 60 days. The company is currently reviewing its credit policies.

To encourage prompt payment, the credit control department has proposed that customers should be given a $2\frac{1}{2}$ per cent discount if they pay within 30 days; for those who do not pay within this period, a maximum of 50 days' credit should be given. The credit department believes that 60 per cent of customers will take advantage of the discount by paying at the end of the discount period with the remainder paying at the end of 50 days.

The credit department believes that bad debts can be effectively eliminated by adopting the above policies and by employing stricter credit investigation procedures, which will cost an additional £20,000 a year. The credit department is confident that these new policies will not result in any reduction in sales.

The business has a £6 million overdraft on which it pays annual interest of 14 per cent.

**Required:**

Calculate the net annual cost (savings) to the company of abandoning its existing credit policies and adopting the proposals of the credit control department.

**9.5** Your superior, the general manager of Plastics Manufacturers Limited, has recently been talking to the chief buyer of Plastic Toys Limited, which manufactures a wide range of toys for young children. At present, Plastic Toys is considering changing its supplier of plastic granules and has offered to buy its entire requirement of 2,000 kilograms a month from you at the going market rate, providing that you will grant it three months' credit on its purchases. The following information is available:

(i)  Plastic granules sell for £10 per kilogram, variable costs are £7 per kilogram and fixed costs £2 per kilogram.

(ii)  Your own company is financially strong and has sales of £15 million a year. For the foreseeable future it will have surplus capacity and it is actively looking for new outlets.

(iii)  Extracts from Plastic Toys' accounts are as follows:

|  | 1999 £000 | 2000 £000 | 2001 £000 |
|---|---|---|---|
| Sales | 800 | 980 | 640 |
| Profit before interest and tax | 100 | 110 | (150) |
| Capital employed | 600 | 650 | 575 |
| **Current assets** |  |  |  |
| Stocks | 200 | 220 | 320 |
| Debtors | 140 | 160 | 160 |
|  | 340 | 380 | 480 |
| **Creditors due within one year** |  |  |  |
| Creditors | (180) | (190) | (220) |
| Overdraft | (100) | (150) | (310) |
|  | (280) | (340) | (530) |
| Net current assets | 60 | 40 | (50) |

**Required:**

(a)  Write some short notes suggesting sources of information you would use to assess the creditworthiness of potential customers who are unknown to you. You should critically evaluate each source of information.

(b)  Describe the accounting controls you would use to monitor the level of your company's trade debtors.

(c)  Advise your general manager on the acceptability of the proposal. You should give your reasons and do any calculations you consider necessary.

*Hint*: In order to answer this question you must weigh the costs of administration and cash discounts against the savings in bad debts and interest charges.

**9.6** Boswell Enterprises Ltd is reviewing its trade credit policy. The business, which sells all of its goods on credit, has estimated that sales for the forthcoming year will be £3 million under the existing policy. Thirty per cent of trade debtors are expected to pay one month after being invoiced and 70 per cent are expected to pay two months after being invoiced. These estimates are in line with previous years' figures.

At present, no cash discounts are offered to customers. However, to encourage prompt payment, the company is considering giving a $2^1/_2$ per cent cash discount to debtors who pay in one month or less. Given this incentive, the company expects 60 per cent of trade debtors to pay one month after being invoiced and 40 per cent of debtors to pay two months after being invoiced. The business believes that the introduction of a cash discount policy will prove attractive to some customers and will lead to a 5 per cent increase in total sales.

Irrespective of the trade credit policy adopted, the gross profit margin of the business will be 20 per cent for the forthcoming year and three months' stock will be held. Fixed monthly expenses of £15,000 and variable expenses (excluding discounts), equivalent to 10 per cent of sales, will be incurred and will be paid one month in arrears. Trade creditors will be paid in arrears and will be equal to two months' cost of sales. The company will hold a fixed cash balance of £140,000 throughout the year, whichever trade credit policy is adopted. No dividends will be proposed or paid during the year. Ignore taxation.

**Required:**
(a) Calculate the investment in working capital at the end of the forthcoming year under:
  - The existing policy
  - The proposed policy.
(b) Calculate the expected net profit for the forthcoming year under:
  - The existing policy
  - The proposed policy.
(c) Advise the business as to whether it should implement the proposed policy.

*Hint*: The investment in working capital will be made up of stock, debtors and cash, *less* trade creditors and any unpaid expenses at the year end.

**9.7** Delphi plc has recently decided to enter the expanding market for minidisc players. The business will manufacture the players and sell them to small TV and hi-fi specialists, medium-sized music stores and large retail chain stores. The new product will be launched next February and predicted sales for the product from each customer group for February and the expected rate of growth for subsequent months are as follows:

| Customer type | February sales £000 | Monthly compound % sales growth | Credit sales (months) |
|---|---|---|---|
| TV and hi-fi specialists | 20 | 4 | 1 |
| Music stores | 30 | 6 | 2 |
| Retail chain stores | 40 | 8 | 3 |

The business is concerned about the financing implications of launching the new product as it is already experiencing liquidity problems. In addition, it is concerned that the credit control department will find it difficult to cope. This is a new market for the company and there are likely to be many new customers who will have to be investigated for creditworthiness.

Workings should be in £000 and calculations made to one decimal point only.

**Required:**
(a) Prepare an ageing schedule of the monthly debtors' balance relating to the new product for each of the first four months of the new product's life, and comment on the results. The schedule should analyse the debts outstanding according to customer type. It should also indicate, for each customer type, the relevant percentage outstanding in relation to the total amount outstanding for each month.
(b) Identify and discuss the factors that should be taken into account when evaluating the creditworthiness of the new business customers.

**9.8** Goliath plc is a retail business operating in Ireland. The most recent accounts of the business are as follows:

**Profit and loss account for the year to 31 May**

|  | £000 | £000 |
|---|---|---|
| Sales |  | 2,400.0 |
| Less Cost of sales |  |  |
| Opening stock | 550.0 |  |
| Add Purchases | 1,450.0 |  |
|  | 2,000.0 |  |
| Less Closing stock | 560.0 | 1,440.0 |
| Gross profit |  | 960.0 |
| Administration expenses | (300.0) |  |
| Selling expenses | (436.0) |  |
| Interest payable | (40.0) | (776.0) |
| Net profit before taxation |  | 184.0 |
| Less Corporation tax (25%) |  | 46.0 |
| Net profit after taxation |  | 138.0 |

**Balance sheet as at 31 May**

|  | £000 | £000 | £000 |
|---|---|---|---|
| **Fixed assets** |  |  |  |
| Machinery and equipment at cost |  | 424.4 |  |
| Less Accumulated depreciation |  | 140.8 | 283.6 |
| Motor vehicles at cost |  | 308.4 |  |
| Less Accumulated depreciation |  | 135.6 | 172.8 |
|  |  |  | 456.4 |
| **Current assets** |  |  |  |
| Stock at cost |  | 560.0 |  |
| Trade debtors |  | 565.0 |  |
| Cash at bank |  | 36.4 |  |
|  |  | 1,161.4 |  |

| | £000 | £000 | £000 |
|---|---|---|---|
| **Creditors: amounts falling due within one year** | | | |
| Trade creditors | (451.0) | | |
| Corporation tax due | (46.0) | (497.0) | 664.4 |
| | | | 1,120.8 |
| **Creditors: amounts falling due after one year** | | | |
| Loan capital | | | (400.0) |
| | | | 720.8 |
| **Capital and reserves** | | | |
| £1 ordinary shares | | | 200.0 |
| Retained profit | | | 520.8 |
| | | | 720.8 |

All sales and purchases are made on credit.

The business is considering whether to grant extended credit facilities to its customers. It has been estimated that increasing the settlement period for debtors by a further 20 days will increase the turnover of the business by 10 per cent. However, stocks will have to be increased by 15 per cent to cope with the increased demand. It is estimated that purchases will have to rise to £1,668,000 during the next year as a result of these changes. To finance the increase in stocks and debtors, the business will increase the settlement period taken for suppliers by 15 days and utilise a loan facility bearing a 10 per cent rate of interest for the remaining balance.

If the policy is implemented, bad debts are likely to increase by £120,000 and administration costs will rise by 15 per cent.

**Required:**
(a) Calculate the increase or decrease to each of the following that will occur in the forthcoming year if the proposed policy is implemented:
   (i)   operating cash cycle (based on year-end figures)
   (ii)  net investment in stock, debtors and creditors
   (iii) net profit after taxation.
(b) Should the company implement the proposed policy? Give reasons for your conclusion.

## CHAPTER 10

# Measuring and controlling divisional performance

## Introduction

Except for fairly small businesses, where it is possible for them to be managed as a separate unit, all businesses are divided into departments or divisions. The reason for this is that it is more practical to manage relatively small units (divisions) than to manage a whole large organisation as a single unit. Naturally managers, both of individual divisions and those to whom those divisional managers are responsible, will be very interested in the performance of each division. This raises the question of how best to assess divisional performance. In turn this raises the issue of how divisions, which provide products or services to other divisions of the same business, should price transfers to the 'buying' division. In this chapter we shall be addressing these two issues of divisional performance measurement and transfer pricing.

## OBJECTIVES

When you have completed this chapter, you should be able to:

- Explain why businesses adopt a divisional structure and what the potential drawbacks of this type of structure are.
- Identify the major methods of measuring the performance of operating divisions and divisional managers and discuss the issues surrounding these measures.
- Explain the problems of determining transfer prices between divisions and outline the methods used in practice.

## Why do businesses divisionalise?

Modern businesses are often extremely complex organisations. Many large businesses, for example, supply a wide range of products and services, have operating units located throughout the world and have an extended management hierarchy. It is not really feasible for those at the top of the management hierarchy to know everything that is going on in the various operating units or to make all the decisions necessary for the running of these units. As a result, it is usually sensible to devolve some decisions to those further down the hierarchy. To do this, the business is often organised into a number of operating **divisions**, usually according to either the products made and/or geographical location, and for the managers of these divisions to be given discretion over various aspects of divisional operations. The extent of the discretion allowed to divisional managers will vary from business to business.

It is possible to identify different types of operating divisions which can be found in practice, and which vary according to the level of managerial discretion allowed. The following are the two major types:

■ **Profit centres**  The divisional manager of a profit centre will have responsibility for production and sales performance and can therefore decide on such matters as pricing, marketing, volume of output, sources of supply, sales mix, etc. The divisional manager will be assigned certain fixed assets and working capital from central management and will be expected to generate profits from the effective use of those assets. Any additional capital expenditure relating to the division would have to be agreed by central management.

■ **Investment centres**  The divisional manager of an investment centre has discretion over capital expenditure and working capital decisions as well as production and sales performance. It is, in many respects, a business within a business.

In both types of division, profit is measured and the divisional manager is held accountable for divisional performance. In practice, it appears that central management is more prepared to allow discretion over production and sales decisions than over capital expenditure decisions. Thus profit centres are more common than investment centres.

The organisational chart for a typical business divisionalised by business activity is shown in Figure 10.1. This hypothetical business has three operating divisions – Brick Manufacturing, Engineering and Food Processing. Each division has a director of the company in charge and is treated as a separate investment centre.

We can see that the divisional directors will report to the managing director of the business. The organisation chart of a company organised along conventional

**Figure 10.1**  **The organisation chart for a business divisionalised along business activity lines**

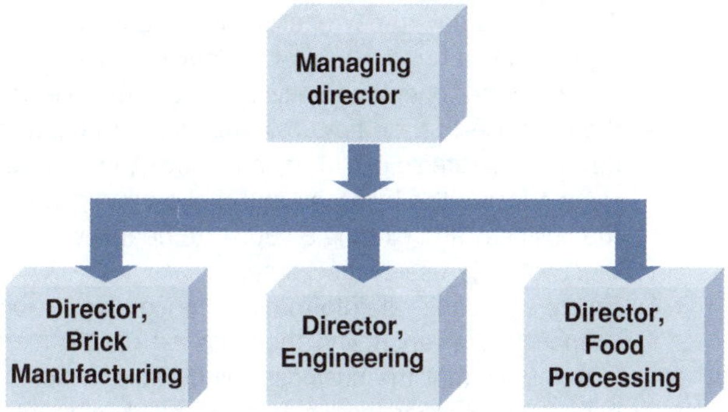

The business is managed as three separate businesses, each dealing with a different type of business activity.

lines would have a marketing director, finance director, production director, etc. reporting to the managing director. In a divisionalised structure, these functional specialists would be employed within each of the operating divisions and so would report to the director of that division.

There are several advantages claimed for dividing business operations into divisions and allowing divisional managers a measure of autonomy.

---

**Activity 10.1**

We have already touched on some of the reasons why businesses operate on divisional lines.

Try to make a list with a brief explanation of the various reasons which you feel lead to businesses being divisionalised.

---

The following reasons occurred to us:

1. *Market information*  Divisional managers will gather an enormous amount of information concerning customers, markets, sources of supply, etc. which may be difficult and costly to transmit to central management. Such information is best used by the divisional managers themselves who might find it impossible to articulate all the knowledge and experience gathered to others.

2. *Management motivation*  Divisional managers are likely to have a greater commitment to their work if they feel they have a significant influence over divisional decisions. The behavioural literature suggests that participation in decision making encourages a sense of responsiblity towards seeing those decisions through. There is a danger that divisional managers will simply 'turn off' if decisions concerning the division are made by central management and then imposed on them.

3. *Management development*  Allowing divisional managers a degree of autonomy should help in their development. They will become exposed to marketing, production, financial problems, etc. which should help them to gain valuable specialist skills. In addition, the opportunity to run a division more or less as a separate business should develop their ability to think in strategic terms. This can be of great benefit to the business when it is looking for successors to the current generation of senior managers.

4. *Specialist knowledge*  Where a business offers a wide range of products and services, it would be difficult for central management to have the expertise to make operating decisions concerning each product. It is more practical to give divisional managers, with the detailed knowledge of the products, responsibility for such matters.

5. *Allowing a strategic role for central managers*  If central managers were given responsibility for the day-to-day operations of each division, they could become bogged down with making a huge number of relatively small decisions. Even if they were capable of making better operating decisions than the divisional managers, this is unlikely to be the best use of their time. Managers operating at the centre of the business should develop a strategic role. They must look to the future to identify the opportunities and threats facing the business and make appropriate plans. By taking a broader view of the business and plotting a course to be followed, senior managers will be making the most valuable use of their time.

6. *Timely decisions*  If information concerning a local division has to be gathered, shaped into a report and then passed up the hierarchy before a decision is made, it is unlikely that the business will be able to act quickly when dealing with changing conditions or emerging issues. In a highly competitive or turbulent environment, the speed of response to market changes can be critical. Divisional managers can usually formulate a response much more quickly than central managers.

**Activity 10.2**

Can you think of any problems that might arise when a business is organised into divisions?

A number of problems may arise as a result of adopting a divisionalised structure. These include:

1. *Goal conflict*   It is possible that the goals of the operating division will be inconsistent with those of either the business as a whole or those of other divisions of the business. For example, an operating division of a business may be unable to sell computer equipment to a particular overseas government because another operating division within the business is selling military equipment to a hostile government. The overall profits of the business, however, may be increased if the military equipment sales ceased in order to allow a new market to develop for the computing equipment sold by the other division.

2. *Risk avoidance*   Where managers of a division are faced with a large project which involves a high level of risk, they may decide against the project even though the potential returns are high. The reason for this may be the consequences of failure for their job security and remuneration. However, investors in the business may prefer to take the risks involved because they view the project as just one of a number of projects undertaken by the business. Whilst each particular project will have its risks, there is an expectation by investors that, overall, the expected returns will outweigh the risks involved. Divisional managers may be unable to take such a detached view, as they may not have a diversified portfolio of projects within the division to help reduce the effect of things going badly wrong.

3. *Management 'perks'*   By allowing divisional managers autonomy, there is a danger that they will award themselves substantial perquisites or 'perks'. These perks may include a generous expense allowance, first-class travel, a chauffeur, etc. These additional benefits may mean that divisional managers receive a far better remuneration package than the market for their services requires. The costs of monitoring divisional manager behaviour, however, may outweigh any benefits arising from identifying and reducing these perks.

4. *Increasing costs*   Additional costs may be borne by the business as a result of organising into divisions. For example, each division may have its own market research department, which may duplicate the efforts of market research departments in other divisions. By organising into smaller operating units, the business may also be unable to take advantage of its size in order to reduce costs. For example, it may be unable to negotiate quantity discounts with suppliers, as each division will be deciding on which supplier it uses and will only be purchasing quantities that are appropriate for its needs.

5. *Competition*   Divisions within the same business offering similar or substitute products may find themselves in competition with each other. Where this competition is intense, prices may be reduced which may, in turn, have the effect of reducing profits of the business as a whole. For this reason, divisionalisation often works best where the different divisions do not offer closely related products or services.

It is clear from the above that divisonalisation is not without its problems. Although these problems usually cannot be eliminated, it may be possible to reduce their severity. Central management must try to devise a divisional framework which reaps the benefits of divisional autonomy and yet minimises the problems which divisionalisation brings.

| Activity 10.3 | Assume that you are the chief executive of a divisionalised business. How might you try to reduce the effects of some of the problems identified above? |

The problems of goal conflict and competition may be dealt with by regulating the behaviour of divisional managers. They should be prevented from making decisions which result in an increase in profits for their particular division, but which reduce the profits of the business as a whole. Although such a policy would cut across the autonomy of divisional managers, it is important for them to appreciate that they are not operating completely independent units and that divisional managers also have responsibilities towards the business as a whole.

The problem of risk avoidance by management is a complex one which may be difficult to deal with in practice. However, it might be possible to encourage divisional managers to take on more risk if the rewards offered reflected the higher levels of risk involved. Both intuition and theory tell us that individuals will often be prepared to take on greater risk provided that they receive compensation in the form of higher rewards. It may also be possible for the business, through the use of budget variance reports, to distinguish between those variances that are outside the control of the divisional manager and those that are within the manager's control. Divisional managers would then only be accountable for the variances within their control. It is not always easy, however, to obtain unbiased information for preparing budgets from divisional managers when they know that such information will be used to evaluate their performance.

Management 'perks' may be controlled, to some extent, by observing the behaviour and actions of divisional managers. Many 'perks' such as luxury cars, chauffeurs, large offices, etc. are quite visible and central management should be alert to any signs that divisional managers are rewarding themselves in this way.

Duplication of effort in certain areas can be extremely costly. For this reason, some businesses prefer particular functions, such as administration, accounting, research and development and marketing, to be undertaken by central staff rather than at the divisional level. Again, this means that divisional managers will have to sacrifice some autonomy for the sake of the performance of the business overall.

Managers are quite often given financial bonuses for achieving their targets. Their promotional opportunities are likely to be enhanced as well. Thus how managers are assessed is an important issue to them and to the business as a whole. Unless the targets against which managers are assessed are carefully established, there is the clear danger that what managers are working towards is not in the best interests of the business, as a whole.

We can see that divisionalisation poses a major challenge for central management. Somehow, it must encourage management discretion at the divisional level whilst trying to ensure that the divisional goals are consistent with the overall goals of the business. This requires sound judgement, as there are really no techniques or models which can be applied to solve this problem. For the management accountant of a divisionalised business there are also major challenges. One such challenge is to provide valid and reliable measures of performance relating to both the division and the divisional managers. It is to this challenge that we now turn.

# Divisional performance measurement

Businesses operate with the primary objective of increasing shareholders' wealth, which on a short-term basis translates into making a profit. It is not surprising, therefore, that profits and profitability are of central importance in **divisional performance measurement** of both the divisional managers and the operating divisions. However, there are various measures of profit which we can use for evaluation purposes. Consider the following divisional profit statement:

### Household Appliances Divisional Profit Statement for last year

|  | £000 |
|---|---|
| Sales | 980 |
| *Less* Variable expenses | 490 |
| **Contribution margin** | 490 |
| *Less* Controllable divisional fixed expenses | 130 |
| **Controllable profit** | 360 |
| *Less* Non-controllable divisional fixed expenses | 150 |
| **Divisional profit** | 210 |
| *Less* Allocated central management expenses | 80 |
| **Divisional net profit (loss)** | 130 |

The words 'controllable' and 'non-controllable' in this statement refer to the ability of the divisional manager to exert influence over them. A fixed expense which is authorised by a senior manager at 'head office' will not be under the control of the divisional manager, despite the fact that the expense may relate to the division. An expense that arises directly from a decision taken by the divisional manager is controllable at divisional level.

This profit statement reveals that there are four measures of performance that could be used when evaluating the division. When deciding on the appropriate measure, it is important to be clear about the purpose for which it is to be used. The **contribution margin** represents the difference between the total sales of the division and the variable expenses incurred. This is a useful measure for gaining an insight into the relationship between costs, output and profit.

---

**Activity 10.4**

Assume that you are the chief executive of a divisionalised business. Would you use the contribution margin as a primary measure of divisional performance?

This measure has its drawbacks for this purpose. The most important drawback is that it only takes account of variable expenses and ignores any fixed expenses incurred. This means that not all aspects of operating performance are considered.

| Activity 10.5 | Assume now that you are a divisional manager. What might you be encouraged to do if the contribution margin were used to assess your performance? |
|---|---|

As variable expenses are taken into account in this measure and fixed expenses are ignored, it would be tempting to arrange things so that fixed expenses rather than variable expenses are incurred wherever possible. In this way, the contribution margin will be maximised. For example, you may decide, as divisional manager, to employ less casual labour and to use machines to do the work instead (even though this may be a more expensive option).

The **controllable profit** deducts all expenses that are within the control of the divisional manager in arriving at a measure of performance. This is viewed by many as the best measure of performance for the divisional manager, as he/she will be in a position to determine the level of expenses incurred. However, in practice, it may be difficult to categorise costs as being either **controllable costs** or **non-controllable costs**. Some expenses may be capable of being influenced by the divisional manager yet not be entirely under his/her control.

Depreciation can be one example of such an expense. The divisional manager may be required to purchase a particular type of computer hardware so that the information systems of the division are compatible with the systems used throughout the business. However, the manager may have some discretion over how often the computer hardware is replaced, as well as over the purchase of particular hardware models that perform beyond the requirement standards needed for the business. By exercising this discretion, the depreciation charge for the year will be different from the one that would arise if the manager stuck to the minimum standards laid down by central management.

The **divisional profit** deducts all divisional expenses (controllable and non-controllable) that are incurred by the division. This provides us with a measure of the contribution of the division to the overall profits of the business.

| Activity 10.6 | Which of the measures so far discussed is most useful for evaluating the performance of:<br>■ The divisional manager, and<br>■ The division? |
|---|---|

It can be argued that the performance of the divisional manager should be judged according to the expenses that are within his/her control. Hence, the controllable contribution would be the most appropriate measure to use. The contribution margin does not take account of all the expenses that are controllable by the divisional manager whilst the divisional contribution takes account of some expenses that are not under the control of the manager. The latter measure, however, may be appropriate for evaluating the performance of the division as it deducts all divisional expenses from the divisional revenues earned. It is a comprehensive measure of divisional achievement.

**Divisional net profit** is derived after deducting a proportion of the central management expenses incurred for the period. The proportion allocated to each division will presumably represent what central management believes is a fair share of the total central management expenses incurred. In practice, the way that these allocations are made between divisions can be extremely contentious. Some divisional managers may be convinced that they have been allocated an unfair share of central management expenses. They may also believe that the divisions are being loaded with expenses over which they have little control and that the divisional net profit figure derived will not truly represent the achievements of the division. These are often compelling arguments for not allocating central management expenses to the various divisions.

| Activity 10.7 | Can you think of any arguments for allocating central management expenses to divisions? |
| --- | --- |

The business as a whole will only make a profit after all central management expenses have been covered, and the allocation of these expenses to the divisions should help make divisional managers more aware of this fact. In addition, central management may wish to compare the results of the division with the results of similar businesses in the same industry that are operating as independent entities. By allocating research and development costs, administration expenses and so on to the divisions, a more valid basis for comparison is provided, as independent businesses will have to bear these kinds of expenses before arriving at their profit for the period. The effect of allocating central management expenses may also help to impose an element of control over these costs. Divisional managers may put pressure on central managers to keep allocated expenses low to minimise the adverse effect on divisional profits.

## Return on investment

➡ **Return on investment (ROI)** is a popular method of evaluating the profitability of divisions. The ratio is calculated in the following way:

$$\text{ROI} = \frac{\text{Divisional profit}}{\text{Divisional investment (assets employed)}} \times 100\%$$

When defining divisional profit for this ratio, the purpose for which the ratio is to be used must be considered. For evaluating the performance of a divisional manager, the controllable contribution is likely to be the most appropriate, whereas for evaluating the performance of a division, the divisional contribution is likely to be more appropriate. The reasons for this have already been discussed above. Different definitions can be employed for divisional investment. The net assets or total assets figure may be used. In addition, assets may be shown at original cost or on some other basis, such as current replacement cost.

The ROI ratio can be broken down into two main elements. These are:

$$\text{ROI} = \frac{\text{Divisional profit}}{\text{Sales}} \times \frac{\text{Sales}}{\text{Divisional investment}}$$

This separation into the two main elements is useful, because it shows that ROI is determined by both the profit margin on each £ of sales and the ability to generate a high level of sales in relation to the investment base.

**Activity 10.8**

The following data relate to the performance and position of two operating divisions which sell similar products:

|  | Kuala Lumpur Division £000 | Singapore Division £000 |
|---|---|---|
| Sales | 300 | 750 |
| Divisional profit | 30 | 25 |
| Divisional investment | 600 | 500 |

**What observations can you make concerning the performance of each division?**

The information shows that the divisions appear to be pursuing different strategies. The profit margins for the Kuala Lumpur and Singapore Divisions are 10 per cent (30/300) and 3.3 per cent (25/750) respectively. The sales to divisional investment ratios for the Kuala Lumpur and Singapore Divisions are 50 per cent (300/600) and 150 per cent (750/500) respectively. Thus, we can see that the Kuala Lumpur Division prefers to sell goods at a higher profit margin than the Singapore Division and this results in a lower sales turnover in relation to assets employed. However, the ROI for both divisions is identical at 5 per cent.

ROI is a measure of **profitability**, as it relates profits to the size of the investment made in the division. This relative measure allows comparisons between divisions of different sizes. However, ROI has its drawbacks. Where it is used as the primary measure of performance for divisional managers, there is a danger that it will lead to behaviour which is not really consistent with the interests of the business overall.

**Activity 10.9**

Russell Francis plc has two divisions, both selling similar products but operating in different geographical areas. The Wessex Division reported a £200,000 controllable contribution from a divisional investment of £1m and the Sussex Division a £150,000 controllable contribution from a divisional investment of £500,000.

The divisional manager of each division has the opportunity to invest £200,000 in the development of a new product line that will boost divisional contributions by £50,000. The finance cost for each division is 16 per cent.

**Which operating division do you think has been the more successful? How might each divisional manager react to the new opportunity?**

Although the Wessex Division has achieved a higher contribution in absolute terms, it has a lower ROI than the Sussex Division. The ROI for Wessex is 20 per cent (£200,000/£1,000,000) compared with 30 per cent (£150,000/£500,000) for the Sussex Division. Using ROI as the measure of performance, the Sussex Division is therefore the better performing division.

The ROI from the new investment is 25 per cent (£50,000/£200,000). Thus, by taking on this investment, the divisional manager of Wessex will increase the ROI of the division which currently stands at 20 per cent. However, the divisional manager of Sussex will reduce the ROI of the division by taking this opportunity as its ROI is below the overall ROI of 30 per cent for the division.

> If ROI is used as the primary measure of divisional performance, the divisional manager of Sussex may decline the opportunity as s/he may feel that a decline in divisional ROI will reflect poorly on her/his performance. However, the returns from the opportunity are 25 per cent, which comfortably exceed the cost of finance of 16 per cent and so failure to exploit the opportunity will mean the profit potential of the division is not fully realised.

A further disincentive to invest can result where the divisional investment in assets is measured in terms of the original cost less any accumulated depreciation to date (that is, net book value or written-down value). Where depreciation is being charged each year, the net book value of the divisional investment will be reduced. Provided that profits stay at the same level, this means that ROI will start to climb.

To illustrate this point, assume the following profits and investment for a division:

| Year | Divisional profit £ | Divisional investment £ | ROI at net book value % |
|---|---|---|---|
| 1 | 30,000 | 200,000 | 15.0 |
| 2 | 30,000 | 180,000 | 16.7 |
| 3 | 30,000 | 160,000 | 18.8 |
| 4 | 30,000 | 140,000 | 21.4 |

We can see that the ROI increases over time simply because the investment base is shrinking. We saw above that divisional managers may be discouraged from investing in further assets where the ROI is below the existing ROI for the division. In this example, the divisional manager may increase the 'hurdle rate' for new investments each year in line with the rise in ROI. This would make new investments increasingly more difficult to accept, even though the need for new investment is likely to increase as the existing assets become fully depreciated.

**Activity 10.10**

How might the problem caused by ROI being boosted simply through a reduction in the investment base be dealt with?

One way around the problem would be to keep the investment in assets at original cost and not to deduct depreciation for purposes of calculating ROI. However, fixed assets normally lose their productive capacity over time, and this fact should really be recognised. Another way around the problem is to use some measure of current market value for the investment in assets.

## Residual income

The weaknesses of the ROI method, particularly the fact that it ignores the cost of financing the division, have led to a search for a more appropriate measure of divisional performance. **Residual income (RI)** has been advocated by a number of commentators as being more acceptable. RI is the amount of income or profit generated by a division which is over and above the minimum acceptable level of income. If we assume the objective of the business is to maximise shareholder wealth, the minimum acceptable level of income to be generated is the amount necessary to cover the cost of capital.

RI is derived by deducting from the divisional profit an imputed interest charge for the capital invested. Let us assume that a division produced a profit of £100,000 and there was a divisional investment of £600,000 with a cost of financing this investment of 15 per cent. The residual income would be as follows:

|  | £ |
| --- | --- |
| Divisional profit | 100,000 |
| *Less* Charge for capital invested | |
| (15% × £600,000) | 90,000 |
| Residual income | 10,000 |

A positive RI (shown above) means that the division is generating returns in excess of the minimum requirements of the business. The higher these excess returns, the better the performance of the division.

---

**Activity 10.11**

Can you see any similarities between the ROI and RI methods discussed above and the methods of investment appraisal dealt with in Chapter 8?

The RI method is similar to the NPV method in many respects. You may recall that, with NPV, a project is accepted where the returns (discounted cash flows) exceed the amount invested. The returns are discounted using the cost of capital. The higher the NPV the greater the wealth generated for shareholders. The ROI is similar in some respects to the IRR method. The IRR method derives a percentage rate of return which is then compared with a 'hurdle rate' to see whether the return is acceptable.

---

**Activity 10.12**

Simonson Pharmaceuticals plc operates a Helena Beauty Care Division, which has reported the following results for last year:

| | |
| --- | --- |
| Divisional investment | £2,000,000 |
| Divisional profit | £300,000 |

The division has the opportunity to invest in a new product. This will require an additional investment in fixed assets of £400,000 and is expected to generate additional profits of £50,000 a year. This company has a cost of capital of 12 per cent.
   Have a go at calculating the residual income of the division for last year.
   Do you believe that the division should produce the new product or not?
   How do you think that the divisional manager might react to the new product opportunity, if ROI were used as the means of evaluating performance?

The residual income for last year is:

|  | £ |
| --- | --- |
| Divisional profit | 300,000 |
| *Less* Charge for capital invested | |
| (12% x £2,000,000) | 240,000 |
| Residual income | 60,000 |

The residual income expected from the new product is:

| | £ |
|---|---|
| Additional divisional profit | 50,000 |
| Less Charge for additional capital | |
| (12% x £400,000) | 48,000 |
| Residual income | 2,000 |

The residual income is positive and, therefore, it would be worthwhile to produce the new product.

The ROI of the division for last year was 15 per cent (that is, £300,000/£2m). However, the new product is only expected to produce an ROI of 12.5 per cent (that is, £50,000/£400,000). The effect of producing the new product will be to reduce the overall ROI of the division (assuming similar results from the existing activities next year). The divisional manager may, therefore, reject the new investment opportunity, despite the fact that acceptance would enhance the shareholders' wealth, because the new product would cover all of the costs, including the cost of financing the investment.

## Divisional performance measures and long-term performance

A problem of both ROI and RI is that divisional managers may focus on short-term divisional performance at the expense of the longer term. There is a danger that investment opportunities will be rejected because they reduce short-term ROI and RI, even though over the longer term they have a positive NPV.

Let us assume that there is an investment opportunity for a division that will require an initial investment of £90,000 and produce the following operating cash flows (net profit before depreciation) over the next five years:

| Year | £ |
|---|---|
| 1 | 18,000 |
| 2 | 18,000 |
| 3 | 25,000 |
| 4 | 50,000 |
| 5 | 60,000 |

Assuming a cost of capital of 16 per cent, the NPV of the project will be:

| Year | Cash flows £ | Disc rate | Present value £ |
|---|---|---|---|
| 1 | 18,000 | 0.862 | 15,516 |
| 2 | 18,000 | 0.743 | 13,374 |
| 3 | 25,000 | 0.641 | 16,025 |
| 4 | 50,000 | 0.552 | 27,600 |
| 5 | 60,000 | 0.476 | 28,560 |
| | | | 101,075 |
| Less Initial investment | | | 90,000 |
| Net present value | | | 11,075 |

This indicates that the NPV is positive and, therefore, it would be in the shareholders' interests to undertake the project.

In order to calculate ROI and RI, we need to derive the divisional profit for each year (that is, deduct a charge for depreciation from the operating cash flows shown above). Assuming that depreciation is charged equally over the life of the assets acquired and there is no residual value for the assets, the annual depreciation charge will be £18,000 (that is, £90,000/5).

After deducting an annual depreciation charge, the divisional profit will be as follows:

| Year | £ |
|---|---|
| 1 | – |
| 2 | – |
| 3 | 7,000 |
| 4 | 32,000 |
| 5 | 42,000 |

**Activity 10.13**

Calculate the project ROI and RI for each of the five years of the project's life. (Base the ROI calculation on the cost of the assets concerned.)

The ROI for the project will be as follows:

| Year | £ | ROI % |
|---|---|---|
| 1 | – | – |
| 2 | – | – |
| 3 | 7,000/90,000 | 7.8 |
| 4 | 32,000/90,000 | 35.6 |
| 5 | 42,000/90,000 | 46.7 |

The RI will be as follows:

| Year | Divisional profit £ | Capital charge £ | RI £ |
|---|---|---|---|
| 1 | – | 14,400 | (14,400) |
| 2 | – | 14,400 | (14,400) |
| 3 | 7,000 | 14,400 | (7,400) |
| 4 | 32,000 | 14,400 | 17,600 |
| 5 | 42,000 | 14,400 | 27,600 |
| | | | 9,000 |

**Activity 10.14**

What do you deduce from the calculations resulting from the previous activity?

We can see that, in the early years, the ROI and RI calculations do not produce good results, even though the situation is reversed in later years. For the first two years the ROI is zero and for the first three years the RI is negative. Divisional managers may, therefore, be discouraged from making investments if they feel that the results in the early years would be viewed unfavourably by central management. Given the results of the NPV analysis, this means that the managers would not be acting in the shareholders' best interests in rejecting the proposal. Note, however, that the RI of the project overall is positive and so provides a result which is consistent with the NPV result.

Various approaches have been proposed in an attempt to avoid the kind of problem described above. It has been suggested, for example, that for the purpose of calculating divisional ROI and RI, the assets employed in the project should not be included in the divisional investment base until the project is generating good returns.

## Further measurement issues

Interpreting divisional performance requires that we have some basis for comparison. There are various bases that can be used:

- *Other divisions within the business*  Comparing the ROI or RI of different divisions within the same business may not be very useful where the divisions operate in different industries. Different types of industries have different levels of risk and this in turn produces different expectations concerning acceptable levels of return.
- *Previous performance of the division*  It is possible to compare current performance with previous performance to see whether there has been any improvement or deterioration. However, it is often necessary to compare performance against some external standard in order to bring to light operating inefficiencies within the division. Also, the economic environment in previous periods may be different from the current environment and so may invalidate comparisons of this nature.
- *Budgeted performance*  This may be useful provided that the basis for the budget targets is reasonable, which should be the case.
- *Similar businesses within the same industry*  The ROI or RI of other divisions or independent entities operating within the same industry can provide a useful basis for comparison. However, there are problems associated with this basis.

| **Activity 10.15** | What problems are you likely to come across, in practice, when seeking to compare the performance of a division within your business with an independent business or similar division of another business? |
|---|---|

You may encounter a number of problems such as:

- *Problems of obtaining the information you require*  This is particularly true for a division within another business. This information may not be available to those outside the business.
- *Differences in accounting policies*  Different depreciation methods, stock valuation methods, etc. may result in different measures of profit.
- *Differences in asset structure*  The different age of fixed assets employed, the decision to rent rather than buy particular assets, and so on may result in differences in the measures derived.

We have seen that a single measure of performance cannot really capture all the various aspects of divisional performance. Moreover, it tends to be the case that 'the things that count are the things that get counted'. This is to say that importance is given to matters that can be measured in figures, irrespective of their real significance. Thus, by focusing on a single measure, there is a risk that managerial actions and behaviour will become distorted. Managers may become more concerned with the particular measure of performance used (and with manipulating its outcome) than the underlying economic reality which it tries to portray. This could, as we have seen, lead to decisions being made which run counter to the interests of the owners of the business.

It may, therefore, be useful to use a variety of different measures of performance which cover both financial and non-financial aspects of performance and which are concerned with both short-term and long-term achievement. Examples of other aspects of the division that may be usefully assessed are:

- *Research and development expenditure*  An evaluation of the level of investment in R&D and the benefits derived over the longer term can be illuminating. If a single measure of performance is used to assess divisional performance, such as ROI or RI, it would be possible to improve these measures in the short term simply by cutting back on this type of expenditure. However, this may be to the detriment of the longer-term profitability of the division.
- *Staff training and morale*  It is widely recognised that, for most businesses, the employees are the most valuable assets. It is, therefore, useful to know how this resource is being cultivated by the divisional managers. Once again, it is possible to improve ROI and RI in the short term by reducing the level of investment in the human assets of the business. Staff morale as revealed by staff turnover and the number of complaints and disputes arising may also help in assessing the management of the division.
- *Product quality*  In a competitive environment, the quality of the products offered can be of vital importance to long-term survival. Maintaining and improving quality, however, may require high levels of investment in equipment with strict tolerance levels, automated inspection methods and staff training.
- *Environmental and social concerns*  In highly industrialised societies, there is increasing pressure on companies to acknowledge their responsibility towards the environment and to assess the impact of their activities on the communities in which they are based. An audit of the policies adopted by the division on such matters as pollution, wildlife protection, employment policies for minorities, etc. can be carried out to see whether it is being a good 'corporate citizen'.
- *Productivity*  The efficiency of the division in producing its output and the level of production achieved may be extremely valuable to central management.

---

**Activity 10.16**

Runne & Co. is a large firm of solicitors which has a property conveyancing division specialising in the purchase and sale of private houses.

How might the productivity of this division be assessed? Can you think of four possible measures of productivity for this division?

Possible measures might include some of the following:

- Total number of conveyances undertaken by the division.
- Total fees generated by the conveyancing division.
- Average time taken to complete conveyances of property.
- Gross income generated per member of conveyancing staff.
- Net income generated per member of conveyancing staff.

---

**? Self-assessment question 10.1**

Andromeda International plc has two operating divisions, the managers of which are given considerable autonomy. In order to assess the performance of divisional managers, the central management uses ROI. For the purposes of this measure the assets employed include both fixed and current assets. The company has a cost of capital of 15 per cent and uses the straight-line method of depreciation for external reporting purposes.

Extracts from the budgets, for each of the two divisions for next year are as follows:

|  | Jupiter division £000 | Mars division £000 |
|---|---|---|
| Net profit | 260 | 50 |
| Fixed assets at cost | 940 | 1,200 |
| Current assets | 290 | 180 |

Since the budgets were prepared, two investment opportunities have been brought to the attention of the relevant divisional managers. These are as follows:

(i) Central management would like to see the productivity of the Mars division improve. To help achieve this, they have informed the divisional manager that equipment costing £300,000 can be purchased which will have a life of five years and which will lead to operating savings of £90,000 each year.

(ii) A new product can be sold by the Jupiter division which will increase sales by £250,000 each year over the next five years. It will be necessary to increase marketing costs by £60,000 a year and stocks held will increase by £90,000. The contribution to sales ratio for the new product will be 30 per cent.

**Required:**

(a) Calculate the expected ROI for each division assuming:
- the investment opportunities are not taken up
- the investment opportunities are taken up.

(b) Comment on the results obtained in (a) and state how the divisional managers and central managers might view the investment opportunities.

(c) Discuss the implications of using net book value (that is after accumulated depreciation) rather than gross book value as a basis for valuing fixed assets when calculating ROI.

Exhibit 10.1 gives some indication of the approaches taken to divisional performance measurement in practice.

---

| Exhibit 10.1 | **Divisional performance measurement in practice** |
|---|---|

The 1993 ACCA survey found that 85 per cent of repondents were divisionalised and that the majority of these (78 per cent of respondents) based their divisions on the nature of their products, that is divisions specialised in particular products or types of product.

The survey also found that businesses seem to use more than one method of measuring divisional performance with various approaches being used as follows:

|  | % of respondents |
|---|---|
| Target ROI | 55 |
| Target RI | 20 |
| Target profit before a finance charge on assets used | 61 |
| A target cash flow figure | 43 |
| Ability to stay within the budget | 57 |

*Source*: Drury, Braund, Osborne and Tayles (see reference (1) at the end of the chapter).

| Exhibit 10.2 | **Divisional performance at Marks and Spencer** |
|---|---|

According to the business's 2000 annual report, Marks and Spencer assesses divisional performance using the residual income approach. In deriving the RI, the business's weighted average cost of capital of 10 per cent is used to calculate the capital charge. The 2001 annual report reveals that divisions are charged a notional rent for the use of premises, even where the business owns the freehold, in deriving divisional profit. The capital charge must, therefore, be based on the assets used by the divisions other than premises. The notional rent covers the use of the premises.

# Transfer pricing

In some cases, one division will sell goods or services to another division within the same business. For example, a brick manufacturing division of a business may sell its products to another division within the same business which is a house-builder. The price at which such transfers between divisions are made can be an important issue. Setting appropriate prices for such inter-divisional trading
→ is known as **transfer pricing**. To the division which is providing the goods or service transfers represent part, or possibly all, of its output. If the performance of the division is to be measured in any useful way, the division should be credited with 'sales revenues' for these goods or services transferred. Failure to credit the supplying division in this way would mean that it would have to bear the expenses of creating the goods or service, but get no credit for it. By the same token, the receiving ('buying') division needs to be charged with the expense of using the goods or service supplied by the other division, if its performance is to be measured in any meaningful way.

Where inter-divisional transfers represent a large part of the total sales or purchases of a division, 'transfer pricing' is a very important issue. Small changes in the transfer price of goods or services can result in large changes in profits for the division concerned. As divisional managers are often assessed according to the profits generated by their division, setting transfer prices may be a sensitive issue between divisional managers.

Whilst the profits of individual divisions will be affected by the transfer prices agreed, the profits of the business as a whole should not normally be affected. An increase in the transfer price of goods or services will lead to an increase in the profits of the selling division, which is normally cancelled out by the decrease in profits of the buying division. However, transfer prices between divisions can indirectly lead to loss of profits to the business as a whole. The level at which the transfer price for a particular good or service is set could lead divisional managers to make decisions which are in the interests of their division but which are not in the interests of the business as a whole. An example of this is a division buying a particular good or service from a supplier outside the business, because the supplier's price is cheaper than the established internal transfer price. In such a situation, the profits of the business as a whole may well be adversely affected.

**Activity 10.17**

What do you think transfer pricing policies should seek to achieve?
    When considering this question, remember what the business as a whole is trying to achieve and why businesses seek to achieve it through divisionalisation.

Transfer pricing seeks to achieve the following:

■ *The independence of divisions*   By allowing divisional managers to set their own trans-fer prices and by allowing other divisions to decide whether or not to trade at the prices quoted, the autonomy of individual divisions is encouraged. This, in turn, should help motivate divisional managers.

■ *The assessment of divisional performance*   Inter-divisional sales will contribute to total revenues for a division which in turn influences divisional profit. Setting an appropriate transfer price can, therefore, be important in deriving a valid measure of divisional profit for evaluation purposes. They should be of value in helping to establish incent-ives for, and promoting accountability of, divisional managers.

■ *Promoting the optimisation of profits for the business*   Transfer prices may seek to optimise profits for the business as a whole. For example, a division may be prevented from quoting a transfer price for goods which will make buying divisions seek cheaper sources of supply from outside the business.

■ *Allocating divisional resources*   Transfer prices will be important in determining the level of output for particular goods and services. The level of return from inter-divisional sales can be important in deciding on the level of sales and investment relating to a particular product or group of products.

■ *Tax minimisation*   Where a business has operations in various countries, it may be beneficial to set transfer prices such that the bulk of profits are reported in divisions where the host country has low corporation tax rates. However, tax laws operating in many countries will seek to prevent this kind of profit manipulation.

**Activity 10.18**

Is there a conflict between any of the objectives identified above? If so, can a single transfer price help achieve all these objectives?

It is quite possible for there to be a conflict between the objectives identified. As a res-ult, a single transfer price is unlikely to be able to achieve all the stated objectives. For example, in order to optimise the profits for the business as a whole it may be necessary to determine transfer prices centrally which would undermine the autonomy of divi-sions. In addition, a centrally imposed transfer price may result in inter-divisional sales at artificially low prices which would disadvantage particular divisions and might result in reported profit figures in both the buying and selling divisions becoming invalid measures of productivity.

## Transfer pricing policies

There are various approaches to setting a transfer price for goods and services between divisions. In this section we shall explore some of the major approaches. Before going on to do this it is probably worth identifying the principle that the best transfer price is one based closely on the **opportunity cost** of the good or ser-vice concerned. This opportunity cost represents the best alternative forgone.

## Market prices

➡ **Market prices** means the prices that exist in the market outside of the business whose divisions are involved in the transfer. Intuition may tell you that market prices should be the appropriate method of setting transfer prices. Using this approach, the transfer price is an objective, verifiable amount which has some real economic credibility. Where there is a competitive and active market for the products, the market price will represent the 'opportunity cost' of goods and services. For the selling division it is the revenue lost by selling to another division rather than to an outside customer. For the buying division, it is the best purchase price available.

However, the market price may not always be appropriate.

| | |
|---|---|
| **Activity 10.19** | Wolf Industries plc has an operating division that produces microwave ovens. The ovens are normally sold to retailers for £120. The division is currently producing 3,000 ovens per month (which is about 50 per cent capacity) and has the following cost structure: |

|  | Cost per oven £ |
|---|---|
| Variable cost | 70 |
| Fixed cost apportionment | 20 |
|  | 90 |

Another division of the company has offered to buy 2,000 ovens for £75 each. How would you respond to such an offer if you were manager of the division making microwave ovens?

---

If the division is operating below capacity, basing the transfer price on market prices may lead to lost sales. Other divisions within the business may prefer to buy from outside sources rather than from the selling division and this loss of sales will not be made good by sales to outside customers. We saw in an earlier chapter that businesses may base selling prices on the variable cost of the goods or services, rather than on the market price where there is a short-term problem of excess capacity. Provided that the selling price exceeds the variable cost of the goods, a contribution will be made towards the profits of the business. This principle can equally be applied to divisions of businesses. Thus, in such circumstances, a selling price somewhere between the variable cost of the product (£70) and the market price (£120) may be the best price for divisional transfers.

Another point to consider when making inter-divisional transfers is that the selling division may make savings owing to the fact that selling and distribution costs may be lower. In such a situation, part of these savings may be passed on to the buying division in the form of lower prices. Thus, some adjustment may be made to the market price of the goods being transferred.

**Activity 10.20**

Apart from the problems, which we have just considered, of trying to base inter-divisional transfer prices on external market prices, there is another, perhaps more fundamental, problem with market prices.
   Can you work out what this problem is?

This problem is that there is often not an external market in existence. It simply may not be possible for the potential 'buying' division to identify external suppliers and a price for the particular good or service required. Still more likely is it that there would be no potential external customer for the 'selling' division's output. It may be so specific to the needs of its fellow division that the division represents the only market there is.

## Variable cost of goods or services

→ We saw above, in the context of market prices, that a **variable cost** approach is appropriate when the division is operating below capacity. This is because, in these particular circumstances, the opportunity cost to the supplying division is not the market price because it will not have to give up selling in the market to enable it to supply its fellow division, since there is a capacity to do both. In these circumstances the opportunity cost is equal to the variable cost of producing the good or service. However, this represents an absolute minimum transfer price and a figure above the variable cost is required for a contribution to be made towards fixed costs and profit. Where the division is operating at full capacity and external customers are prepared to pay above the variable cost of the goods, a variable-cost internal transfer price would mean that inter-divisional sales are less profitable than sales to external customers. Managers of the selling division would therefore have no incentive to agree transfer prices on this basis (even though the business as a whole may benefit). If this pricing method were imposed by central management, divisional autonomy would be undermined.

## Full cost of goods or services

→ Transfers can be made at **full cost**. In such circumstances no profit will be made on the transactions and this can hinder an evaluation of divisional performance. It will also be more difficult when making resources allocation decisions within the division concerning such matters as level of output, product mix and investment levels, as profit cannot be used as a measure of efficiency.
   It is possible to add a mark-up to the full cost of the goods or services in order to derive a profit figure. However, the amount of the mark-up must be justifiable in some way or it will become a contentious issue between buying and selling divisions. A cost-based approach (with or without the use of a mark-up) does not provide any real incentive for divisional managers to keep costs down, since they can pass the costs on to the buying division. This will result in selling divisions transferring their operating inefficiences to buying divisions. Where the mark-up is a percentage of cost, the selling division's profit will be higher if it incurs higher costs. However, where buying divisions have the ability to go to outside suppliers, pressure can be exerted on the selling divisions to control their costs.

Though use of the full cost approach is found in practice (see Exhibit 10.3), it is not an approach which is too logical in principle, since it is not linked to the opportunity cost approach.

## Negotiated prices

It is possible to adopt an approach which allows the divisional managers to arrive at **negotiated prices** for inter-divisional transfers. However, this can lead to serious disputes and where divisional managers are unable to agree a price, central management will be required to arbitrate. However, this can be a time-consuming process and may deflect central management from its more strategic role. It may also result in decisions being made for the benefit of the business as a whole, rather than for the individual divisions. Divisional managers may resent the decisions made by central managers and see these as undermining the autonomy of their divisions.

Negotiated transfer prices probably work best where there is an external market for the goods supplied by the buying and selling divisions and where divisional managers are free to accept or reject offers made by other divisions. Under such circumstances, the negotiated price is likely to be closely related to the external market price of the products. In other circumstances, the negotiated prices may be artificial and misleading. For example, where a division sells the whole of its output to another division, the selling division is likely to be in a weak bargaining position and the transfer price agreed may not provide a valid measure of divisional performance. Negotiated prices are likely to be influenced by the negotiating skills of managers, which can be a problem where the outcome is largely determined by this factor.

Figure 10.2 summarises the various approaches to transfer pricing and Exhibit 10.3 gives some indication of transfer pricing in practice.

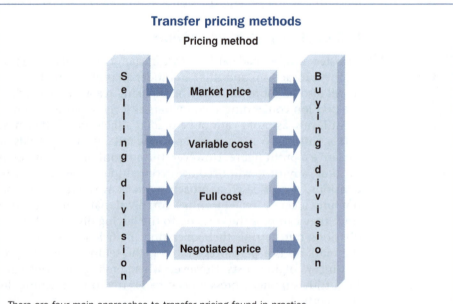

| Figure 10.2 | **Transfer pricing methods** |

**Pricing method**

Selling division → Market price → Buying division

Variable cost

Full cost

Negotiated price

There are four main approaches to transfer pricing found in practice.

| Exhibit 10.3 | **Transfer pricing in practice** |

The 1993 ACCA survey gives some indication of the importance of inter-divisional transfers in practice as follows:

| Internal transfers as a proportion of total external sales | % of divisionalised respondents |
|---|---|
| Under 5% | 36 |
| 5% to 19% | 36 |
| 20% to 49% | 16 |
| Over 50% | 12 |

Thus transfer pricing is an important issue for a very significant proportion of larger businesses. The approaches to setting transfer prices were discovered to be as follows:

| Approach used | % of divisionalised respondents |
|---|---|
| Variable cost | 37 (2) |
| Full cost | 42 (22) |
| Variable cost plus a profit mark-up | 30 (11) |
| Full cost plus a profit mark-up | 52 (27) |
| Market price | 52 (33) |
| Negotiated price | 70 (30) |
| Other methods | 9 (1) |

It is clear from the table that businesses use more than one method, on average. Some of these percentages include 'used rarely' and 'sometimes'. The bracketed figures are percentages of businesses which use the approach 'often' or 'always'. Full cost, which has not too much credibility in theory, seems widely used. The more theoretically respectable variable cost and the market-price-based approaches also seem popular, as do negotiated prices.

*Source*: Drury, Braund, Osborne and Tayles (see reference (1) at the end of the chapter).

## Summary

In this chapter we have examined some of the main issues surrounding divisionalisation. We have seen that measures of divisional performance are not perfect and that it is probably a good idea to develop a range of measures that will look at various aspects of divisional performance over different time periods. Undue emphasis on a single measure is likely to distort management behaviour.

We have also seen that the setting of transfer prices between divisions can be a problem. Once again, there is no single perfect measure which can be applied to all situations. Nevertheless, a market-based approach is generally the most appropriate. We have seen that a transfer pricing method may achieve certain objectives at the expense of others. In particular, there is often a tension between the pursuit of divisional autonomy and the optimisation of profits for the business as a whole.

**→ Key terms**

Divisions  p. 268

Profit centre  p. 269

Investment centre  p. 269

Divisional performance measurement
  p. 273

Controllable costs  p. 274

Non-controllable costs  p. 274

Return on investment (ROI)  p. 275

Residual income (RI)  p. 277

Transfer pricing  p. 284

Opportunity cost  p. 285

Market prices  p. 286

Variable cost  p. 287

Full cost  p. 287

Negotiated prices  p. 288

## Further reading

If you would like to explore the topics covered in this chapter in more depth, we recommend the following books:

**Accounting for Management Decisions**, *Arnold, J.* and *Turley, S.*, Prentice Hall, 3rd edn, 1996, chapter 18.

**Management and Cost Accounting**, *Drury, C.*, Thomson Learning, 5th edn, 2000, chapters 20 and 21.

**Cost and Management Accounting**, *Williamson, D.*, Prentice Hall, 1996, chapters 18 and 19.

**Cost Accounting**, *Horngren, C.*, *Foster, G.* and *Dator, S.*, Prentice Hall International, 10th edn, 2000, chapter 22.

## Reference

1. **A Survey of Management Accounting Practices in UK Manufacturing Companies**, *Drury, C., Braund, S., Osborne, P.* and *Tayles, M.*, Chartered Association of Certified Accountants, 1993.

## ? REVIEW QUESTIONS

**10.1** Research shows that, in practice in the UK, ROI is a much more popular method of assessing divisional performance than RI. However, the literature suggests that RI is conceptually superior to ROI.

Can you explain this apparent paradox?

**10.2** J. Westcott Supplies Ltd has an operating division which produces a single product. Central management wishes to employ other methods of measuring performance and productivity in addition to the conventional RI and ROI measures in order to help evaluate the division.

Identify four possible measures (financial or non-financial) which central management may decide to use.

**10.3** Jerry and Co. is a large computer consultancy firm which has a division specialising in robotics. Can you identify three *non-financial measures* which might be used to help assess the performance of this division?

**10.4** A UK survey of decentralised companies revealed that negotiated prices are the most popular form of transfer pricing method.

How does this finding square with the literature on this topic?

## ? EXERCISES

Questions 10.4–10.8 are more advanced than 10.1–10.3. Those with coloured numbers have answers at the back of the book.

**10.1** In any divisionalised organisation complete autonomy of action is impossible when a substantial level of inter-divisional transfers take place.

**Required:**
(a) In this context, what are a divisionalised organisation and autonomy of action?
(b) Is this autonomy good? Why?
(c) Are there any dangers from permitting autonomy of action and in what ways do inter-divisional transfers make complete autonomy impossible?

**10.2** The management accountant is frequently required to develop a range of measures to monitor managerial performance in a responsibility centre or division.

**Required:**
(a) Explain the computation of such financial performance measures where they are most suitable, and briefly explain, using examples, how the exclusive focus on each single measure may be undesirable.
(b) Suggest three different non-financial measures and consider how such measures, in general, offer improvements when incorporated with financial measures.

**10.3** You have recently taken a management post in a large divisionalised company. A substantial proportion of the business of your division is undertaken through inter-divisional transfers.

**Required:**
(a) What are the objectives of a system of transfer pricing?

(b) Describe the use of and problems associated with, transfer prices based on variable cost and full cost.

(c) Where an external market exists, to what extent is market price an improvement on cost?

**10.4** The following information applies to the planned operations of Division A of ABC Corporation for next year

|  | £ |
|---|---|
| Sales – 100,000 units at £12 | 1,200,000 |
| Variable costs at £8 each | 800,000 |
| Fixed costs (including depreciation) | 250,000 |
| Division A investment (at original cost) | 500,000 |

The minimum desired rate of return on investment is the cost of capital of 20 per cent.

The company is highly profit-conscious and delegates a considerable level of autonomy to divisional managers. As part of a procedure to review planned operations of division A, a meeting has been convened to consider two options:

**Option I**

Division A may sell a further 20,000 units at £11 to customers outside ABC Corporation. Variable costs per unit will be the same as budgeted, but to enable capacity to increase by 20,000 units, one extra piece of equipment will be required costing £80,000. The equipment will have a four-year life and the company depreciates assets on a straight-line basis. No extra cash fixed costs will occur.

**Option II**

Included in the current plan of operations of division A is the sale of 20,000 units to division B also within ABC Corporation. A competitor of division A, from outside the group, has offered to supply division B at £10 per unit. Division A intends to adopt a strategy of matching the price quoted from outside the company to retain the order.

**Required:**

(a) Calculate division A's residual income based on:
  (i)   the original planned operation
  (ii)  option I only added to the original plan
  (iii) option II only added to the original plan,
  and briefly interpret the results of the options as they affect division A.

(b) Assess the implications for division A, division B and the corporation as a whole of option II, bearing in mind that if division A does not compete on price, it will lose the 20,000 units order from division B. Make any recommendations you consider appropriate.

**10.5** The following information applies to the budgeted operations of the Goodman division of the Telling Company.

|  | £ |
|---|---|
| Sales (50,000 units at £8) | 400,000 |
| Variable costs at £6 per unit | 300,000 |
| Contribution (margin) | 100,000 |
| Fixed costs | 75,000 |
| Divisional profit | £25,000 |
| Divisional investment | £150,000 |

The minimum desired return on investment is the cost of capital of 20 per cent.

**Required:**
(a) (i)   Calculate the divisional expected ROI (return on investment).
   (ii)  Calculate the division's expected RI (residual income).
   (iii) Comment on the results of (i) and (ii).
(b) The manager has the opportunity to sell 10,000 units at £7.50. Variable cost per unit would be the same as budgeted, but fixed costs would increase by £5,000. Additional investment of £20,000 would also be required. If the manager accepted this opportunity, by how much and in what direction would the residual income change?
(c) Goodman expects to sell 10,000 units of its budgeted volume of 50,000 units to Sharp, another division of the Telling Company. An outside business has promised to supply the 10,000 units to Sharp at £7.20. If Goodman does not meet the £7.20 price, Sharp will buy from the outside business. Goodman will not save any fixed costs if the work goes outside, but variable costs will be avoided.
   (i)  Show the effect on the total profit of the Telling Company if Goodman meets the £7.20 price.
   (ii) Show the effect on the total profit of the Telling Company if Goodman does not meet the price and the work goes outside.

**10.6**  Glasnost plc is a large group organised on divisional lines. Two typical divisions are East and West. They are engaged in broadly similar activities and, therefore, central management compares their results in order to make judgements on managerial performance. Both divisions are regarded as investment centres.

A summary of last year's performance of the two divisions is as follows:

|  | West £000 | West £000 | East £000 | East £000 |
|---|---|---|---|---|
| Capital employed |  | 2,500 |  | 500 |
| Sales |  | 1,000 |  | 400 |
| Manufacturing cost: |  |  |  |  |
| Direct | 300 |  | 212 |  |
| Indirect | 220 |  | 48 |  |
| Selling and distribution cost | 180 | 700 | 40 | 300 |
| Divisional profit |  | 300 |  | 100 |
| Allocation of uncontrollable |  |  |  |  |
|   central overhead costs |  | 50 |  | 20 |
| Net profit |  | 250 |  | 80 |

At the beginning of last year West division incurred substantial expenditure on automated production lines and new equipment. East has quite old plant. Approximately 50 per cent of the sales of East are inter-company transfers to other divisions within the group. These transfers are based on an unadjusted prevailing market price. The inter-company transfers of West are minimal.

Management of the group focuses on return on investment as a major performance indicator. Their required minimum corporate rate of return and cost of capital is 10 per cent.

**Required:**
(a) Compute any ratios (or other measures) which you consider will help in an assessment of the costs and performance of the two divisions.

(b) Comment on this performance making reference to any matters which give cause for concern when comparing the divisions or in divisional performance generally.

**10.7** The University of Devonport consists of six faculties and an administration unit. Under the university's management philosophy, each faculty is treated, as far as is reasonable, as an independent entity. Each faculty is responsible for its own budget and financial decision making.

A new course in the Faculty of Geography (FG) requires some input from a member of staff of the Faculty of Modern Languages (FML).

The two faculties are in dispute about the 'price' that FG should pay FML for each hour of the staff member's time. FML argues that the hourly rate should be £97.

This is based on the FML budget for this year, which in broad outline is as follows:

|  | £000 |
|---|---|
| Academic staff salaries 45 staff | 1,062 |
| Faculty overheads (nearly all fixed costs) | 903 |
|  | 1,965 |

Each academic is expected to teach on average for 15 hours a week for 33 weeks a year.

FML wishes to charge FG an hourly rate which will cover the appropriate proportion of the member of staff's salary plus a 'fair' share of the overheads plus 10 per cent for a small surplus.

FG is refusing to pay this rate. One of FG's arguments is that it should not have to bear any other cost than the appropriate share of the salary. FG also argues that it could find a lecturer who works at the nearby University of Tavistock and is prepared to do the work for £25 an hour, as an additional, spare-time activity.

FML argues that it has deliberately staffed itself at a level which will enable it to cover FG's requirements and that the price must therefore cover the costs.

The university's Vice-Chancellor (its most senior manager) has been asked to resolve the dispute. You are the university's finance manager.

**Required:**

Make notes in preparation for a meeting with the Vice-Chancellor where you will discuss the problem with her. The Vice-Chancellor is an historian by background and is not familiar with financial matters. Your notes will therefore need to be expressed in language that an intelligent layperson can understand.

Your notes should deal both with the objectives of effective transfer prices and with the specifics of this case. You should raise any issues which seem to you might be relevant.

**10.8** AB Ltd operates retail stores throughout the country. The company is divisionalised. Included in its business are divisions A and B. The work of these divisions is supported by a centralised and automated warehouse which replenishes stock using computer-based systems.

For many years this organisation, which gives considerable autonomy to divisional managers, has emphasised return on investment (ROI) as a composite performance measure. This is calculated after allocation of all actual costs and assets of the company and 'its appropriate service facilities' which includes the costs and assets of the warehouse.

The following information is available for last year:

| | Division A | | Division B | |
|---|---|---|---|---|
| | Actual | Budget | Actual | Budget |
| | £m | £m | £m | £m |
| Sales | 30.0 | 50.0 | 110.0 | 96.0 |
| Assets employed | 20.0 | | 48.0 | |
| Operating profit | 4.3 | | 14.7 | |

These actual figures do not include the allocated costs or assets of the automated warehouse shared by the two divisions. The data available for the warehouse facility for last year are:

| | Warehouse | |
|---|---|---|
| | Actual | Budget |
| | £m | £m |
| Despatches, i.e. sales | 140.0 | 146.0 |
| Assets employed at book value | 8.0 | 8.0 |
| Operating costs: | | |
| Depreciation | 1.6 | 1.6 |
| Other fixed costs | 1.1 | 0.9 |
| Variable storage costs | 0.6 | 0.5 |
| Variable handling costs | 1.3 | 1.1 |
| Total operating costs | 4.6 | 4.1 |

When the warehouse investment was authorised it was agreed that the assets employed and the actual expenses were to be split between the divisions concerned in the proportions originally agreed (50 per cent each). However, it was also pointed out that in the future the situation could be redesigned and there was no need for one single basis to apply. For example, it would be possible to use the information that space occupied by stocks of the two divisions is now A 40 per cent and B 60 per cent.

**Required:**
(a) (i)  Calculate the actual return on investment (ROI) for divisions A and B after incorporating the warehouse assets and actual costs on an equal basis as originally agreed.
   (ii) What basis of allocation of assets and actual costs would the manager of division A argue for in order to maximise the reported ROI of the division? How would you anticipate that the manager of division B might react?
(b) It has been pointed out that a combination of bases may be used instead of just one, such as the space occupied by stocks (A 40 per cent, B 60 per cent) or the level of actual or budgeted sales, and so on. If you were given the freedom to revise the calculation, what bases of allocation would you recommend in the circumstances? Discuss your approach and recalculate the ROI of division A on your recommended basis.

Work to two places of decimals only.

## CHAPTER 11

# Strategic management accounting

## Introduction

Businesses are increasingly being managed along strategic lines where their present position is formally compared with their target position and plans formulated in an attempt to reach the target position, through playing to their strengths and avoiding exposing their weaknesses. This is tending to require that management accounting provides information that will help the managers to work effectively in this strategic framework. This should not be taken to imply that the traditional approach to management accounting is of no use in this framework. Since the framework involves a greater focus on the environment in which the business operates, strategic management accounting tends to look at what is going on outside the business as well as what is happening internally, which has tended to be the focus of the more traditional approach.

**OBJECTIVES**

When you have completed this chapter, you should be able to:

- Explain the nature of strategic management.
- Discuss the role of management accounting in a strategic context.
- Assess a strategic change.
- Undertake a competitor profitability analysis.
- Undertake a customer profitability analysis.
- Explain EVA® and SVA and describe their roles in measuring and delivering shareholder value.
- Discuss the role of the balanced scorecard in providing a framework for management decisions.

## What is strategic management?

Strategic management is an approach where the business seeks to reach its objectives by taking advantage of its strengths, like having a skilled workforce, but at the same time avoiding exposing its weaknesses, like being short of investment finance. This involves strategic plans or strategies that take account not just of the business's strengths and weaknesses, but also of the opportunities offered by the outside world, like an expanding market, and the threats that the business is exposed to by the outside world, such as new competitors entering the market.

→   **Strategic planning** involves five steps:

1. *Establish mission and objectives*

   As we saw in Chapter 6, the mission statement is usually a brief statement of the overall aims of the business. You may recall that Exhibit 6.1 on page 125 reproduced the mission statement of Cadbury Schweppes.

   The objectives are rather more specific than the mission and need to be both quantifiable and consistent with the mission or aims. Exhibit 6.2 on page 125 set out Cadbury Schweppes's objectives.

2. *Undertake a position analysis*

→   With the **position analysis** the business is seeking to establish how it is placed relative to its environment (competitors, markets, technology, the economy, political climate, and so on) given the business's mission and objectives. This is often approached within the framework of an analysis of the business's

→   strengths, weaknesses, opportunities and threats (a **SWOT analysis**). Strengths and weaknesses are internal factors that are attributes of the business itself, whereas opportunities and threats are factors expected to be present in the environment in which the business operates.

---

**Activity 11.1**

Try to suggest some factors that could be strengths, weaknesses, opportunities and threats for a business. Try to think of two for each of these (eight in all).

Strengths could include such things as:

■  a loyal, skilled workforce
■  a strong financial position
■  access to markets.

Weaknesses might include:

■  lack of experience
■  lack of access to new finance
■  lack of access to raw materials.

Opportunities could be such things as:

■  new markets opening up for the business
■  a competitor leaving the market
■  the development of some new technology.

Threats to the business might come from:

■  a new competitor entering the market
■  a decline in the size of the market
■  a change in the law making it harder for the business to operate.

---

A SWOT analysis involves identifying all of the business's strengths and weaknesses and the opportunities and threats provided by the world outside the business.

The SWOT framework is not the only possible approach to undertaking a position analysis, but it seems to be a very popular one.

3. *Identify and assess the strategic options*
   This involves attempting to identify possible courses of action that will enable the business to reach its objectives through using its strengths to exploit opportunities, at the same time avoiding exposing its weaknesses to threats. The strengths, weaknesses, opportunities and threats are, of course, those identified by the SWOT analysis.

4. *Select strategic options*
   Here the business will select what seems to be the best of the courses of action or strategies (identified in step 3) and formulating a strategic plan, in the form of long- and short-term budgets.

5. *Perform, review and control*
   Here the business pursues the plans derived in step 4, using the traditional approach to compare actual performance against budgets, seeking to control where actual performance appears not to be matching plans.

   You may recall that in Chapter 6, we looked at how the business's mission links, through objectives and long-term plans, to detailed budgets. What we have considered so far in this chapter is a more formal structure for the first part of this process. This structure is increasingly the approach taken by businesses.

Figure 11.1 shows the strategic planning framework in diagrammatic form.

**Figure 11.1**

**The strategic planning framework**

Establish mission and objectives

↓

Undertake a position analysis

↓

Identify and assess the strategic options

↓

Select strategic options

↓

Perform review and control

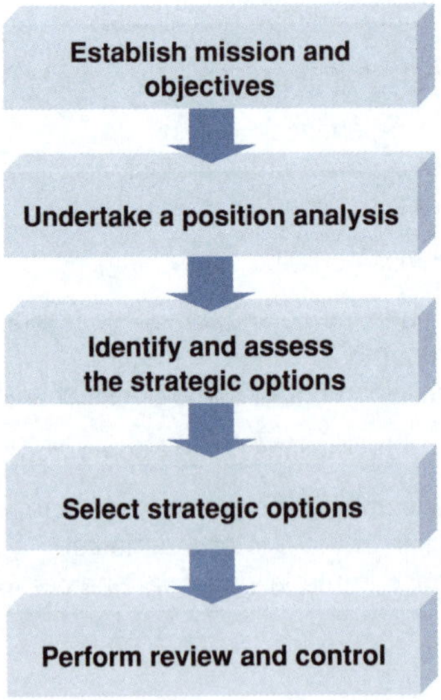

To position itself to play to its strengths and avoid exposing itself to its weaknesses, the business should take steps to draw up and follow strategic plans. By doing this it should most effectively work towards its objectives and mission.

# What is strategic management accounting?

As we have just seen, strategic management is much more concerned with the world outside the business than tends to be the case with the more traditional approach. This requires that strategic management accounting be focused on external factors, like the profitability of its competitors and market share, rather more than the traditional approach, which tends to be inward looking.

# Assessing a strategic change

One way in which management accounting can play a useful part in a strategic approach to management is in analysing the effects of a change in strategy, so that the success of the change can be assessed.

This analysis would usually follow the same broad principles as variance analysis, which we met in Chapter 7. An assessment of strategic change would, in effect, be a comparison of the performance after the change of strategy with that for the period immediately preceding it.

**Example 11.1**

Cosyco is a business that makes ceramic patio heaters. It uses only one raw material to make the heaters. The market for the heaters is now quite competitive, with all of the competitors providing a very similar heater at roughly the same price. The managers of Cosyco have been looking for a way to generate more profit. One strategy considered was to reduce prices in an attempt to gain a greater market share, but this was rejected on the grounds that the increased sales would probably not be sufficient to compensate for the reduced selling prices. Finally, it was decided to pursue a policy of 'product differentiation': that is, to make a better-quality, more attractive heater. This would require the use of a more expensive raw material, which would need to be used in greater quantities than in the present heater. It was believed that the change of strategy would enable the business to charge a higher price for each heater sold and to sell more of them. The strategic change was effective from 1 January 2001.

A summary of Cosyco's trading for 2000, the last year of the old strategy, and 2001, the first year of the new strategy, is as follows:

| Year | 2000 | 2001 |
|---|---|---|
| 1  Number of heaters made and sold | 5,000 | 6,000 |
| 2  Selling price per heater | £40 | £45 |
| 3  Total sales (line 1 × line 2) | £200,000 | £270,000 |
| 4  Direct materials (DM) used per heater | 0.500 kg | 0.533 kg |
| 5  DM cost per kg | £15 | £16 |
| 6  Total DM cost (line 1 × line 4 × line 5) | £37,500 | £51,200 |

The income statements for the two years are, therefore, as follows:

| Year | 2000 | 2001 |
|---|---|---|
| | £ | £ |
| Sales | 200,000 | 270,000 |
| DM | 37,500 | 51,200 |
| Contribution | 162,500 | 218,000 |

It is known that other manufacturing costs are fixed and have not been affected by the change in strategy.

Assuming that the increase in contribution of £56,500 (that is, £218,000 – £162,500) is all caused by the strategic change, it might be useful to Cosyco's management to know in more detail how the additional contribution arose.

The contribution change (£56,500 increase) can be analysed into three aspects:

1. The *growth aspect*, which assesses the extent to which the increased sales alone affected the contribution. Here we ignore the effects of price differences, both the selling and materials purchase price, and the effect of using more materials. We are, therefore, looking at the equivalent of the *sales volume variance* that we met in Chapter 7.
2. The *price aspect*, which arises from the differences both in the selling price and the increased price of the DM. Here we ignore the effect of growth and usage and just concentrate on the effect of price difference. This is equivalent to the *sales price variance* and the *raw material price variance*.
3. The *usage (or productivity) aspect*, which arises from the use of larger amounts of DM for each heater produced. This is, of course, the equivalent of the *DM usage variance*. Here we ignore the effects of growth and price differences and concentrate only on usage differences.

We can now go on to carry out the analysis of Cosyco's change in strategy.

### Growth aspect

1. Revenue growth is the effect of the growth in revenues arising from the volume growth: (units sold in 2001 less units sold in 2000) × 2000 selling price per unit

$$= (6,000 - 5,000) \times £40 = £40,000 \text{ (F)}$$

   (it is 'favourable' because it represents a contribution increase arising from the change in strategy).
2. Cost of growth is the effect on costs of the sales volume growth: (usage of DM for 2001, based on usage of DM per heater that applied in 2000, less usage of DM in 2000) × price of DM in 2000

$$= [(6,000 \times 0.5) - (5,000 \times 0.5)] \times £15 = £7,500 \text{ (A)}$$

   (it is 'adverse' because it represents a contribution decrease arising from the change in strategy).

|  |  | £ |
|---|---|---|
| Summary of growth aspect | Revenue growth | 40,000 (F) |
|  | Cost growth | 7,500 (A) |
|  |  | 32,500 (F) |

### Price aspect

1. Revenue price is the effect of the increase in revenues arising from the price rise: (selling price per unit in 2001 less selling price per unit in 2000) × 2001 sales volume

$$= (£45 - £40) \times 6,000 = £30,000 \text{ (F)}$$

2. Cost price increase effect on costs: (cost per kg of DM in 2001 less cost per kg of DM in 2000) × usage of DM for 2001, based on usage of DM per heater that applied in 2000

$$= (£16 - £15) \times (6,000 \times 0.5) = £3,000 \text{ (A)}.$$

|  | | £ |
|---|---|---|
| Summary of price aspect | Revenue price | 30,000 (F) |
| | Cost price | 3,000 (A) |
| | | 27,000 (F) |

**Usage (or productivity) aspect**

DM usage effect on costs: (actual usage of DM in 2001 less usage of DM for 2001, based on usage of DM per heater that applied in 2000) × 2001 price per kg of DM

$$= [3{,}200 \text{ kg} - (6{,}000 \times 0.5)] \times £16 = £3{,}200 \text{ (A)}$$

| Summary of usage aspect | DM usage | £3,200 (A) |
|---|---|---|

|  | | £ |
|---|---|---|
| **Overall summary:** | Growth aspect | 32,500 (F) |
| | Price aspect | 27,000 (F) |
| | Usage aspect | 3,200 (A) |
| | | 56,300 (F) |

---

| Figure 11.2 | **The aspects of profit, or contribution, increase or decrease, caused by a change of strategy** |
|---|---|

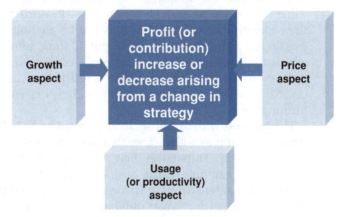

The net effect on profit, or contribution, of a strategic change can be ascribed to three aspects.

---

| Activity 11.2 | **Try to explain briefly, on the basis of the above analysis, why Cosyco's contribution was greater in 2001 than it had been in 2000.** |
|---|---|

We can say that, of the £36,300 additional contribution generated by the change in strategy, £32,500 arose from sales volume growth alone and £27,000 from the higher prices charged, after allowing for the higher cost of the better-quality DM. These growth and price benefits were offset to the extent of £3,200 by increased costs arising from a higher usage of DM.

# Competitor profitability analysis

Nearly all businesses are in a competitive position with all of their products; their customers have a choice of supplier. This means that businesses' ability to meet their objectives depends on their ability to compete effectively. An important tool in the commercial struggle with their competitors is knowledge of their competitors' costs and cost structures. Such knowledge can, for example, enable a particular business to make an informed assessment of what effect a price reduction would have on their competitors. Would a business making a 10 per cent selling price reduction in one of its products be able to be followed by competitors, or would it force them out of the market? If they do not follow the price reduction, would competitors be able to continue to supply, given the likely sales volume reduction that would ensue for the competitors? The business should know what effect such a reduction would have on itself, but traditionally not on its competitors. Yet in a competitive market it is helpful to know the effect on all major players.

Businesses generally seem to be reluctant to release information about themselves, probably partly to avoid their competitors carrying out exactly the type of analysis that we are now considering. In the UK all limited companies are required by law, however, to provide information about themselves in an annual report, to anyone interested. Similar provisions relate to limited companies in most countries in the world. This information tends, however, to be of limited value in **competitor profitability analysis**. Reasons for this include the fact that the competitor to the business may not be a whole company, but just a part of it. Though companies must make public some information about the extent to which their turnover (sales) and profit comes from different activities, this is unlikely to be sufficient to enable a full picture of the competitor to be built up. Nonetheless, a competitor's annual report will usually offer some useful information.

The business will, of course, have detailed knowledge of its own costs and cost structure, so it may well be able to make informed estimates of what these are for the competitor. Differences may well be able to be known and taken into account. For example, if the business knows that the competitor's approach is more capital intensive than its own it may be able to estimate how this would make the competitor's costs different from its own.

It may be possible to gain other information from press coverage of the competitor's business, from talking to customers who trade both with the business and with the competitor, from talking to suppliers to both the business and its competitor, from physical observation, and from government statistics on such matters as the total size of the market. There is a wide range of potential sources of information about competitors. All of these will provide clues that can be pieced together in an attempt to build up as full a picture as possible of each significant competitor. Figure 11.3 shows some of the likely sources of information.

What is likely to be particularly valuable to the business is not so much to know what its competitors' sales and costs were last year, but their cost structures, in terms of the extent that each competitor's costs are fixed and variable. Knowledge of competitors' cost structures would enable the business to make some estimation of the effect on their profit of an increase or decrease in turnover

| Figure 11.3 | **Some sources of information with which to carry out an analysis of competitor profitability** |

The figure shows just some of the more obvious sources of information that would enable a business to analyse the costs, cost structures and profitabilities of its competitors.

volume. This might enable the business to assess how well placed each competitor might be to react to a change in sales volume and/or sales price. For example, a competitor with a high level of fixed costs (high operating gearing) and, consequently, a low margin of safety may not be able to withstand a downturn in sales volume as comfortably as another business with lower operating gearing.

Of course, the business could never normally know everything about its competitors, and there must be a practical limit on how much it is worth the business spending to gain more information. As ever with accounting, it is a question of balancing the potential benefits of having information against the costs involved in obtaining it.

## Customer profitability analysis

➡ **Customer profitability analysis (CPA)** assesses the profitability of the business, customer by customer or type of customer by type of customer. The objective of the business's marketing function is to attract and retain profitable customers. Knowledge of whether a particular customer, or type of customer, is, or is likely to be, profitable to the business, is very valuable information. Analysis that will enable the business to have this knowledge is likely to be worthwhile.

A CPA is essentially an abbreviated 'profit and loss account' for each customer and/or type of customer for the immediately past period.

The CPA will compare the total revenues for the period of the analysis with the associated costs for each customer or type of customer. These costs will obviously include the basic cost of creating or buying in the products (goods or services) supplied to the customer. This cost will already be available from the business's product cost records, perhaps derived using an activity-based costing (ABC) approach. Total customer costs will also include selling and distribution costs. These will encompass such things as the cost to the business of:

- Handling orders from the customer. This encompasses the costs involved with receiving the order and activities relating to it to the point where the goods are despatched, or the service rendered, including the costs of raising invoices and other accounting work.
- Visiting the customer by the business's sales staff. Many businesses have a member of staff visit customers, perhaps to take orders, but often to keep the customer up to date with the latest developments in the business's products.
- Delivering goods to the customer, either using a delivery service provided by another business, or the business's own transport. Naturally the distance travelled and the bulkiness and fragility of the goods will have an effect on this cost.
- Stockholding costs. Some customers may require a particular level of stock to be held by the business. For example, a customer operating a 'just-in-time' raw material stock policy will tend, in effect, to put pressure on the supplier to hold stock.
- Credit costs. The business will have to finance any credit allowed to its customers. This could vary from customer to customer, depending on how promptly they pay.

A customer who places lots of small orders, necessitating numerous deliveries to a distant location, who receives many visits from sales staff, who requires the

| Figure 11.4 | **Factors in a customer profitability analysis** |
|---|---|

The figure shows some of the factors that could be required to be considered in a customer profitability analysis.

business to hold large stocks and who pays slowly is likely to be much less profitable, for the same total sales revenue, than other less demanding customers.

It seems that where CPA is applied in practice, businesses use an ABC approach. Activities like handing sales orders drive costs. The extent to which a particular customer drives order handing costs is likely to be in proportion to the number of orders placed, irrespective of the size of the order. This is likely to be similar for other customer-related costs.

CPA enables management to know which customers generate profit for the business and which do not.

| Activity 11.3 | Amal plc carried out a CPA and discovered that a number of its customers are unprofitable to the business. These tended to be those who placed a number of small orders. |
|---|---|

Can you think of how Amal plc might react to the information provided by the CPA?

We thought of the following:

- Increase prices to the customers concerned.
- Impose a minimum order size: that is, refuse to accept orders below a particular value.
- Increase prices, but allow discounts for larger orders.

| Exhibit 11.1 | **Customer profitability analysis in practice** |
|---|---|

A survey of 176 fairly large UK businesses, conducted during 1999 revealed that seventy-six per cent of respondents analyse the profitability of trading with customers. Nearly two-thirds of those who do this update the analysis monthly and nearly all do so annually or more frequently.

*Source*: Drury and Tayles (see reference (1) at the end of this chapter).

# The quest for shareholder value

For some years, shareholder value has been a 'hot' issue among managers. Many leading businesses now claim that the quest for shareholder value is the driving force behind their strategic and operational decisions. In this section we will begin by asking what is meant by the term 'shareholder value' and in the sections that follow we will look at two of the main approaches to measuring shareholder value.

Let us start by considering what the term 'shareholder value' means. In simple terms, it is about putting the needs of shareholders at the heart of management decisions. It is argued that shareholders invest in a business with a view to maximising their financial returns in relation to the risks that they are prepared to take. As managers are appointed by the shareholders to act on their behalf, management decisions and actions should therefore reflect a concern for maximising shareholder returns. Although the business may have other 'stakeholder' groups, such as employees, customers and suppliers, it is the shareholders that should be seen as the most important group.

This, of course, is not a new idea. As we discussed in Chapter 1, maximising shareholder returns is assumed to be the key objective of a business. However, not everyone accepts this idea. Some believe that a balance must be struck between the competing claims of the various stakeholders. What we can say, however, is that changes in the economic environment over recent years have often forced managers to focus their attention on the needs of shareholders.

In the past, shareholders have been accused of being too passive and of accepting too readily the profits and dividends that managers have delivered. However, this has changed. Nowadays, shareholders are much more assertive, and as owners of the business are in a position to insist that their needs are given priority. Since the 1980s we have witnessed the deregulation and globalisation of business, as well as enormous changes in technology. The effect has been to create a much more competitive world. This has not only meant competition for products and services but also competition for funds. Businesses must now compete more strongly for shareholder funds and so must offer competitive rates of return.

Thus self-interest may be the most powerful reason for managers to commit themselves to maximising shareholder returns. If they do not do this, there is a real risk that shareholders will either replace them with managers who will, or shareholders will allow the business to be taken over by another business, which has managers who are dedicated to maximising shareholder returns.

| | |
|---|---|
| **Exhibit 11.2** | An example of a business that recognises the supremacy of shareholders is the Coca-Cola Company. It has a mission statement that declares: |

> We exist to create value for our shareowners on a long-term basis by building a business that enhances the Coca-Cola Company's trademarks. This is also our ultimate commitment.

An example of a business that takes a broader view of its responsibilities is Cadbury Schweppes plc. The mission statement of this business states:

> Our task is to build our tradition of quality and value to provide brands, products, financial results and management performance that meet the interests of our shareholders, consumers, employees, customers, suppliers and the communities in which we operate.

## Creating shareholder value

Creating shareholder value involves a four-stage process. The first stage is to set objectives for the business that recognize the central importance of maximising shareholder returns. This will set a clear direction for the business. The second stage is to establish an appropriate means of measuring the returns, or value, that have been generated for shareholders. For reasons that we shall discuss later, the traditional methods of measuring returns to shareholders are inadequate for this purpose. The third stage is to manage the business in such a manner as to ensure that shareholder returns are maximised. This means setting demanding targets and then achieving them through the best possible use of resources, the use of incentive systems and the embedding of a shareholder value culture throughout the business. The final stage is to measure the shareholder returns over a period of time to see whether the objectives have actually been achieved.

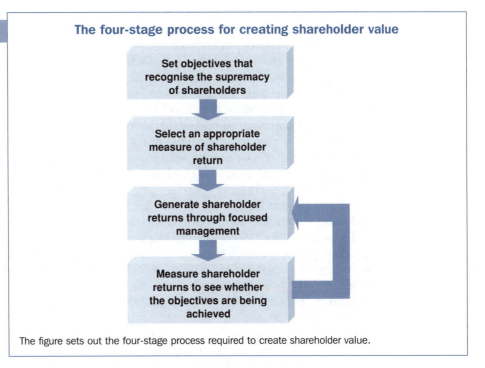

Figure 11.5

**The four-stage process for creating shareholder value**

The figure sets out the four-stage process required to create shareholder value.

## The need for new forms of measurement

Given a commitment to maximise shareholder returns, we must select an appropriate measure that will help us assess the returns to shareholders over time. It is argued that the traditional methods for measuring shareholder returns are seriously flawed and so should not be used for this purpose.

**Activity 11.4**

What are the traditional methods of measuring shareholder returns?

The traditional approach is to use accounting profit or some ratio that is based on accounting profit, such as return on shareholders' funds or earnings per share.

One problem of using accounting profit, or a ratio based on profit, is that profit is measured over a relatively short period of time (usually one year). However, when we talk about maximising shareholder returns, we are concerned with maximising returns over the long term. It has been suggested that using profit as the key measure will run the risk that managers will take decisions that improve performance in the short term but which may have an adverse effect on long-term performance. For example, profits may be increased in the short term by cutting back on staff training and research expenditure. However, this type of expenditure may be vital to long-term survival.

A second problem that arises with conventional methods of measuring shareholder returns is that risk is ignored. A fundamental principle in finance is that there is a clear relationship between the level of returns achieved and the level of risk that must be taken to achieve those returns. The higher the level of returns required, the higher the level of risk that must be taken to achieve the returns. A management strategy that produces an increase in profits can reduce shareholder value if the increase in profits achieved is not commensurate with the increase in the level of risk. Thus profit alone is not enough.

A third problem with the use of profit, or a ratio based on profit, is that it does not take account of all of the costs of the capital invested by the business. The conventional approach to measuring profit will deduct the cost of loan capital (that is, interest charges) in arriving at net profit, but there is no similar deduction for the cost of shareholder funds. (Any dividends payable, which is part of the return to shareholders, is deducted after arriving at the net profit figure.) Critics of the conventional approach point out that a business will not make a profit, in an economic sense, unless it covers the cost of all capital invested, including shareholder funds. Unless this done, the business will operate at a loss and so shareholder value will be reduced.

A final problem is that the accounting profit reported by a business can vary according to the particular policies that have been adopted. Some businesses adopt a very conservative approach, which would be reflected in particular accounting policies such as the immediate writing-off of intangible assets (for example, research and development and goodwill), the use of the reducing-balance method of depreciation (which means high depreciation charges in the early years), and so on. Businesses that do not adopt conservative accounting policies would report higher profits in the early years of owning depreciating assets. The writing-off of intangible assets over a long time period (or perhaps, not writing off intangible assets at all), the use of the straight-line method of depreciation and so on will have this effect. In addition, there may be some businesses that adopt particular accounting policies or carry out particular transactions in a way that paints a picture of financial health that is in line with what those who prepared the financial statements would like to see, rather than what is a true and fair view of financial performance and position. This practice is referred to as 'creative accounting' and has been a major problem for accounting rule makers.

| Exhibit 11.3 | Warren Buffet is probably the world's most successful investor. He has been concerned about the problem of creative accounting for some time and has expressed his views as follows: |
|---|---|

> A growing number of otherwise high-grade managers – CEOs you would be happy to have as spouses for your children or as trustees under your will – have come to the view that it's okay to manipulate earnings to satisfy what they believe are Wall Street's desires. Indeed, many CEOs think this kind of manipulation in not only okay, but actually their duty.

## Net present value (NPV) analysis

To summarise the points made above, we can say that, in order to measure changes in shareholder value, what we really need is a measure that will consider the long term, take account of risk and the cost of shareholders' funds and will not be affected by accounting policy choices. Fortunately, we have a measure that can, in theory, do just this.

Net present value analysis was discussed in Chapter 8. We saw that if we want to know the net present value (NPV) of an asset (whether this is a physical asset such as a machine or a financial asset such as a share in a company) we must discount the future cash flows generated by the asset over its life. Thus:

$$NPV = \frac{C_1}{(1+r)^1} + \frac{C_2}{(1+r)^2} + \frac{C_3}{(1+r)^3} + \ldots$$

where:

$C_1$, $C_2$ and $C_3$ = Cash flows after one year, two years and three years, respectively
$r$ = The required rate of return.

Shareholders have a required rate of return and managers must strive to generate long-term cash flows for shares (in the form of dividends or proceeds from the sale of the shares) that meet this rate of return. A negative present value will indicate that the cash flows generated do not meet the minimum required rate of return. If a business is to create value for its shareholders, it must generate cash flows that exceed the required returns of shareholders. This means that the cash flows generated must produce a positive present value.

The NPV method fulfils the criteria that we mentioned earlier because:

- It considers the long term. The returns from an investment, such as shares, are considered over the whole of its life.
- It takes account of the cost of capital and risk. Future cash flows are discounted using the required rates of returns from investors (that is, both long-term lenders and shareholders). Moreover, this required rate of return will reflect the level of risk associated with the investment. The higher the level of risk, the higher the required level of return.
- It is not sensitive to the choice of accounting policies. Cash rather than profit is used in the calculations and is a more objective measure of return.

## Extending NPV analysis: shareholder value analysis

We know from our earlier study of NPV that, when evaluating an investment project, shareholder wealth will be maximised if we maximise the net present value of the cash flows generated from the project. Leading on from this, the business as a whole can be viewed as simply a portfolio of investment projects and so to maximise the wealth of shareholders the same principles should apply. **Shareholder value analysis (SVA)** is founded on this basic idea.

The SVA approach involves evaluating strategic decisions according to their ability to maximise value, or wealth, for shareholders. To undertake this evaluation, conventional measures are discarded and replaced by discounted cash flows. We have seen that the net present value of a project represents the value of that particular project. Given that the business can be viewed as a portfolio of projects, the value of the business as a whole can, therefore, be viewed as the net present value of the cash flows generated by the business as a whole. SVA seeks to measure the discounted cash flows of the business as a whole and then seeks to identify that part which is available to the shareholders.

**Activity 11.5** If the net present value of future cash flows generated by the business represents the value of the business as a whole, how can we derive that part of the value of the business that is available to shareholders?

A business will normally be financed by a combination of loan capital and ordinary shareholders' funds. Thus holders of loan capital will also have a claim on the total value of the business. That part of the total business value that is available to ordinary shareholders can therefore be derived by deducting from the total value of the business (total NPV) the market value of any loans outstanding. Hence:

Shareholder value = Total business value − Market value of outstanding loans

## Measuring free cash flows

The cash flows used to measure total business value are the **free cash flows**. These are the cash flows generated by the business that are available to ordinary shareholders and long-term lenders. In other words, they are equivalent to the net cash flows from operations after deducting tax paid and cash for additional investment. These free cash flows can be deduced from information contained within the profit and loss account and balance sheet of a business.

It is probably worth going through a simple example to illustrate how the free cash flows are calculated in practice.

**Example 11.2** Sagittarius plc generated sales of £220 million during the year and has an operating profit margin of 25 per cent of sales. Depreciation charges for the year were £8.0m and the cash tax rate for the year was 20 per cent of operating profit. During the year £11.3m was invested in additional working capital and £15.2m was invested in additional fixed assets. A further £8.0m was invested in the replacement of existing fixed assets.

The free cash flows are calculated as follows:

|  | £m | £m |
|---|---|---|
| Sales |  | 220.0 |
| Operating profit (25% × £220m) |  | 55.0 |
| Add Depreciation charge |  | 8.0 |
| Operating cash flows |  | 63.0 |
| Less Cash tax (20% × £55m) |  | 11.0 |
| Operating cash flows after tax |  | 52.0 |
| Less Additional working capital | 11.3 |  |
| Additional fixed assets | 15.2 |  |
| Replacement fixed assets | 8.0 | 34.5 |
| Free cash flows |  | 17.5 |

We can see that to derive the operating cash flows, the depreciation charge is added back to the operating profit figure. We can also see that the cost of replacement of existing fixed assets is deducted from the operating cash flows in order to deduce the free cash flows. When we are trying to predict future free cash flows, one way of arriving at an approximate figure for the cost of replacing existing assets is to assume that the depreciation charge for the year is equivalent to the replacement charge for fixed assets. This would mean that the two adjustments mentioned cancel each other out. In other words, the calculation above could be shortened to:

|  | £m | £m |
|---|---|---|
| Sales |  | <u>220.0</u> |
| Operating profit (25% × £220m) |  | 55.0 |
| Less Cash tax (20% × £55m) |  | <u>11.0</u> |
|  |  | 44.0 |
| Less Additional working capital | 11.3 |  |
| Additional fixed assets | <u>15.2</u> | <u>26.5</u> |
| Free cash flows |  | <u>17.5</u> |

This shortened approach leads us to identify the key variables in determining free cash flows as being:

- Sales
- Operating profit margin
- Cash tax rate
- Additional investment in working capital
- Additional investment in fixed assets.

➡ These are **value drivers** of the business that reflect key business decisions. These decisions convert into free cash flows and finally into shareholder value.

| Figure 11.6 |
|---|

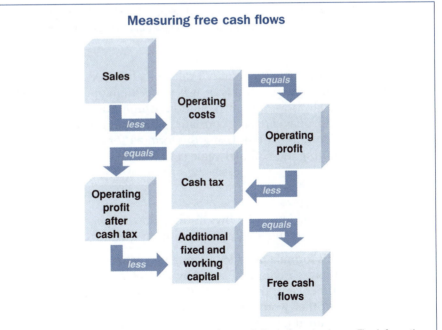

**Measuring free cash flows**

The diagram shows the process of measuring the free cash flows for a business. The information required can be gleaned from the profit and loss account and balance sheet of a business.

The free cash flows should be projected over the life of the business. However, this is usually a difficult task. To overcome the problem, it is helpful to divide the future cash flows into two elements:

- a planning period over which cash flows can be projected with a reasonable level of accuracy
- a terminal calculation to represent the cash flows occurring beyond the planning horizon.

It is a good idea to try and make the planning period as long as possible. This is because the discounting process ensures that values in the distant future are given little weight. As you can imagine, the terminal value of a business can be extremely difficult to forecast with accuracy and so the less weight given to the figure the better.

---

**Activity 11.6**

Libra plc has an estimated terminal value of £100 million. What is the present value of this figure assuming a discount rate of 12 per cent and a planning horizon of:

(a)  5 years?
(b)  10 years?
(c)  15 years?

(You may find it helpful to refer to the discount tables that are appended to Chapter 8.) The answer is:

(a)  £100m × 0.567 = £56.7m
(b)  £100m × 0.322 = £32.2m
(c)  £100m × 0.183 = £18.3m

We can see that there is a dramatic difference in the present value of the terminal calculation between the three time horizons, given a 12 per cent discount rate.

---

To calculate the terminal value of a business, it is usually necessary to make simplifying assumptions. It is beyond the scope of this text to discuss this topic in detail. However, one common assumption is that returns beyond the planning horizon will remain constant (perhaps at the level achieved in the last year of the planning period). Using the formula for a perpetuity, the calculation for determining the terminal value (TV) will be:

$$TV = C_1/r$$

Where:
$C_1$ = the free cash flows in the following year
$r$ = the required rate of return from investors.

This formula provides a capitalised value for future cash flows. Thus if an investor receives a constant cash flow of £100 a year and has a required rate of return of 10 per cent, the capitalised value of these cash flows will be £100/0.1 = £1,000. In other words the future cash flows are worth £1,000, when invested at the required rate of return, to the investor.

At this point it is probably worth going through an example to illustrate the way in which we might calculate shareholder value for a business.

| | | |
|---|---|---|
| **Example 11.3** | The directors of United Pharmaceuticals plc are considering the purchase of all the shares in Bortex plc, which produces vitamins and health foods. Bortex plc has a strong presence in the UK and it is expected that the directors of the company will reject any bids that value the shares of the company at less than £11 per share. | |

Bortex plc generated sales for the most recent year end of £3,000m. Extracts from the balance sheet of the company at the end of the most recent year are as follows:

| | £m |
|---|---|
| **Capital and reserves** | |
| Share capital £1 ordinary shares | 400 |
| Reserves | 380 |
| | 780 |
| | |
| **Creditors due after more than one year** | |
| Loan capital | 120 |

Forecasts that have been prepared by the Business Planning Department of Bortex plc are as follows:

■ Sales will grow at 20 per cent a year for the next five years.
■ The operating profit margin is currently 15 per cent and is likely to be maintained at this rate in the future.
■ The cash tax rate is 25 per cent.
■ Replacement fixed asset investment (RFAI) will be in line with the annual depreciation charge each year.
■ Additional fixed asset investment (AFAI) over the next five years will be 10 per cent of sales growth.
■ Additional working capital investment (AWCI) over the next five years will be 5 per cent of sales growth.

After five years, the sales of the company will stabilise at their year 5 level. The company has a cost of capital of 10 per cent and the loan capital figure in the balance sheet reflects its current market value.

The free cash flow calculation will be as follows:

| | Yr 1 £m | Yr 2 £m | Yr 3 £m | Yr 4 £m | Yr 5 £m | After Yr 5 £m |
|---|---|---|---|---|---|---|
| Sales | 3,300.0 | 3,630.0 | 3,993.0 | 4,392.3 | 4,831.5 | 4,831.5 |
| Operating profit (15%) | 495.0 | 544.5 | 599.0 | 658.8 | 724.7 | 724.7 |
| Less Cash tax (25%) | (123.8) | (136.1) | (149.8) | (164.7) | (181.2) | (181.2) |
| Operating profit after cash tax | 371.2 | 408.4 | 449.2 | 494.1 | 543.5 | 543.5 |
| Less | | | | | | |
| AFAI* | (30.0) | (33.0) | (36.3) | (39.9) | (43.9) | – |
| AWCI** | (15.0) | (16.5) | (18.2) | (20.0) | (22.0) | – |
| Free cash flows | 326.2 | 358.9 | 394.7 | 434.2 | 477.6 | 543.5 |

*Notes*
\* The additional fixed asset investment is 10 per cent of sales growth. In the first year, sales growth is £300m (that is £3,300m – £3,000m). Thus, the investment will be 10 per cent × £300m = £30m. Similar calculations are carried out for the following years.

** The additional working capital investment is 5 per cent of sales growth. In the first year the investment will be 5 per cent × £300m = £15m. Similar calculations are carried out in following years.

Having derived the free cash flows (FCF), the total business value can be calculated as follows:

| Year | FCF £m | Discount rate 10% | Present value £m |
|------|--------|-------------------|------------------|
| 1 | 326.2 | 0.909 | 296.5 |
| 2 | 358.9 | 0.826 | 296.5 |
| 3 | 394.7 | 0.751 | 296.4 |
| 4 | 434.2 | 0.683 | 296.6 |
| 5 | 477.6 | 0.621 | 296.6 |
| Terminal value: | | | |
| 543.5/0.10 | 5,435.0 | 0.621 | 3,375.1 |
| Total business value | | | 4,857.7 |

---

**Activity 11.7**

What is the shareholder value figure for the business?
Would the sale of the shares at £11 per share add value for the shareholders of Bortex plc?

Shareholder value will be the total business value less the market value of the loan capital. Hence, shareholder value is:

£4,857.7m – £120m = £4,737.7m

The proceeds from the sale of the shares to United Pharmaceuticals would yield

400m × £11 = £4,400.0m

Thus, from the point of view of the shareholders of Bortex plc, the sale of the company, at the share price mentioned, would not increase shareholder value.

## Managing the business with SVA

We saw earlier that the adoption of SVA indicates a commitment to managing the business in such a way as to maximise shareholder returns. Those who support this approach argue that SVA can be a powerful tool for strategic planning. For example, SVA can be extremely useful when considering major shifts of direction such as:

■ acquiring new businesses
■ selling existing businesses
■ developing new products or markets
■ reorganizing or restructuring the business.

This is because it takes account of all the elements that determine shareholder value.

To illustrate this point let us suppose that a business develops a new product that is quite different from those within its existing range of products and appeals to a quite different market. Profit forecasts may indicate that the product is likely to be profitable and so a decision to launch the product may be made.

| Figure 11.7 | **Deriving shareholder value** |

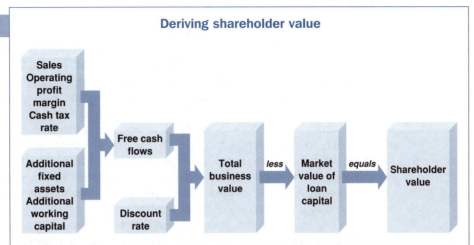

The figure shows how shareholder value is derived. The five value drivers mentioned earlier, sales, operating profit, cash tax, additional fixed assets and additional working capital will determine the free cash flows. These cash flows will be discounted using the required rate of return from investors to determine the total value of the business. If we deduct the market value of any loan capital from this figure, we are left with a measure of shareholder value.

However, this decision may increase the level of risk for the business and, if so, investors will demand higher levels of return. In addition, there may have to be a significant investment in additional fixed assets and working capital in order to undertake the venture. When these factors are taken into account, using the type of analysis shown above, it may be found that the present value of the venture is negative. In other words, shareholder value will be destroyed.

SVA is also useful in focusing attention on the value drivers that create shareholder wealth. For example, we saw earlier that the key variables in determining free cash flows were:

- Sales
- Operating profit margin
- Cash tax rate
- Additional investment in working capital
- Additional investment in fixed assets.

In order to improve free cash flows and, in turn, shareholder value, management targets can be set for improving performance in relation to each value driver and responsibility assigned for achieving these targets.

| Activity 11.8 | **Can you suggest what might be the practical problems of adopting an SVA approach?** |

Two practical problems spring to mind:

1. Forecasting future cash flows lies at the heart of this approach. In practice, forecasting can be difficult and simplifying assumptions will usually have to be made.
2. SVA requires more comprehensive information (for example, information concerning the value drivers) than the traditional measures discussed earlier.

You may have thought of other problems.

## The implications of SVA

It is worth emphasising that supporters of SVA believe that this measure should replace the traditional accounting measures of value creation such as profit, earnings per share and return on ordinary shareholders' funds. Thus, only if shareholder value increases over time can we say that there has been an increase in shareholder wealth. Any change over time can be measured by comparing shareholder value at the beginning and the end of a particular period.

We can see that SVA is really a radical departure from the conventional approach to managing a business. It will require different performance indicators, different financial reporting systems and different management incentive methods. It may also require a change of culture within the business to accommodate the shareholder value philosophy. Not all employees may be focused on the need to maximise shareholder wealth.

If SVA is implemented, it can provide the basis of targets for managers to work towards, on a day-to-day basis, that should promote maximisation of shareholder value.

## Economic value added (EVA®)

➡ **Economic value added (EVA®)** has been developed and trade marked by a US management consultancy firm, Stern Stewart. However, EVA® is based on the idea of economic profit, which has been around for many years. The measure reflects the point made earlier that, for a business to be profitable in an economic sense, it must generate returns that exceed the required returns from investors. It is not enough simply to make an accounting profit, because this measure does not take full account of the returns required by investors.

EVA® indicates whether or not the returns generated exceed the required returns by investors. The formula is as follows:

$$EVA® = NOPAT - (R \times C)$$

Where:

NOPAT = Net operating profit after tax
$R$ = Required returns from investors
$C$ = Capital invested (that is, the net assets of the business)

---

**Activity 11.9**

Does this measure seem familiar to you? Where have we discussed a similar measure to this earlier in the text?

---

This measure is based on the same idea as the residual income measure that we discussed when considering ways of assessing divisional performance (Chapter 10).

---

Only when EVA® is positive can we say that the business is increasing shareholder wealth. To maximise shareholder wealth, managers must increase EVA® by as much as possible.

| Activity 11.10 | Can you suggest what managers might do in order to increase EVA®? (*Hint*: Use the formula shown above as your starting point.) |

The formula suggests that in order to increase EVA® managers may try to:

- Increase NOPAT. This may be done by either reducing expenses or by increasing sales.
- Use capital invested more efficiently. This means selling off any assets that are not generating adequate returns and investing in assets that are generating a satisfactory NOPAT.
- Reduce the required rates of return for investors. This may be achieved by changing the capital structure in favour of loan capital (which tends to be cheaper to service than share capital). However, this strategy can create problems.

EVA® relies on conventional financial statements to measure the wealth created for shareholders. However, the NOPAT and capital figures shown on these statements are used only as a starting point. They have to be adjusted because of the problems and limitations of conventional measures. According to Stern Stewart, the major problem is that profit and capital are understated because of the conservative bias in accounting measurement. Profit is understated as a result of arbitrary write-offs such as goodwill written off or research and development expenditure written off and as a result of excessive provisions being created (such as a provision for doubtful debts). Capital is understated because assets are reported at their original cost (less amounts written off), which can produce figures considerably below current market values. In addition, certain assets, such as internally generated goodwill and brand names, are omitted from the financial statements because no external transactions have occurred.

Stern Stewart has identified more than 100 adjustments that could be made to the conventional financial statements in order to eliminate the conservative bias. However, it is believed that, in practice, only a handful of adjustments will usually have to be made to the accounting figures of any particular business. Unless an adjustment is going to have a significant effect on the calculation of EVA® it is really not worth making. The adjustments made should reflect the nature of the particular business. Each business is unique and so must customise the calculation of EVA® to its particular circumstances. (This aspect of EVA® can be seen as either indicating flexibility or as being open to manipulation depending on whether or not you support this measure!)

The most common adjustments that have to be made are:

- *Research and development (R&D) costs and market costs*   These costs should be written off over the period that they benefit. In practice, however, they are often written off in the period in which they are incurred. This means that any amounts written off immediately should be added back to the assets on the balance sheet, thereby increasing invested capital, and then written off over time.
- *Goodwill*   In theory, goodwill should receive the same treatment as R&D and marketing costs. However, Stern Stewart suggests leaving goodwill on the balance sheet. One argument in favour of this treatment is that goodwill is really a 'catch all' that includes intangible items such as brand names and reputation that have infinite lives. Thus any amounts written off should be added back to assets.

■ *Restructuring costs* This item can be viewed as an investment in the future rather than an expense to be written off. Supporters of EVA® argue that by restructuring the business is better placed to meet future challenges, and so any amounts incurred should be added back to assets.

■ *Marketable investments* Investments in shares and loan capital are not included as part of the capital invested in the business. This is because the income from marketable investments is not included in the calculation of operating profit. (Income from this source will be added in the profit and loss account *after* operating profit has been calculated.)

Let us now consider a simple example to show how EVA® may be calculated.

---

**Example 11.4**

Scorpio plc was established two years ago and has produced the following balance sheet and profit and loss account at the end of the second year of trading.

**Balance sheet as at the end of the second year**

|  | £m | £m | £m |
|---|---|---|---|
| **Fixed assets** | | | |
| Goodwill | | 24.0 | |
| Plant and equipment | | 56.0 | |
| Motor vehicles | | 12.4 | |
| Marketable investment | | 6.6 | 99.0 |
| **Current assets** | | | |
| Stock | | 34.5 | |
| Debtors | | 29.3 | |
| Cash | | 2.1 | |
| | | 65.9 | |
| **Creditors due within one year** | | | |
| Trade creditors | 29.4 | | |
| Taxation | 1.8 | 31.2 | 34.7 |
| | | | 133.7 |
| **Creditors due beyond one year** | | | |
| Loan capital | | | 50.0 |
| | | | 83.7 |
| **Capital and reserves** | | | |
| Share capital | | | 60.0 |
| Reserves | | | 23.7 |
| | | | 83.7 |

**Profit and loss account for the second year**

|  | £m | £m |
|---|---|---|
| Sales | | 148.6 |
| Cost of sales | | 76.2 |
| | | 72.4 |
| Wages | 24.5 | |
| Depreciation of plant and equipment | 8.8 | |
| Goodwill written off | 4.0 | |
| Marketing costs | 22.5 | |
| Provision for doubtful debts | 4.5 | 64.3 |
| Operating profit | | 8.1 |
| Income from investments | | 0.4 |
| | | 8.5 |

|  | £m | £m |
|---|---|---|
| Interest payable |  | 0.5 |
| Ordinary profit before taxation |  | 8.0 |
| Restructuring costs |  | 2.0 |
| Profit before taxation |  | 6.0 |
| Corporation tax |  | 1.8 |
| Profit after taxation |  | 4.2 |

Discussions with the finance director reveal the following:

1. Goodwill was purchased during the first year of trading when another business was acquired. The goodwill cost £32.0m and this amount is being written off over an eight-year period (starting in the first year of the business).
2. Marketing costs relate to the launch of a new product. The benefits of the marketing campaign are expected to last for a three-year period (including this most recent year).
3. The provision for doubtful debts was created this year and the amount of the provision is very high. A more realistic figure for the provision would be £2.0m.
4. Restructuring costs were incurred as a result of a collapse in a particular product market. By restructuring the business, benefits are expected to flow for an infinite period.
5. The business has a 10 per cent required rate of return for investors.

The first step in calculating EVA® is to adjust the net operating profit after tax to take account of the various points revealed from the discussion with the finance director. The revised figure is calculated as follows:

*NOPAT adjustment*

|  | £m | £m |
|---|---|---|
| Operating profit |  | 8.1 |
| *Less* Corporation tax |  | 1.8 |
|  |  | 6.3 |
| *EVA® adjustments (to be added back to profit)* |  |  |
| Goodwill | 4.0 |  |
| Marketing costs ($^2/_3 \times 22.5$) | 15.0 |  |
| Excess provision | 2.5 | 21.5 |
| Adjusted NOPAT |  | 27.8 |

The next step is to adjust the net assets (as represented by capital and reserves and loan capital) to take account of the points revealed.

*Adjusted net assets (or capital invested)*

|  | £m | £m |
|---|---|---|
| Net assets per balance sheet |  | 133.7 |
| *Add* |  |  |
| Goodwill adjustment * | 8.0 |  |
| Marketing costs ** | 15.0 |  |
| Provision for doubtful debts | 2.5 |  |
| Restructuring costs *** | 2.0 | 27.5 |
|  |  | 161.2 |
| *Less* |  |  |
| Marketable investments**** |  | 6.6 |
| Adjusted net assets |  | 154.6 |

> \* The goodwill adjustment takes account of the fact that there was a £4.0m write-off in years 1 and 2.
> \*\* The marketing costs represent two years' benefits added back ($^2/_3 \times$ £22.5m).
> \*\*\* The restructuring costs are added back to the net assets as they provide benefits over an infinite period. (Note that they were not added back to the operating profit, as these costs were deducted *after* arriving at operating profit in the profit and loss account.)
> \*\*\*\* The marketable investments do not form part of the operating assets of the business and the income from these investments is not part of the operating income.

**Activity 11.11**

**Can you work out the EVA® for the second year of the business?**

EVA® can be calculated as follows:

$$\text{EVA}^® = \text{NOPAT} - (R \times C)$$
$$= £27.8m - (10\% \times £154.6m)$$
$$= \underline{£12.3m} \text{ (to one decimal place)}$$

Thus, we can see that the company increased shareholder wealth during the year.

The main advantage of this measure is the discipline to which managers are subjected as a result of the charge for capital that has been invested. Before any increase in shareholder wealth can be recognised, an appropriate deduction is made for the use of business resources. Thus EVA® encourages managers to use these resources efficiently. Where managers are focused simply on increasing profits, there is a danger that the resources used to achieve any increase in profits will not be taken into proper account.

## EVA® and SVA

Although at first glance it may appear that EVA® and SVA are worlds apart, this is not the case. In fact EVA® and SVA are very closely related and, in theory at least, should produce the same figure for shareholder value. The way in which shareholder value is calculated using SVA has already been described. The EVA® approach to calculating shareholder value adds the capital invested to the present value of future EVA® flows and then deducts the market value of any loan capital. Figure 11.8 illustrates the two approaches to determining shareholder value.

Let us go through a simple example to illustrate this point.

**Example 11.5**

Leo Ltd has just been formed and has been financed by a £20m issue of share capital and a £10m issue of loan capital. The proceeds of the issue have been invested in fixed assets with a life of three years and during this period the fixed assets will depreciate by £10m per year. The operating profit after tax is expected to be £15m each year. There will be no replacement of fixed assets during the three-year period and no investment in working capital. At the end of the three years, the business will be wound up and the fixed assets will have no residual value. The required rate of return by investors is 10 per cent.

The SVA approach to determining shareholder value will be as follows:

| Year | FCF | Discount rate | Present value |
|---|---|---|---|
| | £m | 10% | £m |
| 1 | 25.0* | 0.909 | 22.7 |
| 2 | 25.0 | 0.826 | 20.7 |
| 3 | 25.0 | 0.751 | 18.8 |
| | Total business value | | 62.2 |
| | *Less* Loan capital | | 10.0 |
| | Shareholder value | | 52.2 |

\* The free cash flows will be the operating profit after tax *plus* the depreciation charge (that is, £15m + £10m). There are no replacement fixed assets, in this case, against which the depreciation charge can be netted off. It must therefore be added back.

The EVA®approach to determining shareholder value will be as follows:

| Year | Opening capital invested (C) | Capital charge (10% × C) | Operating profit after tax | EVA® | Discount rate 10% | Present value of EVA® |
|---|---|---|---|---|---|---|
| | £m | £m | £m | £m | | £m |
| 1 | 30.0* | 3.0 | 15.0 | 12.0 | 0.909 | 10.9 |
| 2 | 20.0 | 2.0 | 15.0 | 13.0 | 0.826 | 10.7 |
| 3 | 10.0 | 1.0 | 15.0 | 14.0 | 0.751 | 10.5 |
| | | | | | | 32.1 |
| | | | | Opening capital | | 30.0 |
| | | | | | | 62.1 |
| | | | | *Less* Loan capital | | 10.0 |
| | | | | Shareholder value | | 52.1 |

\* The capital invested decreases each year by the depreciation charge (that is, £10m).

---

**Figure 11.8**

## Two approaches to determining shareholder value

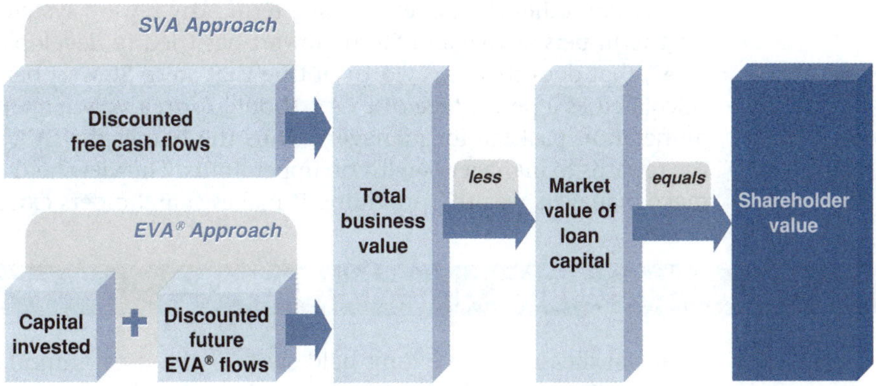

The figure shows how EVA® and SVA can both provide a measure of shareholder value. Total business value can be derived by either discounting the free cash flows over time or by discounting the EVA® flows over time and adding the capital invested. Whichever approach is used, the market value of loan capital must then be deducted to derive shareholder value.

## EVA® or SVA?

Although EVA® and SVA are both consistent with the idea of maximising share-holder wealth and, in theory, should produce the same decisions and results, the supporters of EVA® claim that this measure has a number of practical advantages over SVA. One such advantage is that EVA® sits more comfortably with the conventional financial reporting systems and financial reports. There is no need to develop entirely new systems to implement EVA® as it can be calculated by making a few adjustments to the conventional profit and loss accounts and balance sheets.

It is also claimed that EVA® is more useful as a basis for rewarding managers. Both EVA® and SVA support the idea that management rewards should be linked to increases in shareholder value. This should ensure that the interests of managers are closely aligned to the interests of shareholders. Under the SVA approach, management rewards will be determined on the basis of the contribution made to the generation of long-term cash flows. However, there are practical problems in using SVA for this purpose.

| Activity 11.12 | **Can you think of any practical problems that may arise when using SVA calculations to reward managers?** |
|---|---|

The SVA approach measures changes in shareholder value by reference to predicted changes in future cash flows and it is unwise to pay managers on the basis of predicted rather than actual achievements. If the predictions are optimistic, the effect will be that the business rewards optimism rather than real achievement. There is also a risk that unscrupulous managers will manipulate predicted future cash flows in order to increase their rewards.

Under EVA®, managers can receive bonuses based on actual achievement during a particular period. However, if management rewards are linked to a single period, there is a danger that managers will place undue attention on increases during this period rather than over the long term. Any reward system must encourage a long-term perspective and Stern Stewart has tried to develop a system, based on EVA®, that does this. It is worth noting that Stern Stewart believes that bonuses, calculated as a percentage of EVA®, should form a very large part of the total remuneration package for managers. Thus the higher the EVA® figure, the higher the rewards to managers – with no upper limits. The view held is that EVA® should make managers wealthy providing it makes shareholders extremely wealthy!

## Non-financial measures of performance

Financial measures have long held sway as the most important measures for a business. They provide us with a valuable means of summarising and evaluating business achievement and there is no real doubt about the continued importance of financial measures in this role. In recent years, however, there has been increasing recognition that financial measures alone will not provide managers with sufficient information to manage a business effectively. Non-financial measures must also be used in order to gain a deeper understanding of the business and to achieve the objectives of the business, including the financial objectives.

Financial measures portray various aspects of business achievement (for example, sales, profits, return on capital employed and so on) that can help managers determine whether the business is increasing the wealth of its owners. These measures are vitally important, but in an increasingly competitive environment managers also need to understand what particular things drive the creation of wealth. These value drivers may be such things as employee satisfaction, customer loyalty and the level of product innovation. Often they do not lend themselves to financial measurement, although non-financial measures may provide some means of assessment.

| Activity 11.13 | How might we measure: |
|---|---|

**How might we measure:**

(i)   employee satisfaction?
(ii)  customer loyalty?
(iii) the level of product innovation?

Employee satisfaction may be measured through the use of an employee survey. This could examine attitudes towards various aspects of the job, the degree of autonomy that is permitted, the level of recognition and reward received, the level of participation in decision making, the degree of support received in carrying out tasks and so on. Less direct measures of satisfaction may include employee turnover rates and employee productivity. However, other factors may have a significant influence on these measures.

Customer loyalty may be measured through the proportion of total sales generated from existing customers, the number of repeat sales made to customers, the percentage of customers renewing subscriptions or other contracts and so on.

The level of product innovation may be measured through the number of innovations during a period compared to those of competitors, the percentage of sales attributable to recent product innovations, the number of innovations that are brought successfully to market and so on.

Financial measures are normally 'lag' indicators, in that they tell us about outcomes. In other words, they measure the consequences arising from management decisions that were made earlier. Non-financial measures can be used as lag indicators, of course. However, they can also be used as 'lead' indicators by focusing on those things that drive performance. It is argued that if we measure changes in these value drivers, we may be able to predict changes in future financial performance. For example, a business may find from experience that a 10 per cent fall in levels of product innovation, during one period, will lead to a 20 per cent fall in sales over the next three periods. In this case, the levels of product innovation can be regarded as a lead indicator that can alert managers to a future decline in sales unless corrective action is taken. Thus, by using this lead indicator, managers can identify key changes at an earlier stage and can respond more quickly.

## The balanced scorecard

One of the most impressive attempts to integrate the use of financial and non-financial measures has been the **balanced scorecard**, developed by Robert Kaplan and David Norton (see reference (2) at the end of this chapter). The balanced scorecard is both a management system and a measurement system. In essence, it provides a framework that translates the aims and objectives of the business into a series of key performance measures and targets. This framework is intended to make the strategy of the business more coherent by tightly linking it to particular targets and initiatives. As a result, managers should be able to see more clearly whether the objectives that have been set have actually been achieved.

The balanced scorecard approach involves setting objectives and developing appropriate measures and targets in four main areas:

1. *Financial*   This area will specify the financial returns required by shareholders and may involve the use of financial measures such as return on capital employed, net profit margin, percentage sales growth and so on.
2. *Customer*   This area will specify the kind of customer and/or markets the business wishes to service and will establish appropriate measures such as customer satisfaction, new customer growth levels and so on.
3. *Internal business process*   This area will specify those business processes (for example, innovation, types of operation and after-sales service) that are important to the success of the business and will establish appropriate measures such as percentage of sales from new products, time to market for new products, product cycle times, and speed of response to customer complaints.
4. *Learning and growth*   This area will specify the kind of people, the systems and the procedures that are necessary to deliver long-term business growth. This area is often the most difficult for the development of appropriate measures. However, examples of measures may include employee motivation, employee skills profiles, information systems capabilities and so on.

These four areas are shown in Figure 11.9.

The balanced scorecard approach does not prescribe the particular objectives, measures or targets that a business should adopt; this is a matter for the individual business to decide upon. There are differences between businesses in terms of technology employed, organisational structure, management philosophy, and business environment and so each business should develop objectives and measures that reflect their unique circumstances. The balanced scorecard simply sets out the framework for developing a coherent set of objectives for the business and for ensuring that these objectives are then linked to specific targets and initiatives.

A balanced scorecard will be prepared for the business as a whole (or in the case of large, diverse businesses, for each strategic business unit). However, having prepared an overall scorecard, it is then possible to prepare a balanced scorecard for each sub-unit, such as a department, within the business. Thus, the balanced scorecard approach can cascade down the business and can result in a pyramid of balanced scorecards that are linked to the 'master' balanced scorecard through an alignment of the objectives and measures employed.

Although a very large number of measures, both financial and non-financial, exist and so could be used in a balanced scorecard, only a handful of measures should be employed. A maximum of 20 measures will normally be sufficient to enable the factors that are critical to the success of the business to be captured. (If a business has come up with more than 20 measures it is usually because the managers have not thought hard enough about what the key measures really

**Figure 11.9**

## The balanced scorecard – for translating a strategy into operational processes

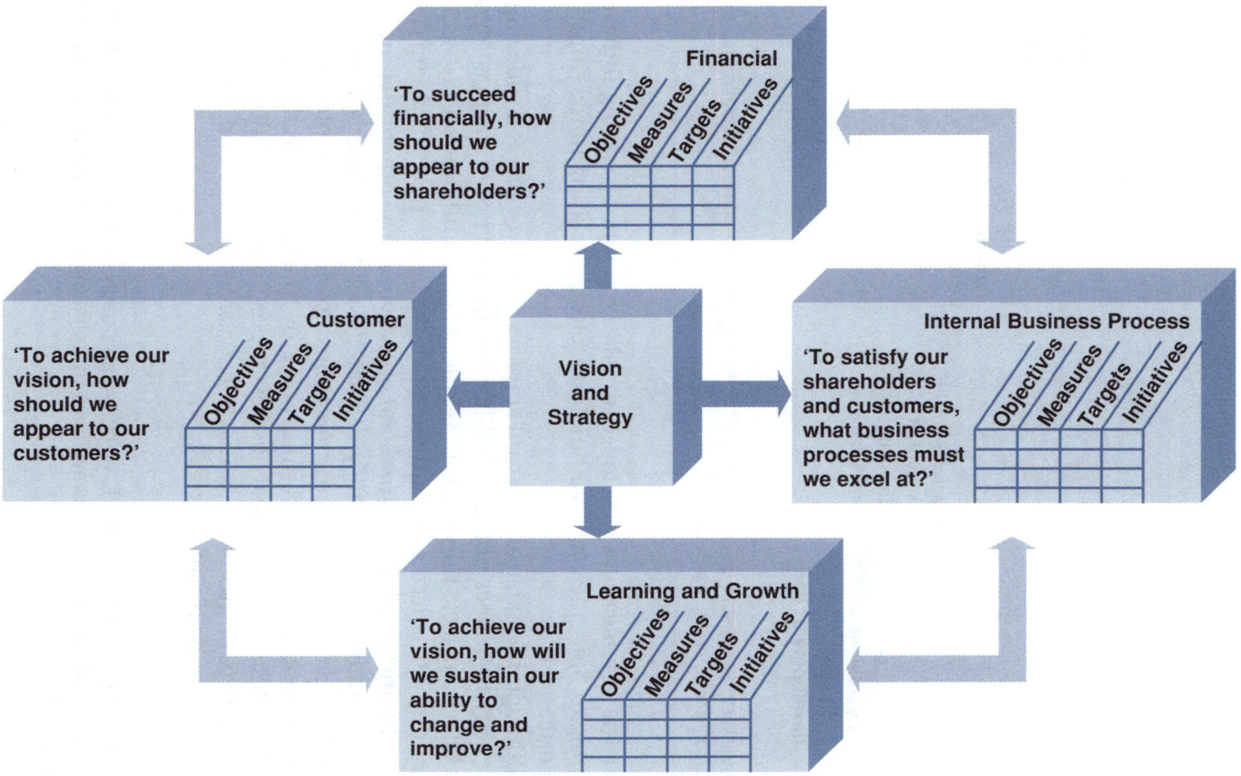

**Financial**

'To succeed financially, how should we appear to our shareholders?'

Objectives | Measures | Targets | Initiatives

**Internal Business Process**

'To satisfy our shareholders and customers, what business processes must we excel at?'

Objectives | Measures | Targets | Initiatives

**Customer**

'To achieve our vision, how should we appear to our customers?'

Objectives | Measures | Targets | Initiatives

**Vision and Strategy**

**Learning and Growth**

'To achieve our vision, how will we sustain our ability to change and improve?'

Objectives | Measures | Targets | Initiatives

The diagram sets out the four main areas covered by the balanced scorecard. Note that, for each area, a fundamental question must be addressed. By answering these questions, managers should be able to develop the key objectives of the business. Once this has been done, suitable measures and targets can be developed that are relevant to those objectives. Finally, appropriate management initiatives will be developed to achieve the targets set.

*Source:* **The Balanced Scorecard** (see reference (2) at end of chapter).

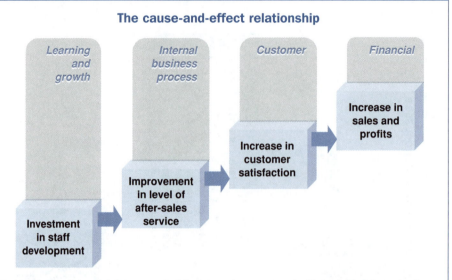

**Figure 11.10**

**The cause-and-effect relationship**

The investment in staff development is linked through a cause-and-effect relationship to the financial objectives of the business.

are!) The key measures developed should be a mix of lagging indicators (those relating to outcomes) and lead indicators (those relating to the things that drive performance).

Although the balance scorecard employs measures across a wide range of business activity, it does not seek to dilute the importance of financial measures and objectives. In fact, the opposite is true. Kaplan and Norton (2) emphasise the point that a balanced scorecard must reflect a concern for the financial objectives of the business and so measures and objectives in the other three areas that have been identified must ultimately be related back to the financial objectives. There must be a clear cause-and-effect relationship. So, for example, an investment in staff development (in the learning and growth area) may lead to improved levels of after-sales service (internal business process area), which, in turn, may lead to higher levels of customer satisfaction (customer area) and, ultimately, higher sales and profits (financial area).

**Activity 11.14**

Do you think this is a rather hard-nosed approach to dealing with staff development? Should staff development always have to be justified in terms of the financial results achieved?

This approach may seem rather hard-nosed. However, Kaplan and Norton (2) argue that unless this kind of link between staff development and increased financial returns can be demonstrated, managers are likely to become cynical about the benefits of staff development and so the result may be that there will be no investment in staff.

You may wonder why this framework is referred to as a *balanced* scorecard. According to Kaplan and Norton there are various reasons. Firstly, it is because it aims to strike a balance between *external* measures relating to customers and shareholders, and internal measures relating to *internal* business process and learning and growth. Secondly, it aims to strike a balance between the measures that portray *outcomes* (lag indicators) and measures that help *predict future perform-ance* (lead indicators). Finally, the framework aims to strike a balance between *hard* financial measures and *soft* non-financial measures.

| Exhibit 11.4 | Kaplan and Norton (2) invite you to imagine the following conversation between you and the pilot of a jet aeroplane in which you are flying: |
| --- | --- |

Q: I'm surprised to see you operating the plane with only a single instrument. What does it measure?
A: Airspeed. I'm really working on airspeed this flight.

Q: That's good. Airspeed certainly seems important. But what about altitude? Wouldn't an alti-meter be helpful?
A: I worked on altitude for the last few flights and I've gotten pretty good on it. Now I have to con-centrate on proper airspeed.

Q: But I notice you don't even have a fuel gauge. Wouldn't that be useful?
A: You're right; fuel is significant, but I can't concentrate on doing too many things well at the same time. So on this flight I'm focusing on airspeed. Once I get to be excellent at airspeed, as well as altitude, I intend to concentrate on fuel consumption on the next set of flights.

The point they are trying to make (apart from warning you against flying with a pilot like this!) is that to fly an aeroplane, which is a complex activity, a wide range of navigation instruments is required. A business, however, can be even more complex to manage than an aeroplane and so a wide range of measures, both financial and non-financial, is neces-sary. Reliance on financial measures is not enough and so the balanced scorecard aims to provide managers with a more complete navigation system.

## ? Self-assessment question 11.1

You have recently heard a fellow student talking about strategic management accounting as follows:

Assessing strategic change is concerned with undertaking a SWOT analysis and then making plans to change strategy.

Customer profitability analysis is about finding out which of your customers are the more profitable companies and trying to encourage the ones that are more profitable to place orders. This is to avoid having customers that go bankrupt.

Shareholder value analysis (SVA) tries to give shareholders their returns in the form that they like. Some shareholders prefer dividends and others prefer profits to be ploughed back. EVA stands for 'equity value analysis' and is an alternative name for SVA.

The 'balanced scorecard' is the American name for what people in the UK call a 'balance sheet'.

### Required:
Critically comment on the student's statement, explaining any technical terms.

## Summary

In this chapter we have looked at how traditional management accounting can be extended to support a strategic management approach. Here the business makes plans, based on strategies, that will have as their goal achievement of the business's objectives and aims. Strategic management tends to be more concerned with factors outside the business than with costs and benefits relating to internal aspects.

If the business is to change its strategy, it is useful to be able to analyse the effect of the change on profit. Assessment of strategic change can do this in a manner quite similar to variance analysis.

To be able to predict the effect on competitors of a business altering its marketing strategy, it can be very valuable to understand the nature of the costs and cost structure of each of its competitors. Competitor profitability analysis tries to build up a picture of each major competitor, gleaning information from such sources as the published annual reports of the businesses concerned and published statistics.

Not all customers are equally profitable for the business, even assuming that they were to buy the same annual volume of goods for similar prices. Differences in such matters as the number of orders placed each year, the cost of transporting goods to customers, the length of trade credit taken and the extent to which particular customers cause the business to hold finished stocks. Customer profitability analysis seeks to assess the relative profitability of the business's customers. This may well reveal that certain customers are not profitable. The analysis, in effect, involves preparing a 'mini' profit and loss account for each customer or, possibly, type of customer.

Pursuit of shareholder value is seen as the key objective of most businesses. Two management accounting approaches have been developed to focus management decision making on this objective. Shareholder value analysis (SVA) has identified a small number of key value drivers which, if focused on, it is claimed will lead to the business generating maximum value for its shareholders.

Economic value added (EVA®), like SVA, focuses on pursuing shareholder value. This approach, however, tends to rely more on the traditional accounting measures of profit as a basis. Accounting profit can be criticised on various grounds for being a limited basis for assessing business success. EVA®, however, advocates recalculating accounting profit so that it can be useful in this regard.

The balanced scorecard is substantially a non-financial approach to measurement of performance. It seeks to balance financial aspects with non-financial ones, external ones with internal ones and lag indicators with lead indicators.

→ **Key terms**

Strategic planning  p. 297
Position analysis  p. 297
SWOT analysis  p. 297
Competitor profitability analysis  p. 302
Customer profitability analysis  p. 303

Shareholder value analysis  p. 309
Free cash flows  p. 310
Value drivers  p. 311
Economic value added (EVA®)  p. 316
Balanced scorecard  p. 323

## Further reading

If you would like to explore topics covered in this chapter in more depth, we recommend the following books:

Management and Cost Accounting, *Drury, C.*, Thomson Learning, 5th edn, 2000, chapter 23.

Cost Accounting, *Horngren, C., Foster, G.* and *Datar, S.*, Prentice Hall International, 10th edn, 2000, chapter 22.

The Balanced Scorecard, *Kaplan, R.* and *Norton D.*, Harvard Business School, 1996.

Fundamentals of Managerial Accounting, *Mills, R.* and *Robertson, J.*, Mars Business Associates, 4th edn, 1999, chapters 5 and 12.

## References

1. **Cost Systems Design and Profitability Analysis in UK Companies**, *Drury, C.* and *Tayles, M.*, CIMA Publishing, 2000.
2. **The Balanced Scorecard**, *Kaplan, R.* and *Norton, D.*, Harvard Business School Press, 1996.

## ? REVIEW QUESTIONS

**11.1** What is the objective of assessment of strategic change and broadly how is this achieved?

**11.2** Both customer A and customer B buy 1,000 units of your business's service each year, paying the same price per unit. Why might your business regard customer A as a desirable customer, but not customer B?

**11.3** What is the principle on which shareholder value analysis is based?

**11.4** What are the four main areas on which the balanced scorecard is based?

## ? EXERCISES

**Questions 11.4–11.8 are more advanced than 11.1–11.3. Those with coloured numbers have answers at the back of the book.**

**11.1** You have been speaking to a friend who owns a small business and she has said that she has read something about strategic planning and that no modern business can afford not to get involved with it. Your friend has little idea what strategic planning involves.

**Required:**
Briefly outline the steps in strategic planning, summarising what each step tends to involve.

**11.2** You have recently heard someone making the following statement about competitor profitability analysis (CPA).

CPA is an assessment of how profitable competitors are, that is carried out in an attempt to establish a benchmark by which one's own business's success can be measured. Usually most of the information for this can be found in the competitors' annual report and accounts. Usually competitors are willing to provide information about their financial results so that any gaps in the CPA can be filled in.

**Required:**
Comment on this statement.

**11.3** Sharma plc makes one standard product for which it charges the same basic price of £20 a unit, though discounts are allowed to certain customers. The company is in the process of carrying out a profitability analysis of all of its customers during the financial year just ended.

Information about Lopez Ltd, one of Sharma's customers, is as follows:

| | |
|---|---|
| Discount on sales price | 5% |
| Number of products sold | 40,000 units |
| Manufacturing cost | £12 |
| Number of sales orders | 22 |
| Number of deliveries | 22 |
| Distance travelled to deliver | 120 miles |
| Number of sales visits from Sharma's staff | 30 |

Sharma uses an activity-based approach to ascribing costs to customers, as follows:

| Cost pool | Cost driver | Rate |
|---|---|---|
| Order handling | Number of orders | £75 an order |
| Delivery costs | Miles travelled | £1.50 a mile |
| Customer sales visits | Number of visits | £230 a visit |

Lopez usually takes two months' credit, of which the cost to Sharma is estimated at 2 per cent per month.

**Required:**
Calculate the net profit that Sharma plc derived from sales to Lopez Ltd during last year.

**11.4** Vitality Ltd imports bottles of French spring water that it markets to shops in the UK. The market is very price competitive. The company's directors believed that a change in marketing strategy would be beneficial. They felt that if the selling price to the shops were lowered, a greater sales volume would be able to be achieved.

In the expectation of additional sales volume, the company was able to negotiate a lower price with the French bottler for all of its purchases. The increased sales volume did not increase the company's fixed costs. The change in marketing strategy took place on 1 January 2001.

Vitality Ltd's water sales results for 2000 and 2001 can be summarised as follows:

| Year | 2000 | 2001 |
|---|---|---|
| 1  Number of bottles bought and sold | 100,000 | 123,000 |
| 2  Selling price per bottle | £0.50 | £0.40 |
| 3  Total sales (line 1 × line 2) | £50,000 | £49,200 |
| 4  Cost price per bottle | £0.30 | £0.28 |
| 5  Total cost of bottles (line 1 × line 4) | £30,000 | £34,440 |

**Required:**
(a) Calculate the change in contribution caused by the change in strategy.
(b) Analyse the figure calculated in (a) into the growth aspect, the price aspect and the usage (profitability) aspect.
(c) Briefly explain and comment on how successful the change in strategy was and why.

**11.5** Jones Dairy Ltd (Jones) operates a 'doorstep' fresh milk delivery service. Two brothers formed the company in the early 1960s when they inherited the business from their father. The business operates from a yard on the outskirts of Trepont, a substantial town in mid-Wales.

Jones expanded steadily until the early 1980s, by which time it employed 25 full-time rounds staff. This was achieved because of four factors: (i) some expansion of the permanent population of Trepont, (ii) expanding Jones's geographical range to the villages surrounding the town, (iii) an expanding tourist trade in the area and (iv) through a positive attitude to 'marketing'.

As an example of the marketing effort, when new residents move into the area, the member of the rounds staff concerned reports this back. One of the directors immediately visits the potential customer with an introductory gift, usually a bottle of milk, a bottle of wine and a bunch of flowers, and attempts to get a regular milk order. Similar methods are used to persuade existing residents to place orders for delivered milk.

By the mid-1980s Jones had a monopoly of doorstep delivery in the Trepont area. A combination of losing market share to Jones and the town's relative remoteness had discouraged the national doorstep suppliers. The little locally based competition there once was had gone out of business.

Supplies of milk come from a bottling plant, owned by one of the national dairy companies, which is located 50 miles from Trepont. The bottlers deliver nightly, except Saturday nights, to Jones's depot. Jones delivers daily, except on Sundays.

Profits, after adjusting for inflation, have fallen since the early 1980s. Sales volumes have fallen by about a third, compared with a decline of about 50 per cent for doorstep deliveries nationally over the same period. New customers are increasingly difficult to find, despite a continuing policy of encouraging them. Many existing customers tend to have less milk delivered. A sufficient profit has been made to enable the directors to enjoy a reasonable income compared with their needs, but only by raising prices. Currently Jones charges 40 pence for a standard pint, delivered. This is fairly typical of doorstep delivery charges around the UK. The Trepont supermarket, which is located in the centre of town, charges 26 pence a pint and other local stores charge between 35 pence and 40 pence.

Currently Jones employs 15 full-time rounds staff, a van maintenance mechanic, a secretary/bookkeeper and the two directors. Jones is regarded locally as a good employer. Regular employment opportunities in the area are generally few. Rounds staff are expected to, and generally do, give customers a friendly, cheerful and helpful service.

The two brothers continue to be the only shareholders and directors and comprise the only level of management. One of the directors devotes most of his time to dealing with the supplier and with issues connected with details of the rounds. The other director looks after administrative matters, like the accounts and personnel issues. Both directors undertake rounds to cover for sickness and holidays.

**Required:**
As far as the information given in the question will allow, undertake an analysis of the strengths, weaknesses, opportunities and threats (SWOT analysis) of the company.

**11.6** Leo plc is considering entering a new market. A new product has been developed at a cost of £5m and is now ready for production. The market is growing and estimates from the finance department concerning future sales of the new product are as follows:

| Year | Sales £m |
|------|----------|
| 1 | 30 |
| 2 | 36 |
| 3 | 40 |
| 4 | 48 |
| 5 | 60 |

After year 5, sales are expected to stabilise at the year 5 level.
You are informed that:

- The operating profit margin from sales in the new market is likely to be a constant 20 per cent of sales.
- The cash tax rate is 25 per cent of operating profit.
- Replacement fixed asset investment (RFAI) will be in line with the annual depreciation charge each year.
- Additional fixed asset investment (AFAI) over the next five years will be 15 per cent of sales growth.
- Additional working capital investment (AWCI) over the next five years will be 10 per cent of sales growth.

The company has a cost of capital of 12 per cent. The new market is considered to be no more risky than the markets in which the business already has a presence.

**Required:**
Using an SVA approach, indicate the effect of entering the new market on shareholder value. (Workings should be to one decimal place.)

**11.7** Pisces plc produced the following balance sheet and profit and loss account at the end of the third year of trading:

**Balance sheet as at the end of the third year**

| | £m | £m |
|---|---:|---:|
| **Fixed assets** | | |
| Goodwill | 40.0 | |
| Machinery and equipment | 80.0 | |
| Motor vans | 18.6 | |
| Marketable investment | 9.0 | 147.6 |
| **Current assets** | | |
| Stock | 45.8 | |
| Debtors | 64.6 | |
| Cash | 1.0 | |
| | 111.4 | |
| **Creditors due within one year** | | |
| Trade creditors | 62.5 | |
| Dividends | | 48.9 |
| | | 196.5 |
| **Creditors due beyond one year** | | |
| Loan capital | | 80.0 |
| | | 116.5 |
| **Capital and reserves** | | |
| Share capital | | 80.0 |
| Reserves | | 36.5 |
| | | 116.5 |

**Profit and loss account for the third year**

| | £m | £m |
|---|---:|---:|
| Sales | | 231.5 |
| Cost of sales | | 143.2 |
| | | 88.3 |
| Wages | 33.5 | |
| Depreciation of machinery and equipment | 14.8 | |
| Goodwill written off | 10.0 | |
| R&D costs | 40.0 | |
| Provision for doubtful debts | 10.5 | 108.8 |
| Operating loss | | 20.5 |
| Income from investments | | 0.6 |
| | | 19.9 |
| Interest payable | | 0.8 |
| Ordinary loss before taxation | | 20.7 |
| Restructuring costs | | 6.0 |
| Profit before taxation | | 26.7 |
| Corporation tax | | – |
| Loss after tax | | 26.7 |

An analysis of the underlying records reveals the following:

1. Goodwill was purchased during the first year of trading when an existing business was acquired. The goodwill cost £70.0m and this amount is being written off over a seven-year period (starting in the first year of the business).
2. R&D costs relate to the development of a new product in the previous year. These costs are written off over a two-year period (starting last year). However, this is a prudent approach and the benefits are expected to last for 16 years.
3. The provision for doubtful debts was created this year and the amount of the provision is very high. A more realistic figure for the provision would be £4.0m.
4. Restructuring costs were incurred at the beginning of the year and are expected to provide benefits for an infinite period.
5. The company has an 8 per cent required rate of return for investors.

**Required:**
Calculate the EVA® for the business for the third year of trading.

**11.8** Aquarius plc has estimated the following free cash flows for its five-year planning period:

| Year | Free cash flows |
|------|-----------------|
|      | £m              |
| 1    | 35              |
| 2    | 38              |
| 3    | 45              |
| 4    | 49              |
| 5    | 53              |

**Required:**
How might it be possible to check the accuracy of these figures? What internal and external sources of information might be used to see whether the figures are realistic?

# Glossary of key terms

**ABC system of stock control**  A method of applying different levels of stock control, based on the value of each category of stock. p. 239

**Accounting**  The process of identifying, measuring and communicating information to permit informed judgements and decisions by users of the information. p. 1

**Accounting information system**  The system used within a business to identify, record, analyse and report accounting information. p. 9

**Accounting rate of return (ARR)**  The average profit from an investment, expressed as a percentage of the average investment made. p. 190

**Activity-based budgeting (ABB)**  A system of budgeting based on the philosophy of activity-based costing (ABC). p. 145

**Activity-based costing (ABC)**  A technique for more accurately relating overheads to specific production or provision of a service. It is based on acceptance of the fact that overheads do not just occur but are caused by activities, like holding products in stores, which 'drive' the costs. p. 99

**Adverse variance**  A difference between planned and actual performance, where the difference will cause the actual profit to be lower than the budgeted one. p. 163

**Ageing schedule of debtors**  A report analysing debtors into categories, depending on the length of time outstanding. p. 248

**Average settlement period for debtors/creditors**  The average time taken for debtors to pay the amounts owing or for a business to pay its creditors. pp. 248 and 259

**Average stock turnover period**  The average period for which stocks are held by a business. p. 238

**Balanced scorecard**  A framework for translating the aims and objectives of a business into a series of key performance measures and targets. p. 323

**Bank overdraft**  A flexible form of borrowing which allows an individual or business to have a negative bank current account balance. p. 259

**Batch costing**  A technique for identifying full cost, where the production of many types of goods and services, particularly goods, involves producing a batch of identical or nearly identical units of output, but where each batch is distinctly different from other batches. p. 87

**Behavioural aspects of budgetary control**  The effect on people's attitudes and behaviour of the various aspects of using budgets as the basis of exercising control over performance. p. 180

**Benchmarking** Identifying a successful business, or part of a business, and measuring the effectiveness of one's own business by comparison with this standard. p. 117

**Break-even analysis** The activity of deducing the break-even point of some activity through analysing costs and revenues. p. 42

**Break-even chart** A graphical representation of the costs and revenues of some activity, at various levels, which enables the break-even point to be identified. p. 43

**Break-even point** A level of activity where revenue will exactly equal total cost, so there is neither profit nor loss. p. 43

**Budget** A financial plan for the short term, typically one year. p. 127

**Budget committee** A group of managers formed to supervise and take responsibility for the budget-setting process. p. 135

**Budget holder** An individual responsible for a particular budget. p. 138

**Budget officer** An individual, often an accountant, appointed to carry out, or take immediate responsibility for having carried out, the tasks of the budget committee. p. 135

**Budgetary control** Using the budget as a yardstick against which the effectiveness of actual performance may be assessed. p. 177

**Cash discount** A reduction in the amount due for goods or services sold on credit in return for prompt payment. p. 247

**Committed cost** A cost which has not yet been incurred, but which must, under some existing contract or obligation, be incurred. p. 26

**Common costs** Costs that relate to more than one business segment. p. 69

**Comparability** The requirement that items which are basically the same should be treated in the same manner for measurement and reporting purposes. Lack of comparability will limit the usefulness of accounting information. p. 6

**Compensating variances** The situation which exists when two variances, both caused by the same factor, one adverse and the other favourable, are of equal size and, therefore, cancel out. p. 176

**Competitor profitability analysis** An assessment of the costs and cost structure of rival businesses with the objective of putting the business in a position to assess how individual competitors might react to strategic moves by the business. p. 303

**Continual (or rolling) budget** A budgeting system which continually updates budgets so that there is always a budget for a full planning period. p. 130

**Contribution (per unit)** Sales revenue per unit less variable costs per unit. p. 46

**Control** Compelling events to conform to plan. p. 127

**Controllable cost** A cost which is the responsibility of a specific manager. p. 274

**Cost** The amount of resources, usually measured in monetary terms, sacrificed to achieve a particular objective. p. 21

**Cost allocation** Dividing costs between cost centres according to the amount of cost which has been incurred in them. p. 81

**Cost apportionment** Dividing costs between cost centres according to the amount of cost which is seen as being fair. p. 81

**Cost behaviour** The manner in which costs alter with changes in the level of activity. p. 71

**Cost centre** Some area, object, person or activity for which costs are separately collected. p. 80

**Cost driver**  An activity which causes costs. p. 99

**Cost-plus pricing**  An approach to pricing output which is based on full cost, plus a percentage profit loading. p. 66

**Cost pool**  The sum of the overhead costs that are seen as being caused by the same cost driver. p. 99

**Cost unit**  The objective for which the cost is being deduced, usually a product or service. p. 72

**Customer profitability analysis (CPA)**  An assessment of the profitability to the business of individual customers, or types of customer. p. 303

**Direct costs**  Costs which can be identified with specific cost units, to the extent that the effect of the cost can be measured in respect of each particular unit of output. p. 69

**Discount factor**  The rate applied to future cash flows to derive the present value of those cash flows. p. 202

**Discretionary budget**  A budget based on a sum allocated at the discretion of top management. p. 139

**Divisional performance measurements**  The activity of assessing the effectiveness of individual departments or sections of a business. p. 273

**Divisions**  Sections or departments through which large businesses are organised and managed. p. 268

**Economic order quantity (EOQ)**  The quantity of stocks which should be purchased in order to minimise total stock costs. p. 240

**Economic value added (EVA®)**  A measure of economic, as opposed to accounting, profit. It is said to be more useful than accounting profit as a measure of business performance because it overcomes some weaknesses of accounting in this context. p. 316

**Elasticity of demand**  The manner in which the level of demand alters with changes in price. p. 105

**Expected net present value (ENPV)**  A weighted average of the possible present value outcomes, where the probabilities associated with each outcome are used as weights. p. 215

**Favourable variance**  A difference between planned and actual performance where the difference will cause the actual profit to be higher than the budgeted one. p. 163

**Feedback control**  A control device where actual performance is compared with planned and where action is taken to deal with future divergences between these. p. 159

**Feedforward control**  A control device where forecast future performance is compared with planned performance and where action is taken to deal with divergences between these. p. 160

**Financial accounting**  The measuring and reporting of accounting information for external users (those users other than the managers of the business). p. 10

**Five Cs of credit**  A checklist of factors to be taken into account when assessing the creditworthiness of a customer. p. 244

**Fixed cost**  A cost which stays the same when changes occur to the volume of activity. p. 37

**Flexible budget**  A budget which is adjusted to reflect the actual level of output achieved. p. 159

**Flex (the budget)** Revising the budget to what it would have been had the planned level of output been different. p. 161

**Forecast** A prediction of future outcomes or of the future state of the environment. p. 129

**Free cash flows** The cash flows generated by the business that are available to the ordinary shareholders and long-term lenders. This is the net cash flow from operating activities, less tax and funds laid out on additional fixed assets. p. 310

**Full cost** The total amount of resources, usually measured in monetary terms, sacrificed to achieve a particular objective. pp. 65 and 287

**Full cost (cost-plus) pricing** Pricing output on the basis of its full cost, normally with a loading for profit. p. 111

**Full costing** Deducing the total direct and indirect (overhead) costs of pursuing some activity or objective. p. 65

**Historic cost** What an asset cost when it was originally acquired. p. 22

**Incremental budgeting** Constructing budgets on the basis of what happened in the previous period, with some adjustment for expected changes in the forthcoming budget period. p. 138

**Indirect costs (or overheads)** All costs except direct costs: that is, those which cannot be directly measured in respect of each particular unit of output. p. 69

**Inflation** The increase in money prices, causing erosion of the value of money. p. 199

**Internal rate of return (IRR)** The discount rate for a project which will have the effect of producing a zero NPV. p. 204

**Investigating variances** The act of looking into the practical causes of budget variances, once those variances have been identified. p. 174

**Investment centre** Some area, object, person or activity in which management is responsible and accountable for all, or most, investment decisions. p. 269

**Irrelevant cost** A cost which is not relevant to a particular decision. p. 22

**Job costing** A technique for identifying the full cost per unit of output, where that output is not similar to other units of output. p. 69

**Just-in-time (JIT) stock management** A system of stock management which aims to have supplies delivered to production just in time for their required use. p. 242

***Kaizen* costing** An approach to cost control where an attempt is made to control costs by trying continually to make cost savings, often only small ones, from one time period to the next. p. 117

**Learning curve** The tendency for people to carry out tasks more quickly as they become more experienced in doing so. p. 172

**Limiting factor** Some aspect of the business (for example, lack of sales demand) which will prevent it achieving its objectives to the maximum extent. p. 136

**Management accounting** The measuring and reporting of accounting information for the managers of a business. p. 10

**Management by exception** A system of control, based on a comparison of planned and actual performance, which allows managers to focus on areas of poor performance rather than dealing with areas where performance is satisfactory. p. 133

**Margin of safety** The extent to which the planned level of output or sales lies above the break-even point. p. 46

**Marginal analysis**   The activity of decision making through analysing variable costs and revenues, ignoring fixed costs. p. 53

**Marginal cost**   The addition to total cost which will be incurred by making/ providing one more unit of output. p. 46

**Marginal cost pricing**   Pricing output on the basis of its marginal cost, normally with a loading for profit. p. 113

**Market prices (as transfer prices)**   Using a price set by the market outside the business as a suitable price for internal, inter-divisional transfers. p. 286

**Master budgets**   A summary of the individual budgets, usually consisting of a budgeted profit and loss account, a budgeted balance sheet and a budgeted cash flow statement. p. 130

**Materiality**   The requirement that material information should be disclosed to users of financial reports. p. 6

**Materials requirement planning (MRP) system**   A computer-based system of stock control which schedules the timing of deliveries of bought-in parts and materials to coincide with production requirements to meet demand. p. 242

**Mission statement**   A brief statement setting out the aims of the business. p. 125

**Negotiated prices**   Transfer prices which are derived as a result of negotiation between managers of the divisions concerned, possibly with the involvement of the business's central management as well. p. 288

**Net present value (NPV)**   A method of investment appraisal based on the present value of all relevant cash flows associated with the project. p. 197

**Non-controllable cost**   A cost for which a specific manager is not held responsible. p. 274

**Non-operating-profit variances**   Differences between budgeted and actual performance which do not lead directly to differences between budgeted and actual operating profit. p. 174

**Objective probabilities**   Probabilities based on information gathered from past experience. p. 218

**Operating cash cycle**   The period between the outlay of cash to purchase supplies and the ultimate receipt of cash from the sale of goods. p. 254

**Operating gearing**   The relationship between the total fixed and the total variable costs for some activity. p. 48

**Opportunity cost**   The cost incurred when one course of action prevents an opportunity to derive some benefit from another course of action. pp. 22 and 285

**Outlay cost**   A cost which involves the spending of money or some other transfer of assets. p. 22

**Overhead (or indirect cost)**   Any cost except a direct cost; a cost which cannot be directly measured in respect of each particular unit of output. p. 69

**Overhead absorption (recovery) rate**   The rate at which overheads are charged to cost units (jobs), usually in a job costing system. p. 73

**Past cost**   A cost which has been incurred in the past. p. 22

**Payback period (PP)**   The time taken for the initial investment in a project to be repaid from the net cash inflows of the project. p. 194

**Penetration pricing**   Setting prices at a level low enough to encourage wide market acceptance of a product or service. p. 114

**Periodic budget**   A budget developed on a one-off basis to cover a particular planning period. p. 129

**Position analysis** A step in the strategic planning process in which the business assesses its present position in the light of the commercial and economic environment in which it operates. p. 297

**Post-completion audit** A review of the performance of an investment project to see whether actual performance matched planned performance and whether any lessons can be drawn from the way in which the investment was carried out. p. 225

**Price skimming** Setting prices at a high level to make the maximum profit from the product or service before the price is lowered to attract the next segment of the market. p. 114

**Process costing** A technique for deriving the full cost per unit of output, where the units of output are exactly similar or it is reasonable to treat them as being so. p. 68

**Product cost centre** Some area, object, person or activity for which costs are separately collected, in which cost units have costs added. p. 80

**Profit centre** Some area, object, person or activity for which its revenues and expenses are compared to derive a profit figure, for which the manager is held accountable. p. 269

**Profit–volume (PV) chart** A graphical representation of the contributions (revenues less variable costs) of some activity, at various levels, which enables the break-even point, and the profit at various activity levels, to be identified. p. 49

**Relevance** The ability of accounting information to influence decisions. Relevance is regarded as a key characteristic of useful accounting information. p. 5

**Relevant cost** A cost which is relevant to a particular decision. p. 22

**Reliability** The requirement that accounting should be free from material error or bias. Reliability is regarded as a key characteristic of useful accounting information. p. 5

**Residual income (RI)** A divisional performance measure. The operating profit of a division, less an interest charge based on the business's investment in the division. p. 277

**Return on investment (ROI)** A divisional performance measure. The operating profit of a division expressed as a percentage of the business's investment in the division. p. 275

**Risk** The likelihood that what is estimated to occur will not actually occur. p. 198

**Risk-adjusted discount rate** A discount rate applied to investment projects which is increased (decreased) in the face of increased (decreased) risk. p. 221

**Rolling (or continual) budget** A budgeting system which continually updates budgets so that there is always a budget for a full planning period. p. 130

**Semi-fixed (semi-variable) cost** A cost which has an element of both fixed and variable cost. p. 41

**Sensitivity analysis** An examination of the key variables affecting a project, to see how changes in each input might influence the outcome. p. 212

**Service cost centre** Some area, object, person or activity for which costs are collected separately, in which cost units do not have cost added, because service cost centres only render services to product cost services and to other service cost centres. p. 80

**Shareholder value analysis (SVA)**  Method of measuring and managing business value based on the long-term cash flows generated. p. 309

**Standard quantities and costs**  Planned quantities and costs (or revenues) for individual units of input or output. Standards are the building blocks used to produce the budget. p. 170

**Stepped fixed cost**  A fixed cost which does not remain fixed over all levels of output but which changes in steps as a threshold level of output is reached. p. 39

**Strategic planning**  The process of setting a course to achieve the business's objectives, taking account of the commercial and economic environment in which the business operates. p. 297

**Subjective probabilities**  Probabilities based on opinion rather than past data. p. 219

**Sunk cost**  A cost which has been incurred in the past; the same as a past cost. p. 26

**SWOT analysis**  A framework in which many businesses set a position analysis. Here the business lists its strengths, weaknesses, opportunities and threats. p. 297

**Target costing**  Where the business starts with the projected selling price and from it deduces the target cost per unit which must be met to enable the company to meet its profit objectives. p. 116

**Total cost**  The sum of the variable and fixed costs of pursuing some activity. p. 42

**Total life-cycle costing**  Paying attention to all of the costs which will be incurred during the entire life of a product or service. p. 116

**Transfer pricing**  The activity of setting prices at which products or services will be transferred from one division of the business to another division of the same business. p. 284

**Understandability**  The requirement that accounting information should be understood by those for whom the information is primarily compiled. Lack of understandability will limit the usefulness of accounting information. p. 6

**Value drivers**  The factors that are seen in shareholder value analysis as being key in generating shareholder value. p. 311

**Variable cost**  A cost which varies according to the volume of activity. pp. 37 and 287

**Variance**  The financial effect, usually on the budgeted profit, of the particular factor under consideration being more or less than budgeted. p. 163

**Variance analysis**  Carrying out calculations to find the area of the business's operations which has caused the budgets not to have been met. p. 170

**Working capital**  Current assets less current liabilities (creditors due within one year). p. 234

**Zero-base budgeting (ZBB)**  An approach to budgeting, based on the philosophy that all spending needs to be justified annually and that each budget should start as a clean sheet. p. 139

# Solutions to self-assessment questions

## 2.1 JB Limited

(a)

| | £ | |
|---|---|---|
| Material M1 | | |
| 1,200 @ £5.50 | 6,600 | The original cost is irrelevant since any stock used will need to be replaced |
| Material P2 | | |
| 800 @ £2.00 (that is, £3.60 – £1.60) | 1,600 | The best alternative use of this material is as a substitute for P4 – an effective opportunity cost of £2.00/kg |
| Part no. 678 | | |
| 400 @ £50 | 20,000 | |
| Labour | | |
| Skilled 2,000 @ £6 | 12,000 | The effective cost is £6/hour |
| Unskilled 2,000 @ £5 | 10,000 | |
| Overheads | 3,200 | It is only the additional cost which is relevant, the method of apportioning total overheads is not relevant |
| Total relevant cost | 53,400 | |
| Potential revenue | | |
| 400 @ £150 | 60,000 | |

Clearly, on the basis of the information available it would be beneficial for the company to undertake the contract.

(b) There is an almost infinite number of possible answers to this part of the question, including:

- If material P2 had not been in stock, it may be that it would not be possible to buy it in and still leave the contract as a beneficial one. In this case the company may be unhappy about accepting a price under the particular conditions that apply, which could not be accepted under other conditions.
- Will the replacement for the skilled worker be able to do the normal work of that person to the necessary standard?
- Is JB Limited confident that the additional unskilled employee can be made redundant at the end of this contract without cost to itself?

### 3.1 Khan Ltd

(a) The break-even point if only product A were made would be:

$$\frac{\text{Fixed costs}}{\text{Sales revenue per unit} - \text{Variable cost per unit}}$$

$$= \frac{£40,000}{£30 - (15 + 6)} = 4,445 \text{ units (a year)}$$

(Strictly it is 4,444.44, but 4,445 is the smallest number that must be produced to avoid a loss.)

(b)

|  | A £/unit | B £/unit | C £/unit |
|---|---|---|---|
| Selling price | 30 | 45 | 20 |
| Variable materials | (15) | (18) | (10) |
| Variable production costs | (6) | (16) | (5) |
| Contribution | 9 | 11 | 5 |
| Time on machines (hr/unit) | 2 | 3 | 1 |
| Contribution/hour on machines | £4.50 | £3.67 | £5.00 |
| Order of priority | 2nd | 3rd | 1st |

(c)

|  | Hours |  | Contribution £ |
|---|---|---|---|
| Produce: |  |  |  |
| 5,000 product C using | 5,000 | generating (that is 5,000 × £5) | 25,000 |
| 2,500 product A using | 5,000 | generating (that is 2,500 × £9) | 22,500 |
|  | 10,000 |  | 47,500 |
|  |  | Less fixed costs | 40,000 |
|  |  | Profit | 7,500 |

Leaving a demand for 500 units of product A and 2,000 units of product B unsatisfied.

### 4.1 Hector and Co. Ltd

(a) Job costing basis

|  |  |  | £ |
|---|---|---|---|
| Materials: | Metal wire | 1,000 × 2 × £2.20 | 4,400 |
|  | Fabric | 1,000 × 0.5 × £1.00 | 500 |
| Labour: | Skilled | 1,000 × (10/60) × £7.50 | 1,250 |
|  | Unskilled | 1,000 × (5/60) × £5.00 | 417 |
| Overheads |  | 1,000 × (15/60) × (50,000/12,500) | 1,000 |
| Total cost |  |  | 7,567 |
| *Add* profit loading |  | 12.5% thereof | 946 |
| Total tender price |  |  | 8,513 |

(b) Minimum contract price (relevant cost basis)

|  |  |  | £ |
|---|---|---|---|
| Materials: | Metal wire | 1,000 × 2 × £2.50 (replacement cost) | 5,000 |
|  | Fabric | 1,000 × 0.50 × £0.40 (scrap value) | 200 |
| Labour: | Skilled | (there is no effective cost of skilled staff) | – |
|  | Unskilled | 1,000 × 5/60 × £5.00 | 417 |
| Minimum tender price | | | 5,617 |

The difference between the two prices is partly that the relevant costing approach tends to look to the future, partly that it considers opportunity costs, and partly that the job-costing basis total has a profit loading.

### 5.1 Psilis Ltd

(a) Full cost (present basis)

|  | Basic £ |  | Super £ |  |
|---|---|---|---|---|
| Direct labour (all £5/hour) | 20.00 | (4 hours) | 30.00 | (6 hours) |
| Direct material | 15.00 |  | 20.00 |  |
| Overheads | 18.20 | (£4.55* × 4) | 27.30 | (£4.55* × 6) |
|  | 53.20 |  | 77.30 |  |

* Total direct labour hours worked = (40,000 × 4) + (10,000 × 6) = 220,000 hours. Overhead recovery rate = £1,000,000/220,000 = £4.55.

Thus the selling prices are currently:

| Basic: | £53.20 + 25% = £66.50 |
|---|---|
| Super: | £77.30 + 25% = £96.63 |

(b) Full cost (activity basis)
Here, the cost of each cost-driving activity is apportioned between total production of the two products.

| Activity | Cost £000 | Basis of apportionment | Basic £000 | | Super £000 | |
|---|---|---|---|---|---|---|
| Machine set-ups | 280 | Number of set-ups | 56 | (20/100) | 224 | (80/100) |
| Quality inspection | 220 | Number of inspections | 55 | (500/2,000) | 165 | (1,500/2,000) |
| Sales order processing | 240 | Number of orders processed | 72 | (1,500/5,000) | 168 | (3,500/5,000) |
| General production | 260 | Machine-hours | 182 | (350/500) | 78 | (150/500) |
| Total | 1,000 | | 365 | | 635 | |

The overheads per unit are:

$$\text{Basic:} \quad \frac{£365,000}{40,000} = £9.13$$

$$\text{Super:} \quad \frac{£635,000}{10,000} = £63.50$$

Thus on an activity basis the full costs are as follows:

| | Basic £ | | Super £ | |
|---|---|---|---|---|
| Direct labour (all £5/hour) | 20.00 | (4 hours) | 30.00 | (6 hours) |
| Direct material | 15.00 | | 20.00 | |
| Overheads | 9.13 | | 63.50 | |
| Full cost | 44.13 | | 113.50 | |
| Current selling price | £66.50 | | £96.63 | |

(c) It seems that the Supers are being sold for less than they cost to produce. If the price cannot be increased, there is a very strong case for abandoning this product. At the same time, the Basics are very profitable to the extent that it may be worth considering lowering the price to attract more sales.

The fact that the overhead costs can be related to activities and, more specifically, to products does not mean that abandoning Super production would lead to immediate overhead cost savings. For example, it may not be possible or desirable to dismiss machine-setting staff overnight. It would certainly rarely be possible to release factory space occupied by machine setters and make immediate cost savings. Nevertheless, in the medium term these costs can be avoided and it may be sensible to do so.

### 6.1 Antonio Ltd

(a) (i) Raw materials stock budget for the six months ending 31 December (physical quantities):

| | July units | Aug units | Sept units | Oct units | Nov units | Dec units |
|---|---|---|---|---|---|---|
| Opening stock (Current month's production) | 500 | 600 | 600 | 700 | 750 | 750 |
| Purchases (Balancing figure) | 600 | 600 | 700 | 750 | 750 | 750 |
| | 1,100 | 1,200 | 1,300 | 1,450 | 1,500 | 1,500 |
| Less Issues to production (From question) | 500 | 600 | 600 | 700 | 750 | 750 |
| Closing stock (Next month's production) | 600 | 600 | 700 | 750 | 750 | 750 |

Raw materials' stock budget for the six months ending 31 December (in financial terms), that is, the physical quantities × £8:

|  | July £ | Aug £ | Sept £ | Oct £ | Nov £ | Dec £ |
|---|---|---|---|---|---|---|
| Opening stock | 4,000 | 4,800 | 4,800 | 5,600 | 6,000 | 6,000 |
| Purchases | 4,800 | 4,800 | 5,600 | 6,000 | 6,000 | 6,000 |
|  | 8,800 | 9,600 | 10,400 | 11,600 | 12,000 | 12,000 |
| Less Issues to production | 4,000 | 4,800 | 4,800 | 5,600 | 6,000 | 6,000 |
| Closing stock | 4,800 | 4,800 | 5,600 | 6,000 | 6,000 | 6,000 |

(ii) Creditors budget for the six months ending 31 December:

|  | July £ | Aug £ | Sept £ | Oct £ | Nov £ | Dec £ |
|---|---|---|---|---|---|---|
| Opening balance (Current month's payment) | 4,000 | 4,800 | 4,800 | 5,600 | 6,000 | 6,000 |
| Purchases (From raw materials stock budget) | 4,800 | 4,800 | 5,600 | 6,000 | 6,000 | 6,000 |
|  | 8,800 | 9,600 | 10,400 | 11,600 | 12,000 | 12,000 |
| Less Payments | 4,000 | 4,800 | 4,800 | 5,600 | 6,000 | 6,000 |
| Closing balance (Next month's payment) | 4,800 | 4,800 | 5,600 | 6,000 | 6,000 | 6,000 |

(iii) Cash budget for the six months ending 31 December:

|  | July £ | Aug £ | Sept £ | Oct £ | Nov £ | Dec £ |
|---|---|---|---|---|---|---|
| **Inflows** |  |  |  |  |  |  |
| Receipts: |  |  |  |  |  |  |
| Debtors (40% of sales of two months previous) | 2,800 | 3,200 | 3,200 | 4,000 | 4,800 | 5,200 |
| Cash sales (60% of current month's sales) | 4,800 | 6,000 | 7,200 | 7,800 | 8,400 | 9,600 |
| Total inflows | 7,600 | 9,200 | 10,400 | 11,800 | 13,200 | 14,800 |
| **Outflows** |  |  |  |  |  |  |
| Creditors (from creditors budget) | (4,000) | (4,800) | (4,800) | (5,600) | (6,000) | (6,000) |
| Direct costs | (3,000) | (3,600) | (3,600) | (4,200) | (4,500) | (4,500) |
| Advertising | (1,000) | – | – | (1,500) | – | – |
| Overheads: 80% | (1,280) | (1,280) | (1,280) | (1,280) | (1,600) | (1,600) |
| 20% | (280) | (320) | (320) | (320) | (320) | (400) |
| New plant |  |  | (2,200) | (2,200) | (2,200) |  |
| Total outflows | (9,560) | (10,000) | (12,200) | (15,100) | (14,620) | (12,500) |
| Net inflows (outflows) | (1,960) | (800) | (1,800) | (3,300) | (1,420) | 2,300 |
| Balance c/f | 5,540 | 4,740 | 2,940 | (360) | (1,780) | 520 |

The balances carried forward are deduced by deducting the deficit (net outflows) for the month from (or adding the surplus for the month to) the previous month's balance.

Note how budgets are linked; in this case the stock budget to the creditors budget and the creditors budget to the cash budget.

(b) The following are possible means of relieving the cash shortages revealed by the budget:

- Make a higher proportion of sales on a cash basis.
- Collect the money from debtors more promptly, for example during the month following the sale.
- Hold lower stocks, both of raw materials and of finished goods.
- Increase the creditor payment period.
- Delay the payments for advertising.
- Obtain more credit for the overhead costs; at present only 20 per cent are on credit.
- Delay the payments for the new plant.

## 7.1 Toscanini Ltd

(a) and (b)

| | Budget | | | Actual | |
|---|---|---|---|---|---|
| | Original | Flexed | | Actual | |
| Output (units) (production and sales) | 4,000 | 3,500 | | 3,500 | |
| | £ | £ | | £ | |
| Sales | 16,000 | 14,000 | | 13,820 | |
| Raw materials | (3,840) | (3,360) | (1,400 kg) | (3,420) | (1,425 kg) |
| Labour | (3,200) | (2,800) | (700 hr) | (2,690) | (690 hr) |
| Fixed overheads | (4,800) | (4,800) | | (4,900) | |
| Operating profit | 4,160 | 3,040 | | 2,810 | |

| | £ | | Manager accountable |
|---|---|---|---|
| Sales volume variance (4,160 − 3,040) | (1,120) | (A) | Sales |
| Sales price variance (14,000 − 13,820) | (180) | (A) | Sales |
| Materials price variance (1,425 × 2.40) − 3,420 | 0 | | – |
| Materials usage variance [(3,500 × 0.4) − 1,425] × £2.40 | (60) | (A) | Production |
| Labour rate variance (690 × £4) − 2,690 | 70 | (F) | Personnel |
| Labour efficiency variance [(3,500 × 0.20) − 690] × £4 | 40 | (F) | Production |
| Fixed overhead spending (4,800 − 4,900) | (100) | (A) | Various depending on the nature of the overheads |
| Total net variances | (1,350) | (A) | |
| Budgeted profit | 4,160 | | |
| Less Total net variance | 1,350 | | |
| Actual profit | 2,810 | | |

(c) Feasible explanations include the following:

- Sales volume  Unanticipated fall in world demand would account for $400 \times £2.24 = £896$ of this variance. The remainder is probably caused by ineffective marketing, though a lack of availability of stock to sell may be a reason.
- Sales price  Ineffective selling seems the only logical reason.
- Materials usage  Inefficient usage of material, perhaps because of poor performance by labour or substandard materials.
- Labour rate  Less overtime worked or lower production bonuses paid as a result of lower volume of activity.
- Labour efficiency  More effective working, perhaps because fewer hours were worked than planned.
- Overheads  Ineffective control of overheads.

(d) Clearly, not all of the sales volume variance can be attributed to poor marketing, given a 10 per cent reduction in demand.

It will probably be useful to distinguish between that part of the variance that arose from the shortfall in general demand (a planning variance) and a volume variance, which is more fairly attributable to the manager concerned. Thus accountability will be more fairly imposed.

|  | £ |
| --- | --- |
| Planning variance $(10\% \times 4,000) \times £2.24$ | 896 |
| 'New' sales volume variance | |
| $\quad [4,000 - (10\% \times 4,000) - 3,500] \times £2.24$ | 224 |
| Original sales volume variance | 1,120 |

## 8.1 Beacon Chemicals plc

(a) Relevant cash flows are as follows:

| | Year 0 £000 | Year 1 £000 | Year 2 £000 | Year 3 £000 | Year 4 £000 | Year 5 £000 |
| --- | --- | --- | --- | --- | --- | --- |
| Sales revenue | – | 80 | 120 | 144 | 100 | 64 |
| Loss of contribution | | (15) | (15) | (15) | (15) | (15) |
| Variable costs | | (40) | (50) | (48) | (30) | (32) |
| Fixed costs (Note 1) | | (8) | (8) | (8) | (8) | (8) |
| Operating cash flows | | 17 | 47 | 73 | 47 | 9 |
| Working capital | (30) | | | | | 30 |
| Capital cost | (100) | | | | | |
| Net relevant cash flows | (130) | 17 | 47 | 73 | 47 | 39 |

*Notes:*

1. Only the fixed costs that are incremental to the project (only existing because of the project) are relevant. Depreciation is irrelevant because it is not a cash flow.

2. The research and development cost is irrelevant since it has been spent irrespective of the decision on X14 production.

(b) The payback period is as follows:

|  | Year 0 £000 | Year 1 £000 | Year 2 £000 | Year 3 £000 |
|---|---|---|---|---|
| Cumulative cash flows | (130) | (113) | (66) | 7 |

Thus the equipment will have repaid the initial investment by the end of the third year of operations.

(c) The net present value is as follows:

|  | Year 0 £000 | Year 1 £000 | Year 2 £000 | Year 3 £000 | Year 4 £000 | Year 5 £000 |
|---|---|---|---|---|---|---|
| Discount factor | 1.00 | 0.926 | 0.857 | 0.794 | 0.735 | 0.681 |
| Present value | (130) | 15.74 | 40.28 | 57.96 | 34.55 | 26.56 |
| Net present value | 45.09 | (that is the sum of the present values for years 0 to 5) | | | | |

### 9.1 Williams Wholesalers Ltd

|  | £ | £ |
|---|---|---|
| Existing level of debtors (£4m × 70/365) |  | 767,123 |
| New level of debtors: £2m × 80/365 | 438,356 |  |
| £2m × 30/365 | 164,384 | 602,740 |
| Reduction in debtors |  | 164,383 (say £165,000) |
| **Costs and benefits of policy** |  |  |
| Cost of discount (£2m × 2%) |  | 40,000 |
| Less Savings |  |  |
| Interest payable (£165,000 × 13%) | 21,450 |  |
| Administration costs | 6,000 |  |
| Bad debts (20,000 − 10,000) | 10,000 | 37,450 |
| **Net cost of policy** |  | 2,550 |

The above calculations reveal that the company will be worse off by offering the discounts.

### 10.1 Andromeda International plc

(a)

| Jupiter | Mars |
|---|---|
| (i) (260/1,330) × 100% | (50/1,380) × 100% |
| = 19.5% | = 3.6% |
| (ii) (275/1,430[a]) × 100% | (80/1,680[b]) × 100% |
| = 19.2% | = 4.8% |

[a] The profit will increase by £15,000 ((£250,000 × 0.30) − £60,000). Assets will increase by £90,000.

[b] Profit will increase by £30,000 (£90,000 − £60,000 depreciation). Assets will increase by £300,000.

(b) The investment opportunity for Jupiter division will result in an ROI of 16.7 per cent (i.e. 15/90) which is above the cost of capital for the company. As a result central management is likely to view the opportunity favourably. However, the effect of taking the opportunity will be to lower the existing ROI of the division.

This may mean that the divisional manager will be reluctant to take on the opportunity.

The investment opportunity for the Mars division provides an ROI of 10 per cent (i.e. 30/300) which is below the cost of capital of the company. As a result central management would not wish for this opportunity to be taken up. However, the opportunity will increase the ROI of the Mars division overall and, as a result, the divisional manager may be keen to invest in the opportunity.

There may be reasons for investing in each opportunity which are not given in the question but which may be compelling. For example, it may be necessary to introduce the new product into the Jupiter division in order to ensure that the range of products offered to customers is complete. Failure to do so may result in a decline in overall sales. It may be that investment in the Mars division is important to ensure that productivity over the longer term does not slip behind that of its competitors.

(c) Ideally, ROI should be calculated using the current value of the assets employed. By so doing we can see whether or not the returns are satisfactory as compared with the alternative use of those resources. Using costs (or cost less accumulated depreciation) as the basis for ROI will be measuring current performance against past outlays.

Gross book value fails to take account of the age of the assets held. It may be that the assets are all near the end of their useful lives and are, therefore, highly depreciated. In such a case, the gross book value may produce a low ROI and may provide too high a 'hurdle' rate for new investment opportunities. Gross book value in such circumstances would also provide a poor approximation to the current value of the assets.

Using net book value would overcome the problem mentioned above but, during a period of inflation, this measure may be significantly lower than the current value of the assets employed. In addition, there is the problem that ROI can improve over time simply because of the declining value of the assets employed. Divisional managers may be less inclined to replace old assets where this will lead to a decline in ROI.

**11.1** The student is talking about strategic planning, not about assessment of strategic change. Strategic planning is concerned with going through a process of identifying the aim or mission of the business, turning them into objectives, assessing the current position of the business (perhaps through a SWOT analysis) and planning strategies to achieve the objectives, given the current position.

On the other hand, assessing strategic change is carrying out an analysis, not unlike variance analysis, to investigate the success of a new strategy, relative to the old one, following the first operating period after the change.

Customer profitability analysis is concerned with assessing how profitable particular customers are to one's own business, as customers. This involves preparing a 'mini P and L account' for each customer or, perhaps, group of customers. Here all of the costs of providing the business's goods or services to the customer are taken into account. This includes not just the cost of providing the basic goods or service, but also other costs that probably vary between customers, such as delivery costs, warehousing (stores) costs and the costs of providing trade credit. The student is wrong; how profitable the customer is as a business is not the subject of customer profitability analysis, though this would be of interest to the supplying business.

SVA is an approach to management that focuses on the generally accepted business objective of maximisation of shareholder wealth. It does this by identifying a number of 'value drivers' that are seen as key to delivering value for shareholders. Plans can be made in respect of each of these key value drivers. These plans can be used as the basis of day-to-day management targets, against which managers can be assessed. SVA has little to do with the preferences of individual shareholders for dividends rather than retained profits.

EVA stands for 'economic value added', not 'equity value analysis'. It tries to measure the extent to which a period of trading has led to value being created for shareholders. It tries to assess whether the profit generated by the business exceeds the minimum required to hold the shareholders' wealth steady. The latter is based on the shareholders' required return and a fair assessment of the value of the assets in use in generating that profit. Though SVA and EVA are quite closely linked, in that they both focus on achieving shareholder wealth maximisation, they approach this in rather different ways and are certainly not the same thing.

The 'balanced scorecard' is certainly not another name for the balance sheet. It is an attempt to provide financial and non-financial targets for managing the business. It seeks to strike a balance between financial and non-financial, external and internal and predictive and historic factors. The balance sheet deals only with financial matters and has no connection with the balanced scorecard, except that both use the word 'balance' in their names.

# Solutions to selected exercises

## Chapter 2

**2.1** Lombard Ltd

Relevant costs of undertaking the contract are:

|  | £ |
|---|---:|
| Equipment costs | 200,000 |
| Component X (20,000 × 4 × £5) | 400,000 |
| Component Y (20,000 × 3 × £8) | 480,000 |
| Additional costs (20,000 × £8) | 160,000 |
|  | 1,240,000 |
| Revenue from the contract (20,000 × £80) | 1,600,000 |

Thus from a purely financial point of view the project is acceptable. (Note that there is no relevant labour cost since the staff concerned will be paid irrespective of whether the contract is undertaken or not.)

**2.2** The local authority

(a) **'Normal' monthly surplus**

Revenues per performance for a full house:

|  | £ |
|---|---:|
| 200 @ £6 = | 1,200 |
| 500 @ £4 = | 2,000 |
| 300 @ £3 = | 900 |
|  | 4,100 |

|  |  | £ | £ |
|---|---|---:|---:|
| Ticket revenues at 50% capacity for 20 performances (£4,100 × 50% × 20) |  |  | 41,000 |
| Refreshment sales |  |  | 3,880 |
| Programme advertising |  |  | 3,360 |
|  |  |  | 48,240 |
| *Less* | Full-time staff | 4,800 |  |
|  | Artistes | 17,600 |  |
|  | Costumes | 2,800 |  |
|  | Scenery | 1,650 |  |
|  | Heating and light | 5,150 |  |
|  | Administration costs | 8,000 |  |
|  | Casual staff | 1,760 |  |
|  | Refreshments | 1,180 |  |
|  |  |  | 42,940 |
| 'Normal' surplus |  |  | 5,300 |

**Touring company surplus**

Revenues per performance for a full house:

$$£$$

$$200 \text{ @ } £5.50 = 1,100$$
$$500 \text{ @ } £3.50 = 1,750$$
$$300 \text{ @ } £2.50 = \underline{\phantom{0}750}$$
$$\underline{3,600}$$

|  |  | £ | £ |
|---|---|---|---|
| Ticket revenues ($£3,600 \times 10 \times 50\%$) |  |  | 18,000 |
| ($£3,600 \times 15 \times \frac{2}{3} \times 50\%$) |  |  | 18,000 |
| Refreshment sales |  |  | 3,880 |
| Programme advertising |  |  | 3,360 |
|  |  |  | 43,240 |
| Less | Full-time staff | 4,800 |  |
|  | Artistes | 17,600 |  |
|  | Heating and light | 5,150 |  |
|  | Administration costs | 8,000 |  |
|  | Refreshments | 1,180 |  |
|  |  |  | 36,730 |
| Touring company surplus |  |  | 6,510 |

Thus on financial grounds, the approach by the touring company will be accepted.

(b) (i) With only the 10 full performances, the deficit for the month would be:

£18,000 – 6,510 = £11,490 (that is, £18,000 less than the expected surplus)

If $y$ is the required occupancy rate, then:

$$£3,600 \times 15 \times y \times 50\% = £11,490$$

$$y = \frac{11,490}{3,600 \times 15 \times 50\%} = 42.56 \text{ per cent occupancy}$$

Thus, to avoid a deficit there would need to be a 42.56 per cent occupancy rate for the other 15 performances.

(ii) With only the ten full performances the deficit for the month, relative to a 'normal' month, would be

£11,490 + 5,300 = £16,790 (that is,
a deficit of £11,490 instead of a surplus of £5,300)

If $y$ is the required occupancy rate, then:

$$£3,600 \times 15 \times y \times 50\% = £16,790$$

$$y = \frac{16,790}{3,600 \times 15 \times 50\%} = 62.19 \text{ per cent occupancy}$$

Thus the occupancy rate for the other 15 performances would need to be 62.19 per cent to generate the same surplus as in a normal month.

(c) Other possible factors to consider include:

■ The reliability of the estimations, including the assumption that programme and refreshment sales will not be altered by the level of occupancy.

- A desire to offer theatre goers the opportunity to see another group of players.
- Dangers of loss of morale of staff not employed, or employed to do other than their usual work.

**2.3** Andrews and Co. Ltd

Minimum contract price

| | | | £ |
|---|---|---|---:|
| *Materials* | Steel core: | 10,000 × £2.10 | 21,000 |
| | Plastic: | 10,000 × 0.10 × 0.10 | 100 |
| *Labour* | Skilled: | | – |
| | Unskilled: | 10,000 × 5/60 × £5 | 4,167 |
| Minimum tender price | | | 25,267 |

**2.6** The local education authority

(a) One-off financial net benefits of closing:

| | No schools | D only | A and B | A and C |
|---|---:|---:|---:|---:|
| Capacity reduction | 0 | 800 | 700 | 800 |
| | £m | £m | £m | £m |
| Property developer (A) | – | – | 14.0 | 14.0 |
| Shopping complex (B) | – | – | 8.0 | – |
| Property developer (D) | – | 9.0 | – | – |
| Safety (C) | (3.0) | (3.0) | (3.0) | – |
| Adapt facilities | | (1.8) | | |
| Total | (3.0) | 4.2 | 19.0 | 14.0 |
| Ranking based on total one-off benefits | 4 | 3 | 1 | 2 |

(Note that all past costs of buying and improving the schools are irrelevant.)

Recurrent financial net benefits of closing:

| | No schools £m | D only £m | A and B £m | A and C £m |
|---|---:|---:|---:|---:|
| Rent (C) | – | – | – | 0.3 |
| Administrators | – | 0.2 | 0.4 | 0.4 |
| Total | – | 0.2 | 0.4 | 0.7 |
| Ranking based on total of recurrent benefits | 4 | 3 | 2 | 1 |

On the basis of the financial figures alone, closure of either A and B or A and C looks best. It is not possible to add the one-off and the recurring costs directly, but the large one-off cost saving associated with closing schools A and B makes this option look attractive. (In Chapter 8 we shall see that it is possible to add one-off and recurring costs in a way that should lead to sensible conclusions.)

(b) The costs of acquiring and improving the schools in the past are past costs or sunk costs. The costs of employing the chief education officer is a future cost, but irrelevant because it is not differential between outcomes, it is a common cost.

(c) There are many other factors, some of a non-quantifiable nature. These include:

- Accuracy of projections of capacity requirements.
- Locality of existing schools relative to where potential pupils live.
- Political acceptability of selling schools to property developers.
- Importance of purely financial issues in making the final decision.
- The quality of the replacement sporting facilities compared with those at school D.
- Political acceptability of staff redundancies.
- Possible savings/costs of employing fewer teachers, which might be relevant if economies of scale are available by having fewer schools.
- Staff morale.

**2.7** Rob Otics Ltd

(a) The minimum price for the proposed contract would be:

|  | £ |
|---|---:|
| Materials | |
| Component X   $2 \times 8 \times £180$ | 2,880 |
| Component Y | 0 |
| Component Z   $[(75 + 32) \times £20] - (75 \times £25)$ | 265 |
| Other miscellaneous items | 250 |
| Labour | |
| Assembly   $(25 + 24 + 23 + 22 + 21 + 20 + 19 + 18) \times £48*$ | 8,256 |
| Inspection   $8 \times 6 \times £18$ | 864 |
| Total | 12,515 |

*£60 − £12 = £48.

Labour is an irrelevant cost here because it will be incurred irrespective of which work the staff do. Thus the minimum price is £12,515.

(b) Other factors include:

- Competitive state of the market.
- The fact that the above figure is unique to the particular circumstances at the time – for example, having component Y in stock but having no use for it. Any subsequent order might have to take account of an outlay cost.
- Breaking even (that is, just covering the costs) on a contract will not fulfil the company's objective.
- Charging a low price may cause marketing problems. Other customers may resent the low price for this contract. The current enquirer may expect a similar price in future.

## Chapter 3

**3.1** Alpha, Beta and Gamma

(a) and (b) Deduce the total contribution per product and deduce the contribution per £1 of labour and hence the relative profitability of the three products, given a shortage of labour. Strictly, we should use the contribution per hour, but we do not know the number of hours involved. Since all labour is paid at the same rate, using labour cost will give us the same order of priority as using hours.

|  | Alpha<br>£ | Beta<br>£ | Gamma<br>£ |
|---|---|---|---|
| Variable costs: | | | |
| Materials | (6,000) | (4,000) | (5,000) |
| Labour | (9,000) | (6,000) | (12,000) |
| Expenses | (3,000) | (2,000) | (2,000) |
| Total variable cost | (18,000) | (12,000) | (19,000) |
| Sales | 39,000 | 29,000 | 33,000 |
| Contribution | 21,000 | 17,000 | 14,000 |
| Contribution per £ of labour | 2.333 | 2.833 | 1.167 |
| Order of profitability | 2nd | 1st | 3rd |

Since 50 per cent of each budget (and, therefore, £13,500 of labour) is committed, only £6,500 (£20,000 – £13,500) of labour is left uncommitted. The £6,500 should be deployed as:

|  | £ |
|---|---|
| Beta | 3,000 |
| Alpha | 3,500 |
|  | 6,500 |

Total labour committed to each product and resultant profit are as follows:

|  | Alpha<br>£ | Beta<br>£ | Gamma<br>£ | Total<br>£ |
|---|---|---|---|---|
| Labour | | | | |
| 50% of budget | 4,500 | 3,000 | 6,000 | |
| Allocated above | 3,500 | 3,000 | – | |
| Total | 8,000 | 6,000 | 6,000 | 20,000 |
| Contribution per £ of labour | 2.333 | 2.833 | 1.167 | |
| Contribution per product* | 18,664 | 16,998 | 7,002 | 42,664 |
| Less Fixed costs | | | | 33,000 |
| Maximum profit (after rounding) | | | | 9,664 |

* The contribution per £ of labour × total labour.

(c) Other factors that might be considered include the following:

■ Could all of the surplus labour be used to produce Betas (the most efficient user of labour)? In other words, could the business sell more than £29,000 of this product? It might be worth reducing the price of the Beta, though still keeping the contribution per £1 of labour above £2.33, in order to expand sales.
■ Could the commitment to 50 per cent of budget on each product be dropped in favour of producing the maximum of the higher-yielding products?
■ Could another source of labour be found?
■ Could the labour-intensive part of the work be subcontracted?

**3.2** (a) Lannion and Co.

|  | October | November |
|---|---|---|
| Sales (units of the service) | 200 | 300 |
| Sales (£) | 5,000 | 7,500 |
| Costs (balancing figure, £) | (4,000) | (5,300) |
| Operating profit (£) | 1,000 | 2,200 |

The increase in output of 100 units (300 − 200) gives rise to additional costs of £1,300 (£5,300 − £4,000) or £13 per unit (£1,300/100). This is the variable cost. Since there were no price changes, the £1,300 can only have arisen from additional sales.

We do not know how much of each month's costs figure is fixed and how much is variable, but we can work it out. For October, total variable cost = 200 × £13 = £2,600. Thus, the fixed cost must be £1,400 (£4,000 − £2,600). This can be checked using the November figures: total variable cost = 300 × £13 = £3,900; fixed cost = £5,300 − £3,900 = £1,400. Fixed costs, by definition, must be the same each month.

Sales revenue per unit = £5,000/200 or 7,500/300 = £25. Therefore:

$$\text{Break-even point} = \text{Fixed cost/contribution} = \frac{£1,400}{£25 - £13}$$

$$= 116.67, \text{ or } 117 \text{ units per month}$$

(b) Knowledge of the break-even point is useful because it enables management to judge how close the planned level of activity is to the point at which no profit will be made. This enables some assessment of riskiness to be made.

**3.3** The hotel group

(a) The variable element and, by implication, the fixed element of the hotel's costs can be deduced by comparing any two quarters, for example:

| Quarter | Sales £000 | Profit(loss) £000 | Total cost £000 |
|---|---|---|---|
| 1 | 400 | (280) | 680 |
| 2 | 1,200 | 360 | 840 |
| Difference | 800 |  | 160 |

Thus the variable element of the sales price is 20 per cent (160/800). Now:

The fixed costs for quarter 1 = Total costs − Variable costs

= £680,000 − (20% × 400,000) = £600,000

To check that this calculation is correct and consistent for all four quarters, we can 'predict' the total costs for the other three quarters and then check the predicted results against those which can be deduced from the question, as follows:

Quarter 2

Total cost = fixed costs + variable costs

= £600,000 + (20% × 1,200,000)

= £840,000    Agrees with the question

Quarter 3

Total cost = fixed costs + variable costs

$= £600,000 + (20\% \times 1,600,000)$

$= £920,000$      Agrees with the question

Quarter 4

Total cost = fixed costs + variable costs

$= £600,000 + (20\% \times 800,000)$

$= £760,000$      Agrees with the question

Had the fixed and variable elements been deduced graphically, the consistency of the fixed and variable cost elements over the four quarters would have been obvious because a straight line would have emerged.

The provisional results for this year are as follows:

| | Total | Per visitor (50,000 visitors) |
|---|---|---|
| | £000 | £ |
| Sales | 4,000 | 80 |
| Variable costs (20% of sales) | (800) | (16) |
| Contribution | 3,200 | 64 |
| Fixed costs (that is fixed costs per quarter × 4) | (2,400) | (48) |
| Profit | 800 | 16 |

(b) (i) At the same level of occupancy as this year and incorporating the increase in variable costs of 10 per cent, the sales revenue for next year will need to be:

| | £000 |
|---|---|
| Fixed costs | 2,400 |
| Variable costs (800,000 × 110%) | 880 |
| Total costs | 3,280 |
| Target profit | 1,000 |
| Sales target | 4,280 |

Hence the sales revenue per visitor is:

$$\frac{£4,280,000}{50,000} = £85.60$$

(ii) If the sales revenue per visitor remains at the current rate, the contribution per visitor will be:

$$£80 - (£16 \times 110\%) = £62.40$$

To cover the fixed costs and the target profit, would take:

$$\frac{£2,400,000 + 1,000,000}{£62.40} \approx 54,487 \text{ visitors}$$

(c) The major assumptions of profit–volume analysis are that costs can be analysed as those that vary with the volume of activity (and with that factor alone) and those that are totally unaffected by volume changes. A further assumption is that variable costs vary at a steady rate (straight-line relationship) with volume.

These assumptions are unlikely to be strictly valid in reality. Variable costs are unlikely to vary in a truly straight-line manner relative to volumes. For example, at higher levels of output there may be economies of scale in purchasing (for example, bulk discounts) or the opportunity to use materials or labour more effectively. On the other hand, the opposite may be the case. At higher levels of output, cost per unit increases because a shortage may be created by the higher output level.

**3.5** Products A, B and C

(a) Total time required on cutting machines is:

$$(2,500 \times 1.0) + (3,400 \times 1.0) + (5,100 \times 0.5) = 8,450 \text{ hours}$$

Total time available on cutting machines is 5,000 hours. Therefore this is a limiting factor.

Total time required on assembling machines is:

$$(2,500 \times 0.5) + (3,400 \times 1.0) + (5,100 \times 0.5) = 7,200 \text{ hours}$$

Total time available on assembling machines is 8,000 hours. Therefore this is not a limiting factor.

| | A (per unit) £ | B (per unit) £ | C (per unit) £ |
|---|---|---|---|
| Selling price | 25 | 30 | 18 |
| Variable materials | (12) | (13) | (10) |
| Variable production costs | (7) | (4) | (3) |
| Contribution | 6 | 13 | 5 |
| Time on cutting machines | 1.0 hour | 1.0 hour | 0.5 hour |
| Contribution per hour on cutting machines | £6 | £13 | £10 |
| Order of priority | 3rd | 1st | 2nd |

Therefore, produce:

| | |
|---|---|
| 3,400 product B using | 3,400 hours |
| 3,200 product C using | 1,600 hours |
| | 5,000 hours |

(b) Assuming that the company would make no saving in variable production costs by subcontracting, it would be worth paying up to the contribution per unit (£5) for product C, which would therefore be £5 × (5,100 − 3,200) = £9,500 in total.

Similarly it would be worth paying up to £6 per unit for product A – that is, £6 × 2,500 = £15,000 in total.

**3.6** Darmor Ltd

(a) Contribution per hour of unskilled labour of product A is:

$$\frac{(£30 - 6 - 2 - 12 - 3)}{(6/6)} = £7$$

Given the scarcity of skilled labour, if the management is to be indifferent between the products then the contribution per skilled-labour hour must be the same. Thus for product B the selling price must be:

$$[£7 \times (9/6)] + 9 + 4 + 25 + 7 = £55.50$$

(that is, the contribution plus the variable costs)
and for product C the selling price must be:

$$[£7 \times (3/6)] + 3 + 10 + 14 + 7 = £37.50$$

(b) The company could pay up to £13 an hour (£6 + £7) for additional hours of skilled labour. This is the potential contribution per hour, before taking account of the labour rate of £6 per hour.

## Chapter 4

| 4.1 | Offending phrase | Explanation |
|---|---|---|
| | 'necessary to divide the business up into departments' | This can be done but it will not always be beneficial to do so. Only in quite restricted circumstances will it give significantly different job costs. |
| | 'Fixed costs (or overheads)' | This implies that fixed costs and overheads are the same thing. They are not really connected with one another. 'Fixed' is to do with how costs behave as the level of output is raised or lowered, 'overheads' are to do with the extent to which costs can be directly measured in respect of a particular unit of output. Though it is true that many overheads are fixed, not all are. Also, direct labour is usually a fixed cost. |
| | | All of the other references to fixed and variable costs are wrong. The person should have referred to indirect and direct costs. |
| | 'Usually this is done on the basis of area' | Where overheads are apportioned to departments, they will be apportioned on some logical basis. For certain costs – for example, rent – the floor area may be the most logical; for others, such as machine maintenance costs, the floor area would be totally inappropriate. |
| | 'When the total fixed costs for each department have been identified, this will be divided by the number of hours that were worked' | Where overheads are dealt with on a departmental basis, they may be divided by the number of direct-labour hours to deduce a recovery rate. However, this is only one basis of applying overheads to jobs. For example, machine hours or some other basis may be more appropriate to the particular circumstances involved. |
| | 'It is essential that this approach is taken in order to deduce a selling price' | It is relatively unusual for the 'job cost' to be able to dictate the price at which the manufacturer can price its output. Job costing may have its uses, but setting prices is not usually one of them. |

**4.2** All three of the costing techniques listed in the question are means of deducing the full cost of some activity. The distinction between them lies essentially with the difference in the style of the production of the goods or services involved. Thus:

- *Job costing* is used where each unit of output, or 'job', differs from others produced by the same business. Because the jobs are not identical, it is not normally acceptable to those who are likely to use the cost information to treat the jobs as if they were identical. This means that costs need to be identified, job by job. For this purpose, costs fall into two categories: direct costs and indirect costs (or overheads).

    Direct costs are those that can be measured directly in respect of the specific job, such as the amount of labour that was directly applied to the job, or the amount of material that has been incorporated in it. To this must be added a share of the indirect costs. This is usually done by taking the total overheads for the period concerned and charging part of them to the job. This, in turn, is usually done according to some measure of the job's size and importance, relative to the other jobs done during the period. The number of direct-labour hours worked on the job is the most commonly used measure of size and/or importance.

    The main problem with job costing tends to be the method of charging indirect costs to jobs. Indirect costs, by definition, cannot be related directly to jobs and must, if full cost is to be deduced, be charged on a basis that is more or less arbitrary. If indirect costs accounted for a small proportion of the total, the arbitrariness of charging them would probably not matter. Indirect costs, in many cases, however, form the majority of total costs and so arbitrariness is a problem.

- *Process costing* is the approach taken where all output is of identical units. These units can be treated, therefore, as having identical cost. Sometimes a process costing approach is taken even where the units are not strictly identical. This is because process costing is much simpler and cheaper to apply than the only other option, namely job costing. Provided that users of the cost information are satisfied that treating units as identical is acceptable, the additional cost and effort of job costing is not justified.

    In process costing, the cost per unit of output is found by dividing total costs for the period by the total number of units produced in the period.

    The main problem with process costing tends to be that, at the beginning and end of any period, there will probably be partly completed units of output. An adjustment needs to made for this work in progress if the resulting cost unit figures are not to be distorted.

- *Batch costing* is really an extension of job costing. Batch costing tends to be used where production is in batches. A batch consists of more than one identical unit of output. The units of output differ from one batch to the next. For example, a clothing manufacturing business may produce 500 identical jackets in one batch, followed by a batch of 300 identical skirts in another batch.

    Each batch is costed as one job, using a job-costing approach. The full cost of each garment is then found by dividing the cost of the batch by the number of garments in the batch.

    The main problem of batch costing is exactly that of job costing, of which it is an extension: that of dealing with overheads.

**4.3** Bodgers Ltd

(a) The company predetermines the rate at which overheads are to be charged to jobs because, for most of the reasons that full costing information could be useful, costs usually need to be known either before the job is done or very soon afterwards.

The two main reasons why businesses identify full costs are for pricing decisions and for income-measurement purposes.

For pricing, the customer will usually want to know the price in advance of placing the order. Thus it is not possible to wait until all of the costs have been incurred, and are known, before the price can be deduced. Even where production is not for an identified customer, the business still needs to have some idea of whether it can produce the goods or service at a price that the market will bear.

In the context of income measurement, valuing work in progress is the purpose for which full costs are required. If managers and other users are to benefit as much as possible from accounting information, that information must speedily follow the end of the period to which it relates. This usually means that waiting to discover actual cost is not practical.

(b) Predetermining the rate at which overheads are charged to jobs requires that three judgements are made:

(i)   Predicting the overheads for the period concerned.

(ii)  Deciding on the basis of charging overheads to jobs (for example, rate per direct labour hour).

(iii) Predicting the number of units of the basis factor (for example, number of direct labour hours) which are expected to occur during the period concerned.

Judgements (i) and (iii) are difficult to make, but there will normally be some past experience to provide guidance. Judgement (ii) is purely a matter of opinion.

(c) The problems of using predetermined rates are really linked to the ability to predict (i) and (iii) in (b) above. The desired result is that the total of the overheads, but no more than this, become part of the cost of the various jobs worked on in the period. Only if (i) and (iii) are both accurately predicted will this happen, except by lucky coincidence. There is clearly the danger that jobs will either be undercharged or overcharged with overheads, relative to the total amount of overheads incurred during the period. In fact, it is almost certain that one of these two will happen to some extent simply because perfect prediction is virtually impossible. Minor errors will not matter, but major ones could well lead to bad decisions.

**4.6** Promptprint Ltd

(a) The budget may be summarised as:

| | £ | |
|---|---|---|
| Sales revenue | 196,000 | |
| Direct materials | (38,000) | |
| Direct labour | (32,000) | |
| Total overheads | (77,000) | (2,400 + 3,000 + 27,600 + 36,000 + 8,000) |
| Profit | 49,000 | |

The job may be priced on the basis that both overheads and profit should be apportioned to it on the basis of direct labour cost, as follows:

| | £ | |
|---|---|---|
| Direct materials | 4,000 | |
| Direct labour | 3,600 | |
| Overheads | 8,663 | (£77,000 × 3,600/32,000) |
| Profit | 5,513 | (£49,000 × 3,600/32,000) |
| | 21,776 | |

This answer assumes that variable overheads vary in proportion to direct labour cost.

Various other bases of charging overheads and profit loading the job could have been adopted. For example, materials cost could have been included (with direct labour) as the basis for profit-loading, or even apportioning overheads.

(b) This part of the question is, in effect, asking for comments on the validity of 'full cost-plus' pricing. This approach can be useful as an indicator of the effective long-run cost of doing the job. On the other hand, it fails to take account of relevant opportunity costs as well as the state of the market and other external factors. For example, it ignores the price that a competitor printing business may quote.

(c) Revised estimates of direct material costs for the job:

| | £ | |
|---|---|---|
| Paper grade 1 | 1,500 | (£1,200 × 125%) This stock needs to be replaced |
| Paper grade 2 | 0 | It has no opportunity cost value |
| Card | 510 | (£640 – 130: using the card on another job would save £640, but cost £130 to achieve that saving.) |
| Inks, etc. | 300 | This stock needs to be replaced |
| | 2,310 | |

---

**4.7** Bookdon plc

(a) To answer this question, we need first to allocate and apportion the overheads to product cost centres, as follows:

| | | | Department | | | |
|---|---|---|---|---|---|---|
| Cost | Basis of apportionment | Total | Machine shop | Fitting section | Canteen | Machine maintance section |
| | | £ | £ | £ | £ | £ |
| Allocated items | Specific | 90,380 | 27,660 | 19,470 | 16,600 | 26,650 |
| Rent, rates, heat, light | Floor area | 17,000 | 9,000 (3,600/ 6,800) | 3,500 (1,400/ 6,800) | 2,500 (1,000/ 6,800) | 2,000 (800/ 6,800) |
| Depreciation and insurance | Book value | 25,000 | 12,500 (150/ 300) | 6,250 (75/ 300) | 2,500 (30/ 300) | 3,750 (45/ 300) |
| | | 132,380 | 49,160 | 29,220 | 21,600 | 32,400 |
| Canteen | Number of employees | – | 10,800 (18/36) | 8,400 (14/36) | (21,600) | 2,400 (4/36) |
| | | 132,380 | 59,960 | 37,620 | – | 34,800 |
| Machine maintenance section | Specified % | – | 24,360 (70%) | 10,440 (30%) | – | (34,800) |
| | | 132,380 | 84,320 | 48,060 | – | – |

Note that the canteen overheads were reapportioned to the other cost centres first because the canteen renders a service to the machine maintenance section but does not receive a service from it.

Calculation of the overhead absorption (recovery) rates can now proceed:

(i) Total budgeted machine hours are:

|  | Hours |
| --- | --- |
| Product X (4,200 × 6) | 25,200 |
| Product Y (6,900 × 3) | 20,700 |
| Product Z (1,700 × 4) | 6,800 |
|  | 52,700 |

Overhead absorption rate for the machine shop is:

$$\frac{£84,320}{52,700} = £1.60/\text{machine hour}$$

(ii) Total budgeted direct labour cost is:

|  | £ |
| --- | --- |
| Product X (4,200 × £12) | 50,400 |
| Product Y (6,900 × £3) | 20,700 |
| Product Z (1,700 × £21) | 35,700 |
|  | 106,800 |

Overhead absorption rate for the fitting section is:

$$\frac{£48,060}{£106,800} \times 100\% = 45\% \text{ or } £0.45 \text{ per £ of direct labour}$$

(b) The cost of one unit of product X is calculated as follows:

|  | £ |
| --- | --- |
| Direct materials | 11.00 |
| Direct labour |  |
| Machine shop | 6.00 |
| Fitting section | 12.00 |
| Overheads |  |
| Machine shop (6 × £1.60) | 9.60 |
| Fitting section (£12 × 45%) | 5.40 |
|  | 44.00 |

Therefore, the cost of one unit of product X is £44.00.

## Chapter 5

**5.1** Woodner Ltd

| A<br>Output | B<br>Sales<br>price<br>per<br>unit | C<br>Total<br>sales<br>revenue<br>(A × B) | D<br>Marginal<br>unit<br>sales<br>revenue | E<br>Total<br>variable<br>cost<br>(A × £20) | F<br>Total cost<br>(variable<br>cost<br>+ £2,500) | G<br>Marginal<br>cost<br>per<br>unit | H<br>Profit/<br>(loss) |
|---|---|---|---|---|---|---|---|
| units | £ | £ | £ | £ | £ | £ | £ |
| 0 | 0 | 0 | 0 | 0 | 2,500 | – | (2,500) |
| 10 | 95 | 950* | 95** | 200 | 2,700 | 20 | (1,750) |
| 20 | 90 | 1,800 | 85 | 400 | 2,900 | 20 | (1,100) |
| 30 | 85 | 2,550 | 75 | 600 | 3,100 | 20 | (550) |
| 40 | 80 | 3,200 | 65 | 800 | 3,300 | 20 | (100) |
| 50 | 75 | 3,750 | 55 | 1,000 | 3,500 | 20 | 250 |
| 60 | 70 | 4,200 | 45 | 1,200 | 3,700 | 20 | 500 |
| 70 | 65 | 4,550 | 35 | 1,400 | 3,900 | 20 | 650 |
| 80 | 60 | 4,800 | 25 | 1,600 | 4,100 | 20 | 700 |
| 90 | 55 | 4,950 | 15 | 1,800 | 4,300 | 20 | 650 |
| 100 | 50 | 5,000 | 5 | 2,000 | 4,500 | 20 | 500 |

\* (10 × £95)
\*\* ((950 – 0)/(10 – 0))

An output of 80 units each week will maximise profit at £700 per week. This is the nearest, given the nature of the input data, to the level of output where marginal cost per unit equals marginal revenue per unit. (For the mathematically minded this question could have been solved by using calculus to find the point at which slopes of the total sales revenue and total costs lines were equal.)

**5.2** Cost-plus pricing means that prices are based on calculations/assessments of how much it costs to produce the goods or service, and includes a margin for profit. 'Cost' in this context might mean relevant cost, variable cost, direct cost or full cost. Usually cost-plus prices are based on full costs.

If a business charges the full cost of its output as a selling price, it will in theory break even. This is because the sales revenue will exactly cover all of the costs. Charging something above full cost will yield a profit. Thus, in theory, cost-plus pricing is logical.

If a cost-plus approach to pricing is to be taken, the question that must be addressed is the level of profit required from each unit sold. This must logically be based on the total profit that is required for the period. Normally, businesses seek to enhance their wealth through trading. The extent to which they expect to do this is normally related to the amount of wealth that is invested to promote wealth enhancement. Businesses tend to seek to produce a particular percentage increase in wealth. In other words, they seek to generate a particular return on capital employed. It seems logical, therefore, that the profit loading on full cost should reflect the business's target profit and that the target should itself be based on a target return on capital employed.

An obvious problem with cost-plus pricing is that the market may not agree with the price. Put another way, cost-plus pricing takes no account of the market demand function (the relationship between price and quantity demanded). A business may fairly deduce the full cost of some product and then add what might be regarded as a reasonable level of profit, only to find that a rival producer is offering a similar product for a much lower price, or that the market simply will not buy at the cost-plus price.

Most suppliers are not strong enough in the market to dictate pricing; most are 'price takers', not 'price makers'. They must accept the price offered by the market or they do not sell any of their wares. Cost-plus pricing may be appropriate for price makers, but it has less relevance for price takers.

The cost-plus price is not entirely useless to price takers. When contemplating entering a market, knowing the cost-plus price will tell the price taker whether it can profitably enter the market or not. As has been said above, the full cost can be seen as a long-run break-even selling price. If entering a market means that this break-even price, plus an acceptable profit, cannot be achieved, then the business should probably stay out. Having a breakdown of the full cost may put the business in a position to examine where costs might be capable of being cut in order to bring the full cost-plus profit to within a figure acceptable to the market.

Being a price maker does not always imply that the business dominates a particular market. Many small businesses are, to some extent, price makers. This tends to be where buyers find it difficult to make clear distinctions between the prices offered by various suppliers. An example of this might be a car repair. Though it may be possible to obtain a series of binding estimates for the work from various garages, most people would not normally do so. As a result, garages normally charge cost-plus prices for car repairs.

| 5.3 | Kaplan plc |

(a) At present, the company makes each model of suitcase in a batch. The direct materials and labour costs will be recorded in respect of each batch. To these costs will be added a share of the overheads of the business for the period in which production of the batch takes place. The basis of the batch absorbing overheads is a matter of managerial judgement. Direct-labour hours spent working on the batch, relative to total direct-labour hours worked during the period, is a popular method. This is not the 'correct' way, however. There is no correct way. If the activity is capital intensive, some machine-hour basis of dealing with overheads might be more appropriate, though still not 'correct'. Overheads might be collected department by department and charged to the batch as it passes through each department. Alternatively, all of the overheads for the entire production facility might be totalled and the overheads dealt with more globally. It is only in restricted circumstances that overheads charged to batches will be affected by a decision to deal with them departmentally, rather than globally.

Once the 'full cost' (direct costs plus a share of indirect costs) has been ascertained for the batch, the cost per suitcase can be established by dividing the batch cost by the number in the batch.

(b) The uses to which full cost information can be put have been identified as:

- *For pricing purposes.* In some industries and circumstances, full costs are used as the basis of pricing. Here the full cost is deduced and a percentage is added on for profit. This is known as cost-plus pricing. A solicitor handling a case for a client probably provides an example of this.

  In many circumstances, however, suppliers are not in a position to deduce prices on a cost-plus basis. Where there is a competitive market, a supplier will probably need to accept the price that the market offers – that is, most suppliers are 'price takers' not 'price makers'.

- *For income-measurement purposes.* To provide a valid means of measuring a business's income, it is necessary to match expenses with the revenues realised in the same accounting period. Where manufactured stock is made or partially made in one period but sold in the next, or where a service is partially rendered in one accounting period but the revenue is realised in the next, the full cost (including an appropriate share of overheads) must be carried from one accounting period to the next. Unless we are able to identify the full cost of work done in one period, which is the subject of a sale in the next, the profit figures of the periods concerned will become meaningless.

Unless all production costs are charged in the same accounting period as the sale is recognised in the profit and loss account, distortions will occur that will render the profit and loss account much less useful. Thus it is necessary to deduce the full cost of any production undertaken completely or partially in one accounting period but sold in a subsequent one.

(c) Whereas the traditional approach to dealing with overheads is just to accept that they exist and deal with them in a fairly broad manner, ABC takes a much more enquiring approach. ABC takes the view that overheads do not just 'occur', but that they are caused or 'driven' by 'activities'. It is a matter of finding out which activities are driving the costs and how much cost they are driving.

For example, a significant part of the costs of making suitcases of different sizes is resetting machinery to cope with a batch of a different size from its predecessor batch. Where a particular model is made in very small batches, because it has only a small market, ABC would advocate that this model is charged directly with its machine-setting costs. The traditional approach would be to treat machine setting as a general overhead that the individual suitcases (irrespective of the model) might bear equally. ABC, it is claimed, leads to more accurate costing and thus to more accurate assessment of profitability.

(d) The other advantage of pursuing an ABC philosophy and identifying cost drivers is that, once the drivers have been identified, they are likely to become much more susceptible to being controlled. Thus the ability of management to assess the benefit of certain activities against their cost becomes more feasible.

**5.6** GB Company – the International Industries (II) enquiry

(a) The minimum acceptable price of 120,000 motors to be supplied over the next four months is:

|  | £000 |  |
|---|---|---|
| Direct materials | 600 | (120,000 × £5.00) |
| Direct labour | 720 | (120,000 × £6.00) |
| Variable manufacturing overheads | 360 | (120,000 × £3.00) |
| Fixed manufacturing overheads | 60 | (4 × £15,000) |
| Total | 1,740 |  |

The offer price is:

$$120,000 \times £19.00 = £2,280,000$$

On this basis, the price of £19 per machine could be accepted, subject to a number of factors identified in (b) below.

(b) The assumptions on which the above analysis and decision in (a) are based include the following:

- That the contract can be accommodated within the 30 per cent spare capacity of GB. If this is not so, then there will be an opportunity cost relating to lost 'normal' production, which must be taken account of in the decision.

- That sales commission and freight costs will not be affected by the contract.
- It is unlikely that work more remunerative to GB than this contract will be available during the period of the contract.

There are also some strategic issues involved in the decision, including:

- The possibility that the contract could lead to other and better remunerated work from II.
- A problem of selling similar products in the same market at different prices. Other customers, knowing that GB is selling at marginal prices, may make it difficult for the business to resist demand from other customers for similarly priced output.

**5.7** Sillycon Ltd

(a)

### Overhead analysis

|  | Electronics £000 | Testing £000 | Service £000 |
|---|---|---|---|
| Variable overheads | 1,200 | 600 | 700 |
| Apportionment of service dept (800 : 600) | 400 | 300 | (700) |
|  | 1,600 | 900 | – |
| Direct labour hours | 800 | 600 |  |
| Variable overheads per direct labour hour | £2.00 | £1.50 |  |

|  | Electronics £000 | Testing £000 | Service £000 |
|---|---|---|---|
| Fixed overheads | 2,000 | 500 | 800 |
| Apportionment of service dept (equally) | 400 | 400 | (800) |
|  | 2,400 | 900 | – |
| Direct labour hours | 800 | 600 |  |
| Fixed overheads per direct labour hour | £3.00 | £1.50 |  |

### Product cost (per unit)

|  |  | £ |  |
|---|---|---|---|
| Direct materials |  | 7.00 |  |
| Direct labour | electronics | 40.00 | (4 × £10.00) |
|  | testing | 18.00 | (3 × £6.00) |
| Variable overheads | electronics | 8.00 | (4 × £2.00) |
|  | testing | 4.50 | (3 × £1.50) |
| Total variable cost |  | 77.50 | (assuming direct labour to be variable) |
|  |  |  |  |
| Fixed overheads | electronics | 12.00 | (4 × £3.00) |
|  | testing | 4.50 | (3 × £1.50) |
| Total 'full' cost |  | 94.00 |  |
| Add mark-up, say 30% |  | 28.20 |  |
|  |  | 122.20 |  |

On the basis of the above, the business could hope to compete in the market at a price that reflects normal pricing practice.

(b) At this price, and only taking account of incremental fixed overheads, the break-even point (BEP) would be given by:

$$\text{BEP} = \frac{\text{Fixed costs}}{\text{Contribution per unit}} = \frac{£150,000^*}{£122.20 - £77.50} = 3,356 \text{ units}$$

*(£13,000 + £100,000 + £37,000) namely the costs specifically incurred.

As the potential market for the business is around 5,000 to 6,000 units a year, the new product looks viable.

## Chapter 6

**6.1** | Daniel Chu Ltd

(a) The finished goods stock budget for the six months ending 30 September (in units of production) is:

|  | April units | May units | June units | July units | Aug units | Sept units |
|---|---|---|---|---|---|---|
| Opening stock (note 1) | 0 | 500 | 600 | 700 | 800 | 900 |
| Production (note 2) | 500 | 600 | 700 | 800 | 900 | 900 |
|  | 500 | 1,100 | 1,300 | 1,500 | 1,700 | 1,800 |
| Less Sales (note 3) | 0 | 500 | 600 | 700 | 800 | 900 |
| Closing stock | 500 | 600 | 700 | 800 | 900 | 900 |

(b) The raw materials stock budget for the six months ending 30 September (in units) is:

|  | April units | May units | June units | July units | Aug units | Sept units |
|---|---|---|---|---|---|---|
| Opening stock (note 1) | 0 | 600 | 700 | 800 | 900 | 900 |
| Purchases (note 2) | 1,100 | 700 | 800 | 900 | 900 | 900 |
|  | 1,100 | 1,300 | 1,500 | 1,700 | 1,800 | 1,800 |
| Less Production (note 4) | 500 | 600 | 700 | 800 | 900 | 900 |
| Closing stock | 600 | 700 | 800 | 900 | 900 | 900 |

The raw materials stock budget for the six months ending 30 September (in financial terms) is:

|  | April £ | May £ | June £ | July £ | Aug £ | Sept £ |
|---|---|---|---|---|---|---|
| Opening stock (note 1) | 0 | 24,000 | 28,000 | 32,000 | 36,000 | 36,000 |
| Purchases (note 2) | 44,000 | 28,000 | 32,000 | 36,000 | 36,000 | 36,000 |
|  | 44,000 | 52,000 | 60,000 | 68,000 | 72,000 | 72,000 |
| Less Production (note 4) | 20,000 | 24,000 | 28,000 | 32,000 | 36,000 | 36,000 |
| Closing stock | 24,000 | 28,000 | 32,000 | 36,000 | 36,000 | 36,000 |

(c) The trade creditors budget for the six months ending 30 September is:

| | April £ | May £ | June £ | July £ | Aug £ | Sept £ |
|---|---|---|---|---|---|---|
| Opening balance | | | | | | |
| (note 1) | 0 | 44,000 | 28,000 | 32,000 | 36,000 | 36,000 |
| Purchases (note 5) | 44,000 | 28,000 | 32,000 | 36,000 | 36,000 | 36,000 |
| | 44,000 | 72,000 | 60,000 | 68,000 | 72,000 | 72,000 |
| Less Cash payment | 0 | 44,000 | 28,000 | 32,000 | 36,000 | 36,000 |
| Closing balance | 44,000 | 28,000 | 32,000 | 36,000 | 36,000 | 36,000 |

(d) The trade debtors budget for the six months ending 30 September is:

| | April £ | May £ | June £ | July £ | Aug £ | Sept £ |
|---|---|---|---|---|---|---|
| Opening balance (note 1) | 0 | 0 | 50,000 | 60,000 | 70,000 | 80,000 |
| Sales (note 3) | 0 | 50,000 | 60,000 | 70,000 | 80,000 | 90,000 |
| | 0 | 50,000 | 110,000 | 130,000 | 150,000 | 170,000 |
| Less Cash received | 0 | 0 | 50,000 | 60,000 | 70,000 | 80,000 |
| Closing balance | 0 | 50,000 | 60,000 | 70,000 | 80,000 | 90,000 |

(e) The cash budget for the six months ending 30 September is:

| | April £ | May £ | June £ | July £ | Aug £ | Sept £ |
|---|---|---|---|---|---|---|
| **Inflows** | | | | | | |
| Share issue | 300,000 | | | | | |
| Receipts – debtors | | | | | | |
| (note 6) | 0 | 0 | 50,000 | 60,000 | 70,000 | 80,000 |
| | 300,000 | 0 | 50,000 | 60,000 | 70,000 | 80,000 |
| **Outflows** | | | | | | |
| Payments to | | | | | | |
| creditors | | | | | | |
| (note 7) | 0 | 44,000 | 28,000 | 32,000 | 36,000 | 36,000 |
| Labour (note 3) | 10,000 | 12,000 | 14,000 | 16,000 | 18,000 | 18,000 |
| Overheads: | | | | | | |
| Production | 17,000 | 17,000 | 17,000 | 17,000 | 17,000 | 17,000 |
| Non-production | | | | | | |
| (note 8) | 10,000 | 10,000 | 10,000 | 10,000 | 10,000 | 10,000 |
| Fixed assets | 250,000 | | | | | |
| Total outflows | 287,000 | 83,000 | 69,000 | 75,000 | 81,000 | 81,000 |
| Net inflows | | | | | | |
| (outflows) | 13,000 | (83,000) | (19,000) | (15,000) | (11,000) | (1,000) |
| Balance c/f | 13,000 | (70,000) | (89,000) | (104,000) | (115,000) | (116,000) |

*Notes*
1. The opening balance is the same as the closing balance from the previous month.
2. This is a balancing figure.
3. This figure is given in the question.
4. This figure derives from the finished stock budget.
5. This figure derives from the raw materials stock budget.
6. This figure derives from the trade debtors budget.
7. This figure derives from the trade creditors budget.
8. This figure is the non-productive overheads less depreciation, which is not a cash expense.

**6.2** (a) A budget is a financial plan for a future period. A forecast is an assessment/estimation of what is expected to happen in the environment. 'Plan' implies an intention to achieve. Thus a budget is a plan of what is intended to be achieved during the period of the budget. Relevant forecasts may well be taken into account when budgets are being prepared, but there is a fundamental difference between budgets and forecasts.

Though a year is a popular period for detailed budgets to be drawn up, there is no strong reason in principle why they have to be of this length.

(b) The layout described is generally regarded as a useful approach. Budgets are documents exclusively for the use of managers within the business. For this reason, those managers can use whatever layout best suits their purpose and tastes. In fact, there is no legal requirement that budgets should be prepared at all, let alone that they are prepared in any particular form.

(c) It is probably true to say that any manager worth employing would not want to work for a business that did not have an effective system of budgeting. Without budgeting, the advantages of:

- co-ordination
- motivation
- focusing on the future, and
- provision of the basis of a system of control

would all be lost.

Any good system of budgeting would almost certainly have individual managers participating heavily in the preparation of their own budgets and targets. It would also be providing managers with demanding, but rigorous, targets. This would give good managers plenty of scope to show flair and initiative, yet be part of a business that is organised, in control and potentially successful.

(d) All budgeting must take account of the planned volume of activity. ABB takes an ABC approach to the identification of overheads and to trying to ensure that managers who have control over the activities that drive the costs are held accountable for those costs. Similarly, ABB seeks to ensure that managers who have no effective control over particular costs are not held accountable for them.

(e) Any sensible person would probably start with the budget for the area in which the limiting factor lies – that is, that factor that will, in the end, prevent the business from achieving its objectives to the extent that would have been possible were it not for that factor.

It is true that, in practice, sales demand is often the limiting factor. In those cases, the sales budget is the best place to start. The limiting factor could, however, be a shortage of suitable labour or materials. In this case, the labour or materials budget would be the sensible place to start.

The reason why the starting point is important is simply that it is easier to start with the factor that is expected to limit the other factors and for those other factors to fit in.

**6.4** Linpet Ltd

(a) Cash budgets are extremely useful for decision-making purposes. They allow managers to see the likely effect on the cash balance of the plans that they have set in place. Cash is an important asset and it is necessary to ensure that it is properly managed. Failure to do so can have disastrous consequences for the business. Where the cash budget indicates a surplus balance, managers must decide whether this balance should be reinvested in the business or distributed to the owners. Where the cash budget indicates a deficit balance, managers must decide how this deficit should be financed or how it might be avoided.

(b) Cash budget to 30 November

| | June £ | July £ | Aug £ | Sept £ | Oct £ | Nov £ |
|---|---|---|---|---|---|---|
| **Receipts** | | | | | | |
| Cash sales | | | | | | |
| (Note 1) | 4,000 | 5,500 | 7,000 | 8,500 | 11,000 | 11,000 |
| Credit sales | | | | | | |
| (Note 2) | – | – | 4,000 | 5,500 | 7,000 | 8,500 |
| | 4,000 | 5,500 | 11,000 | 14,000 | 18,000 | 19,500 |
| **Payments** | | | | | | |
| Purchases | | | | | | |
| (Note 3) | – | 29,000 | 9,250 | 11,500 | 13,750 | 17,500 |
| Overheads | 500 | 500 | 500 | 500 | 650 | 650 |
| Wages | 900 | 900 | 900 | 900 | 900 | 900 |
| Commission | | | | | | |
| (Note 4) | – | 320 | 440 | 560 | 680 | 880 |
| Equipment | 10,000 | | | | | 7,000 |
| Motor vehicle | 6,000 | | | | | |
| Freehold | 40,000 | | | | | |
| | 57,400 | 30,720 | 11,090 | 13,460 | 15,980 | 26,930 |
| Cashflow | (53,400) | (25,220) | (90) | 540 | 2,020 | (7,430) |
| Opening bal. | 60,000 | 6,600 | (18,620) | (18,710) | (18,170) | (16,150) |
| Closing bal. | 6,600 | (18,620) | (18,710) | (18,170) | (16,150) | (23,580) |

Notes:
1. 50% of the current month's sales.
2. 50% of sales of two months' previous.
3. To have sufficient stock to meet each month's sales will require purchases of 75% of the month's sales figures (25% is profit). In addition, each month the business will buy £1,000 more stock than it will sell. In June, the business will also buy its initial stock of £22,000. This will be paid for in the following month. For example, June's purchases will be (75% × £8,000) + £1,000 + £22,000 = £29,000, paid for in July.
4. This is 5% of 80% of the month's sales, paid in the following month. For example, June's commission will be 5% × 80% × £8,000 = £320, payable in July.

**6.5** Lewisham Ltd

(a) The finished goods stock budget for the three months ending 30 September (in units of production) is:

| | July '000 units | Aug '000 units | Sept '000 units |
|---|---|---|---|
| Opening stock (note 1) | 40 | 48 | 40 |
| Production (note 2) | 188 | 232 | 196 |
| | 228 | 280 | 236 |
| Less Sales (note 3) | 180 | 240 | 200 |
| Closing stock | 48 | 40 | 36 |

(b) The raw materials stock budget for the two months ending 31 August (in kg) is:

|  | July '000 kg | Aug '000 kg |
|---|---|---|
| Opening stock (note 1) | 40 | 58 |
| Purchases (note 2) | 112 | 107 |
|  | 152 | 165 |
| *Less* Production (note 4) | 94 | 116 |
| Closing stock | 58 | 49 |

(c) The cash budget for the two months ending 30 September is:

|  | Aug £ | Sept £ |
|---|---|---|
| **Inflows** |  |  |
| Debtors – Current month (note 5) | 493,920 | 411,600 |
| Preceding month (note 6) | 151,200 | 201,600 |
| Total inflows | 645,120 | 613,200 |
| **Outflows** |  |  |
| Payments to creditors (note 7) | 168,000 | 160,500 |
| Labour and overheads (note 4) | 185,600 | 156,800 |
| Fixed overheads | 22,000 | 22,000 |
| Total outflows | 375,600 | 339,300 |
| Net inflows/(outflows) | 269,520 | 273,900 |
| Balance c/f | 289,520 | 563,420 |

*Notes*
1. The opening balance is the same as the closing balance from the previous month.
2. This is a balancing figure.
3. This figure is given in the question.
4. This figure derives from the finished stock budget.
5. This is 98 per cent of 70 per cent of the current month's sales revenue.
6. This is 28 per cent of the previous month's sales.
7. This figure derives from the raw materials stock budget.

**6.6** Newtake Records Ltd

(a) The cash budget for the period to 30 November is:

|  | June £000 | July £000 | Aug £000 | Sept £000 | Oct £000 | Nov £000 |
|---|---|---|---|---|---|---|
| **Cash receipts** |  |  |  |  |  |  |
| Sales (Note 1) | 227 | 315 | 246 | 138 | 118 | 108 |
| **Cash payments** |  |  |  |  |  |  |
| Administration (Note 2) | (40) | (41) | (38) | (33) | (31) | (30) |
| Goods purchased | (135) | (180) | (142) | (94) | (75) | (66) |
| Finance expenses | (5) | (5) | (5) | (5) | (5) | (5) |
| Selling expenses | (22) | (24) | (28) | (26) | (21) | (19) |
| Tax paid |  |  | (22) |  |  |  |
| Shop refurbishment |  | (14) | (18) | (6) |  |  |
|  | (202) | (264) | (253) | (164) | (132) | (120) |

| | June £000 | July £000 | Aug £000 | Sept £000 | Oct £000 | Nov £000 |
|---|---|---|---|---|---|---|
| Cash surplus (deficit) | 25 | 51 | (7) | (26) | (14) | (12) |
| Opening balance | (35) | (10) | 41 | 34 | 8 | (6) |
| Closing balance | (10) | 41 | 34 | 8 | (6) | (18) |

*Notes:*
1. (50% of the current month's sales) + (97% × 50% of those sales). For example, the June cash receipts = (50% × £230,000) + (97% × 50% × £230,000) = £226,550.
2. The administration expenses figure for the month, *less* £15,000 for depreciation (a non-cash expense).

(b) The stock budget for the six months to 30 November is:

| | June £000 | July £000 | Aug £000 | Sept £000 | Oct £000 | Nov £000 |
|---|---|---|---|---|---|---|
| Opening balance | 112 | 154 | 104 | 48 | 39 | 33 |
| Stock purchased | 180 | 142 | 94 | 75 | 66 | 57 |
| | 292 | 296 | 198 | 123 | 105 | 90 |
| Cost of stocks sold (60% sales) | (138) | (192) | (150) | (84) | (72) | (66) |
| Closing balance | 154 | 104 | 48 | 39 | 33 | 24 |

(c) The budgeted profit and loss account for the six months ending 30 November is:

| | £000 | £000 |
|---|---|---|
| Sales turnover | | 1,170 |
| *Less* Cost of goods sold | | 702 |
| Gross profit | | 468 |
| Selling expenses | (136) | |
| Admin. expenses | (303) | |
| Credit card charges | (18) | |
| Interest charges | (6) | (463) |
| Net profit for the period | | 5 |

(d) We are told that the company is required to eliminate the bank overdraft by the end of November. However, the cash budget reveals that this will not be achieved. There is a decline in the overdraft of nearly 50 per cent over the period, but this is not enough and ways must be found to comply with the bank's requirements. It may be possible to delay the refurbishment programme that is included in the forecasts or to obtain an injection of funds from the owners or other investors. It may also be possible to stimulate sales in some way. However, there has been a decline in the sales since the end of July and the November sales are approximately one-third of the July sales. The reasons for this decline should be sought.

The stock levels will fall below the preferred minimum level for each of the last three months. However, to rectify this situation it will be necessary to purchase more stock, which will, in turn, exacerbate the cash-flow problems of the business.

The budgeted profit and loss account reveals a very low net profit for the period. For every £1 of sales, the company is only managing to generate 0.4p in profit. The company should look carefully at its pricing policies and its overhead expenses. The administration expenses, for example, absorb more than one-quarter of the total sales turnover. Any reduction in overhead expenses will have a beneficial effect on cash flows.

## Chapter 7

**7.1** (a) A favourable direct-labour rate variance can only be caused by something that leads to the rate per hour paid being less than standard. Normally, this would not be linked to efficient working. Where, however, the standard envisaged some overtime working, at premium rates, the actual labour rate may be below standard if efficiency has removed the need for the overtime.

(b) The statement is true. The action will lead to an adverse sales-price variance and may well lead to problems elsewhere, but the sales volume variance must be favourable.

(c) It is true that below standard material could lead to adverse materials usage variances because there may be more than a standard amount of scrap. This could also cause adverse labour efficiency variances because labour time would be wasted by working on materials that would not form part of the output.

(d) Higher than budgeted sales could well lead to an adverse labour rate variance because producing the additional work may require overtime working at premium rates.

(e) The statement is true. Nothing else could cause such a variance.

**7.2** Pilot Ltd

(a) and (b)

| | Budget | | | Actual | |
|---|---|---|---|---|---|
| | Original | Flexed | | Actual | |
| Output (units) (production and sales) | 5,000 | 5,400 | | 5,400 | |
| | £ | £ | | £ | |
| Sales | 25,000 | 27,000 | | 26,460 | |
| Raw materials | (7,500) | (8,100) | (2,700 kg) | (8,770) | (2,830 kg) |
| Labour | (6,250) | (6,750) | (1,350 hr) | (6,885) | (1,300 hr) |
| Fixed overheads | (6,000) | (6,000) | | (6,350) | |
| Operating profit | 5,250 | 6,150 | | 4,455 | |

| | £ | | Manager accountable |
|---|---|---|---|
| Sales volume variance (5,250 − 6,150) | 900 | (F) | Sales |
| Sales price variance (27,000 − 26,460) | (540) | (A) | Sales |
| Materials price variance (2,830 × 3) − 8,770 | (280) | (A) | Buyer |
| Materials usage variance [(5,400 × 0.5) − 2,830] × £3 | (390) | (A) | Production |
| Labour rate variance (1,300 × £5) − 6,885 | (385) | (A) | Personnel |
| Labour efficiency variance [(5,400 × 0.25) − 1,300] × £5 | 250 | (F) | Production |
| Fixed overhead spending (6,000 − 6,350) | (350) | (A) | Various – depends on the nature of the overheads |
| Total net variances | (£795) | (A) | |

| | | |
|---|---|---|
| Budgeted profit | £5,250 | |
| *Less* total net variance | (795) | |
| Actual profit | £4,455 | |

**7.4** (a) Flexing the budget identifies what the profit would have been, had the only difference between the the original budget and the actual figures been concerned with the difference in volume of output. Comparing this profit figure with that in the original budget reveals the profit difference (variance) arising solely from the volume difference (sales volume variance). Thus, flexing the budget does not mean at all that volume differences do not matter. Flexing the budget is the means of discovering the effect on profit of the volume difference.

In one sense, all variances are 'water under the bridge', to the extent that the past cannot be undone, and so it is impossible to go back to the last control period and put in a better performance. Identifying variances can, however, be useful in identifying where things went wrong, which should enable management to take steps to ensure that the same things do not to go wrong in the future.

(b) Variances will not tell you what went wrong. They should, however, be a great help in identifying the manager within whose sphere of responsibility things went wrong. That manager should know why it went wrong. In this sense, variances identify relevant questions, but not answers.

(c) Identifying the reason for variances may well cost money, usually in terms of staff time. It is a matter of judgement in any particular situation, of balancing the cost of investigation against the potential benefits. As is usual in such judgements, it is difficult, before undertaking the investigation, to know either the cost or the likely benefit.

In general, significant variances, particularly adverse ones, should be investigated. Persistent (over a period of months) smaller variances should also be investigated. It should not automatically be assumed that favourable variances can be ignored. They indicate that things are not going according to plan, possibly because the plans (budgets) are flawed.

(d) Research evidence does not show this. It seems to show that managers tend to be most motivated by having as a target the most difficult goals that they find acceptable.

(e) Budgets normally provide the basis of feedforward and feedback control. During a budget preparation period, potential problems (for example a potential stock shortage) might be revealed. Steps can then be taken to revise the plans in order to avoid the potential problem. This is an example of a feedforward control: potential problems are anticipated and eliminated before they can occur.

Budgetary control is a very good example of feedback control, where a signal that something is going wrong triggers steps to take corrective action for the future.

**7.5** Bradley-Allen Ltd

(a)

| | Budget | | Actual |
|---|---|---|---|
| | Original | Flexed | |
| Output (units) | 800 | 950 | 950 |
| (production and sales) | | | |

| | £ | £ | | £ | |
|---|---|---|---|---|---|
| Sales | 64,000 | 76,000 | | 73,000 | |
| Raw materials – A | (12,000) | (14,250) | (285 kg) | (15,200) | (310 kg) |
| – B | (16,000) | (19,000) | (950 m) | (18,900) | (920 m) |
| Labour – skilled | (4,000) | (4,750) | (950 hr) | (4,628) | (890 hr) |
| – unskilled | (10,000) | (11,875) | (2,968.75 hr) | (11,275) | (2,750 hr) |
| Fixed overheads | (12,000) | (12,000) | | (11,960) | |
| Operating profit | 10,000 | 14,125 | | 11,037 | |

### Sales variances

| | | |
|---|---|---|
| Volume: | $(10,000 - 14,125) = £4,125$ | (F) |
| Price: | $(76,000 - 73,000) = £3,000$ | (A) |

### Direct material A variances

| | | |
|---|---|---|
| Usage: | $[(950 \times 0.3) - 310] \times £50 = £1,250$ | (A) |
| Price: | $(310 \times £50) - £15,200 = £300$ | (F) |

### Direct material B variances

| | | |
|---|---|---|
| Usage: | $[(950 \times 1) - 920] \times £20 = £600$ | (F) |
| Price: | $(920 \times £20) - £18,900 = £500$ | (A) |

### Skilled direct labour variances

| | | |
|---|---|---|
| Efficiency: | $[(950 \times 1) - 890] \times £5 = £300$ | (F) |
| Rate: | $(890 \times £5) - £4,628 = £178$ | (A) |

### Unskilled direct labour variances

| | | |
|---|---|---|
| Efficiency: | $[(950 \times 3.125) - 2,750] \times £4 = £875$ | (F) |
| Rate: | $(2,750 \times £4) - £11,275 = £275$ | (A) |

### Fixed overhead variances

| | | |
|---|---|---|
| Spending: | $(12,000 - 11,960) = £40$ | (F) |

| | | | | |
|---|---|---|---|---|
| **Budgeted profit** | | | | £10,000 |
| Sales: | Volume | 4,125 | (F) | |
| | Price | (3,000) | (A) | 1,125 |
| Direct material A: | Usage | (1,250) | (A) | |
| | Price | 300 | (F) | (950) |
| Direct material B: | Usage | 600 | (F) | |
| | Price | (500) | (A) | 100 |
| Skilled labour: | Efficiency | 300 | (F) | |
| | Rate | (178) | (A) | 122 |
| Unskilled labour: | Efficiency | 875 | (F) | |
| | Rate | (275) | (A) | 600 |
| Fixed overheads: | Expenditure | | | 40 |
| **Actual profit** | | | | £11,037 |

(b) The statement in (a) is useful to management because it enables them to see where there have been failures to meet the original budget and to be able to quantify the extent of such failures. This means that junior managers can be held accountable for the performance of their particular area of responsibility.

| 7.6 | Mowbray Ltd

|  | Budget | | Actual |
|---|---|---|---|
|  | Original | Flexed |  |
| Output (units) (production and sales) | 1,200 | 1,000* | 1,000* |
|  | £ | £ | £ |
| Sales | 24,000 | 20,000 | 18,000 |
| Raw materials | (9,000) | (7,500) (3,000 kg) | (7,400) (2,800 kg) |
| Labour | (2,700) | (2,250) (500 hr) | (2,300) (510 hr) |
| Fixed overheads | (4,320) | (4,320) | (4,100) |
| Operating profit | 7,980 | 5,930 | 4,200 |

\* The sales of £18,000 were at 10 per cent below standard price, at £18 each. Sales volume was, therefore, 1,000 units (that is, £18,000/18).

**Sales variances**

| | | |
|---|---|---|
| Volume: | $(7,980 - 5,930) = £2,050$ | (A) |
| Price: | $(20,000 - 18,000) = £2,000$ | (A) |

**Direct material variances**

| | | | |
|---|---|---|---|
| Usage: | $[(1,000 \times 3) - 2,800] \times £2.50 =$ | £500 | (F) |
| Price: | $(2,800 \times £2.50) - £7,400 =$ | £400 | (A) |

**Direct labour variances**

| | | | |
|---|---|---|---|
| Efficiency: | $[(1,000 \times 0.5) - 510] \times £4.50 =$ | £45 | (A) |
| Rate: | $(510 \times £4.50) - £2,300 =$ | £5 | (A) |

**Fixed overhead variances**

| | | | |
|---|---|---|---|
| Spending: | $(4,320 - 4,100) =$ | £220 | (F) |

(The budgeted fixed overheads were $£3.60 \times 1,200 = £4,320$)

| **Budgeted profit** $(1,200 \times £6.65)$ | | | | $= £7,980$ |
|---|---|---|---|---|
| **Variances** | | | | |
| Sales: | Volume | 2,050 | (A) | |
| | Price | 2,000 | (A) | (4,050) |
| Direct materials: | Usage | 500 | (F) | |
| | Price | 400 | (A) | 100 |

| Direct labour: | Efficiency | 45 | (A) | |
| | Rate | 5 | (A) | (50) |
| Fixed overheads: | Expenditure | | | 220 |
| **Actual profit** | | | | **£4,200** |

Since the low sales demand, and the reaction to it of dropping sales prices, seems to be caused by factors outside the control of managers of Mowbray Ltd, there are strong grounds for dividing the sales volume and price variances into those that are controllable and those that are not (planning variances).

## Chapter 8

8.1 Mylo Ltd

(a) The annual depreciation of the two projects is:

$$\text{Project 1: } \frac{(£100,000 - £7,000)}{3} = £31,000$$

$$\text{Project 2: } \frac{(£60,000 - £6,000)}{3} = £18,000$$

Project 1

(i)

| | Year 0 £000 | Year 1 £000 | Year 2 £000 | Year 3 £000 |
|---|---|---|---|---|
| Net profit(loss) | | 29 | (1) | 2 |
| Depreciation | | 31 | 31 | 31 |
| Capital cost | (100) | | | |
| Residual value | | | | 7 |
| Net cash flows | (100) | 60 | 30 | 40 |
| 10% discount factor | 1.000 | 0.909 | 0.826 | 0.751 |
| Present value | (100.00) | 54.54 | 24.78 | 30.04 |
| **Net present value** | 9.36 | | | |

(ii) Clearly the IRR lies above 10 per cent; try 15 per cent:

| | | | | |
|---|---|---|---|---|
| 15% discount factor | 1.000 | 0.870 | 0.756 | 0.658 |
| Present value | (100.00) | 52.20 | 22.68 | 26.32 |
| **Net present value** | 1.20 | | | |

Thus the IRR lies a little above 15 per cent, perhaps around 16 per cent.

(iii) To find the payback period, the cumulative cash flows are calculated:

| | | | | |
|---|---|---|---|---|
| Cumulative cash flows | (100) | (40) | (10) | 30 |

Thus the payback will occur after about 2 years 3 months (assuming that the cash flows accrue equally over the year), or 3 years if we assume year-end cash flows.

Project 2

(i)

| | Year 0 £000 | Year 1 £000 | Year 2 £000 | Year 3 £000 |
|---|---|---|---|---|
| Net profit(loss) | | 18 | (2) | 4 |
| Depreciation | | 18 | 18 | 18 |
| Capital cost | (60) | | | |
| Residual value | | | | 6 |
| Net cash flows | (60) | 36 | 16 | 28 |
| 10% discount factor | 1.000 | 0.909 | 0.826 | 0.751 |
| Present value | (60.00) | 32.72 | 13.22 | 21.03 |
| Net present value | 6.97 | | | |

(ii) Clearly the IRR lies above 10 per cent; try 15 per cent:

| | | | | |
|---|---|---|---|---|
| 15% discount factor | 1.000 | 0.870 | 0.756 | 0.658 |
| Present value | (60.00) | 31.32 | 12.10 | 18.42 |
| Net present value | 1.84 | | | |

Thus the IRR lies a little above 15 per cent; perhaps around 17 per cent.

(iii) The cumulative cash flows are:

| | | | | |
|---|---|---|---|---|
| Cumulative cash flows | (60) | (24) | (8) | 20 |

Thus, the payback will occur after about 2 years 3 months (assuming that the cash flows accrue equally over the year) or 3 years (assuming year-end cash flows).

(b) Presuming that Mylo Ltd is pursuing a wealth-maximisation objective, project 1 is preferable since it has the higher NPV. The difference between the two NPVs is not significant, however.

(c) NPV is the preferred method of assessing investment opportunities because it fully addresses each of the following:

■ *The timing of the cash flows.* Discounting the various cash flows associated with each project, according to when they are expected to arise, takes account of the fact that cash flows do not all occur simultaneously. Associated with this is the fact that by discounting, using the opportunity cost of finance (namely the return that the next best alternative opportunity would generate), the net benefit, after financing costs have been met, is identified (as the NPV).

■ *The whole of the relevant cash flows.* NPV includes all of the relevant cash flows irrespective of when they are expected to occur. It treats them differently according to their date of occurrence, but they are all taken into account in the calculation of the NPV and they all have, or can have, an influence on the decision.

■ *The objectives of the business.* NPV is the only method of appraisal where the output of the analysis has a direct bearing on the wealth of the business. (Positive NPVs enhance wealth; negative NPVs reduce it.) Since most private-sector businesses seek to increase their value and wealth, NPV is clearly the best approach to use.

**8.3** Haverhill Engineers Ltd

(a) The first step is to calculate the cash savings from the new machine:

|  | Per-unit cash flow | |
| --- | --- | --- |
|  | Old line | New line |
|  | p | p |
| Selling price | 150 | 150 |
| Less   Materials | (40) | (36) |
| Labour | (22) | (10) |
| Variable overheads | (14) | (14) |
| Cash contribution | 74 | 90 |

The cash saving per unit is (90p − 74p) = 16p. Hence, the cash saving for 1,000,000 units a year is:

$$1{,}000{,}000 \times 16p = £160{,}000$$

The incremental cash flows arising from the project are:

|  | Year 0 £000 | Year 1 £000 | Year 2 £000 | Year 3 £000 | Year 4 £000 | Year 5 £000 |
| --- | --- | --- | --- | --- | --- | --- |
| Cash savings |  | 160 | 160 | 160 | 160 | 160 |
| New machine | (700) |  |  |  |  | 100 |
| Old machine residual value | 50 |  |  |  |  |  |
| Working capital | 160 |  |  |  |  | (160) |
| Net cash flows | (490) | 160 | 160 | 160 | 160 | 100 |

(b)

|  | | | | | | |
| --- | --- | --- | --- | --- | --- | --- |
| Discount factor | 1.000 | 0.909 | 0.826 | 0.751 | 0.683 | 0.621 |
| Present value | (490) | 145.4 | 132.2 | 120.2 | 109.3 | 62.1 |
| NPV | 79.2 | | | | | |

Thus the project's NPV is £79,200.

(c)

|  | | | | | | |
| --- | --- | --- | --- | --- | --- | --- |
| Discount factor (20%) | 1.000 | 0.833 | 0.694 | 0.579 | 0.482 | 0.402 |
| Present value | (490.0) | 133.3 | 111.0 | 92.6 | 77.1 | 40.2 |
| NPV | (35.8) (that is, NPV of £35,800 negative) | | | | | |

We can see that increasing the discount rate from 10 per cent to 20%, an increase of 10 percentage points, decreases the NVP from +79.2 to −35.8, a decrease of 115. This is an average decrease of 11.5 per 1% increase in the discount rate. The rate at which the project would have a zero NPV (the IRR) is therefore about 10% + (79.2/11.5) = 16.9%, that is about 17%.

(d) NPV is the difference between the future cash inflows and outflows relating to a project after taking account of the time value of money. The time value of money is taken into account by discounting the future cash flows, using the cost of finance as the appropriate discount rate. The decision rule for NPV is that projects with a positive NPV should be accepted, as this will lead to an increase in shareholder wealth.

The internal rate of return is the discount rate that, when applied to the projected cash flows of the project, produces a zero NPV. The IRR is compared with a 'hurdle rate', determined by management, to see whether the project should be undertaken.

The IRR approach is currently as popular as the NPV method among practising managers. Managers appear to like to use percentage figures, as a basis for evaluating projects, rather than absolute figures. However, the IRR method has disadvantages compared with the NPV method, which were discussed in the chapter.

Normally, the two methods will give the same solution concerning acceptance/rejection of a project and will usually give the same solution concerning the ranking of projects. However, where a difference occurs, it is the NPV method that provides the more reliable answer. As a result, the NPV approach is considered to be the more appropriate method to adopt.

**8.4** Lansdown Engineers Ltd

(a)

| | System A | | | System B | | |
|---|---|---|---|---|---|---|
| | Cash flow | Discount factor at 12% | NPV | Cash flow | Discount factor at 12% | NPV |
| | £000 | | £000 | £000 | | £000 |
| Initial outlay (year 0) | (70) | 1.000 | (70) | (150) | 1.000 | (150) |
| Annual cost (years 1 to 10) | (140) | 5.651 | (791)* | (120) | 5.651 | (678) |
| Residual value (year 10) | 14 | 0.322 | 4 | 30 | 0.322 | 10 |
| | | | (857) | | | (818) |

(b)

| | System B | Existing system | Incremental cost |
|---|---|---|---|
| | £000 | £000 | £000 |
| Initial outlay (year 0) | (150) | 0 | (150) |
| Residual value (year 0) | – | 5 | 5 |
| Overhaul (year 0) | – | 20 | 20 |
| | | | (125) |
| Annual cost (years 1 to 10) | 120 | 145 | 25 |
| Residual value (year 10) | 30 | 10 | 20 |

(c) We can only find the IRR by trial and error. Let us use 15 per cent for the first try.

| | Cash flow | Discount factor at 15% | NPV |
|---|---|---|---|
| | £000 | | £000 |
| Year 0 | (125) | 1.000 | (125) |
| Years 1 to 10 | 25 | 5.019** | 125 |
| Year 10 | 20 | 0.247 | 5 |
| | | | 5 |

Since the NPV is only +5, 15 per cent is fairly close to the IRR but slightly below it. Let us try 16%.

| | Cash flow | Discount factor at 16% | NPV |
|---|---|---|---|
| | £000 | | £000 |
| Year 0 | (125) | 1.000 | (125) |
| Years 1 to 10 | 25 | 4.833*** | 121 |
| Year 10 | 20 | 0.227 | 5 |
| | | | 1 |

We can now say that the IRR is very close to 16% (slightly over).

\* This calculation is a bit of a short cut. Since each year has the same cash flow (that is, 140), instead of multiplying each of the ten 140s by its appropriate discount rate, depending on which year it occurs, and adding the ten resulting figures together, we can adopt a slight variation. This is to add the discount factors for the years 1 to 10 inclusive, and multiply this total (5.651) by 140. If you look at the present value table in the appendix to this chapter, you will see that the figures in the 12% column are 0.893 for 1 year, 0.797 for 2 years and so on until year 10 when it is 0.322. Adding these ten figures together gives 5.651.
\*\* 5.019 is the equivalent to 5.651, but for a 15% discount rate.
\*\*\* 4.833 is the equivalent to 5.651 and 5.019, but for a 16% discount rate.

(d) B is cheaper than A. It is also cheaper than the existing system. The company should, therefore, consider installing system B.

**8.5** Chesterfield Wanderers

(a) and (b)

**Player option**

| | 0 £000 | 1 £000 | 2 £000 | 3 £000 | 4 £000 | 5 £000 |
|---|---|---|---|---|---|---|
| Sale of player | 220 | | | | | 100 |
| Purchase of Bazza | (1,000) | | | | | |
| Sponsorship, etc. | | 120 | 120 | 120 | 120 | 120 |
| Gate receipts | | 250 | 130 | 130 | 130 | 130 |
| Salaries paid | | (80) | (80) | (80) | (80) | (120) |
| Salaries saved | | 40 | 40 | 40 | 40 | 60 |
| Net cash received (paid) | (780) | 330 | 210 | 210 | 210 | 290 |
| Discount factor 10% | 1.000 | 0.909 | 0.826 | 0.751 | 0.683 | 0.621 |
| Present values | (780) | 300.0 | 173.5 | 157.7 | 143.4 | 180.1 |
| NPV | 174.7 | | | | | |

**Ground improvement option**

| | 1 £000 | 2 £000 | 3 £000 | 4 £000 | 5 £000 |
|---|---|---|---|---|---|
| Ground improvements | (1,000) | | | | |
| Increased gate receipts | (180) | 440 | 440 | 440 | 440 |
| | (1,180) | 440 | 440 | 440 | 440 |
| Discount factor 10% | 0.909 | 0.826 | 0.751 | 0.683 | 0.621 |
| Present values | (1,072.6) | 363.4 | 330.4 | 300.5 | 273.2 |
| NPV | 194.9 | | | | |

(c) The ground improvement option provides the higher NPV and is therefore the preferable option, based on the objective of shareholder wealth maximisation.

(d) A professional football club may not wish to pursue an objective of shareholder wealth maximisation. It may prefer to invest in quality players in an attempt to enjoy future sporting success. If this is the case, the NPV approach will be less appropriate because the club is not pursuing a strict wealth maximisation objective.

**8.6** Newton Electronics Ltd

(a)

**Option 1**

| | Year 0 £m | Year 1 £m | Year 2 £m | Year 3 £m | Year 4 £m | Year 5 £m |
|---|---|---|---|---|---|---|
| Plant and equipment | (9.0) | | | | | 1.0 |
| Sales | | 24.0 | 30.8 | 39.6 | 26.4 | 10.0 |
| Variable costs | | (11.2) | (19.6) | (25.2) | (16.8) | (7.0) |
| Fixed costs (ex. depreciation) | | (0.8) | (0.8) | (0.8) | (0.8) | (0.8) |
| Working capital | (3.0) | | | | | 3.0 |
| Marketing costs | | (2.0) | (2.0) | (2.0) | (2.0) | (2.0) |
| Opportunity costs | | (0.1) | (0.1) | (0.1) | (0.1) | (0.1) |
| | (12.0) | 9.9 | 8.3 | 11.5 | 6.7 | 4.1 |
| Discount factor 10% | 1.000 | 0.909 | 0.826 | 0.751 | 0.683 | 0.621 |
| Present value | (12.0) | 9.0 | 6.9 | 8.6 | 4.6 | 2.5 |
| NPV | 19.6 | | | | | |

**Option 2**

| | Year 0 £m | Year 1 £m | Year 2 £m | Year 3 £m | Year 4 £m | Year 5 £m |
|---|---|---|---|---|---|---|
| Royalties | – | 4.4 | 7.7 | 9.9 | 6.6 | 2.8 |
| Discount factor 10% | 1.000 | 0.909 | 0.826 | 0.751 | 0.683 | 0.621 |
| Present value | – | 4.0 | 6.4 | 7.4 | 4.5 | 1.7 |
| NPV | 24.0 | | | | | |

**Option 3**

| | Year 0 | Year 2 |
|---|---|---|
| Instalments | 12.0 | 12.0 |
| Discount factor 10% | 1.000 | 0.826 |
| Present value | 12.0 | 10.0 |
| NPV | 22.0 | |

(b) Before making a final decision, the board should consider the following factors:

- The long-term competitiveness of the business may be affected by the sale of the patents.
- At present, the company is not involved in manufacturing and marketing products. Would a change in direction be desirable?

- The company will probably have to buy in the skills necessary to produce the product itself. This will involve costs, and problems will be incurred. Has this been taken into account?
- How accurate are the forecasts made and how valid are the assumptions on which they are based?

(c) Option 2 has the highest NPV and is therefore the most attractive to shareholders. However, the accuracy of the forecasts should be checked before a final decision is made.

## Chapter 9

**9.1**  Hercules Wholesalers Ltd

(a) The liquidity ratios of the company seem low. The current ratio is only 1.1 (that is, 306/285) and its acid test ratio is 0.6 (that is, 163/285). This latter ratio suggests the company has insufficient liquid assets to pay its short-term obligations. A cash-flow projection for the next period would provide a better insight to the liquidity position of the business. The bank overdraft seems high and it would be useful to know whether the bank is pressing for a reduction and what overdraft limit has been established for the company.

(b) The operating cash cycle can be calculated as follows:

**No. of days**

Average stockholding period:

$$\frac{[(\text{Opening stock} + \text{Closing stock})/2] \times 360}{\text{Cost of sales}} = \frac{[(125 + 143)/2] \times 360}{323} = 149$$

*Add* Average settlement period for debtors:

$$\frac{\text{Trade debtors} \times 360}{\text{Credit sales}} = \frac{163}{452} \times 360 = \underline{130}$$

$$279$$

*Less* Average settlement period for creditors:

$$\frac{\text{Trade creditor} \times 360}{\text{Credit purchases}} = \frac{145}{341} \times 360 = \underline{153}$$

$$\underline{126}$$

(c) The company can reduce the operating cash cycle in a number of ways. The average stockholding period seems quite long: at present, average stocks held represent almost five months' sales. This period may be reduced by reducing the level of stocks held. Similarly, the average settlement period for debtors seems long at more than four months' sales. This may be reduced by imposing tighter credit control, offering discounts, charging interest on overdue accounts, and so on. However, any policy decisions concerning stocks and debtors must take account of current trading conditions.

The operating cash cycle could also be reduced by extending the period of credit taken to pay suppliers. However, for the reasons mentioned in the chapter, this option must be given careful consideration.

9.4 | Dylan Ltd
New proposals from credit department

|  | £000 | £000 |
|---|---|---|
| Current level of investment in debtors | | |
| [£20m × (60/365)] | | 3,288 |
| Proposed level of investment in debtors | | |
| [(£20m × 60%)(30/365)] | (986) | |
| [(£20m × 40%)(50/365)] | (1,096) | (2,082) |
| Reduction in level of investment | | 1,206 |

The reduction in overdraft interest as a result of the reduction in the level of investment will be:

$$£1,206,000 × 14\% = £169,000$$

Thus

|  | £000 | £000 |
|---|---|---|
| Cost of cash discounts offered (£20m × 60% × 2½%) | | 300 |
| Additional cost of credit administration | | 20 |
| | | 320 |
| Bad debt savings | (100) | |
| Interest charge savings (see above) | (169) | (269) |
| Net annual cost of new credit policy | | 51 |

These calculations show that the company would incur additional annual costs in order to implement this proposal. It would, therefore, be cheaper to stay with the existing credit policy.

9.6 | Boswell Enterprises Ltd

(a)

|  | Current policy | | New policy | |
|---|---|---|---|---|
|  | £000 | £000 | £000 | £000 |
| Debtors | | | | |
| [(£3m × 1/12 × 30%) | | | | |
| + (£3m × 2/12 × 70%)] | | 425.0 | | |
| [(£3.15m × 1/12 × 60%) + | | | | |
| (£3.15m × 2/12 × 40%)] | | | | 367.5 |
| Stocks | | | | |
| {[£3m − (£3m × 20%)] × 3/12} | | 600.0 | | |
| {[£3.15m − (£3.15m × 20%)] × 3/12} | | | | 630.0 |
| Cash (fixed) | | 140.0 | | 140.0 |
| | | 1,165.0 | | 1,137.5 |
| Creditors | | | | |
| {[£3m − (£3m × 20%)] × 2/12} | (400.0) | | | |
| {[£3.15m − (£3.15m × 20%)] × 2/12} | | | (420.0) | |
| Accrued variable expenses | | | | |
| [£3m × 1/12 × 10%] | (25.0) | | | |
| [£3.15m × 1/12 × 10%] | | | (26.3) | |
| Accrued fixed expenses | (15.0) | (440.0) | (15.0) | (461.3) |
| Investment in working capital | | 725.0 | | 676.2 |

(b) The forecast net profit for the year

| | Current policy | | New policy | |
|---|---|---|---|---|
| | £000 | £000 | £000 | £000 |
| Sales | | 3,000.0 | | 3,150.0 |
| Cost of goods sold | | (2,400.0) | | (2,520.0) |
| Gross profit (20%) | | 600.0 | | 630.0 |
| Variable expenses (10%) | (300.0) | | (315.0) | |
| Fixed expenses | (180.0) | | (180.0) | |
| Discounts | – | (480.0) | (47.3) | 542.3 |
| Net profit | | 120.0 | | 87.7 |

(c) Under the proposed policy we can see that the investment in working capital will be slightly lower than under the current policy. However, profits will be substantially lower as a result of offering discounts. The increase in sales resulting from the discounts will not be sufficient to offset the additional costs of making the discounts to customers. It seems that the company should, therefore, stick with its current policy.

**9.7** Delphi plc

(a) The debtors ageing schedule is:

| | Number of months outstanding | | | | | | | |
|---|---|---|---|---|---|---|---|---|
| | 1 month or below £000 | % | 1 to 2 months £000 | % | 2 to 3 months £000 | % | Total debtors £000 | % |
| **February** | | | | | | | | |
| TV and hi-fi | 20.0 | (22.2) | | | | | 20.0 | (22.2) |
| Music | 30.0 | (33.3) | | | | | 30.0 | (33.3) |
| Retail | 40.0 | (44.5) | | | | | 40.0 | (44.5) |
| | 90.0 | (100.0) | | | | | 90.0 | (100.0) |
| **March** | | | | | | | | |
| TV and hi-fi | 20.8 | (12.5) | | | | | 20.8 | (12.5) |
| Music | 31.8 | (19.2) | 30.0 | (18.1) | | | 61.8 | (37.3) |
| Retail | 43.2 | (26.1) | 40.0 | (24.1) | — | — | 83.2 | (50.2) |
| | 95.8 | (57.8) | 70.0 | (42.2) | — | — | 165.8 | (100.0) |
| **April** | | | | | | | | |
| TV and hi-fi | 21.6 | (10.0) | | | | | 21.6 | (10.0) |
| Music | 33.8 | (15.6) | 31.8 | (14.7) | | | 65.6 | (30.3) |
| Retail | 46.6 | (21.4) | 43.2 | (19.9) | 40.0 | (18.4) | 129.8 | (59.7) |
| | 102.0 | (47.0) | 75.0 | (34.6) | 40.0 | (18.4) | 217.0 | (100.0) |
| **May** | | | | | | | | |
| TV and hi-fi | 22.4 | (9.6) | | | | | 22.4 | (9.6) |
| Music | 35.8 | (15.4) | 33.8 | (14.6) | | | 69.6 | (30.0) |
| Retail | 50.4 | (21.7) | 46.6 | (20.1) | 43.2 | (18.6) | 140.2 | (60.4) |
| | 108.6 | (46.7) | 80.4 | (34.7) | 43.2 | (18.6) | 232.2 | (100.0) |

We can see that the debtors figure will increase substantially in the first four months. The retail chains will account for about 60 per cent of the total debtors outstanding by May as this group has the fastest rate of growth. There is also a significant decline in the proportion of total debts outstanding from TV and hi-fi shops over this period.

(b) In answering this part of the question, you should refer to the 'five Cs of credit' that were discussed in detail in the chapter.

**9.8** Goliath plc

(a) (i) The existing operating cash cycle can be calculated as follows:

| | No. of days |
|---|---|
| Stockholding period = $\dfrac{\text{Stock at year end}}{\text{Cost of sales}} \times 365$ | |
| $= \dfrac{560}{1,440} \times 365 =$ | 142 |
| Add Debtors settlement period = $\dfrac{\text{Debtors at year end}}{\text{Sales}} \times 365$ | |
| $= \dfrac{565}{2,400} \times 365 =$ | 86 |
| | 228 |
| Less Creditors settelement period = $\dfrac{\text{Creditors at year end}}{\text{Purchases}} \times 365$ | |
| $= \dfrac{451}{1,450} \times 365 =$ | (114) |
| Operating cash cycle | 114 |

The new operating cash cycle is:

| | No. of days |
|---|---|
| Stockholding period = $\dfrac{(560 \times 1.15)}{(2,400 \times 1.10) \times 0.60} \times 365 =$ | 148 |
| Debtors settlement period = 86 + 20 | 106 |
| | 254 |
| Less Creditors settlement period = 114 + 15 | (129) |
| | 125 |
| New operating cash cycle | 125 |
| Existing operating cash cycle | (114) |
| Increase (decrease) in operating cash cycle (days) | 11 |

(ii)

|  | £000 |
|---|---|
| Increase (decrease) in stock held [(560 × 1.15) − 560] | 84.0 |
| Increase (decrease) in debtors [((2,400 × 1.1) × (106/365)) − 565] | 201.7 |
|  | 285.7 |
| (Increase) decrease in creditors [1,668 × (129/365) − 451] | (138.6) |
| Increase (decrease) in net investment | 147.1 |

(iii)

|  | £000 | £000 |
|---|---|---|
| Gross profit increase [(2,400 × 0.1) × 0.40] |  | 96.0 |
| *Adjust for* |  |  |
| Admin. expenses increase (15%) | (45.0) |  |
| Bad debts increase | (120.0) |  |
| Interest (10%) on borrowing for increased net investment in working capital (147.1) | (14.7) | (179.7) |
| Increase (decrease) in net profit before tax |  | (83.7) |
| Decrease in tax charge for the period (25% × 83.7) |  | 20.9 |
| Increase (decrease) in net profit after tax |  | (62.8) |

(b) There has been an increase in the operating cash cycle and this will have an adverse effect on liquidity. The existing debtors period and stockholding period already appear to be quite high, and any increase in either of these periods must be justified. The planned increase in the creditors period must also be justified because it may risk the loss of goodwill from suppliers. Although there is an expected increase in turnover of £240,000 from adopting the new policy, the net profit after taxation will decrease by £62,800. This represents a substantial decrease when compared with the previous year. (The increase in bad debts is a major reason why the net profit is adversely affected.) There is also a substantial increase in the net investment in stocks, debtors and creditors, which seems high in relation to the expected increase in sales. The new policy requires a significant increase in investment and is expected to generate lower profits than are currently being enjoyed. It should, therefore, be rejected.

## Chapter 10

**10.1** (a) A divisional organisation is one which divides itself into operating units in order to deliver its range of products or services. Divisionalisation is, in essence, an attempt to deal with the problems of size and complexity.

Autonomy of action relates to the amount of discretion the managers of divisions have been given by central management over the operations of the division. Two forms of autonomy are discussed in the chapter: profit centres and investment centres. Though divisionalisation usually leads to decentralisation of decision-making this need not necessarily be the case.

(b) The benefits of allowing divisional managers autonomy are dealt with in the chapter. These include:

- Better use of market information.
- Increase in management motivation.
- Providing opportunities for management development.

- Making full use of specialist knowledge.
- Giving central managers time to focus on strategic issues.
- Permitting a more rapid response to changes in market conditions.

(c) The chapter also identified certain problems with this approach which include:

- Goal conflict between divisions or between divisions and central management.
- Risk avoidance on the part of divisional managers.
- The growth of management 'perks'.
- Increasing costs due to inability to benefit from economies of scale.

Transfers between divisions can create problems for a business. Managers of the selling division may wish to obtain a high price for the transfers in order to achieve certain profit objectives. However, the managers of the purchasing division may wish to buy as cheaply as possible in order to achieve their profit objectives. This can create conflict and central managers may find that they are spending time arbitrating disputes. It may be necessary for central managers to impose a solution on the divisions where agreement cannot be reached which will, of course, undermine their autonomy.

**10.2** (a) Contribution margin represents the difference between the total sales of the division and the variable expenses incurred. This is a useful measure for understanding the relationship between costs, output and profit. However, it ignores any fixed expenses incurred and so not all aspects of operating performance are considered.

The *controllable contribution* deducts all expenses within the control of the divisional manager when arriving at a measure of performance. This is viewed by many as the best measure of performance for divisional managers as they will be in a position to determine the level of expenses incurred. However, in practice, it may be difficult to categorise expenses as being either controllable or non-controllable. This measure also ignores the investment made in assets. For example, a manager may decide to hold very high levels of stock which may be an inefficient use of resources.

Return on investment (ROI) is a widely used method of evaluating the profitability of divisions. The ratio is calculated in the following way:

$$ROI = \frac{\text{Division profit}}{\text{Divisional investment (assets employed)}} \times 100\%$$

The ratio is seen as capturing many of the dimensions of running a division.

When defining divisional profit for this ratio, the purpose for which the ratio is to be used must be considered. When evaluating the performance of a divisional manager, the controllable contribution is likely to be the most appropriate, whereas for evaluating the performance of a division, the divisional contribution is likely to be more appropriate. Different definitions can be employed for divisional investment. The net assets or total assets figure may be used. In addition, assets may be shown at original cost or some other basis such as current replacement cost.

(b) There is a number of non-financial measures available to evaluate a division's performance. Example of these measures have been cited in the chapter. Further example include:

- Plant capacity utilised
- Percentage of rejects in production runs
- Ratio of customer visits to customer orders
- Number of customers visited.

By using a broad range of financial and non-financial measures covering different time horizons there is a better chance that all of the major dimensions of management and divisional performance will be properly assessed. By focusing on a few short-term financial objectives there is a danger that managers will strive to achieve these at the expense of the longer-term objectives. We have seen in the chapter that ROI can be increased in the short term by cutting back on discretionary expenditure such as staff training and research and development and by not replacing heavily depreciated assets.

**10.4** ABC Corporation

(a) (i) Residual income calculation – original plan:

|  | £000 |
|---|---|
| Sales | 1,200 |
| Less Variable costs | 800 |
| Contribution margin | 400 |
| Fixed costs | 250 |
| Divisional profit | 150 |
| Capital charge (£500,000 @ 20%) | 100 |
| Residual income | 50 |

(ii) Residual income calculation – original plan and option I:

|  | £000 |
|---|---|
| Sales | 1,420 |
| Less Variable costs | 960 |
| Contribution margin | 460 |
| Fixed costs | 270 |
| Divisional profit | 190 |
| Capital charge (£580,000 @ 20%) | 116 |
| Residual income | 74 |

(iii) Residual income calculation – original plan and option II:

|  | £000 |
|---|---|
| Sales | 1,160 |
| Less Variable costs | 800 |
| Contribution margin | 360 |
| Fixed costs | 250 |
| Divisional profit | 110 |
| Capital charge (£500,000 @ 20%) | 100 |
| Residual income | 10 |

(b) Division A is unlikely to find the price reduction for division B attractive. Division B, on the other hand, will benefit by £40,000 (20,000 × £2) from the price reduction. However, overall, the total profits of the business will be unaffected as the increase in division B's profits will be cancelled out by the decrease in division A's profit.

If an outside supplier is used, the profits of the business overall will fall by the amount of the lost contribution (20,000 × (£10 – £8) = £40,000).

Another option would be to allow the outsiders to supply division B and to use the released production capacity to sell outside customers 20,000 units @ £11 per unit. In this way, additional equipment costs would be avoided.

**10.5** Telling Company

(a)
$$\text{ROI} = \frac{\text{Division profit}}{\text{Divisional investment (assets employed)}} \times 100\%$$

$$= \frac{25,000}{150,000} \times 100\%$$

$$= 16.7\%$$

| | £ |
|---|---|
| RI = Divisional profit | 25,000 |
| Required return 20% × £150,000 | 30,000 |
| Residual income (loss) | (5,000) |

The results show that the ROI is less than the required return of 20% and the residual income is negative. The results must therefore be considered unsatisfactory.

(b)

| | £ |
|---|---|
| Increase in sales (£7.5 × 10,000) | 75,000 |
| Increase in variable costs (£6 × 10,000) | 60,000 |
| Increase in contribution margin | 15,000 |
| Increase in fixed costs | 5,000 |
| Increase in divisional profit | 10,000 |
| Increase in cost of capital (20% × £20,000) | 4,000 |
| Increase in RI | 6,000 |

(c) Though the divisional profits of Goodman and Sharp will each be affected by a change in the transfer price, the total profits of Telling Co. will be unaffected. The increase in profit occurring in one division will be cancelled out by the decrease in profit in the other division and so the overall effect will be nil.

　　If the work goes outside, Goodman would lose £20,000 in contribution (that is, 10,000 × £2) and Sharp would gain £8,000 by the reduction in the buying-in price (that is, 10,000 × (£8 − £7.20)). The net effect on the business as a whole will therefore be a loss of £12,000 (£20,000–£8,000).

**10.6** Glasnost plc

(a)

| | West £000 | East £000 |
|---|---|---|
| **Residual income:** | | |
| 300 − (2,500 × 10%) | 50 | |
| 100 − (500 × 10%) | | 50 |

Return on investment (ROI):

| | West | East |
|---|---|---|
| **Based on net profit** | | |
| (250/2,500) × 100% | 10% | |
| (80/500) × 100% | | 16% |
| **Based on divisional profit** | | |
| (300/2,500) × 100% | 12% | |
| (100/500) × 100% | | 20% |

Expenses to sales ratio:

| | | |
|---|---|---|
| Direct manufacturing | 30% | 53% |
| Indirect manufacturing | 22% | 12% |
| Selling and distribution | 18% | 10% |
| Central overhead | 5% | 5% |

(b) The ROI ratios indicate that East is the better performing division. However, we are told in the question that East has older plant than West, which has recently modernised its production lines. This difference in the age of the plant is likely to mean that the ROI of East is higher due, at least in part, to the fact that the plant has been substantially written down. Some common base is required for comparison purposes (for example unadjusted historical cost).

We are told that ROI is used as the basis for evaluating performance. We can see that, whichever measure of ROI is used, the two divisions meet the minimum returns required. If ROI is being used to assess managerial performance then the divisional profit rather than net profit figure should be used in the calculation. This is because the net profit figure is calculated after non-controllable central overheads have been deducted.

The company should consider the use of RI as another measure of divisional performance. This measure reveals the same level of performance for the current year from each division.

The expenses to sales ratios are revealing. West has a lower direct manufacturing cost to sales ratio but a higher indirect manufacturing cost to sales ratio than East. This is consistent with the introduction of modern labour-saving plant.

West has a higher selling expenses to sales ratio than East. This is probably due to the fact that inter-company transfers are minimal whereas for East they represent 50 per cent of total sales.

## Chapter 11

**11.1** Strategic planning involves five steps:
1. *Establish mission and objectives*   The mission statement is usually a brief statement of the overall aims of the business. The objectives are rather more specific than the mission and need to be both quantifiable and consistent with the mission or aims.
2. *Undertake a position analysis*   Here the business is seeking to establish how it is placed relative to its environment (competitors, markets, technology, the economy, political climate, and so on), given the business's mission and objectives. This is often approached within the framework of an analysis of the business's strengths, weaknesses, opportunities and threats (a SWOT analysis). Strengths and weaknesses are internal factors that are attributes of the business itself, whereas opportunities and threats are factors expected to be present in the environment in which the business operates. The SWOT framework is not the only possible approach to undertaking a position analysis, but it seems to be a very popular one.
3. *Identify and assess the strategic options*   This involves attempting to identify possible courses of action that will enable the business to reach its objectives in the light of the position analysis undertaken in step 2.
4. *Select strategic options*   Here the business will select what seems to be the best of the courses of action or strategies (identified in step 3) and will formulate a strategic plan in the form of long- and short-term budgets.

5. *Perform, review and control*   Here the business pursues the plans derived in step 4, using the traditional approach to compare actual performance against budgets, seeking to control where actual performance appears not to be matching plans.

**11.3** Sharma plc Analysis of trading with Lopez during last year

|  |  | £ |
|---|---|---|
| Gross sales revenue | (40,000 × £20) | 800,000 |
| Discount allowed | (£800,000 × 5%) | 40,000 |
| Manufacturing cost | (40,000 × £12) | 480,000 |
| Sales order handling | (22 × £75) | 1,650 |
| Delivery costs | (22 × 120 × £1.50) | 3,960 |
| Customer sales visits | (30 × £230) | 6,900 |
| Credit costs | [(£800,000 − £40,000) × 2/12 × 2] | 2,533 |
|  |  | 535,043 |
| Net profit from the customer for the year |  | 264,957 |

**11.4** Vitality Ltd

The income statements for the two years are as follows:

| Year | 2000 | 2001 |
|---|---|---|
|  | £ | £ |
| Sales | 50,000 | 49,200 |
| Cost of bottles | 30,000 | 34,440 |
| Contribution | 20,000 | 14,760 |

The change in strategy led to a decline in contributions of £5,240 (that is, £20,000 − £14,760). This can be analysed as follows:

**Growth aspect**

1. Revenue growth is the effect of the growth in revenues arising from the volume growth:
   (units sold in 2001 less units sold in 2000) × 2000 selling price per unit = (123,000 − 100,000) × £0.50 = £11,500 (F) (it is 'favourable' because it represents a contribution increase arising from the change in strategy).
2. Cost of growth is the effect on costs of the sales volume growth:
   (number of bottles for 2001 less number of bottles in 2000) × price per bottle in 2000 = [(123,000 − 100,000)] × £0.30 = £6,900 (A) (it is 'adverse' because it represents a contribution decrease arising from the change in strategy).

|  |  | £ |
|---|---|---|
| Summary of growth aspect | Revenue growth | 11,500 (F) |
|  | Cost growth | 6,900 (A) |
|  |  | 4,600 (F) |

**Price aspect**

1. Revenue price is the effect of the decrease in revenues arising from the price reduction: (selling price per bottle in 2001 less selling price per bottle in 2000) × 2001 sales volume = (£0.40 − £0.50) × 123,000 = £12,300 (A)
2. Cost price decrease effect on costs:
   (cost per bottle of DM in 2001 less cost per bottle of DM in 2000) × number of bottles sold in 2001 = (£0.38 − £0.40) × 123,000 = £2,460 (F)

|  | | £ |
|---|---|---|
| Summary of price aspect | Revenue price | 12,300 (A) |
| | Cost price | 2,460 (F) |
| | | 9,840 (A) |

### Usage (or productivity) aspect

Since the number of bottles needed to make each sale remained at one (as it had to), there is no usage aspect to this analysis.

|  | | £ |
|---|---|---|
| **Overall summary:** | Growth aspect | 4,600 (F) |
| | Price aspect | 9,840 (A) |
| | Usage aspect | zero |
| | | 5,240 (A) |

The change in strategy was clearly a mistake. Though making extra sales taken alone generated an additional £4,600 of contribution, this was overwhelmed by the effect of the lower price, even taking account of the benefit of the reduced cost price to the company. This led to a reduction of more than 25 per cent of the 2000 contribution.

Clearly for this strategy to work at the selling and cost prices applying in 2001, rather greater sales volume was required than was able to be generated. Possibly with more determined marketing, highlighting to customers the low price, it could be made to work.

**11.5** SWOT analysis of Jones Dairy Ltd

### Strengths

- A portfolio of identifiable customers who show some loyalty to the company.
- Good cash flow profile. Though credit will be given, a week is the normal credit period.
- An apparently sound distribution system.
- A monopoly of doorstep delivery in the area.
- Barriers to entry. There are probably relatively high fixed costs, which implies a 'critical mass' of volume is necessary.
- Good employees and ease of recruitment.
- Differentiated product; clearly different from what is supplied by the supermarket in that it is delivered to the door.
- Apparently good marketing, since the decline in business is less than the national average.
- Good knowledge of the local market.
- Tendency for people to shop infrequently means that doorstep delivery may be the only practical means of having fresh milk.

### Weaknesses

- Ageing managers.
- Success might be dependent on the present management continuing to manage.
- Narrow product range.
- High price necessary to generate acceptable level of profit.
- Available substitute, that is non-delivered milk.
- High operating gearing (probably) means that profit suffers disproportionately with a downturn in demand.
- Single supplier.

### Opportunities

- Possibility of extending the product range to include other dairy and non-dairy products to existing customers.
- Possible geographical expansion to cover other local towns and villages.
- Possibly move to act as a wholesaler to local stores at differentiated prices. It is probable that the bottlers would supply Jones more cheaply than they would supply individual small stores.
- Using plant for some other purpose, such as letting coldstore facilities.

### Threats

- Apparently strong trend against doorstep delivery driven by price differential.
- Trend away from dairy products for health/cultural reasons.
- The probability that Jones is entirely dependent on the only local bottler. More geographically remote bottlers may not be prepared to supply at any acceptable price.
- Increasing strength of supermarket buying power.

## 11.6 Leo plc

*Free cash flows*

|  | Yr 1 £m | Yr 2 £m | Yr 3 £m | Yr 4 £m | Yr 5 £m | After Yr 5 £m |
|---|---|---|---|---|---|---|
| Sales | 30.0 | 36.0 | 40.0 | 48.0 | 60.0 | 60.0 |
| Operating profit (20%) | 6.0 | 7.2 | 8.0 | 9.6 | 12.0 | 12.0 |
| Less | | | | | | |
| Cash tax (25%) | 1.5 | 1.8 | 2.0 | 2.4 | 3.0 | 3.0 |
| Operating profit less cash tax | 4.5 | 5.4 | 6.0 | 7.2 | 9.0 | 9.0 |
| Less | | | | | | |
| AFAI (15%) | (4.5)* | (0.9) | (0.6) | (1.2) | (1.8) | |
| AWCI (10%) | (3.0)* | (0.6) | (0.4) | (0.8) | (1.2) | – |
| Free cash flows | (3.0) | 3.9 | 5.0 | 5.2 | 6.0 | 9.0 |
| 12% discount factor | 0.893 | 0.797 | 0.712 | 0.636 | 0.567 | 0.567 |
| Present value | (2.7) | 3.1 | 3.6 | 3.3 | 3.4 | 42.5** |
|  | 53.2 | | | | | |

\* In the first year, the additional sales will be £30m and so the calculations for fixed assets and working capital must be based on this figure.

\*\* The terminal value is $(9.0/0.12 \times 0.567) = 42.5$.

Total business value will increase by £53.2m. As there has been no change to the level of borrowing, shareholder value should increase by this amount.

# Index